GLOBAL DEVELOPMENT OF TIENS GROUP

SWAP, TRANSCENDENCE AND CHINESE SUCCESS

LI JINYUAN

Published by
LID Publishing
An imprint of LID Business Media Ltd.
The Record Hall, Studio 304,
16-16a Baldwins Gardens,
London EC1N 7RJ, UK

info@lidpublishing.com
www.lidpublishing.com

A member of:
BPR
businesspublishersroundtable.com

Printed by Severn, Gloucester

ISBN: 978-1-911687-02-3
ISBN: 978-1-911687-03-0 (ebook)

Cover and page design: Caroline Li

GLOBAL DEVELOPMENT OF TIENS GROUP

SWAP, TRANSCENDENCE AND CHINESE SUCCESS

LI JINYUAN

LID

MADRID | MEXICO CITY | LONDON
NEW YORK | BUENOS AIRES
BOGOTA | SHANGHAI | NEW DELHI

CONTENTS

Part IV
Swap Process and Transcendence Practice III: 'One Body with Multiple Wings' Model
Zhao Qilan

Part V
Swap Promotes Transcendence: Corporate Governance Model Innovation in Direct-Selling Enterprises
Ju Jinwen

Part VI
Self-transcendence Creates Glory: From Household Consumption to Household Business Consumption
Feng Lei

Part VII
Global Expansion Creates the Future: Self-transcendence Promotes Swap Practice
Peng Lihong

PREFACE

Confidence and success in business and in life comes from clear targets, high standards, pushing boundaries and breaking through. This approach and the energy it creates allows businesses and people to carry forward their success, take advantage of momentum, continue to work hard and strive to be the best they can. These are some of the main messages in this book about swap and transcendence.

Of course, these things are not always easy to do, and this book sets out not only the theory to help readers understand the concepts, but also provides the methods to help apply the principles of swap and transcendence.

When I talk with those in Tiens Group around the world, I try to deliver some important messages about doing business in a world that continues to change before our eyes.

First, we must advance with the times, reacting to truth with a pragmatic approach. As long as the strategic direction is clear and effective implementation is in place, then the result will be a strong, harmonious competitiveness. The recent cross-border e-commerce of JTMM has successfully achieved global online coverage, and the new overseas direct sales have been incorporated into Tiens' global cross-border social membership. The successful implementation of the new strategy of terminal experience stores has formed a new mechanism and a new model of swap and transcendence for the third entrepreneurship of "driving the development of stores with the network and promoting the development of the network with stores." This will surely achieve new breakthroughs, new leapfrog opportunities and new developments.

Second, businesses and individuals must persist in education and training. I have always believed that to seize any market and to expand any business, education is the soul, the guide, the foundation and the core. To a large degree, Tiens Group, through its regional companies and national branches, continues to be successful because it attaches great importance to education and training, and fully supports both.

Third, in the competitive world in which we live, businesses must keep adding new and important products from around the world. In the final analysis, market competition is product and service competition. Customers always pursue products that offer an experience and function that is of a high standard and high quality. We must only present consumers with the absolute best. Tiens works constantly, with the principles of swap and transcendence, to expand the number of leading products, strengthen our product reserves, and strengthen the market competitiveness of our products and services.

Fourth, businesses must always strengthen their work process management. We must pursue the best results in all our work, and we must insist that performance, profit and work efficiency are paramount. A good process has a good result, and a good result needs a good process to ensure survival. Tiens aims to strengthen process management, pay attention to the process, review the process, modify, shorten and evaluate the process in order to achieve the best results.

Fifth, businesses must understand themselves very well, including through market surveys and research. Without investigative work, there is no right to speak, and without knowing the truth, there is no right to make decisions. Since the beginning, the business expansion of Tiens has been the front line, and the performance we have pursued is success in the market. Tiens has aimed to serve the market and to actively understand the business and the experience of our competition. Knowledge must be grasped and conveyed and I've always shared knowledge with the whole family of Tiens. If you can solve a problem on the spot, then the problem should be solved on the spot. If it can't be solved on the spot, then it is through the help and wisdom of others in the family that is Tiens that an authentic solution can be found.

Sixth, it is necessary to build strong organizational capabilities, including cultivating members' organizational management and focus management, and training employees to consider problems in an overall thinking way and common perspectives. This often involves being willing to delegate management power to lower levels and to authorize market managers to use their autonomy and decision-making rights. Thinking that can't be taken into action is pale, and action can only happen with valued and valuable employees. Employees must have a sense of faith, mission, expectation, values, accomplishment and meaning. For our employees, we adopt a strategy of integrating mission-drive and material incentives and work closely both to help them achieve self-value and to create value to the enterprise.

And this brings me to my seventh and last point, which is that in business and in life, we must persist in showing loyalty and integrity and we must take responsibility. Loyalty, integrity and responsibility are the minimum professional qualities and requirements, and they are important principles and the bottom line for being a person. These are key characteristics that have carried Tiens through 26 years of successful experiences.

I believe that the principles of swap and transcendence set out in this book provide a good environment for working together to achieve outstanding results in business. These principles have served Tiens well and will continue to do so.

I hope that readers find information, whether through academic theory or practical application, in this book that will help them not only understand Tiens better, but also help them overcome any business difficulties they are having to carry forward their success and to bring new glory to themselves through excellent performance.

Li Jinyuan
Tiens Group

PREFACE

Joseph Schumpeter created a well-known term, 'Creative Destruction.' In his 1911 book, *The Theory of Economic Development*, he made a penetrating analysis that the so-called entrepreneur was essentially "the leader in economic development" as well as the innovator who "realized the re-combination of production factors." By destroying the old combination of production factors and constructing the new, the entrepreneur is striving for creative destruction and the better development of the enterprise. The phenomena and actions of creative destruction have been emerging in an endless stream through the efforts of entrepreneurs and the support of technological innovation. Creative destruction not only promotes the reform of the economic system, but also facilitates the development of economy and technology. Industries are exposed to great changes and re-organization during the economic development as a result of science and technology innovation and the invention and wide application of countless internet technologies.

Tiens Group started with direct selling of health products; achieved the second start-up and take-off by building the new model of transnational development of 'three-network integration' and 'seven-network interaction'; and is now ushering in the new stage of the third start-up by using the 'Internet+' and 'blockchain+.' The history of Tiens is one of constant exploration to acquire success and development, as well as a process of subversion to rise to challenges and transcend itself.

By understanding the concepts and practices of global development and systematically summarizing its global development experiences as theory, Tiens can guide further development and provide a new perspective and model for more national enterprises to go global and realize transcendence and development.

This book has been written by experts who have made an in-depth investigation of Tiens, explored and summarized the concepts and experiences of the global development of Tiens, and set out the theory of 'Swap and Transcendence' that complies with the demands of the development of Chinese national enterprises and features global insights and guiding significance.

Swap and Transcendence carries forward the spirit of the book *New Swap and Alternative Theory*, published in 2003. Despite a timespan of almost two decades, the previous book has laid the foundation for the content and logic of the new book.

The previous book focused on 'swap and alternative' in empirical analysis and theory exposition, aiming to clarify how a national enterprise acquired high-quality and high-level development through the integration and swap of internal and external resources and the construction of the new combination of factors and efficient mechanism. This book applies empirical analysis and comparative study to discuss and explain how a national enterprise based on swap adopts the latest information technology, network management and communication technology, and intelligent combination and connection technology and achieves cross-industry subversion by integrating the traditional industries and the modern network information technologies, then 'transcends' itself and its opponents and finally leads the world. In other words, in this book, 'swap' constitutes the logical and practical foundation for 'transcendence,' and 'transcendence' means to effectively integrate and reorganize internal and external resources of an enterprise in a scientific manner and thus "subvert the past self," "transcend the present self" and "surpass future opponents."

The body of this book comprises 26 chapters across seven sections. The three chapters in the first section mainly analyse and clarify the scope, connotation and theoretical foundation of swap and transcendence and its innovation and development, as well as the history of how a Direct-Selling enterprise achieves self-transcendence by means of swap and new forms of market changes, including emerging economic theories and practices such as sharing economy, experience economy and fans economy. The second section includes three chapters, which mainly explain the 'three-network integration' and market model swap, the conditions and realization of three-network integration and the experiences and effect of three-network integration in the swap. The four chapters in the third section analyse the basic connotation of 'multi-network interaction' and its manifestation in the process of swap and transcendence, its structure and economic spillover effect, its operating mechanism and its benefit evaluation and distribution mechanism.

The fourth section, with four chapters, explains the basic connotation, framework, factors and internal structure of 'one body with multiple wings,' the conditions, process, mechanism and effect of the strategy and its role in improving the value chain, swap chain and ecological chain, and advancing the competitiveness of the Direct-Selling enterprise. In the fifth section, the five chapters focus on the Direct-Selling enterprise's governance model and its innovation and analyse the relation between the corporate governance and management model and swap, the evolution of the Tiens model, the process of transcendence, the Direct-Selling model and its incentive system and incentive efficiency. The sixth section consists of four chapters, which clarify the occurrence of household consumption and its development and evolution to household business consumption, reveal the relation between the consumption chain and consumption ecological chain, and discuss the transcendence concept of household consumption and product integration, household business consumption and consumer surplus and the transcendence and wealth-creation mechanism of Internet+ Direct-Selling. The three chapters in the seventh section discuss how to upgrade the swap and global exploration to create a better future for the Direct-Selling enterprise, analyse the conditions, model and process of the Direct-Selling enterprise's global exploration as well as the opportunities and challenges it will meet, and explain the strategic focus, blueprint, vision and implementation of the exploration. We hope this book, which displays the research findings combining both case analysis and theoretical exploration, will provide basic theoretical guidance and vigorous logical support for Tiens and many other Direct-Selling enterprises to grow faster and healthier with higher quality.

Liu Yingqiu
Research Group of China Research Society of Urban Development

FOREWORD

During increasing times of globalization and human economic and social development, Tiens Group has taken the reality of the situation in China into consideration and taken the lead in exchanging internal and external corporate resources. Tiens Group has efficiently integrated various applicable operational and market development factors. These efforts have laid solid foundations for the entrepreneurial development of multinational operations.

Tiens Group quickly grew into a huge enterprise by taking exploratory and innovative actions, such as combining property organization, corporate structure and personal business performance management. They applied leading technology like 'Internet+' and implemented a combination of multiple interacting networks: "One body with multiple wings." They focused on their idea of 'interconnecting and interchanging' resources. Tiens Group also developed 'JTMM e-commerce' and promoted the concept: "Family consumption generates wealth; operating family consumption generates even more wealth."

Tiens Group's strength and success has set an example for other Chinese domestic enterprises. The experience is well worth learning from. Based on detailed research and careful analysis, this book reports on the normative and positive, rational and logical, and empirical and comparative methods that Tiens Group has used. The book indicates that Tiens encourages no limits on human creativity and personal development. This personal development can enhance corporate development; with better individual energy behind corporate development, there will then be more contributions to social development.

I send my heartfelt congratulations to Tiens Group for being featured as an example of an iconic enterprise.

Ban Ki-moon
Former Secretary-General of the United Nations
Chairman of the Board of Boao Forum for Asia

ACKNOWLEDGMENTS

Over almost four years, Liu Yingqiu and members of the Research Group of China Research Society of Urban Development investigated and analysed the global development concept and practice of Tiens Group. As well as deep discussions with Li Jinyuan, the members collected, summarized and learned from the successful experience of domestic and foreign Direct-Selling enterprises.

The research group was honoured to be invited to do this work by Li Jinyuan, and deeply thanks him for his guidance and assistance.

In addition to Liu Yingqiu, the members of the research group who were involved in the investigation, research and writing of this book include leading economists who had previously carried out in-depth research of Tiens: Feng Lei (Professor and Doctoral Supervisor of the National Academy of Economic Strategy, Chinese Academy of Social Sciences [CASS], writing Part VI of this book); Zhao Qilan (Professor and Doctoral Supervisor of Beijing Jiaotong University, writing Part IV of this book); Guo Qingfang (Professor and Master Supervisor of China University of Petroleum, writing Part III of this book); and Ming Anshu (Professor of the Institute of Quantitative & Technical Economics, CASS, Secretary of the research group, responsible for the organization and management of the research group).

The members also include leading economists that newly joined for this book: Ju Jinwen (Professor and Doctoral Supervisor of the Institute of Economics, CASS, writing Part V of this book); Zhang Wanming (Dean, Professor and Doctoral Supervisor of the Business School of the University of CASS, writing Part I of this book); Lv Fengyong (Doctor and Executive Researcher of National Academy of Economic Strategy, CASS, writing Part II and compiling the book); Peng Lihong (Professor and Doctoral Supervisor of the School of Economics, Renmin University of China) and Wang Xinling (Lecturer of Beijing International Studies University, Doctor of Economics of CASS, academic secretary and English translator of the research group). Ming Anshu provided excellent assistance as administrative secretary of the research group.

The book was written in Chinese and Wang Xinling provided the initial English translation. Professor Kevin McConkey, Senior Consultant, International Affairs, Tiens Group, assisted with editing that translation and with the process of publication in English. Those involved in the book are grateful also to Martin Liu and his colleagues at LID Publishing for their support and commitment to this book.

Li Jinyuan is honoured that Ban Ki-moon provided a Foreword for this book, and expresses gratitude for his words and understanding of Tiens Group.

PART I

SWAP AND TRANSCENDENCE: CONNOTATION, THEORY AND PRACTICE

ZHANG WANMING

Swapping is when an enterprise systematically integrates its available resources and factors of production, not only the traditional human resources, financial resources and material resources of an enterprise but also the resources of market, location and institutional variance. Swapping enables the rapid expansion and development of an enterprise by lowering operating costs, avoiding business risks, allocating some production factors outside the enterprise, and integrating more external forces in the internal operations of the enterprise.

Transcendence refers to the process of how an enterprise understands, challenges and surpasses others to achieve success. It reflects the theoretical findings obtained by enterprises when they apply modern economics, management theory and theory on emerging economies such as sharing economy, experience economy and fans economy to practice.

CHAPTER 1

SWAP AND TRANSCENDENCE: SCOPE AND CONNOTATION

SECTION 1
BACKGROUND AND SIGNIFICANCE OF SWAP AND TRANSCENDENCE

I. Background of Swap and Transcendence

1. The Constant Deepening and Development of the Reform and Opening Up has Brought New Opportunities to Swap and Transcendence

Initiated in 1978, the reform and opening-up has progressively changed China from a highly centralized planned economy to a socialist market economy, and thus brought about new opportunities to the common development of diverse forms of ownership. With the constant deepening of the reform, the market has played an increasingly important role in resource allocation; the government has further streamlined administration and delegated power to lower levels, and thus improved the efficiency of market operations; and, as affected by economic globalization, China has become more vulnerable to the impact of inflation or financial crisis but meanwhile benefited from the introduction of foreign advanced technologies and the rapid growth of international trade. In a word, the reform and opening-up has brought enterprises unprecedented opportunities.

First, the enterprise ownership structure has become diversified. With the transition from a planned economy to a market economy in China, the original monopoly of public ownership of the means of production has been broken, and nonpublic enterprises have developed from nothing and grown strong. Therefore, a market pattern with the public sector remaining dominant and diverse sectors of the economy competing equally and developing side-by-side has been formed. The diversified ownership structure not only lays a solid social and economic basis for the reform of state-owned enterprises, but also provides new space for the development of small and medium-sized enterprises. The Third Plenary Session of the

18th Communist Party of China (CPC) Central Committee put forward the new goal of a socialist market economy system with Chinese characteristics in the new stage, which was to deepen the reform of state-owned enterprises and develop a mixed-ownership economy. Since then, the Chinese market has embraced more diversified entities, seen more fierce competition, and given priority to quality and efficiency, offering new opportunities for enterprises to allocate resources more effectively and achieve transcendence.

Second, the supply-side structural reform has allowed a new platform for the development of enterprises. In 2015, the Central Economic Working Conference proposed the idea to implement the supply-side structural reform and clarified the task of "capacity reduction, de-stocking, deleverageing, cost reduction and improving underdeveloped areas," which defined the direction of enterprise reform and brought about new opportunities. In the supply-side structural reform, technological innovation and industrial upgrading constitute an important part. Hence, by issuing new policies on innovation and entrepreneurship, building innovation centres and constructing innovation platforms, the government has promoted the change of enterprises from low-cost competition to high-tech innovation competition, and brought the enterprises to the middle and high end of the global value chain. Under these circumstances, enterprises in China have ushered in new opportunities to allocate resources more effectively and attain transcendental development.

2. Internet Technologies Support Swap and Transcendence

Internet technologies now support swap and transcendence because human society has developed into the information age, where information is acquired, transmitted, processed and used through computer applications. Based on modern communication, the internet as well as database and its processing technologies, internet sharing has remarkably improved the efficiency of information acquisition and transmission. Internet technologies constitute important technological support for enterprises to effectively integrate resources and achieve transcendental development.

First, internet technologies can be applied to significantly improve the efficiency of enterprise management. The application of information technologies assists enterprises in realizing network-based information communication and flat management, and thus leads to the qualitative changes of the enterprise management information system, office automation system and analysis, decision-making and feedback system and significantly raises the efficiency of enterprise management.

Second, internet technologies can be applied to improve the efficiency of enterprise operations. Enterprises that make use of information technologies can rapidly acquire information on market supply and demand of products, effectively allocate resources for production and operations, lower operations costs and then enhance the efficiency of enterprise operation.

Finally, internet enterprises can be applied to facilitate business innovation of enterprises. The application of information technologies promotes the transformation of the manufacturing and operations modes of an enterprise and even the form of the whole industry. According to futurist Jeremy Rifkin, collaborative sharing of zero marginal cost created by the internet will probably become the dominant economic system worldwide. Sharing economy facilitates the circulation and reorganization of social idle resources and increases the efficiency of temporal and spatial allocation of resources. In addition, the commercialization of extensive internet technologies greatly expands the market boundary of enterprises and boosts enterprises' business model innovations such as e-commerce, online shopping and cross-border marketing.

3. The Development of Market Economy Creates a New Environment for Swap and Transcendence
   As a major characteristic of a market economy, the production and marketing of an enterprise is guided by the price mechanism. Since the reform and opening-up, China has constructed a socialist market economy system with public ownership remaining dominant and diverse forms of ownership competing equally and developing side-by-side. The Third Plenary Session of the 18th CPC Central Committee made a resolution to deepen the all-round reform, which expressly raised the requirement on dealing well with the relationship between government and market, making market play a decisive role in resource allocation and having government point out the development direction of a socialist market economy. By deepening the reform, it further facilitates the free and full circulation of various production factors, improves the efficiency of resource allocation, and creates an external free-competition environment for the development of swap and transcendence of enterprises.

4. The Rise of De-globalization and Trade Protectionism Poses New Challenges to Swap and Transcendence
   Currently, as the world economic growth slows down, market demand picks up insignificantly and international competition becomes increasingly intensified. As demonstrated by Britain exiting from the EU, the rise of far-right political parties in Europe, the US announcing to withdraw from the Trans-Pacific Partnership Agreement (TPP), Global Compact on Migration of the UN and the United Nations Educational, Scientific

and Cultural Organization (UNESCO), populism has resurfaced in some developed economies, 'de-globalization' has become a new phenomenon in current world economic development and the authority of the multilateral trading system is severely weakened. Various deep-rooted structural imbalances and interest conflicts in the current world economy pose a threat to the steady and healthy development of international trade and the world economy and also become a new obstacle and challenge to Chinese enterprises' swap and transcendence.

II. Theoretical Value and Practical Significance of Swap and Transcendence

1. Theoretical Value and Practical Significance of Swap

As the name suggests, swap means swapping one element for another element. It is distinguished from some other similar concepts including 'replacement,' 'displacement' and 'substitution' with specific technical connotations, since, for example, 'substitution' is generally applied to chemistry, commerce and mathematics. Many concepts in economic theory are associated with 'swap,' such as property rights exchange, financial swap and equivalent exchange of goods. However, these concepts focus on 'exchange' of things, but not their 'placement,' the systematic integration of the enterprise's available resources.

Swap initially referred to swapping the life-tenure labour relationship of unlimited liability between the enterprise and employees for the new labour relationship adapted to the market economy during the reform of state-owned enterprises. According to law, state-owned enterprises should pay compensation to employees and then terminate the unlimited liability system to eliminate the unlimited dependence of employees on state-owned enterprises, thus to turn employees into 'market men.' Afterwards, swap mainly indicated the swap of property rights, which mainly reflected the relationship between the original property rights owners and other subjects involved in the swap. Swap here essentially meant exchange, transferring the property rights of an enterprise through the property rights market to acquire other property rights.

In addition to containing the meaning of exchanges described above, the concept of swap in this book also represents the more systematic swapping process. It is the swap conducted in an interactive system, which is a way for the enterprise to integrate available resources and factors instead of individual swaps simply for the sake of transaction.

In the modern market economy, an enterprise has diversified available resources. In addition to traditional production factors such as human resources, financial resources and material resources, the resources of market, location and institutional variance also constitute the precious resources and factors for the development of enterprises. On the basis of swap theory, the development and utilization of market resources will place focus on the swap of common resources and functional interaction, but not the market itself. Through the swap and interaction, the market that did not exist or that could only be formed upon further development will be automatically created during the integration of network resources. Therefore, an important point of an enterprise's swap is to spread the products of developed countries and regions to backward regions and countries, and to transport the resources of backward countries to developed countries.

Moreover, swap is also a new operations and management mode. Traditional management theory believes that an enterprise can operate effectively only by scientifically manageing seven operating factors: human resources, financial resources, material resources, production, supply, sales and storage. However, according to swap theory, to lower operating costs and avoid operating risks, an enterprise can place some factors outside and introduce more external forces into enterprise operations through the swap, thus to realize the rapid expansion and development of the enterprise.

2. Theoretical Value and Practical Significance of Transcendence

Transcendence is a new theoretical category emerging along with the market competition of modern enterprises. It summarizes the theoretical findings obtained by enterprises when they comprehensively apply modern economics, management theory and theory on emerging economies such as sharing economy, experience economy and fans economy to practice. Transcendence refers to the process of how an enterprise understands, challenges, and overcomes itself, and finally surpasses others and achieves success.

First, transcendence means to transcend the enterprise itself. An enterprise can achieve a sharp rise of profits, expand its market share, and increase the enterprise value by integrating and reorganizing the interior organization, operations mechanism and ownership structure of the enterprise. An enterprise's organization modes are collectively known as the interior organization. This interior organization enables the communication of management decisions between the high and the low, so its efficiency determines the quality and efficiency of the enterprise's work. By optimizing the interior organization, the enterprise can speed up information transmission, save the time cost and lay the foundation for self-transcendence. The operations mechanism of an enterprise describes the enterprise's internal function and operations mode that support its existence and development. This mechanism covers the basic rules and corresponding regulations that guide and restrict the enterprise's business decisions and all activities associated with human, financial and material resources, as well as all internal and external factors and correlations that decide the enterprise's business behaviours. It determines the profit model, operations methods and marketing methods of an enterprise. Therefore, an enterprise can combine new management philosophy to optimize the ownership structure and solve the agency problem, adjust the ownership structure to expand the enterprise's business to new areas, and finally achieve the enterprise's transcendental development.

Second, transcendence refers to transcending competitors of the industry. In a market economy, to attain transcendental development, an enterprise must seize its special advantages, create a separate school in terms of the organization, market mode, ownership structure and operations mechanism and win customers' support with its unique advantages. These enterprises have either a high brand value, or unique marketing means, or a hi-tech network and information system. Only by "being unique, being excellent, being special and being the best" can an enterprise surpass competitors of the industry.

Finally, an enterprise's transcendence adheres to the supreme goal of leading the development of the industry. It means that an enterprise pursuing transcendence will apply new management theory to practice, forecast the trend of industry development, lead the whole industry with the innovative thinking pattern and product technology, create new modes of the industry and set new standards for the industry. By leading the development of the whole industry, an enterprise will enjoy various forms of gains in terms of cost, profit, scale and reputation. This is the supreme goal of an enterprise's transcendence.

3. Relation Between Swap and Transcendence

Swap and transcendence are respectively the means and the goal. Through swap, an enterprise can realize the optimum allocation and effective utilization of production factors, innovate its operations mode and business pattern, improve its management, better its management regulations, construct its new operations network and create the ecosphere for its transcendental development. The practice of the swap and transcendence theory is essentially the process of how an enterprise utilizes theory to drive development. An enterprise will inevitably confront many difficulties and obstacles during development. In this situation, the enterprise will seriously consider the strategies to solve these difficulties and obstacles; for instance, adopting the strategy of product differentiation or low-cost competition, the strategy of regional concentration or multinational collaboration, the strategy of individual proprietorship or merger and reorganization for win-win cooperation.

SECTION 2
SCOPE AND CONNOTATION OF SWAP

I. Concept of Swap

1. Definition of Swap

By swap, we generally mean ownership swap, which differs from exchange or replacement. In this book, we will discuss and explain the 'new swap.' According to existing research, new swap can be defined as the cross-factor, cross-sector, cross-product, cross-region, cross-market and even cross-border swap performed with human resources development and application as the basis, network direct selling as the pivot point and the brand effect as the support; and during the systematic swap, the enterprise can integrate internal and external resources, promote its competitiveness, development and expansion and finally achieve its transcendental development.

It is of profound theoretical background and practical significance to attain an enterprise's transcendental development through swap. As an enterprise is a collection of resources, the competition among enterprises mainly focuses on the struggle for and utilization of resources. The market standing of an enterprise depends on not only the quantity and quality of its resources but also its efficiency of resource utilization. Hence, the effective utilization of resources constitutes the key point to maintain the enterprise's survival and development and improve the enterprise's competitive edge, the important foundation for the enterprise to "defeat the strong by the weak," as well as the core objective that drives the enterprise to enhance its management efficiency.

With the development of economic globalization and information technology, production factors such as human resources, capital, land, technology and information have transcended the limit of time and space and are flowing worldwide. After China's accession to the WTO, seeing the fierce international market competition, Chinese enterprises must allocate their production factors in the global economic system and realize the swap and effective allocation of various production factors on a global scale.

2. Characteristics of Swap

First, the network is the main carrier for swap. The 'network' here not only includes the interconnection network mainly represented by the internet, but also covers the marketing network formed during the enterprise's production and operations and various network resources for the enterprise's production and operations management such as the human resources network and the Internet of Things.

Second, the effective allocation of resources is the main content of swap. In addition to human resources, capital, land and technology, modern enterprises also embrace the resources of information and market. In view of different resource endowments in different regions and sectors, an enterprise can swap its resources for new factor endowments to achieve transcendental development. Among the resource and factor endowments of an enterprise, human resources, market resources and corresponding endowments are of great significance. Human resources and their swap and integration can be transcultural, transethnic and even transregional and transnational. By swapping and integrating human resources of different countries, regions, cultures and nations, it will assist the enterprise in localizing human resources, avoiding the conflicts among different cultures and advancing the fusion and cooperation of different ethnic groups, and thus improve the enterprise's international marketing and competitiveness in the international market. Moreover, the enterprise can also swap and integrate the status and function of the operator and consumers, so as to change the status of consumers in the traditional economic life, internalize consumer behaviours as the production and operations behaviours of the enterprise and have consumers participate in the enterprise's production and operations and share the profits.

Finally, the constant innovation of the mechanism is the important institutional support to swap. Traditional private enterprises mostly adopts family operations, which is characterized by highly centralized power. This operations mode shows evident advantages in lowering the cost of the enterprise's internal coordination and avoiding noncooperation risk but may result in unplanned or biased operations decisions or wrong investment decisions of the enterprise. Therefore, the enterprise must constantly reform and innovate its mechanism and optimize its ownership structure and governance structure to prevent the decision risks and operations risks of private enterprises.

II. Connotation and Effect of Swap

1. Connotation of Swap

Swap not only involves the integration of an enterprise's internal resources, but also includes the integration of external social resources of an enterprise. Typically, swap consists of cross-factor swap, cross-border swap and cross-market swap.

Cross-factor swap means that an enterprise integrates resources based on its advantage in factor endowments. In cross-factor swap, the enterprise aims to remove its low-quality resources and acquire new factor endowments. Swap is the means and method to effectively integrate both internal and external production factors of an enterprise. By applying cross-factor swap, it helps the enterprise break through the limit of its own resource endowments and enables it to integrate and reorganize different factors at a higher level.

Cross-border swap indicates that an enterprise integrates international resources by making use of the differences of factor endowments among various countries. The enterprise's goal of cross-border swap is to acquire the resources lacking in its own country and advance the enterprise's resource endowment edge. Cross-border swap is not only the important means for an enterprise to integrate international market resources, but also the important approach for an enterprise to upgrade its resources, products and services. It will assist the enterprise in overcoming its shortage of resource endowments and making full use of high-quality resources from different countries.

Cross-market swap refers to an enterprise allocating and integrating resources from different markets. The enterprise conducts cross-market swap with the goal of lowering its production and operations cost and increasing the channels to gain profits. Cross-market swap is an important means for the enterprise to integrate resource advantages of different markets, as well as an important way for the enterprise to achieve transcendental development. Through cross-market swap, the enterprise can lower the production and operations cost, acquire the benefits of scope economy, break the barriers among different product markets and realize the cross-market layout.

Swap is holistic and systematic. Enterprises can improve their operations efficiency and achieve long-term healthy and steady development through the cross-temporal and cross-spatial integration and swap among different resources, countries and markets.

2. Effect of Swap

The effect of swap refers to the benefits and results of the enterprise's resource swap and integration. First, swap leads to the effect of market exploration. Through the swap and integration of production resources, human resources and market resources, the enterprise improves the efficiency of resource allocation, optimizes the structure of human resource allocation and expands the market, which reflects the swap's effect of market exploration.

Second, swap presents the innovation effect. By swapping and integrating business models and internal and external market resources, the enterprise expands its scope of business, develops its business scale, improves its organization and innovates its business models, which constitutes the innovation effect.

Finally, swap shows the effect of the superimposition of advantages. An enterprise's competitiveness depends on its core competence, while its core competence originates from its ability to integrate and reorganize its resource and factor endowments. Through the integration and swap of factor endowments, the enterprise takes the initiative to promote the dynamic role of its superior resources in its production and operations, changes the traditional way of resource allocation and integration, turns the original inferior resource endowments to superior endowments and introduces external resource endowments inside the enterprise. This is the effect of the superimposition of advantages.

III. Implementation Paths of Swap

1. Category of Swap

Swap is divided into the following categories based on the content and nature.

First, subject swap. The subject swap indicates the swap of the ownership nature of an enterprise. The enterprise can adjust its original ownership nature through the ownership swap, transfer or sell part of the enterprise ownership to professional managers and thus have the professional managers engage in enterprise operations and management as owners to avoid the agency risk. By the means of subject swap, an enterprise can implement effective property rights constraints and incentives and improve competitiveness. Subject swap can be conducted by transforming the family-based property relation to the partnership or stock system, or by changing state-holding ownership to stock-holding ownership.

Second, factor swap. Also known as cross-factor swap, it suggests the swap among different factors including capital, labour and technology. For example, in an industrial society, the labour intensive can be swapped for the capital intensive by increasing capital investment; and in an information society, the capital intensive can be swapped for the technology intensive. In recent years, enterprises have started changing their development methods. They have increased the research and development (R&D) expense, lowered the labour cost, replaced the capital intensive with the technology intensive, swapped heavy assets for light assets, transformed their capital structure and improved the efficiency of capital operations.

Third, endogenous swap and exogenous swap. Endogenous swap refers to the swap of production factors inside the enterprise, such as increasing the investment on R&D to develop new products and reducing the staff or adjusting the structure of personnel to improve operations efficiency. Exogenous swap indicates the swap between production factors inside and outside the enterprise, such as the swap of production factors between domestic enterprises and foreign enterprises, which is typically realized by mergers and acquisitions by transnational enterprises and the strategic alliance of enterprises. With endogenous swap and exogenous swap, the enterprise can perfect its industrial chain, acquire market access through business acquisitions, incorporate external resources in enterprise operations and thus achieve the goal of lowering costs, simplifying the structure and improving efficiency.

Fourth, static swap and dynamic swap. Static swap mainly means the one-time swap that achieves the goal of enterprise development, such as the property rights swap. Dynamic swap refers to the constant swap behaviours that exert constant influence, like constantly swapping backward technologies for new and high technologies and constantly swapping low-ability talents for high-ability talents.

2. Choices of Swap Paths
To realize the rational and effective allocation of enterprise resources, the enterprise can choose from multiple swap paths as follows:

The first choice is the swap with human resource development as a breakthrough. In the era of a knowledge economy, innovative talents are regarded as the key to the development of enterprises. By developing human resources rationally, it will improve the efficiency of human capital and advance the core competitiveness of the enterprise. The development and swap of human resources mainly consist of the following: (1) Educate and train enterprise employees. Increase investment in employee training, better employees' knowledge structure and improve the efficiency of human capital; (2) Carry out employee incentive measures. An effective employee incentive mechanism will encourage advanced employees, spur on backward employees and improve employees' work efficiency; (3) Explore and implement employee stock ownership. To adopt employee stock ownership, the enterprise can change the year-end bonus to equity, so as to render long-term incentives; and (4) Explore and implement management buy-out. It means that management, including the managers, can acquire enterprise equity with their own disposable incomes, or achieve the swap of enterprise equity through management's options. In this way, the enterprise can attract excellent talent, promote human capital efficiency and advance its competitiveness.

Second, the swap with transnational investment and trade as the main form. This kind of swap mainly comprises cross-border swap and cross-market swap. Cross-border swap refers to the resource swap and integration performed through transnational investment by the enterprise. Relying on transnational investment, the enterprise can expand its room for the swap of production factors, and meanwhile acquire more high-quality factors and resources. Cross-market swap is mainly carried out through transnational trade. In this kind of swap, the enterprise can exchange domestic commodities for foreign currency, pay attention to changes in the exchange rate of international financial markets and purchase foreign high-quality commodities with a manufacturing cost lower than those made in China. Hence, it can acquire greater comparative advantages in international trade through this cross-market swap.

Finally, the swap with network and information technology as the carrier. As China has transformed from a traditional industrial society to an information society, the acquisition and effective transmission of information have become the major factors contributing to the success of an enterprise. The key to the existence, development and success of an enterprise lies in whether the enterprise can effectively swap and integrate internal and external resources with network and information technology as the main carrier. Network and information technology can be applied to all aspects of enterprise operations and management. First, the management and control of the enterprise organization. The application of network and information technology can reduce management levels, realize a flat structure of enterprise organization, and improve management efficiency. Second, the control of the time cost and expense of enterprise operations and management. The global coverage of network constitutes important technical support to enterprise operations and management, since it can lower the time cost and management expense of the enterprise and prevent information asymmetry. Third, the revolution of the means of payment in enterprise production and operations. Along with the development of network and information technology, online sales are occupying an increasing proportion compared to offline sales. Therefore, it is of great significance to effectively apply network and information technology, as well as the development and use of big data, as it can help the enterprise innovate the means of payment, improve its production management and operations, lower marketing costs and raise marketing efficiency.

SECTION 3
SCOPE AND CONNOTATION OF TRANSCENDENCE

Transcendence, literally meaning to advance and surpass, generally refers to the qualitative leap and development after a long time of quantitative changes. Distinguished from the traditional industrial upgrading of an enterprise that simply suggests technological upgrading, personnel turnover and market change, transcendental development means to reform the operations mode, transform the business model and innovate the development concept of an enterprise.

I. Definition of Transcendence

Despite near-synonyms, transcendence has its own different meaning. First of all, distinguished from 'leap,' it places more emphasis on the process of a change, the process from the quantitative change to the qualitative change, and describes how to achieve a certain goal or status in this process. Second, transcendental development also differs from the development ahead of the times, since the latter is an unscientific and impractical development method that overuses resources or overestimates the development capacity. Third, transcendence is also different from disruption. While disruption is inclined to overthrow the old structure and set new standards in the process of creation, transcendence aims to improve and upgrade the original structure. To seek transcendental development, an enterprise attaches more importance to planning the development direction and goal in the light of market changes and achieve transcendental development through resource integration and upgrading.

In accordance with the maturity of the organizational structure of current enterprises and the status of the Chinese market economy, transcendence mainly covers following processes of qualitative changes. First, the transcendence of the enterprise system clears away all obstacles inside the enterprise. The family operations mode of "one family talks only" can no longer adapt to the current market conditions. Seeing the diversified development of enterprise businesses, the owner-and-manager-in-one operations mode greatly lowers the efficiency of decision-making. By comparison, the modern enterprise system that separates ownership from execution will help entrepreneurs play a bigger role and promote the enterprise's transcendental development through innovation.

Second, the transcendence of the enterprise management model provides the enterprise with a low-cost, high-efficiency organizational structure. The transformation from the 'pyramid' to the 'flat' management style symbolizes the start to reduce information asymmetry. Moreover, the transcendence from a single business entity to multi-business interaction constructs the platform for the enterprise to run scope economy. Compared to small-sized enterprises where the scale economy of a single business is the key to success, the large transnational enterprises construct the business information network, talent network and sales network during the process from the quantitative changes of business expanding to the qualitative change of business collaboration, thus to realize the transcendence of the business structure. In the meantime, along with the constant progress of science and technology and the development of emerging business models, the operations models based on the internet such as 'experience economy' and 'sharing economy' have created a new dimension of enterprises' business models; and the model innovation driven by the innovation of production factors also advances the transcendental development of enterprises.

In other words, an enterprise can practise swaps, adopt scientific management concepts and modern management measures, rely on emerging business models as the breach, open the mind and transform development methods, promote in-depth reform by means of cross-factor, cross-market and cross-border swaps, and finally transcend itself, other enterprises and the whole industry.

By transcending the enterprise itself, it means that the enterprise changes its structure of resource allocation and management through swaps, builds the new operations and management system, and exceeds its original level of development.

By transcending other enterprises, it means that the enterprise improves its organization and management ability and innovation ability in the process of swaps, thus to cultivate comparative advantages and transcend other enterprises.

By transcending the whole industry, it means that the enterprise has already surpassed other excellent enterprises and is further swapping and integrating internal and external resources and showing its powerful industrial leadership.

II. Contents and Implementation Paths of Transcendence

1. Main Contents of Transcendence

Transcendence is the reform of an enterprise in terms of its development ideas, operations models and business models, and mainly consists of the following four aspects.

First, the transcendence of development ideas. Rigid thinking patterns and development ideas can never lead to the healthy growth of an enterprise, not to mention its innovative development. Therefore, the transcendence of development ideas constitutes the primary task to be solved by the enterprise. Development ideas here comprise two aspects: the idea of enterprise development and the idea of market exploration. The idea of enterprise development determines the development direction, scale, quality and speed of an enterprise. Without a clear and scientific idea of enterprise development, the enterprise can hardly meet the requirements of the times, find the correct development direction, or attain the appropriate scale, the higher development quality, and the more sustainable development mode. As Internet+ is applied to an increasing number of enterprises, the enterprise can only transform its operations mode, innovate its marketing mode and acquire scientific and effective transcendental development by closely combining the network and information technology in the enterprise's development ideas and applying the technology to every link of the enterprise's operations.

Second, the transcendence of the operations model. Constructed on the basis of the enterprise's operations and development tenet, the operations model of an enterprise is a general term for all operations methods and approaches adopted to realize the enterprise's values and secure its development orientation. It includes the scope and content of business determined based on the enterprise's values, the position of the enterprise in the industrial chain and its approaches and methods to decide its values and improve its benefits. The transcendence of the operations model is an important means for the enterprise to change its development mode, choose its own profit mode and complete its transformation. In the practice of transcendence, the enterprise will stand in the height of a new age, new period and new development, depend on its advantages in resource endowments and choose the operations model and development method adapting to the times, market and its own conditions, which is the key to the transcendental development of the operations model.

Third, the transcendence of the business model. The business model mentioned here mainly consists of the operations model, the profit mode and the development strategy. As the overall strategy for transcendental development, the business model of an enterprise will be chosen according to the development stage and the superior resource endowments of the enterprise. If the enterprise is exposed to large-scale development, the standard production and marketing of products will be considered as the fundamental basis for the choice of the business model; if the enterprise is developing high-end consumer customization, the differentiated product design and manufacturing will be the basis; and if the enterprise is in the development stage of Internet+, the necessary basis to choose the business model will be whether the model constructs a sharing platform and realizes zero-cost intermediary business. The key to the transcendence of the business model lies in the enterprise accurately recognizing its own development stage and choosing the business model that is appropriate for its own development.

Fourth, the transcendence of the enterprise system. The enterprise system mainly comprises the ownership structure, the corporate governance structure and the enterprise governance structure. Deeply rooted inside the enterprise, the enterprise system plays a decisive role in the enterprise's development. Institutional arrangements, including ownership and management rights, the distribution of profits and the relationship between the parent enterprises and subsidiary enterprises, all exert significant influence on the enterprise operations. During the diversified development of family enterprises, a clear ownership structure and an independent legal person system will assist the enterprise in expanding its assets and achieving diversification.

2. Choices of Transcendence Paths

Enterprises in different development stages necessarily choose different paths to achieve transcendence. Three available choices of transcendence paths are listed below.

First, the transcendence of the ownership structure. The ownership structure and the corporate governance structure constitute the primary foundation and premise for the enterprise to achieve economies of scale and lower the transaction cost. The ownership structure is generally divided into the family ownership, partnership and shareholding system. With unitary subject of ownership and the source of funds confined to the family, family ownership restricts the amount of funds the enterprise can raise and makes it difficult to achieve economies of scale. Furthermore, the unclear ownership among family members will inevitably result in internal ownership dispute. The partnership, essentially the embryo of the shareholding system, was created by private enterprises during the reform and opening-up in China. The shareholding system is a typical form of a modern ownership system, which features the advantages of lowering the transaction cost, broadening the sources of funds, reducing the financing cost and expanding the enterprise's asset scale. The ownership structure is considered as the primary and fundamental factor to the development of an enterprise, so the transcendence of the ownership structure is an important approach for the enterprise to achieve transcendental development.

Second, the transcendence of the corporate governance structure. The corporate governance structure, consisting of the board of directors, the general manager and the board of supervisors, is essentially a structural institutional arrangement that defines the mutual checks and balances between the enterprise's ownership and management rights based on fiduciary duties. Two points of the corporate governance structure influence the success or failure of the enterprise. The first is how to coordinate the interest relationship between shareholders and the enterprise. In the enterprise where ownership is separated from management rights, shareholders may easily lose their power of control and be exposed to the agency problem, which goes against the long-term development of the enterprise. The enterprise can rationally coordinate the relationship between management's interests and investors' interests by providing stock options to management, to assure the healthy operations of the enterprise. The second point is how to coordinate the enterprise's relationship with other enterprises and the government. Market competition becomes increasingly fierce along with the development of a market economy. Therefore, a perfect corporate government structure must be constructed to help the enterprise achieve constant growth and healthy development. The transcendence of the enterprise's governance structure can ease the interest contradictions of all parties inside and outside the enterprise and enhance its ability to withstand risks.

Third, the transcendence of the incentive mechanism and consumption stickiness. The incentive mechanism here refers to the incentive measures adopted by the enterprise to build consumer stickiness. The incentive mechanism for consumers is generally divided into two categories. The first is membership to increase customers' repeat purchases and drives them to introduce new customers by means of price concessions. The other mechanism relies on the market strength created by consumers and the corresponding value expression. As the third capital form in addition to currency capital and knowledge capital, this value expression is manifested by the shares and options of consumers. This incentive mechanism transcends the traditional relationship between consumers and operators, changes their roles, builds a favourable sales relationship between the enterprise and consumers, and secures a stable source of customers for the enterprise. With the transcendence of the incentive mechanism and consumption stickiness, the enterprise can cultivate steady and sticky consumers and acquire greater market strength.

CHAPTER 2

SWAP AND TRANSCENDENCE: THEORETICAL BASIS AND INNOVATIVE DEVELOPMENT

The swap and transcendence theory is not only a summary of enterprises' practical experiences, but also a new theoretical exploration and development of modern economics and management. This chapter mainly analyses and explains the basic theoretical basis for swap and transcendence, as well as its development and innovation in practice.

SECTION 1
THEORETICAL BASIS OF SWAP

I. Enterprise Growth Theory, Enterprise Management Theory and Basis of Swap

With the enterprise as the research object, the enterprise growth theory explores the general law of the growth of enterprises and probes into the comprehensive theory that determines an enterprise's growth and development. On the basis of the factors influencing enterprise development, the enterprise growth theory can be divided into two types: the enterprise exogenous growth theory and the enterprise endogenous growth theory. Explaining the role of external factors and internal factors in enterprise development, the enterprise growth theory constitutes the theoretical support to the transcendental development of enterprises.

1. Main Content of the Enterprise Growth Theory

An enterprise's essential characteristics lie in the returns from different resources and factors confirmed by contract. The contract is the form of enterprise existence, instead of the cause of enterprise emergence. The enterprise contract is established based on the enterprise's acquisition and use of resources. Neoclassical economists represented by Roger Penrose regard an enterprise as a production function and believe that the enterprise growth is basically affected by exogenous factors and an enterprise adjusts its production scale according to the cost curve and the demand curve. Considering the relation between income and cost, the enterprise growth comprises three stages: increasing returns to scale, constant returns to scale and decreasing returns to scale. The key to achieve increasing returns to scale rests in the innovation of the production or operations modes of products or services. Innovation originates inside the enterprise. The Austrian School represented by Joseph Schumpeter considers the entrepreneur as the most important factor influencing enterprise growth. In the book *The Theory of Economic Development*, Schumpeter pointed out: "Entrepreneurs' innovation activities are the primary force that drives the economic system to develop from one kind of balance to another kind of balance. Traditional theories only consider the economy's adaption to external changes as the origin of economic development and growth. However, as a matter of fact, the entrepreneur also makes up the internal factor of an economy, whose creative behaviours play a revolutionary role in the enterprise development. By determining the mode of resource allocation and utilization, the entrepreneur can promote enterprise upgrading and growth. Entrepreneurs can innovate enterprises in five ways: (1) Produce new products. Promote the enterprise upgrading from the aspect of products by improving the product quality or releasing new products that consumers are unfamiliar with; (2) Adopt new methods of production. Advance the enterprise development with new production methods of low cost and high efficiency; (3) Explore new sales markets. New markets, which are mainly explored by establishing transnational corporations, exert significant influence on the market size; (4) Acquire new sources of the supply of raw materials. New sources are generally characterized by high quality or lower costs and enable enterprises to acquire comparative advantages; and (5) Build a new organization, such as achieving a monopoly or breaking the original industrial layout."

Distinguished from managers, the entrepreneur bears the primary task to make strategic decisions. The enterprise depends on the entrepreneur's innovation behaviours to explore new methods of production and realize the reintegration and reorganization of production factors. The enterprise growth theory of Joseph Schumpeter constitutes a theoretical support to swap. The entrepreneur's innovation, which is essentially the process of systematic swap in swap theory, means to upgrade the enterprise management measures and production methods through technical swap, explore new sales markets with transnational swap, and innovate enterprise products and cover multidomain markets by means of product swap.

2. Different Management Modes in Different Development Stages of the Enterprise

Different operations and management modes are adopted by the enterprise in different development stages. The selection of the enterprise's operations and management model depends on both endogenous and exogenous factors of the enterprise in the specific development stage. By swapping and integrating the enterprise's resources in different development stages, the enterprise aims to realize the conversion between endogenous and exogenous resources and thus adapt to different operations and management goals in different development stages. The operations and management modes in different development stages of the enterprise include the following.

First, the line management mode. At the initial stage of an enterprise, the manager generally adopts the line management mode considering the small enterprise scale, the small number of employees and the small market size. Based on line management, the enterprise can directly guide production, operations, marketing and making decisions. The enterprises adopting line management show a greater effect in organization management, operations management, cost management and sales management.

Second, the systematic multi-level management mode. As to the enterprises at the mid stage of development, managers generally give up the line management mode that directly guides production, operations, marketing and making decisions, in view of the larger enterprise size, more employees and larger market size. In this stage, the enterprise usually applies the systematic multi-level management mode. This mode overcomes the shortage of the line management mode that the overall situation is affected by the error of a single decision; but meanwhile it may lower the efficiency of information transmission and result in the failure of the information feedback mechanism since it features multiple levels of management and a more complex system. Therefore, this management mode also encounters new challenges along with the development of the enterprise.

Third, the operations and management mode of equity incentive. For enterprises in the mature development stage, production and operations activities also rely on managers and employees of enterprises in addition to their owners. Under these conditions, according to the empirical conclusion that equity incentive has positive correlation with the enterprise's performance based on the demand of market development and modern economics of property rights, the enterprise owners take the initiative to transfer part of their equity to management and employees and build the operations and management mode of equity incentive. With this mode, the enterprise can arouse the enthusiasm of management and employees, improve the efficiency of management, production and operations, and advance its ability of innovative development, transformation and upgrading.

Fourth, the flat operations and management mode. With regard to enterprises in the development stage of the wide application of network and information technology, their major operations and management characteristic lies in their emphasis on applying the network and information technology to enterprise management. The network and information technology can promote the efficiency of information transmission and feedback among department managers and employees of the enterprise, as well as between managers of different levels and the senior management of the enterprise. By introducing the network and information technology, it can reduce the levels of management and thus improve the efficiency of the enterprise's operations and management.

3. Management Modes and Swap

Neoclassical economists regard an enterprise as a 'black box.' According to this opinion, the enterprise is essentially a market subject that shares an equal position with consumers. While consumers pursue maximum efficiency, the enterprise seeks maximum profits. The enterprise black-box theory sees all factors controlled by the enterprise as the capital of the enterprise. To maximize profits, the enterprise must satisfy market demand through internal and external flow of capital, thus to constantly increase the enterprise value. The enterprise acquires economic resources, material resources, human resources and information resources from the market through swap, which is an important method for the enterprise to seek greater development and maximize profits in a modern market economy.

Which way of swap the enterprise chooses depends on several factors. One of these factors is the operations mode of the enterprise. With different operations modes, enterprises adopt different ways of swap. The enterprise of line management mainly conducts swap directly. The enterprise of systematic multi-level management mode performs swap in a multi-level, systematic and complex manner. The swap of the equity-incentive enterprise mainly presents the symmetry between power and interests and the balance between incentive and efficiency. As to the enterprise of flat management, the swap is conveniently conducted by placing production factors on the network upon the main support of information technology.

The relations between the operations and management model and swap mentioned above have been demonstrated by the practices of numerous enterprises. Despite the different manifestations of these models, they share basically the same connotation. With its rapid development, enterprises are exploring and applying the network and information technology as the platform for enterprises' operations and management, through which enterprises realize the efficient transmission, real-time feedback and effective sharing of resource information and management directives. By means of institutional optimization and systematic swap of original human resource management, it can perfectly integrate advanced technologies, advanced management methods and the modern enterprise management system, and thus promote the innovation of the enterprise management system and improve the overall management level and efficiency of the enterprise.

II. Human Capital Theory and Swap

1. Basic Connotation of Human Capital Theory

Among various factors that influence economic development, the human factor is the most essential. Economic development mainly relies on the advancement of human capital instead of non-natural resources or capital itself. In modern society, the investment in human capital enjoys a higher rate of return compared to other investments. Theodore W. Schultz compared the relation curve of the income and age of skilled workers and unskilled workers and found the curve of unskilled workers steeper. Through the quantitative study of the relation between American education investment and economic growth between 1929 and 1957, he concluded that the average rate of return of education investment reached 17%. Therefore, the investment in human capital plays a significant positive role in the economic development of the enterprise and even the whole of society.

Human capital management is established on the basis of human resource management. An enterprise invests in and manages people as its capital and adjusts and swaps human resources and the corresponding structure according to the different value goals in different development stages to acquire the long-term return of value. Human capital management consists of the quantitative and qualitative management of human resources. The former maintains the optimum ratio between the quantity of human resources and the scale of enterprise development by cultivating, organizing and coordinating personnel, so as to give the best play to human resources and material resources. The latter effectively identifies, guides and manages people's thoughts, behaviours and skills and fully mobilizes people's initiative and hence improves work efficiency.

Human resource management built on the basis of the human capital theory generally originates in three different management concepts. The first is the human resource management concept led by the enterprise manager, the core of which is the performance management of human resources. The enterprise manager makes the best use of human resources by systematically designing, manageing and regulating human resources. On the basis of this concept, the enterprise is more inclined to adopt such modes as human resource outsourcing and electronic human resource management. The second is the human resource management concept led by enterprise employees. As to this concept, the enterprise employee formulates and also implements the human resource management system and policies. Since man is not merely a natural man with physiological needs but also a social man with interest demands, the human resource management of the enterprise will take into account both the natural needs and social needs of people. The enterprises adopting this concept prefer to apply the human resource management mode of equity incentive. The third is the human resource management concept led by enterprise stakeholders. With this concept, the enterprise will strive for the effective matching between internal employees and their positions, as well as the harmonious development of the external market. In this case, the enterprise generally adopts the human resource management mode of 'paid public welfare leave' (which is a paid leave provided by the enterprise to encourage enterprise employees to experience public-welfare programs and activities and help others as volunteers) and 'the employer brand' (which is an emotional relationship between the employer and employees with the enterprise brand as the carrier. In this enterprise human resource management mode, with the employer as the subject and core employees as the carrier, the employer and enterprise stakeholders provide high-quality and featured services to employees in the enterprise and even in society, to build a good image as an employer worthy of expectation and respect and improve the popularity and reputation of the employer in the talent market). The human capital theory theoretically supports the practice of enterprise swap and promotes the innovation of enterprise human resource management.

2. Human Capital and Swap
   As human capital plays an important role in enterprise development, human capital management constitutes an important part of enterprise management. The enterprise manages human capital through swap, which is mainly manifested by the swap between human capital development and people themselves and between human capital property and people's status.

   First, the swap between human capital development and people themselves. Compared with material capital, human capital presents the following features. First, with the greater stock and higher quality of human capital, the per-capital output and labour productivity are higher. Second, with the increasing capital investment, human capital increases, but the marginal revenue of material capital is decreasing. Third, the increase of human capital improves the efficiency of material capital and thus raises the marginal revenue of material capital. In other words, the increase of human capital not only develops its own marginal revenue, but also raises the marginal revenue of investment in other material capital, thus increasing the return to scale of the whole social economy. The special role of human capital in economic growth has altered people's understanding of the source of economic growth, so the new growth theory centring on human capital is generated. The emphasis of the enterprise's human capital investment will be placed on the education of employees. It can swap low-quality labour resources for high-quality labour resources by building the enterprise's human resource education and training platform.

Second, the swap between human capital property and people's status. As determined by the special role of human capital in market competition, the modern enterprise competition is not simply the competition of the institution, but also the competition of talents. Particularly, in the modern market economy where the network and information technology ushers in rapid development, talents have become the first capital support to improve enterprise competitiveness. Therefore, the enterprise will attach importance to the development and application of human capital and select effective incentive systems to retain high-end talent. By designing and applying the talent incentive system and changing the status of people in the enterprise, the enterprise can swap the status of managers, operators and marketers and fully explore and give full play to employees' enthusiasm, initiative and creativity, thus advancing the efficiency of other production factors and improving the enterprise's competitiveness and development ability.

The human capital incentive system mainly comprises three aspects. The first is the equity incentive. Issue equity to employees and turn employees into enterprise owners, so as to mobilize employees' enthusiasm and increase the enterprise value. The second point is the incentive of rights and status. Develop the superior and weed out the inferior of enterprise human capital by selecting and employing the CEO, adjusting the positions of general employees, and promoting or dismissing employees. The third is the cultural incentive. It means to build a favourable environment of the enterprise, assure the harmonious competition and cooperation of employees, enhance team cohesion, and cultivate employees' sense of belonging and fulfilment. The enterprise can turn employees into enterprise owners and profit sharers to maximize the return from the enterprise's investment in human capital.

III. International Trade, Investment Theory and Swap

To improve competitiveness and promote the growth and development of an enterprise, an important approach is to achieve cross-region, cross-border and cross-market resource integration and improve efficiency through swap. The theory of international trade and investment has systematically revealed the general rules of the enterprise's cross-border supply of commodities and services and investment, which provides important theoretical support for the enterprise to explore the space for development through swap.

1. Comparative Advantages and Product Differentiation Advantages are the Premise and Foundation for the Swap of Commodities and Services

To embrace greater market competitiveness, an enterprise must acquire advantages in competition first. The advantages in competition can be divided into three different types. The first is the absolute advantage, which suggests that a country can produce products that cannot be produced by other countries. The second is the comparative advantage. It means that a country can produce products at a lower cost, though other countries can produce products of the same kind. The third is the product differentiation advantage. In this case, the enterprise enjoys constant innovation ability and is able to produce products different from other enterprises while assuring a lower production cost. Among the three advantages above, the absolute advantage is special since it depends on the special resource endowment, and the other two advantages rely on the effective utilization and integration of resource endowments. Hence these two different groups of advantages complement each other. This constitutes an important factor driving the product and service trade of enterprises in different countries.

The enterprise that transacts cross-border swap of products or services must show its own advantages. As proved by swap practices, most of the enterprises having performed swap successfully enjoy capital advantage, technology advantage or brand advantage. The different advantages of different enterprises urge the enterprises to swap different advantageous resources. By incorporating high-quality production factors and products at home and abroad in the enterprise through cross-border marketing, the enterprise can give full play to the comparative advantage and product differentiation advantage of the enterprise.

2. The Key is to Realize Swap is Transforming Internalization to Externalization

During the swap, the enterprise adheres to the important goal of exploring and playing to advantages, lowering the cost and achieving the transcendental development of the enterprise. In this process, internalization and externalization are generally adopted as the important means and measures of the enterprise to lower the cost and improve efficiency. The theory of internalization aims to avoid the expensive cost of external transactions. It believes that an enterprise can reduce its cost of external transactions (such as the negotiation cost, enforcement cost, supervision and punishment cost) by transforming external transactions to internal activities of the enterprise. Internalization of external transactions assists the enterprise in expanding its size, lowering the transaction cost and maintaining the advantage of lower costs.

The theory of externalization discusses the integration of the enterprise's external resources, which is mainly realized through outsourcing.

Outsourcing means that the enterprise makes full use of external resources, transfers its internal production to external production by signing a contract with a business contractor, solves geographical restrictions and technical difficulties based on external resource advantages, and supports its development with more external resources.

Internalization enables the enterprise to bring its own resource advantages into play, lower transaction expenses and operating costs and achieve economies of scale, while externalization helps the enterprise adopt flexible modes of operation, integrate internal and external resource advantages, and promote operations performance and enterprise competitiveness.

3. International Trade and Multinational Investment Expands the Space for Swap

International trade and multinational investment are considered to be important methods for the enterprise to expand the space for swap. They are not only an important means for the enterprise to explore the overseas market, but also an important approach for the enterprise to complete its strategic layout overseas. By means of integration and swap of internal and external resources, the enterprise can satisfy local market demands and also realize its overseas layout and industrial optimization.

Economic globalization has promoted market competition and advanced the development of the global economy. The rise of 'de-globalization' is challenging developing countries that are involved in international divisions of labour and international competition, including China. It also makes China and developing countries and regions replace developed countries and regions as the main battlefield of international market competition. Under these circumstances, the important factor that determines whether an enterprise can successfully explore the international market, grab opportunities and acquire further development rests in whether the enterprise chooses the development strategy conforming to the requirements of the international market and whether it can successfully complete cross-space and cross-market swap and integration of domestic and foreign resources through international trade and multinational investments.

IV. Modern Circulation Theory and Swap

In the modern market economy, it is of great significance for the enterprise to achieve transcendental development in how the enterprise realizes cross-product, cross-sector, cross-region, cross-market and cross-border swap and resource integration against the de-globalization trend. Modern logistics represented by supply chain management and e-commerce has emerged along with the development of network and information technology, which will assist the enterprise in swapping and integrating internal and external resources. Thus, the modern logistics theory becomes the important theoretical support to swap.

1. Supply Chain Management is the Necessary Condition for Successful Swap
The supply chain refers to the whole process by which the enterprise manufactures final products and delivers the products to consumers through marketing channels and retailers. Supply chain management essentially means the management and control of goods, capital and information flow, which effectively connects commodities and consumers by integrating the management of raw material suppliers, product manufacturers, market distributors and retailers, and consumers.
In the process of supply chain management, the network and information technology can be applied to improve the efficiency of information communication among scattered members of the supply chain and advance the coordination and cooperation efficiency between production and processing enterprises and logistics and transportation enterprises. Scientific supply chain management plays an important part in simplifying the process of enterprise production and operations, raising the efficiency of all links associated with enterprise production and operations and lowering the transaction cost of operations and management. Effective supply chain management plays an irreplaceable role in shortening the circulating time of products, increasing the rate of capital turnover, reducing enterprise stock, avoiding operating risk, and achieving a constant growth of profits. As it is widely applied, supply chain management shows an increasingly significant effect on the management of enterprise logistics, cash flow and information flow, and even becomes the important approach for the enterprise to achieve transcendental development.

2. E-commerce and Network Marketing are Important Technical Means to Improve the Quality and Speed of Swap
Distinguished from a traditional sales mode, e-commerce is a transaction conducted through the internet instead of business activity carried out through physical exchange or direct physical contact. E-commerce can be completed through online shopping, online payment and supporting logistics. As an advanced form of e-commerce, network marketing constitutes an integral part of the enterprise's overall marketing strategy. It includes various operating and sales activities performed online with the technical support of the internet, aiming to achieve the enterprise's overall business objective. Network marketing is performed in multiple forms, including trading e-commerce marketing, content site marketing and social network marketing. All marketing activities carried out mainly on the internet can be called network marketing. As emerging formats of marketing, e-commerce

and networking marketing are developing vigorously, the transaction modes mainly consist of: manufacturer to business (M2B); business to business (B2B); business to customer (B2C); customer to customer (C2C); customer to business (C2B); and so on. In practice, the enterprise mostly adopts the online to offline (O2O) model for network marketing.

Compared to traditional transaction modes, e-commerce and network marketing feature evident advantages. First, e-commerce and network marketing go beyond the temporal and spatial constraints of traditional markets and can conduct transactions worldwide 24 hours a day. Second, they simplify the transaction procedure and save on transaction costs. In the traditional transaction mode, the product is sold by the manufacturer to the agent or wholesaler, then distributed to the retailer and, finally, sold to the consumer. In this mode, the product price paid by the end customer is much higher than the ex-factory price of the product due to the price markups of all the links in this long process. Therefore, the traditional offline sales model is much less effective. Third, they improve the transaction efficiency and precisely allocate supply and demand. In the traditional transaction mode, information asymmetry between the producer and the customer leads to mismatching between consumption and production. In comparison, in e-commerce and network marketing that is free from any spatial and temporal constraints, both the supply and demand sides display and need relatively little information, so they can effectively achieve the optimum allocation of supply and demand resources.

E-commerce and network marketing have become important technical measures and means for the enterprise to raise its efficiency of resource swap and integration. According to *2016 Analysis Report of the Big Data of China's E-commerce Industry*, online retail sales had exceeded 5 trillion by 2016, accounting for 14.9% of total retail sales of social consumer goods, and 64% of all internet users had joined online shopping. Online sales are taking the market shares from offline sales, and e-commerce has become the necessary means for the sales of an enterprise.

SECTION 2
PROCESS AND THEORETICAL INNOVATION OF TRANSCENDENCE

I. Enterprise's Merger and Reorganization and Transcendence

1. Connotation of Enterprise's Merger and Reorganization

The enterprise's merger and reorganization mean that it transforms its ownership structure, organizational structure, and operations and management mode through equity transfer and organization integration between enterprises according to certain procedures stipulated by law, with the purpose of effectively allocating and integrating enterprise resources. It is a kind of strategic arrangement by which the enterprise breaks the constraints of the market, region, country and ownership, introduces external resources in the enterprise, expands the business scale, extends the scope of business, and thus achieves greater development. The basic rules that the enterprise will abide by during the merger and reorganization include the following: the principle of voluntary consultation and mutual benefit; the principle of complementary advantages, structure optimization and efficiency first; the principle of revitalizing stock and expanding increments; the principle of giving priority to assuring the rights and interests of creditors and employees; the principle of exchange of equal values and fair competition; and the principle of improving the enterprise's innovation ability and competitiveness.

2. Modes of Enterprise's Merger and Reorganization and their Transcendence Effect

In general, the enterprise's merger and reorganization is mainly realized across these modes: first, the acquirer undertakes all the creditor's rights and liabilities of the acquired; second, the acquirer purchases all assets of the acquired at a market price; third, the acquirer obtains the controlling stake of the acquired through acquisition or asset transfer; fourth, the acquirer accepts the authorization of the acquired to operate all the assets of the acquired; and fifth, several enterprises are combined to become a new enterprise according to the merger agreement.

Merger and reorganization of the enterprise can be divided into horizontal and vertical merger and acquisition by the object and scope of resources integration and swap of the enterprise. The horizontal merger and acquisition are the cross-industry merger and acquisition implemented by the enterprise for synergistic effect. With the merger and acquisition of different businesses, the enterprise can realize the effective allocation and integration of the enterprise's internal resources, reduce the external transaction cost, explore the economies of scope and cultivate a comparative advantage. The vertical merger and acquisition are performed between different enterprises respectively at the upstream and downstream of the industrial chain, to lower the transaction cost, transportation cost and operation and management cost and rebuild the high-quality industrial chain. By means of vertical and horizontal merger and reorganization, the enterprise can push forward its deep development in the same field or expand its presence to different industries.

Merger and reorganization of the enterprise shows significant transcendence effect. First, it enables cooperative cooperation. Through merger and acquisition, two or more enterprises can integrate their own advantageous resources, complement and benefit each other and create greater value of the enterprise. Second, it raises the market share. The market share of the enterprise's products and services rapidly rise based on merger and reorganization, which will assist the enterprise in gaining greater market advantage and comparative advantage. Third, it boosts the transformation and upgrading of the enterprise. Merger and reorganization will help the enterprise cultivate new growing points and adjust the market position of the products and services, and therefore drives the transformation and upgrading of the enterprise. Finally, it strengthens the enterprise's risk management and control. By means of merger and reorganization, the enterprise's ability of risk identification, management and control can be advanced. Hence, merger and reorganization are regarded as an important means for the enterprise to meet fierce market competition at home and abroad and achieve transcendental development.

II. Enterprise's Cross-temporal Swap and Transcendence

The rapid development and wide application of the network and information technology lays the foundation for an enterprise's cross-temporal swap and transcendence. The network and information technology not only helps the enterprise break the time limit on resource allocation, but also assists it in realizing the inter-temporal allocation of resources.

1. The Network and Information Technology Breaks the Time Limit on Resource Allocation

The development of the network and information technology drives the progress of e-commerce, cloud connectivity, big data analysis and enterprise intelligent management. By developing and applying the network and information technology, it technically supports the allocation and swap of internal and external resources of the enterprise and enables the enterprise to break the time limit on resource allocation. For example, the turnover of Tmall had exceeded 1 billion yuan within merely 52 seconds after the initiation of the 2016 Single's Day Shopping Carnival; three minutes later, Cainiao Logistics had received over 1 million orders; and by 09:39,

Alipay had reached a peak of 120,000 payments per second. Moreover, the 2017 Carnival outperformed 2016. According to the statistics, e-commerce and network marketing have expanded the sales channels for the enterprise, enhanced the speed and efficiency of the enterprise's cross-temporal allocation of product sales and broken the time limit on the enterprise's resource allocation.

2. The network and information technology improves the efficiency of the enterprise's inter-temporal allocation of resources

   The development and wide application of the network and information technology renders important technical support to the timely and efficient interconnection between enterprises and global consumers. The network and information technology can be applied to assist the enterprise in efficient, convenient and real-time transactions of products and services and help the enterprise to significantly improve the efficiency of inter-temporal allocation of products and services. For example, the network and information technology connects the marketing and transaction of offline market subjects and the marketing and transaction of online market subjects, which goes beyond the time limit on marketing and transaction of market subjects in the traditional transaction mode, and improves time efficiency, thus making the enterprise's inter-temporal allocation of resources more convenient and efficient.

III. Enterprise's Cross-spatial Swap and Transcendence

An enterprise's cross-spatial swap and transcendence is performed on the basis of effective swap between its exogenous and endogenous factors. The effective swap between exogenous and endogenous factors of the enterprise facilitates the spatial integration and cross-spatial allocation of its factors, which drives its transcendental development. The enterprise's cross-spatial allocation of resources consists of the cross-spatial allocation of single resources and the allocation of overall resources. The realization of the cross-spatial swap and transcendence of an enterprise depends on whether single resources or overall resources are exposed to resource allocation and whether any difference exists between them.

1. Cross-spatial Allocation of Single Resources and Its Realization

   Considering an enterprise's available resources may be single or overall, the cross-spatial allocation of resources will be correspondingly different. The single resource refers to the resource with a single individual characteristic or a single cluster characteristic that can be independently identified in available resources. In the early and medium stage of enterprise development, most of its available resources are single resources.

The cross-spatial allocation of the enterprise's single resources suggests the allocation and swap of its available single resources in different spaces, different regions and even different countries. The cross-spatial allocation of single resources is mainly realized by exploring and discovering the potential and advantage of cross-spatial allocation of available resources and seeking the mode and path of the cross-spatial allocation of available single resources, so as to achieve the ultimate goal of improving efficiency and achieving transcendental development. According to *2016-2020 China's Logistics Industry Investment Analysis and Forecasting Report*, the total transaction volume of logistics in China had grown from 96.7 trillion to 213.5 trillion yuan from 2009 to 2014, reaching an average annual growth of 17.3%. This fact demonstrates the increasingly important role of the cross-spatial allocation of enterprise resources in enterprise development.

2. Cross-spatial Allocation of Overall Resources and its Realization

The overall resources mean the sum of all available resources of the enterprise, which are holistic and systematic with integrated clusters. In the medium and advanced stage, the enterprise's available resources are mostly exposed to overall coordination linkage. The swap and integration of these available resources are technically supported by modern logistics based on the network and information technology, which not only breaks the spatial limit on the enterprise's resource allocation, but also provides the technical platform that enables the cross-spatial allocation of enterprise resources.

Being the supporting system to e-commerce and network marketing platforms, modern logistics realizes the free circulation and convenient transaction of various enterprise resources among different enterprises, regions and countries and even in the whole world, and assures material transfer and effective allocation as the important foundation for the cross-spatial allocation of resources worldwide. With the rapid development of e-commerce and network marketing, an increasing number of enterprises have started to construct their modern logistics network adapting to their own development, to support the effective allocation of enterprise resources inside the enterprise or among different enterprises or regions in the whole country or the world.

The cross-spatial allocation of the enterprise's overall resources is mainly achieved through merger and reorganization of the enterprise or the strategic alliance and international division of labour. In a strategic alliance, enterprises establish a strategic partnership to share resources and risks by integrating with other stakeholders. A strategic alliance can be built in multiple ways such as production outsourcing, project entrustment, franchising and joint development. By establishing a strategic alliance, it can save the transaction cost of the enterprise's merger and reorganization and help the enterprise to expand its presence in or outside the industry. Its typical representatives include the production alliance and R&D alliance. On the basis of alliances, the enterprise can complete its production, R&D outside and transcend its business forms by means of resource sharing and complementary advantages.

As a result of the development of social productivity, the pattern of international division of labour was formed based on different resource endowments in different regions since modern times. It demonstrates that the social labour division of a country has gradually gone beyond the border and suggests the change from production socialization to internationalization. The development of international division of labour makes the cross-spatial allocation of enterprise resources possible.

SECTION 3 THEORETICAL EXPANSION OF SWAP AND TRANSCENDENCE

New ideas about the production, operations and management of enterprises are growing along with the emergence and development of new technologies. In this new period and new stage, enterprises must think about how to effectively utilize the network and information technology to integrate technology with production, operations and management and to innovate operations models and business models. Seeing the wide application of the network and information technology and the rise of de-globalization, the important premise of transcendental development rests in whether the enterprise can choose the appropriate operations and business models for itself.

I. Swap and Transcendence in the Sharing Economy

The sharing economy is a new economic model in which the use rights of idle resources are temporarily transferred to the people and market subjects in need to obtain return. In this economy, various idle resources offline in forms of material, labour, education and health are integrated through the internet, and the subjects pay and benefit in different ways and share the economic dividends generated by the integration.

The concept of the sharing economy was first put forward by Professor Marcus Felson from the Texas State University and Professor Joel Spaeth from University of Illinois in their thesis *Community Structure Collaborative Consumption: A Routine Activity Approach*. The sharing economy comprises three major parts: the demander of commodities or services, the supplier and the sharing economy platform. This economic model operates depending on information technology-based market platforms constructed by the third party. By means of these platforms, participants in market transactions exchange their idle materials, share their knowledge and experiences, and raise funds for certain innovative projects from enterprises.

The sharing economy establishes a series of mechanisms including the mobile LBS application, dynamic algorithm and pricing and mutual evaluation system based on the network and information technology, helps the supplier and demander trade on the sharing economy platform and becomes a new economic mode on the basis of big data analysis and integration of various information. The emergence and development of this economic model mentally inspire and practically support the formation and development of the swap and transcendence theory.

Consumers or producers, natural people or enterprises engaged in production or operations, are all demanders or suppliers of products or services, which changes the demand and supply structure of the traditional market and expands the scope of demand and supply. The third-party platform connects the supplier and the demander of idle resources through big data matching and thus evidently improves the efficiency of the allocation and swap of production factors.

The swap and transcendence theory is closely associated with the sharing economy. As a modern method of the swap and effective allocation of idle resources, the sharing economy constitutes a new carrier and approach for an enterprise to effectively allocate and swap internal idle resources, and meanwhile provides new ideas for it to lighten assets, lower financial leverage and increase the efficiency of asset operations, so as to achieve innovative and transcendental development. By sharing and swapping resources, an enterprise can not only effectively allocate and utilize its idle resources, but can also share and swap resources with external resource demanders and suppliers, laying the foundation for its transcendental development.

II. Swap and Transcendence in the Experience Economy

The experience economy is an economic activity in which an enterprise adopts the means of production or service of creating consumption experience, provides the product of consumers' actual experience, regards consumer experience feelings or status as the product quality and creates and obtains remuneration in this way. As a new business model, the experience economy presents four characteristics: (1) The experience product is produced in a short time but is consumed in a long time. The production cycle of the experience economy on the network platform is merely several minutes or even several seconds. However, this product or service exerts continuous influence on consumers and brings them a long-term consumption experience, which significantly increases gains for them;

(2) The experience product is invisible. Experience products mainly satisfy consumers' spiritual needs instead of material needs; (3) Consumers of the experience products directly participate in production. Compared to the traditional economy where production is separated from consumers, the experience products need consumers to complete the production and swap of products during the experience and become one of the subjects that create product value; and (4) Products of the experience economy are differentiated. In the consumer-centred experience economy, customization constitutes the outstanding characteristic of the experience economy.

B. Joseph Pine and James H. Gilmore point out that "work is a show", that work is no longer a tedious task to be completed quietly but becomes a 'performance' to interact with customers. In the retail industry, the cashiers at the market 'perform' their skill of rapidly scanning the bar code, and the sales assistants 'perform' their psychological skills of deeply exploring customers' demands. All these performances aim to provide customers with unique shopping experiences and thus enhance the overall brand reputation of the enterprise.

With the emergence and development of the experience economy, experience marketing has gradually become the emerging marketing model, which is widely applied by an increasing number of employees. Since the focus of consumption is gradually upgraded from the material to the spiritual, the factor determining the customers' purchase gradually changes from the commodity itself to the experience. In this process, the customer-centred experience marketing gradually replaces the traditional commodity-centred marketing. Based on the practical experience provided by experience marketing, consumers can directly perceive the internal values and spiritual values of the products and therefore show stickiness to the experience products and their suppliers. Having transformed the traditional business model of enterprises, the experience economy is considered as a new stage of social and economic development following the agricultural economy, industrial economy and service economy.

III. Swap and Transcendence in the Fans Economy

The fans economy refers to the new marketing and income-generating activity constructed on the relationship between the following and the follower. This new business model enhances consumers' stickiness by means of word-of-mouth (WOM) marketing and then acquires economic and social benefits. As to the fans economy, the followers mainly follow stars, idols and celebrities of certain industries, and purchase their products or services. In this way, their stickiness to these products or services is established. With the development of the network and information technology, the fans economy is widely applied to product marketing, cultural and entertainment activities, or other service economies. An enterprise cultivates its followers and fans through the network marketing platform and provides diversified and customized commodities and services to fans, thus converting fans to consumers and finally increasing the profit and value of the enterprise.

In the fans economy, stars, idols and celebrities of certain industries are followed in most cases. For example, the fans of a singer will purchase the singer's albums and concert tickets, as well as the commodities that the singer likes or endorses. Through the fans' consumption, relevant products or services are sold and the consumption stickiness of fans is formed. A successful enterprise can also be a 'star' or an 'idol' followed by consumers. Once the enterprise fans are cultivated, those of high loyalty to the enterprise will satisfy most of their demands through the products or services of the star or idol enterprise. This fact creates a good environment for the enterprise to perform cross-area, cross-region and even cross-border marketing.

IV. Swap and Transcendence of Consumption Capital

During the transition from an industrial society to post-industrial society, productivity levels rise ceaselessly, and the market economy constantly develops, so the material resources are becoming more abundant and the product supply is growing sharply. As the market economy gradually transforms from the seller's market to the buyer's market, the consumption choice is playing an increasingly important part in economic development. With the goal to maximize unity, consumers will choose products with the optimum cost performance. With the goal to maximize the profit, the enterprise will produce products satisfying consumers' demands. Along with the development of the network and information technology, the enterprises and consumers begin to integrate. Consumers start to influence the production and business operations by means of consumption capital, leading to the capitalization of consumption.

Consumption capital can be defined in either a broad sense or a narrow sense. The consumption capital in a broad sense refers to the total market forces and values created by the consumer during the consumption of products and services. The consumption capital in a narrow sense indicates the values created by the total consumption capital of the market in the enterprise within a certain period. Consumption capital is considered as the third form of capital in addition to money capital and knowledge capital.

According to the theory of consumption capital, consumption capital is essentially the reinvestment of consumers on enterprise production, by which consumers extend their influence to the area of production and business operations and share the results of the enterprise's growth and development. Consumption capital is mainly realized by consumers holding equity or options. As demonstrated by the consumption agglomeration, scale economies and capital precipitation effect, consumption capital can promote the development of an enterprise. In the traditional market economy, the consumer is merely a consuming subject of the enterprise's product. However, after consumption capital is introduced to the enterprise, consumers become a special group who are consumers and business owners at the same time. Not only acquiring consumer utility, they also attract more consumers to the enterprise and establish a stable customer base for the enterprise. With the agglomeration and expansion of the stable customer base, the enterprise sees a growing reputation and market scale and then achieves the scale economies effect.

CHAPTER 3

SWAP AND TRANSCENDENCE: EVOLUTION AND PRACTICAL CLUES OF ENTERPRISE GROWTH PATH

As an exploratory practice of an enterprise, swap and transcendence is barely mentioned in traditional economic theories. However, it is essentially supported by these modern economic theories. Each theoretical innovation, from the neoclassical firm theory of Alfred Marshall, the enterprise boundary and transaction cost theory to the post-modern enterprise theory, has brought about the evolution of the enterprise growth path. In particular, the swap and transcendence theory shows a disruptive effect.

SECTION 1
TRADITIONAL PATHS AND CONSTRAINTS OF ENTERPRISE GROWTH

I. Nature of Enterprise Growth

Enterprise growth refers to the whole process from the founding to the development of an enterprise, which is a result of the rational organization and effective allocation of the enterprise's endowments and resources. First, enterprise growth is acquired on the basis of reasonable division of labour. Adam Smith conducted a profound analysis and elaboration of this point in *The Wealth of Nations*. With a small needle factory as an example, he argued that the division of labour was essentially the productivity. With the development of human society and the division of labour, the division of labour has become more mature and production has become more specialized. Meanwhile, the division of labour and production specialization of an enterprise is subject to the constraints of the enterprise's factor endowments, which constitute the foundation for the division of labour and specialized production. Therefore, enterprises always provide products of different categories, quantities and qualities based on their different factor endowments.

For example, for an enterprise with abundant labour resources, its better choice is to produce and supply labour-intensive products; and a capital-rich enterprise would better supply capital-intensive products. In other words, the resource endowments of an enterprise determine its production mode and operations mode. Only by fully considering its factor endowments and resource structure can an enterprise fully discover, explore and bring into play its advantages in factor endowments and maximize the efficiency of its resource allocation.

Second, enterprise growth is mainly manifested as the expansion of the scale, the improvement of the internal structure, the optimization of functions and the whole development of the enterprise. The internal structure of an enterprise mentioned here refers to its organizational, institutional and cultural composition and their relations; and the function of an enterprise indicates the role that the enterprise's organizational, institutional and cultural components play and their response and adaption to the environment. An enterprise will select the rational scale, improve the internal structure and optimize the functions to achieve the final goal of the enterprise's overall development. Typically, enterprise growth is divided into several stages, when the major strategies adopted include technological innovation, economies of scale, economies of scope and diversity.

Finally, enterprise growth is closely associated with the enterprise's factor endowments and the efficiency of factor allocation. This can be explained from two perspectives. The factor endowments and their quantity and quality make up the basic element that influences and even determines the production efficiency and output values of the enterprise; and meanwhile, the allocation method and management system of factor endowments constitute the mechanism to effectively utilize the basic element. With a given institutional system, the enterprise will necessarily seek the method of factor allocation that maximizes the revenue. Hence, in the final analysis, enterprise growth aims to acquire maximum benefits by means of the effective allocation of resource endowments and then achieve long-term healthy growth and transcendental development of the enterprise.

II. Traditional Paths of Enterprise Growth

In the whole process from the founding, operations and growth to the development of the enterprise, the effective allocation of production factors always plays an important part. According to classical economics and neoclassical economics, the ultimate purpose of human economic activities is to satisfy the needs of human survival and development. For this reason, people will attempt to maximize the utility and benefits in production and operations by rationally choosing and effectively allocating various available resources. The enterprise is always growing along a specific development path under given conditions, and enterprises in different stages follow different growth paths. To date, the paths of enterprise growth can be divided into traditional paths and modern paths.

In traditional paths, with the given technologies, the enterprise will increase the capital and labour investment to raise the output. In the short run, as the production scale of an enterprise is gradually expanding, the revenue can be maximized when the marginal benefit of the enterprise is equal to its marginal cost. In this case, if the enterprise continues to increase the investment, the marginal benefit will decrease progressively and even become a negative number. In the long run, the optimum production scale of the enterprise will assure its marginal cost at the lowest point of the curve of the long-term average cost.

The quality and the use efficiency of the enterprise's available resources constitute the key factor contributing to the growth and development of the enterprise. On the one hand, the type and quality of its available resources exert decisive influence on the direction of the growth and development of the enterprise. The initial available resources of the enterprise not only decide its market positioning, but also make up an important foundation for the enterprise owners and managers to conduct business. Therefore, they have determined the direction of the enterprise's growth and development to some extent. On the other hand, the essence of the enterprise's growth and development rests in effectively utilizing resources, so the utilization efficiency of its available resources decides the success of its growth and development. In a word, the traditional paths of enterprise growth strive to achieve constant growth and development by optimizing the structure and utilization efficiency of the enterprise's available resources, upgrading the quality of human resources, and improving the management and operations system, with the technology unchanged.

III. Breakthroughs of the Traditional Paths of Enterprise Growth

With the development of a modern market economy and information technology, and constant changes and adjustments of the industrial structure, the traditional paths of enterprise growth start to hit a bottleneck. To sustain healthy development, the enterprise must make a breakthrough in the traditional growth path.

First, the growth and development of the enterprise will be driven by innovation instead of by production factors. The traditional paths of enterprise growth mostly depend on advantages in resources and factors. Therefore, they are increasingly subject to the constraints of insufficient resources and the environment. In particular, in view of the gradual disappearance of the original demographic dividend and the ageing of population, it is difficult to acquire the enterprise's continuous growth completely depending on low-cost labour, low-price natural resources and heavy capital investment. In the future, enterprise growth must rely on technological innovation, product innovation, organizational innovation and market innovation.

Second, the positioning of the enterprise will develop from the lower end to the middle and high end of the industrial value chain. As manifested in the development of a modern market economy, the costs of entry to the low, middle and high end of the industrial value chain vary significantly. Generally, the cost of entry to the low end is lower, and the entry cost of the middle and high end is higher. Therefore, as restricted by the scale of assets and capital strength, the enterprise at its early stage often chooses to enter the low end of the industrial chain at a lower cost, which is the so-called 'low-end embedded' long path. Also, the enterprise of insufficient technological innovation, management innovation, organizational innovation and market innovation is also inclined to adopt the growth path starting from the low end of the industrial chain.

Seeing the rapid development of the modern market economy and increasingly fierce market competition, the key to the long-term sustainable and healthy development of an enterprise rests in whether it can upgrade itself from the low end to the middle and high end of the industrial chain. To this end, the enterprise must break through its original growth path, focus on technological innovation, elevate its position in the global industrial value chain by means of brand innovation and operations and marketing channel update and exploration, and seek a new path of growth and development.

Third, the enterprise will expand its regional layout to global layout. The major problem and challenge facing the enterprise during its production layout and marketing always lies in the distance between the market and the enterprise and the cost incurred by this distance. Considering this, the enterprise is inclined to enter the industrial chain at a position suitable for its own development level in the region of high-degree industrial agglomeration. With the development of economic globalization and the wide application of the network and information technology, the industrial selection and market selection of a certain region show a less-restrictive effect on the growth and development of an enterprise. Therefore, the important strategy for the enterprise to achieve sustainable growth and transcendental development is to shake off the traditional regional restrictions and plan for a global layout.

In conclusion, only by transferring from factor-driven growth to innovation-driven growth, upgrading from the low end to the middle and high end of the industrial value chain and changing from regional selection to global layout can an enterprise break through the traditional growth path and maintain healthy development.

SECTION 2
MODERN PATH CHOICES FOR ENTERPRISE GROWTH

Along with the rapid development of a modern market economy and the wide application of the network and information technology, the paths of enterprise growth and development have been exposed to an enormous change, from traditional paths to modern paths. Under new historical conditions and a development environment, the enterprise is no longer a 'black box' decided by the investment of external factors, since it starts to clearly and accurately understand the factors that decide enterprise growth, the driving mechanism for enterprise growth and the source of the enterprise's competitive advantages. In other words, in the new context, the enterprise is a resource collection restricted by the administrative framework but flexibly adapting to the demands of market development.

The development of a modern enterprise is no longer completely decided by the force of market equilibrium but depends more on the enterprise's ability to effectively utilize available resources. To acquire timely product supply and effective service, the enterprises all cultivate their unique characteristics and develop themselves based on the rational integration, allocation and effective utilization of resource endowments and technology. With the development of the network and information technology, timely reform and modernization of the enterprises' management method, system and mode become a key factor contributing to their growth and development. The modern management method enables the enterprise to improve its production and operations efficiency and lower the operations and transaction cost. For the purpose of shifting from the traditional growth path to modern growth and realize sustainable and healthy growth and transcendental development, it is of great significance for the enterprise to break free of the traditional development path and extend and deepen the value chain of enterprise growth by means of swap and integration of the enterprise's available resources. The modern path of enterprise growth consists of both the management mode and value increment method.

I. The Selection of the Enterprise's Management Mode: Flat Management

The management mode makes up an important part in the selection of the enterprise's production, operations and development mode. Along with constant development of the network and information technology, as well as management philosophy, enterprises are also exploring the more scientific and efficient organizational management mode to promote its healthy growth and sustainable development. As a result of the innovation of traditional enterprise management modes, flat management adopts the principles of network design, simplifies the process and lowers the cost of information transmission. By reducing the levels of management, combining management functions, compressing management organizations and cutting down redundant personnel, flat management helps deliver the decision information rapidly to the front end of the enterprise's production and marketing and thus evidently improves the enterprise's efficiency of decision implementation. This new mode circumvents the shortages of the traditional pyramid management mode.

Traditional enterprises mostly adopt the pyramid-type organizational management, with senior management at the spire, whose instructions are conveyed to the primary level through layers of management. Then the feedback information acquired from the instruction implementation is sent back to the decision level after filtering by layers of management. This management structure lowers the efficiency of information transmission and even leads to information distortion due to multiple levels and the complex process.

Flat management stresses the transformation of the management structure, which means to reduce the levels of management longitudinally and widen the limits of authority of each management level transversely. Flat management facilitates the timely transmission, communication and sharing of enterprise information and achieves the goal of streamlining the organization, lowering costs and improving efficiency. Compared to traditional multi-level management, flat management presents obvious advantages. First, it reduces the management process, improves management efficiency, and thus promotes the overall efficiency of the enterprise. Second, it strengthens people's consciousness of responsibility and power and enhances management effectiveness. Since each level is provided with greater administrative authority, the employees of each level have greater power and also greater responsibilities. The unification of administrative power and responsibility upgrades the efficiency of the management system. Finally, it reduces information distortion and improves information quality. With accurate information, the enterprise can respond to market changes timely, better adapt to the market and promote its own market competitiveness.

The rapid development of the network and information technology renders important technological support for enterprises to change from the growth path of the traditional multi-level management mode to the flat management of modern enterprises. Facing the market varying from minute to minute, modern enterprises must make a response and decision rapidly and timely convey the decision information to the primary level of the enterprise for implementation, thus to assure their market responsiveness, adaption and competitiveness. To meet requirements on the timely, efficient, accurate and convenient transmission of information, enterprises will necessarily adopt the flat management mode based on the network and information technology during their growth and development and step on the modern growth path.

The institutionalized management, information-based organization and high-quality employees constitute the important organizational and institutional support to the enterprise's transformation from the traditional multi-level management mode to flat management. Modern enterprise management adheres to clear power and responsibilities, self-management, real-time supervision, timely feedback and orderly operations, and is therefore scientific and efficient.

II. The Selection of the Enterprise's Value Increment Modes: Short- and Long-term Gains and their Realization

The growth path of the modern enterprise determines the value increment mode of the enterprise. The major basis for the selection of the enterprise's value increment modes lies in technological innovation and industrial structure adjustment. In the short run, under the premise of an existing technological level and industrial structure, the value increment modes of the enterprise include: the low-cost mode and product differentiation mode. In the long run, since the technological level and industrial structure of an enterprise may be exposed to changes, the value increment modes include the internal value and goodwill value promotion mode, technological innovation mode, brand mode and specialized development mode.

1. Short-term Value Increment Modes of the Enterprise and their Realization Path

Revenue and cost constitute the major factor that determines the short-term profits and sustainable development of an enterprise. Profit is considered as the leading indicator of the enterprise's short-term development. The short-term value increment modes of an enterprise mainly include the low-cost mode and product differentiation mode.

The low-cost value increment mode means that an enterprise lowers the cost of production and operations, obtains a price advantage with low total cost, and thus acquires a bigger market share and a greater advantage in market competition. Enterprises of different industries, different stages and different scales have their different ways to acquire the cost advantage. The enterprises engaged in production and operations mainly win their cost advantages by means of patented and innovative technologies. As to the enterprises in their early and middle stages of development, their human resource advantages achieved by one employee assuming the duties of multiple posts help lower their costs. With regard to the enterprises of a relatively big scale in the middle and late stage of development, the favourable prices of raw material procurement and large-scale production constitute the major factor contributing to their low costs. In the short run, the key to realize value increment of the enterprise lies in having the sustainable low-cost advantage greater than that of the competition while satisfying customer requirements.

The differentiation mode is a development model by which the enterprise differentiates itself from other competitors with different products and services. In this mode, an enterprise provides consumers with a consumption experience worth more than its cost depending on its technology advantage or customization. Since the differentiated products or services show greater marginal utility for consumers, they also bring higher marginal returns to the enterprise, thus promoting the enterprise's bargaining capability and product competitiveness. Once production differentiation is achieved, customers' dependence on the products will construct a solid industry barrier that protects the enterprise's monopoly and monopolistic return in the market in the short term.

2. Long-term Value Increment Modes of the Enterprise and their Realization Path

According to the theory of the enterprise's long-term development, the key indicators to measure the long-term growth and development of an enterprise include the rise of output, the increase of scale, the expansion of boundaries and the improvement of quality. The quality improvement here mainly embodies the development of the technological innovation capability, the upgrading of the product quality, the optimization of the organizational structure and the perfection of the operations and management system. Meanwhile, the quantity increase is mainly manifested as the increase of the operations scale, the growth of the output and the expansion of the business scope. There are three realization paths for the long-term value increment modes of the enterprise, including technological innovation, brand building and diversified growth.

Technological innovation means that an enterprise adopts new technologies; develops new processes; researches and develops new products; adopts new production, operations and management modes; and effectively integrates available resources to acquire a larger market share and realize the long-term value increment of the enterprise. With regard to brand building, the enterprise builds its products or services with high quality, a large market share and an extensive popularity as its representative brand during its production and operations, and finally makes it an enterprise brand of market appeal, influence and consumption stickiness through meticulous cultivation and long-term maintenance. Diversified growth is a mode by which the enterprise operates products or services of different functions and purposes to achieve long-term value increment of the enterprise. Diversified operations can be conducted by means of the merger and reorganization of available resources, or a strategic alliance, to achieve the goals of avoiding risks, lowering costs, improving competitiveness and realizing value increment.

SECTION 3
PATH INNOVATION FOR THE GROWTH AND DEVELOPMENT OF DIRECT-SELLING ENTERPRISES - SWAP AND TRANSCENDENCE

I. Choices of the Growth and Development Paths of Direct-Selling Enterprises: New Opportunities and New Challenges

In the new period of economic development, how to effectively make use of the network and information technology, save costs, avoid risks and improve efficiency becomes an issue that should be considered when all enterprises, particularly Direct-Selling enterprises, choose their development paths. With the rapid development of the Chinese market economy and the significant improvement of people's living standards, the national consumption structure and preference have been exposed to great changes. Correspondingly, the main contradiction in China's social development has also been transformed from the contradiction between the growing material and cultural needs of the people and backward productive forces to the contradiction between people's growing needs for a better life and unbalanced and inadequate development. These changes of the economic development environment and conditions at home and abroad have brought new opportunities as well as new challenges to Direct-Selling enterprises' selection of growth and development paths.

1. New Opportunities for Direct-Selling Enterprises' Selection of Growth Paths

First, the wide application of the network and information technology renders new technological support to the development of Direct-Selling enterprises. The application of the new technology offers new possibilities and opportunities for the innovation of the organizational modes of Direct-Selling enterprises. It not only removes the obstacles against the flat management adopted by the Direct-Selling enterprise, but also creates a convenient communication environment and information flow channels for the construction of the flat structure. Hence it reduces the asymmetry of management information and efficiency loss to a great extent and makes the flat management of the enterprise more scientific, accurate and efficient.

Second, it provides more choices for the innovation of the operations modes of Direct-Selling enterprises. The traditional operations modes of enterprises mainly depend on investments for production, depend on sales promotion for market, depend on products for competition and depend on marketing for income. With the wide application of the network and information technology, Direct-Selling enterprises see their production and operations activities increasingly associated with the network and information technology, their market increasingly dependent on the application of the network and information technology and the expansion of the marketing network, their competition increasingly relying on the scale of the marketing network and the marketing quality and their income increasingly counting on the application of information technology instead of the investment of tangible capital. The application of the network and information technology provides more choices for the innovation of Direct-Selling enterprises' operations modes.

Third, it furnishes new opportunities to the innovation of the sales modes of Direct-Selling enterprises. Though having institutionally broken through the traditional marketing modes and extricated themselves from the multi-link supply chain marketing, Direct-Selling enterprises still need to transfer a considerable part of profits to their sales teams of multiple levels due to their sales mode of a multi-level team. In this situation, the wide application of the network and information technology significantly improves the efficiency and quality of Direct-Selling enterprises, providing new opportunities for them to lower their market information costs and production and operations costs.

Fourth, the emergence of the 'new retailing' mode and format brings new opportunities to the innovation of Direct-Selling enterprises' operations modes. Distinguished from the traditional retail mode that mostly depends on physical stores including large shopping centres, supermarkets and chain stores, 'new retailing' is a new sales mode that is established based on big data analysis with e-commerce as the important carrier, deeply integrates online and offline sales and realizes rapid and convenient direct supply and marketing by means of the internet. The new retailing system not only helps the enterprise build the marketing platform, completely integrating online and offline sales, but also precisely creates the 'personas' based on consumer preferences and propensity by conducting big data analysis of consumers' behaviours through cloud computing. Therefore, the new retailing mode directly guides the enterprise in its R&D of products and enables it to understand and correctly judge the market and customers' demands in the first place, thus to timely seize the market heights and take the lead in market competition.

The new retailing mode is not a fundamental denial of the traditional retail mode but has fully developed what is useful or healthy and discarded what is not in the traditional mode. Meanwhile, this new mode brings new opportunities to the innovation of Direct-Selling enterprises. The new retailing mode's function of big data analysis partitions the market demands for Direct-Selling enterprises and helps them seize the market segment; and its function of online and offline integration assists Direct-Selling enterprises in building a new consumption mode that combines online direct sales and the offline experience of consumers, products and consumption scenarios.

Finally, the development of a market economy creates a better external environment and institutional support to the format innovation and development of Direct-Selling enterprises. Characterized by the equal competition among market subjects, the market economy adheres to the basic principle of exchange of equal value. With the constant deepening and development of China's reform of the market economic system, the resource allocation system based on administrative directives and planning in the traditional planned economy has been altered, and the equal competition and exchange of equal value have been established among market subjects. Also, in pace with the development of the market economy in China, the market is playing an increasingly decisive role in resource allocation, thus government control becomes more scientific and reasonable, and enterprises enjoy a better environment for their survival, growth and development. Instead of allocating resources by exploiting social connections, getting government approvals or applying for loans, enterprises depend on their independent decision-making capability and competitiveness to win success in their production and operations activities. As a special product of the development of the market economy, direct sales are highly dependent on a healthy market environment and a favourable market mechanism. Therefore, the constant and healthy development of China's market economy creates a better external environment and institutional support to the format innovation and development of Direct-Selling enterprises.

2. New Challenges for Direct-Selling Enterprises' Selection of Growth Paths

Direct-Selling enterprises are faced with new challenges during their development in the new period of economic development, particularly with the wide application of the network and information technology. The major challenges for Direct-Selling enterprises include the new retailing revolution, multi-channel integration of the sales mode and the changes to the subjects, objects and spaces of market transactions.

First, when choosing the growth and development path, Direct-Selling enterprises are challenged by the demand cocreation of new retailing. New retailing is a revolution of traditional retailing. Though traditional retailing also aims to satisfy consumers' demands, enterprises in this mode are always thinking over "how to sell." Distinguished from traditional retailing, new retailing adheres to the basic principle of demand cocreation by consumers and enterprises, where enterprises are considering "what to sell." How to realize demand cocreation by consumers and enterprises makes up a great challenge to Direct-Selling enterprises. Since Direct-Selling enterprises put great efforts to solve the issue of "how to sell" the given products, their marketing mainly adopts consumption demonstration and direction promotion of product functions by direct sellers. However, for the sake of demand cocreation, the enterprises need to fully obtain consumers' information and integrate resources to the greatest extent to satisfy consumers' demands. Moreover, scene experience is regarded as a necessary condition for demand cocreation. Though most Direct-Selling enterprises have their own special stores, they still fall far behind the requirement of establishing spiritual links with consumers and experiential scenes for the cocreation of demand. Therefore, demand cocreation becomes a new challenge for Direct-Selling enterprises' selection of growth paths.

Second, Direct-Selling enterprises also encounter the challenge of multi-channel integration when choosing the growth and development path. The development of the network and information technology leads to the expansion of the network marketing of enterprises, making multi-channel integration imperative. However, Direct-Selling enterprises mainly grasp the marketing information on the data of product sales and personal performance of direct sellers but lack the resources for whole-scene information analysis and whole-channel information integration. In the meantime, Direct-Selling enterprises mostly adopt the marketing method of direct in-person contact between direct sellers and consumers and have inadequate capability of online and offline linkage. To meet the development needs, Direct-Selling enterprises must vigorously transform and integrate the existing marketing system and reconstruct consumer's cognition, customer relationship, partnership, and internal link; otherwise, they can hardly realize multi-channel integration.

Finally, Direct-Selling enterprises' selection of the growth and development path is also challenged by the changes to the subjects, objects and spaces of market transactions. As a result of the development of the network and information technology, the market transactions of the retail sector are involving an increasing number of subjects and objects and covering a wider space. Anyone who wants to become a subject of market transactions can become a subject in some way. Retailing activities are no longer the exclusive privilege of a certain group. With the popularization of retail subjects, traditional physical retail stores have been virtualized and been replaced by online retailers or WeChat retailers, and even the retail industry has been moved from the consumer end to the factory end. Since any articles or services can be endued with value, the objects of transaction can be in any form in addition to articles or services and extricate themselves from ownership restriction, so their connotation and denotation have been unprecedentedly broadened. As long as there is demand, the transaction objects, articles or services can be transacted in some way in a different time and space in any situation, either online or offline. Under the above conditions, it is a huge challenge for Direct-Selling enterprises to win consumers in the fierce market competition.

II. Path Innovation for the Growth and Development of Enterprises - Swap and Transcendence

The key factors contributing to the traditional way of enterprises' growth and development generally include the quantity and quality of capital and labour investment and technological improvement and upgrading, which are invested following the principles of the easy before the difficult, the direct before the indirect, labour before capital and general practical technologies before high-grade, high-precision and advanced technologies. Then, the enterprises strive for their growth and development by centring on the effective allocation and integration of their available resources and production factors. However, in a modern market economy, enterprises, particularly Direct-Selling enterprises, will not only follow and improve the traditional paths of enterprise growth and development, but also make innovations different from the traditional paths.

1. Innovation of Direct-Selling Platforms
   E-commerce and network marketing have risen rapidly along with the development of the network and information technology, which has led to enormous changes in people's consumption preferences and consumption methods. Under these circumstances, the offline marketing method adopted by Direct-Selling enterprises by which direct sellers and consumers communicate face-to-face no longer meets the needs of enterprise development. According to practical demand, Direct-Selling enterprises will need to keep pace with the times and make new choices and innovations. In other words, they will continue to cultivate their offline consumption platforms and provide consumers with more comprehensive and convenient offline experiences, while putting forth great efforts to construct online platforms. By combining offline and online sales, they can simultaneously realize the excellent experience, high efficiency and great convenience of sales.

2. Innovation of Direct-Selling Modes
   Since cloud computing, the Internet of Things, big data, and some other latest technologies have been widely applied to enterprise operations, many Direct-Selling enterprises start to incorporate big data in their innovation of Direct-Selling modes. With the support of big data, Direct-Selling enterprises collect and organize the big data about direct sellers and customers on a long-term basis. On one hand, they are doing so to analyse the consumer group. They classify the data by the frequency, scale, income and varieties of sales, as well as the gender, age and regional distribution of customers, then provide targeting services to different customer groups, enlarge and explore consumer demands and potential demands, and increase the sales scale and consumers' stickiness. Direct-Selling enterprises also create 'personas' of consumer groups, based on the data, to describe customers' habits, preferences, behaviours, capability, level and frequency of consumption, and thus supply products precisely meeting customers' demands as well as more satisfactory services. In this way, they can maximize customer value, promote the enterprises' recognition, reputation and goodwill, and increase enterprises' values.

On the other hand, these technologies constitute the technical support to direct sellers. By replacing the traditional Direct-Selling modes with the network and information technology-based Direct-Selling platforms, it can facilitate the online communication between direct sellers and more customers, expand the scope of customers and the space for product display, lower the cost of production exhibition and customer communication and thus improve the Direct-Selling enterprises' efficiency of economies of scale.

3. Innovation of the Direct-Selling Industry and Direct-Selling Products

Industrial innovation constitutes an important factor that promotes economic development. The emerging new technologies, which are essentially the creative destructions of the old industrial structure, give birth to a new economic structure. Jointly driven by the changes of customers' demands, technological innovation and the enhancement of enterprise managers' innovative consciousness, industrial innovation can be divided into three categories. The first is industrial transfer. Enterprises carry out industrial transfer and upgrading according to the characteristics of the population, economy, environment and development changes in various regions. The second is industrial cluster. Enterprises depend on large-scale agglomeration in a certain spatial scope and specialized division of labour to improve their competitiveness and achieve an agglomeration effect. The third is industrial convergence, which means that enterprises break the traditional industry boundaries with technological progress and deregulation and realize technological convergence of different industries, to seek new opportunities of industrial innovation. In the current stage, the Direct-Selling industry must lead the development path of industrial innovation to satisfy the demands of different customer groups.

By now, the products of Direct-Selling enterprises in China are subject to single variety and homogenization due to the administration system and Direct-Selling policies of China. The whole Direct-Selling industry is exposed to the increasingly intensified 'red sea state.' The red sea state refers to bloody and brutal competition. In a red sea, the boundary and competition rules of each industry are well known to the people. As the market becomes more crowded, the profit and growth potential of enterprises in this industry are declining. Competitors here have to compete fiercely, thus turning the market into a bloody red sea. In this situation, to attain faster and better development, Direct-Selling enterprises will have to solve the urgent and prominent problem of how to differentiate their products and services and how to precisely satisfy the different demands of different customer groups with the Direct-Selling products and services.

To rise to the red sea state, Direct-Selling enterprises will innovate their Direct-Selling products in two ways. First, according to the principle of 'product differentiation,' Direct-Selling enterprises will conduct differentiation-oriented innovation of their products and services, adhere to the concept of being unique, being special, being excellent and being the best, provide better products and more considerate services than others, supply practically useful and perfect products and services and develop consumers' psychological recognition to consumption recognition. Second, they will innovate their products and services by means of 'Internet+ direct selling' under the guidance of the 'Internet+' idea. To win consumers of Direct-Selling enterprises and products, it is of great significance to give full play to the wide, broad and precise influence of 'Internet+' swap the traditional direct contact between direct sellers and customers, provide more customer groups with differentiated products and services and maintain a larger group of customers with a closer connection.

4. Direct-Selling Institutional Innovation and Cultural Innovation

Institutional innovation lays the foundation for the enterprise's transcendental development. The institutional innovation of Direct-Selling enterprises mainly consists of the innovation of institutional arrangements and organizational structure design, as well as the normalization of operations modes. Direct-Selling enterprises mostly achieve institutional innovations in two ways. First, they innovate their ownership structure. The primary goal of enterprise institutional innovation is to establish the scientific and normative operations modes and institutionally divide the functions and duties of the board of directors, shareholders' meetings and management. In the meantime, as an important part of ownership institution innovation, Direct-Selling enterprises introduce the corporate governance structure, assign professional managers to manage different business sectors and integrate the internal resources. Second, they innovate their marketing network. The marketing network innovation starts from the innovation of enterprises' management modes. The transformation from the linear and pyramid management mode to the flat management mode has accelerated information feedback and lowered management costs. In the flat management mode, the Direct-Selling system is not merely a matter of sales, but becomes a bi-directional sales channel integrating both sales and data feedback. This bi-directional sales channel provides the technological platform for the integration of the enterprises' and consumers' goals. Hence, the fact that the network management mode replaces the pyramid management mode constitutes an important manifestation of the institutional innovation of Direct-Selling enterprises.

The cultural innovation of Direct-Selling enterprises focuses on experience and sharing. It is of great significance for Direct-Selling enterprises to cultivate their own fans, who essentially make up an important cultural tool for Direct-Selling enterprises to seek greater development. With the development of the modern market economy, the market becomes increasingly prosperous with diversified commodities and services. In this event, experience becomes the important basis for an increasing number of consumers to make consumption decisions. In a manner of speaking, we have ushered in 'the age of experience economy.' In this age, consumers are buying the experience from perception to feeling, from cognition to identification and from the material to the spiritual, instead of buying commodities or services themselves.

Though some 'experience-based' activities are involved in traditional Direct-Selling businesses, experience does not make up the only element of direct selling. For a new business, modern direct selling will not only involve experience, but also upgrade experience to be the basic element, to spiritually connect enterprises and customers through experience-oriented consumption. Hence, offline experience venues and experience centres replace traditional Direct-Selling stores, which wins customers' product identification and satisfies their demands by providing them with practical experience.

The essence of a sharing economy lies in the fragmented and precise interfacing between supply and demand by means of the network and information technology. As to Direct-Selling enterprises, sharing plays a more important role than experience in corporate culture. The promotion of the sharing concept and the sharing culture is considered an important part in Direct-Selling enterprises' cultural innovation. A sharing economy, sharing culture and win-win cooperation are not only the common choice of modern enterprises, but also the foundation for Direct-Selling enterprises to search for better development with cultural innovation. By establishing a sharing culture and forming the community of shared undertakings, shared future and shared development, it builds a bridge among enterprise managers, distributors, direct sellers and the majority of customers and finally achieves the goal of sharing and win-win cooperation. This is the ultimate aim and spirit of a sharing culture. The idea that the exclusive and the unshared will be replaced by the shared and win-win cooperation has gradually become a cultural view among modern Direct-Selling enterprises, as well as the 'golden key' for modern Direct-Selling enterprises to acquire greatness and glory.

Finally, regional innovation is the major means for Direct-Selling enterprises to broaden market scope and expand market capacity. When developing in foreign countries, Direct-Selling enterprises will need to choose the appropriate products adapting to local conditions in view of different demographic and geographical features in different countries, which is the main method of Direct-Selling enterprises' regional innovation. The rise of internet technology and the new retailing mode clear the obstacles for the transnational development of Direct-Selling enterprises. Meanwhile, with regional innovation, Direct-Selling enterprises usher in new development opportunities for the innovation of Direct-Selling products and the exploration of new Direct-Selling modes.

PART II

SWAP PROCESS AND TRANSCENDENCE PRACTICE I: 'CONSOLIDATION OF THREE NETWORKS'

LV FENGYONG

The 'consolidation of three networks' is a new Direct-Selling mode that centres on direct selling. In this mode, the human resources and marketing networks, the product and R&D network and the finance and capital network mutually support and connect each other, finally establishing a face-to-face multi-level sales system based on interpersonal relationships.

The consolidation of three networks produces a new human resource relation and service concept, realizes the close integration of production, consumption and distribution, and gives full play to the incentive effect of the bonus system. It features the unique competitive edge of stronger customer stickiness and more diversified products, and thus reduces production waste and lowers the inventory cost. In practice, it effectively improves the enterprises' capability and efficiency of human resources exploration, product R&D and market supply, global resources integration and flexible response to market demands. Meanwhile, it also presents the characteristics of a network such as a wide scope, economies of scale, platform display, diversity and expansiveness, laying the foundation for the construction of a new retailing model of multi-network interaction.

CHAPTER 4
CONSOLIDATION OF THREE NETWORKS AND SWAPPING OF MARKET MODEL

SECTION 1
ESSENCE OF SWAPPING IN CONSOLIDATION OF THREE NETWORKS

I. Swapping of Market Model and Consolidation of Three Networks

1. Swapping of Market Model

An essential point that distinguishes swapping from upgrading lies in that swapping completely discards the dross of old resources of traditional modes and absorbs and cultivates newly emerging things. As to the development of enterprises, the selection of the market model directly determines how product supply and demand connect to each other, how demanders accept the products supplied and how competitive the enterprise is in the market compared to other enterprises.

Though with marketing as an important part, the market model goes beyond the concept of marketing and involves strategic and organizational elements. If marketing is compared to a battle, the market model is a war. According to the definition given by the American Marketing Association (AMA) in 2013, marketing refers to a series of activities, processes and systems that bring value to consumers, customers, partners and the whole of society during creation, connection, communication and product exchange. The market factors traditionally comprise '4Ps': the product, price, promotion, and place and distribution. The different combinations of factors constitute the enterprise's marketing strategy. Being a superordinate concept to marketing, the market model deconstructs and reorganizes the enterprise's strategies, organizational structure and human, financial and material resources after the basic marketing methods are determined upon the market factors, and turns marketing strategies from general enterprise activities to unique and vital models of the enterprise.

Since then, all marketing strategies and specific marketing activities will be carried out and conducted under the modes.

In various forms, marketing models involve every link of the operation from the R&D of products, production, and sales to services. They can be divided into the product-oriented, consumer-oriented, competition-oriented and relation-oriented models by the concept, and into the brand marketing, positioning marketing, trade marketing, commodity promotion and terminal marketing models by the marketing carrier. In addition, some new marketing models are constantly emerging, including the emotional marketing, conceptual marketing, service marketing and network marketing models, which place more emphasis on people's diverse emotions and desires and attach greater importance to the role of the network technology in marketing.

The market model is distinguished from any marketing model mentioned above but is established upon the refinement and integration of the above models. In general, if simply considering the external forms of product distribution, market models can be divided into pyramid selling, direct selling, agency selling, distributor selling, network selling (B2C), catalogue selling and telemarketing. Each enterprise, with a simple market model as the core, cultivates a more advanced and energetic market model that adapts to the enterprise's characteristics by means of the meticulous design of the organizational structure, perfect coordination of the flow of people, materials, funds and information and the construction of the enterprise's cultural concepts. This advanced and energetic market model will guide the supply and marketing activities of the whole enterprise and continuously boost the enterprise's development.

Among these modes, direct selling always shows its distinct character. Provided that the enterprise's products meet certain conditions, the Direct-Selling model can effectively mobilize the enthusiasm of human resources in product R&D, production, sales and consumption, form a semi-closed loop of production, supply and marketing, promote customers' loyalty to products and consumption stickiness, and help the enterprise constantly expand and develop its market. Two Direct-Selling scholars in the USA, Professor Robert A. Peterson from the University of Texas at Austin, and Professor Thomas R. Wotruba from San Diego State University, simply and precisely defined direct selling as face-to-face selling without a fixed retail outlet. Direct selling generally shows the following characteristics: (1) Sellers can be either enterprise employees or independent direct sellers, the latter of which are more commonly seen; (2) Direct sellers can be either full-time or part-time, while part-time personnel take up a considerable proportion; and (3) Selling can be conducted in a single-level or multi-level system, but the multi-level system shows a better incentive effect and is adopted by most Direct-Selling enterprises.

Products suitable for direct selling will embrace three characteristics: otherness, low logistics cost and repeat sales. Direct selling can also be applied to products without these characteristics but will only constitute an occasional and secondary part of the enterprise instead of becoming its dominant market model. According to research, the top four types of products for direct selling in Taiwan (of China), respectively, include nutritious health food, beauty products, household cleaning supplies and water purifiers/filters, which all show two or three of the characteristics mentioned above.

Then, what makes direct selling competitive in the market? Direct selling, stressing on face-to-face communication, undoubtedly incorporates sentiment in the products, thus to promote consumers' purchasing, increase their stickiness to products and constantly improve the market share. Therefore, many enterprises are crazy about the Direct-Selling model since it enjoys the market competition advantage incomparable to other general distribution modes. However, when a large number of enterprises producing products of the same kind adopt the Direct-Selling mode, the market competitiveness of this model will be undoubtedly lowered in homogeneous competition. Therefore, enterprises will depend on their incisive political judgments and market judgment and seize market opportunities through rapid swapping of the model instead of gradual reform.

For instance, Tiens (formerly known as Tianjin Tiens Economic Development Company) is an excellent enterprise that always seizes the right time and contends for first place. In 1995, the group had finally developed Tiens' high-calcium supplement after having experienced untold hardships and setbacks. Despite the extremely satisfactory product quality and effect, it could not open the market in a short period and suffered from a serious input-output imbalance due to huge investment in the early stage and too long a period of market cultivation in the traditional marketing mode. It was almost on the verge of bankruptcy. Since May 1995, Tiens had prepared itself for the adoption of the modern marketing method of direct selling, and decisively ended store sales of Tiens products. On August 3 1995, Baojinfa Trading Company, founded by Tiens, acquired the approval for operation. This is the birthday chosen by Tiens people when Tiens got up again like a phoenix rising from the ashes.

2. 'Consolidation of Three Networks' and New Direct-Selling Model

In 1995, direct selling was still a brand-new market model just known to Chinese people. The swapping of the traditional marketing model was not completed naturally, but required enterprises to elaborately combine and organize their resources and give full play to their own potential energy, thus to escort enterprises on their way to explore the market. For example, instead of creating the concrete Direct-Selling mode at one stroke, Tiens had put great efforts to constantly explore and test the model before finally establishing the new Direct-Selling model of 'consolidation of three networks.' This model has proven to be highly effective by practice for quite a long time.

Centring on direct selling, the consolidation of three networks has the human resources and marketing network, the product and R&D network, and the finance and capital network that support and connect each other, and finally builds a face-to-face multi-level sales system based on interpersonal relationships. In short, the so-called consolidation of three networks perfectly incorporates interpersonal relationships, R&D power, and incentives in the whole process covering production, marketing and financial allocation, constructs three relatively independent block networks including the human resources and marketing network, the product and R&D network, and the finance and capital network, and finally forms a Direct-Selling network in a form of blockchain based on organizational and managerial guidance and the link of enterprise value chain.

(1) Concrete Manifestation of the 'Three Networks' in the 'Consolidation of Three Networks'

A. Human Resources and Marketing Network

The core element of the human resources and marketing network is human resources and special stores of the products, which, combining the subject elements and spatial scope, is regarded as the consolidation of three networks in a narrow sense for a period. Internationally, the spatial scope can expand the denotation of the human resources and marketing network and provide more opportunities for the survival or development of multi-level sales.

The subject elements are still considered as the core of the human resources and marketing networks. Among them, human resources constitute the live and motile subject element, while special stores are called the static and physical subject element. The tight combination of the two significantly promotes the influence of the human resources and marketing network and drives the deepening and widening of the network.

The human resources and marketing network in a broad sense also covers the relationship between direct sellers and managers. As managers also make up a part of human resources and direct sellers and managers need to cooperate with each other, they too are collectively referred to as the 'human resources network.' This human resources network connects and interacts with special stores of the products worldwide, giving birth to the 'human resources and marketing network.'

Tiens has accomplished extraordinary achievements in designing and establishing the human resources and marketing network. Only one year later, in 1996, the number of sellers of Tiens high-calcium supplement and other health products had exceeded 600,000. Tiens started in overseas markets in 1998, when the human resources team were developing geometrically. At present, Tiens has expanded its presence to over 190 countries and attracted approximately 40 million families as its stable consumers and partners. These special stores and human resources worldwide jointly constitute the human resources network and special stores network of a large size and close connections, boosting the constant advancement of Tiens. The human resources network, special stores network and global marketing network were regarded as the consolidation of three networks in a narrow sense in the early stage of Tiens, which laid more emphasis on the important role of marketing in the development of the enterprise.

B. Product and R&D Network

The key element of the product and R&D network rests in products of rich varieties and the corresponding great R&D capability. The product is the object element that connects producers and consumers and realizes producers' values and consumer utility, with the product category and quality as the fundamental guarantee.

For either developing new products or upgrading traditional products, Direct-Selling enterprises attach great importance to the low production cost and irreplaceability of products. To accomplish this goal, the enterprises will conduct meticulous R&D centring on market or production to constantly increase the added value of products and consumer utility. In this sense, although the production of products is different to the R&D of products, the processes and results of both links are embodied in the products put to the market and form a product and R&D network of mutual dependence.

We still use Tiens as an example here. By 2016, Tiens had launched over 1,000 types of products in five major categories, with health food as the lead and household products, beauty and skin-care products, health products and fashion products as the main part; and has built production bases and OEM plants in many countries and regions, including China, Vietnam, Spain, Russia, Indonesia and India. Despite their rich categories and diversified forms, these products are connected by the concept of healthcare in a broad sense. While enriching the product categories, Tiens has always been concerned with the building of the product R&D team and the cultivation of the R&D ability. The R&D force of Tiens is also in a form of network. Tiens has not only established its own R&D department at headquarters, but also looks for enterprises with excellent R&D teams in the world and cooperates with them in product research, development and production. In this way, it fully facilitates, instead of hindering, the development of the

Tiens R&D force along with the increase of the product category, forms an expanding R&D network, perfectly integrates it with the worldwide product network, and thus creates an orderly product and R&D network.

C. Finance and Capital Network

The core elements of the finance and capital network include the incentive mechanism related to the interest distribution between the enterprise and distributors and among distributors, as well as the corresponding finance and capital settlement network. The fundamental goal of economic subjects is to acquire benefits through labour or operations activities. One of the major differences between the Direct-Selling model and the traditional marketing model rests in their different interest distribution system. Associated with the multi-level sales system, the interest distribution system of the Direct-Selling model attaches greater importance to the role of repeat sales and the incentive effect of alternate-level sales, extricates direct selling from the limitation of single products for sales and has an interpersonal relation attached to material products. In this way, the incentive role of the interest distribution system for economic subjects has been significantly promoted.

Moreover, this new interest distribution system also breaks through the limitation of partial and local interests. It maintains the relatively independent operations of each team, associates the interest distribution of the teams to the business performance of the whole enterprise and has the enterprise accountable for overall planning and precise calculation. In addition, it concentrates financial capital at headquarters and distributes the interests among different operations teams worldwide based on the performance accounting and interest distribution calculation. In this way, the finance and capital network with the distribution and incentive system as the core, financial settlement as the means and capital distribution as the goal is formed.

The distribution and incentive system is mainly embodied in the Direct-Selling business plans characterized by the point system, which directly affect the enterprises' financial settlement and capital distribution and guide the generation of the finance and capital network. After adopting the different forms of the distribution incentive mechanism, including the gradation system and dual-rule system, many enterprises start to explore and implement new composite business plans to integrate all institutional advantages.

Award setting is the essential content of many enterprises' new business plans, as well as the major foundation for their financial settlement and capital distribution. For example, the standard new business plan overseas of Tiens has received eight awards, respectively the service award, expansion award, cultivation award, sales award, leadership award, excellence award, glorious title award and special award, which respectively promotes expansion performance and retail performance and involves the expansion rank system and direct-seller rank system.

(2) Integration Method of the 'Consolidation' in the 'Consolidation of Three Networks'

The consolidation of three networks includes not only the unification but also the mutual connection and agreement of the human resources and marketing network, product and R&D network, and finance and capital network. Only by successfully 'consolidating' the three networks can the new Direct-Selling mode be gradually perfected.

The connections among the three networks are artificially designed rather than being naturally established. These artificially designed connections can only loosely combine these networks, but the networks can only be perfectly 'consolidated' when numerous organizational and managerial factors are swapped and the contents, responsibilities and models are endowed with new intensions and extensions.

The consolidation of the three networks is mainly realized through four connection methods:

1. Value chain. This is the essential but intangible connection, which achieves the branding effect for marketing with the product and R&D network, realizes the incentive effect for the human resource team with the finance and capital network, and creates the viscosity effect for product consumption with the human resources and marketing network, gradually intensifies the branding effect, incentive effect and viscosity effect and becomes the best adhesive that closely connects and integrates the three networks and realizes the 'consolidation.'
2. Information chain. This tangible connection is also essential for the consolidation of the three networks. The human resources and marketing network acquires the market information feedback; based on the information, the product and R&D network develops new products or organizes the production of new products; and the finance and capital network makes an overall plan for the use of funds according to the new information on market and product development and production, records the use of funds with the advanced global financial management software and provides the record to the human resources and marketing network and the product and R&D network for reference. In this way, consolidation of the three networks can be achieved through information exchange and sharing.
3. Logistics chain. The logistics chain here, made up by tangible resources, is a generalized concept including the capital chain. The logistics chain

lays the foundation for consolidation of the three networks. It enables the information management function of the finance and capital network and the outcomes of the product and R&D network to extend to the human resources and marketing network in the most economic, efficient, rapid and convenient manner as finished products. Then, the returns created by the human resources and marketing network flow back to the finance and capital network in the form of funds and are allocated to these networks in a certain method by the finance and capital network. Hence, the rational distribution of logistics and capital flow are realized among the three networks.

4. Capital chain. Capital chain plays a very important part in the construction of corporate culture and team talent, which achieves the ultimate goal of talent cultivation and motivation, as well as finance and capital settlement and distribution. Mainly based on the reward system, post and rank of the human resource team and management and work process, the capital chain is essentially the material manifestation of institutional arrangements, and connects the human resources and marketing network, product and R&D network, and finance and capital network at the cultural and spiritual level rather than the material level. Therefore, it is the adhesive that effectively integrates the three networks.

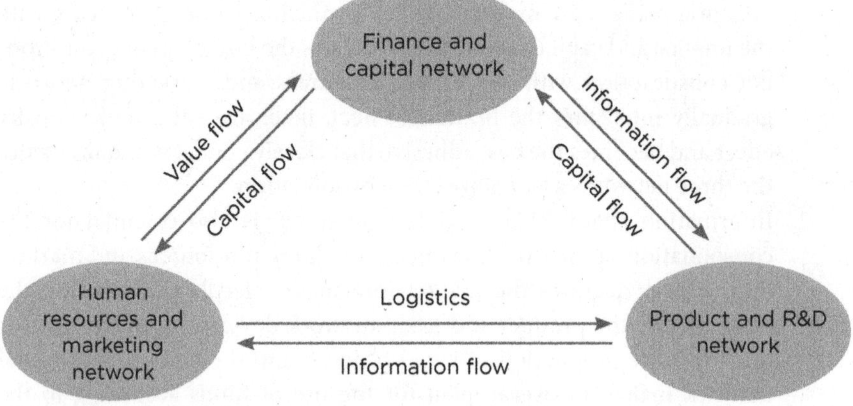

Figure 4-1 Connections of the 'Consolidation of Three Networks'

II. Core Characteristics of Consolidation of Three Networks

Being a new Direct-Selling model, consolidation of three networks embraces characteristics distinguished from traditional marketing models and traditional Direct-Selling models. It is these characteristics that make the market model of consolidation of three networks vigorous and competitive and boost the constant advancement and development of enterprises. This Direct-Selling model of powerful incentive effect and market competitiveness is created upon the integration of the new global marketing method, the product composition structure, and the capital settlement system.

1. Manpower is the Core

In the new Direct-Selling model of consolidation of three networks, human resources, the importance of which has been significantly upgraded, have become the most important and energetic resource for enterprises' development. In a traditional market model, rich human resources do not necessarily guarantee the market expansion or business income increase. However, in the model of consolidation of three networks, the increase of human resources essentially means the expansion of the product market, as well as the development of enterprises' ability to further explore the market in the future. This is because human resources have been integrated with the product market in the model of consolidation of three networks instead of being isolated. Distributors are the sellers and loyal consumers of the enterprises at the same time. Therefore, they can display and sell products to other potential consumers based on their own consumption experience. In this way, they can achieve better marketing results than that in the model where consumption and marketing are separated.

2. Product is the Foundation

In the model of consolidation of three networks, products show their own characteristics and generate more repeat sales for their significant effect. Such products will attract the human resource team of the enterprise as the first-level loyal customers and boost their confidence and enthusiasm to promote and sell products. In particular, corporate culture is also fully embodied in the product, which can improve the market image of the enterprise and achieve a macro-marketing effect that could never be reached by the individual marketing model. For instance, Tiens holds high the banner of 'comprehensive health,' applies this concept to the product quality, type and category, builds a favourable image in the comprehensive health market and thus embraces greater appeal and mobilization power than general enterprises do. In this way, it paves the way for marketing of the human resource team and drives the constant development of comprehensive health undertakings of the enterprise.

3. Finance is the Guarantee
   Though not the core, finance plays the most fundamental role in consolidation of three networks. Only with financial settlement and the overall plan of capital can enterprises' activities be executed orderly. Though it is not the decision-making centre for the enterprise's operations, it is the information hub that enables the enterprise's operations. Finance shows a stronger incentive and guiding effect in the model of consolidation of three networks than in other general market models where finance merely transfers and processes operations information. By constructing a whole set of calculation formulas for capital distribution, finance fully guarantees the implementation of the human resources incentive system and the smooth running of product R&D, production and distribution. In view of this, finance is the key and indispensable factor to the 'consolidation' of the 'three networks,' and is regarded as one of its core characteristics.

4. Integration is the Driving Force
   The human resources and marketing network, product and R&D network, and finance and capital network, which are formed independently, can unleash enormous vitality and vigorously advance the enterprise's development when the product flow, information flow and capital flow can be connected and perfectly integrated through the management platform of the enterprise. The human resources and marketing network makes a strong demand on the product and R&D network. Only with products of rich varieties, perfect quality and famous brands can the human resources and marketing network give full play to its unique advantages. Meanwhile, the product and R&D network depends on the promotion and demonstration activities of the human resources and marketing network to explore and improve itself. The integration of the two networks can build a favourable brand image of Tiens products in the short term and also advance a more extensive expansion of the human resources and marketing network and the product and R&D network. Simultaneously, the finance and capital network provides information and capital support to the expansion of the human resources and marketing network and the product and R&D network by processing and sharing the information flow and the revenue-expenditure accounting of the capital flow; and it also motivates relevant stakeholders in the human resources and marketing network and the product and R&D network. In other words, the finance and capital network is guiding and inspiring the other two networks and thus constitutes an indispensable part in the consolidation of three networks.

5. Incentive is the Soul

   What most directly distinguishes the new Direct-Selling relationship from traditional marketing methods lies in their different incentive systems. In traditional marketing methods, consumption and production are separated. Their relationship ends after the producer provides products to the consumer and the consumer pays the producer. In comparison, in the direct selling of consolidation of three networks, the producer returns part of the payment to the consumer based on the amount of consumption after the end of the trade, and also makes payment to the consumer based on the number of consumers they bring. It means that the consumer will get a rebate or reward according to the amount of the consumer's 'self-consumption' and relevant 'others' consumption,' which makes the consumer an operator of the producer to a certain degree and connects the consumer with the enterprise development. Hence, the consumer and producer have established a bilateral and netlike relationship. Since no operation lies between them, the consumer and producer have a closer relationship. This incentive system for the consumer lays the foundation for the development of the consolidation of three networks and becomes the soul.

III. Theoretical Basis of Consolidation of Three Networks

Characterized by strong vitality and market competitiveness, consolidation of three networks essentially reflects a new Direct-Selling relationship from the perspective of marketing. Then, what relationship does it embody on a deeper level, for example, from the perspective of political economics? How does this relationship influence resource allocation, production allocation and product circulation? By exploring these questions, we can better understand the fundamental attribute of consolidation of three networks from a theoretical point of view, in addition to the simple and direct perception from a practical aspect. Also, by discussing these questions, we can apply this model to practice more flexibly and improve it, thus to make the consolidation of three networks a net model for more enterprises to swap resources and improve efficiency and finally advance the efficiency of resource allocation and production of the whole of society.

1. Consolidation of Three Networks Is a New Way to Organize Production

   Consolidation of three networks removes the commodities' attributes to a certain extent, since production and consumption here present the characteristic of 'self-producing and self-marketing' at a social level instead of the traditional family level. As a matter of fact, consolidation of three networks has reintegrated and reallocated the producer surplus of the enterprise, the consumer surplus of consumers and consumers' labour remuneration, and is essentially the production relations of self-producing and self-marketing that are open but confined to a certain social scope. The only difference is that the 'self-producing' unit in the production relations here is the enterprise rather than the front-line workers, and the remuneration is distributed according to 'sales' (including the sales made by oneself or by others relevant to oneself) instead of work. Consumption and sales here are also united.

2. Consolidation of Three Networks Is a New Circulation Relationship
   Consolidation of three networks is essentially a Direct-Selling model, which reduces the circulation links of commodities, saves the circulation cost, maximizes the enterprise's profits and consumer surplus, improves the efficiency of social resource allocation to a certain extent and reflects a new circulation relationship. In essence, it represents a new circulation relationship that tightly combines circulation and consumption, by which buyers of enterprise products are consumers and sellers at the same time. In this circulation relationship, the human resources and marketing network is the core, while the product and R&D network and the finance and capital network assure that the human resources and marketing network plays a full role in promoting the close integration of circulation and consumption.

3. Consolidation of Three Networks Is a New Supply and Demand Relationship
   As a new circulation relationship, consolidation of three networks closely combines consumption and finally leads to the supply-demand balance, when a new supply-demand relationship is formed. Based on consolidation of three networks, the circulation links between production and consumption are cut down, which enables the almost-perfect combination of production and consumption, significantly reduces and even prevents blind production and eliminates the disconnection between supply and demand to a large extent. By adopting consolidation of the three networks, the enterprise avoids the principal contradiction of commodity economy, the disconnection between supply and demand, and meanwhile adapts the products to consumers' demands, increases consumer surplus and finally drives the formation of a new supply-demand relationship.

4. Consolidation of Three Networks Is a New Distribution Relationship
   Consolidation of three networks is a new distribution relationship, as it breaks the traditional triangular relationship among 'firm – distributor – consumption,' closely combines the three, internalizes the triangular relationship by extending the market border, and has the internal organization instead of the market guide the interest distribution among the three. In this model, the production chain of the firm, consumption management chain and interest distribution chain are closely connected with each other, and the production activities, distribution activities and consumption

activities constitute a closed loop. To a certain extent, it realizes 'communism' and eliminates 'single-handed' work. The interests of the firm, distributor and consumers are distributed according to 'central planning' instead of market competition. In addition, central planning effectively gets rid of 'equalitarianism' and establishes an incentive mechanism of significant effect based on the finance and capital network to mobilize the enthusiasm of relevant personnel. This closed loop is always open to people, since it actively attracts consumers or distributors outside the loop.

It can be seen from the above analysis that consolidation of three networks, distinguished from traditional production relations, shows its unique characteristics in production, circulation, consumption and distribution. These characteristics assure the higher efficiency of this model in resource allocation. From the perspective of the basic system, consolidation of three networks is essentially a planned economy with market selection and, to a certain degree, it is a self-fulfilment of a planned economy at a higher development stage and a higher level. In the meantime, the new distribution relationship in the capital settlement network supports this model by guaranteeing its competitiveness, incentive effect and motive force for operations.

SECTION 2
SWAP ATTRIBUTES AND CORE VALUES EMBODIED IN CONSOLIDATION OF THREE NETWORKS

I. Swap Attributes of Consolidation of Three Networks

Why does Tiens apply the market model of consolidation of three networks? The theoretical basis of consolidation of three networks implies the competitive advantages of the consolidation of three networks model. Dynamically, these competitive advantages are acquired under the premise of resource swap. Only by means of a series of swap of the traditional operations mechanisms can the potential competitive advantage of consolidation of three networks be turned into reality.

The 'consolidation' of 'three networks' means not breaking the multi-relationships among major components of these networks and reorganizing the components, but refers to maintaining the relevant independence of these networks. This depends on certain mechanisms to effectively connect these networks, make up a comprehensive network consisting of the integrated and also segmented networks, improve the efficiency, coordinate the behaviours and assure the consistent targets of the three networks, and finally advance the enterprise's competitiveness.

1. Consolidation of Three Networks and Customer Swap
In the model of consolidation of three networks, product customers are consumers and distributors at the same time. Their amount of consumption and distribution are directly associated with their interest distribution and progressively and significantly inspire customers' loyalty to products and customer stickiness. Since most customers are consumers and distributors at the same time, they have direct experience and feelings about the products and therefore can deeply understand the consumption experience and feelings of new customers. In this way, they can feed back the market information to the product and R&D department of the enterprise, which will further improve the category and quality of products through the product and R&D network. Compared to the traditional market model where customers are more inactive, this new model can help enterprises perfect the product library. With customer swap and a powerful incentive system, consolidation of three networks considerably enhances customer stability and the ability of product optimization.

2. Consolidation of Three Networks and Market Swap
Consolidation of three networks is also distinguished from traditional market models for its market swap. In the model of consolidation of three networks, enterprises can choose products that generate repeat sales, are easy to transport and embrace high added value for market sales. Also, the human resource team adopts face-to-face marketing and self-marketing to replace the advertising and promotion activities of poor effect and no precise target. Then, enterprises appropriately internalize the existing market while opening to the outside, closely bind consumers, distributors and the producer through consolidation of three networks and substitute market-oriented distribution with internal interest-oriented distribution. By doing this, enterprises can expand market size and meanwhile maintain market stability. By means of market swap, consolidation of three networks considerably enhances the low-cost expansion of a market and assures the constant rise of the enterprise's market share.

3. Consolidation of Three Networks and Cost Swap
Cost swap makes another important factor that distinguishes consolidation of three networks from traditional market models. Adopting the Direct-Selling model, consolidation of three networks combines distributors and consumers, purchases goods directly from the enterprise, performs unified accounting with the production and sales of the enterprise and thus lowers transaction costs such as the transportation cost, advertising cost and store rental, as well as the inventory cost and ineffective loss. The benefits from the cost reduction will be redistributed between the producer and consumers

as profit or surplus. Consolidation of three networks also attempts to provide products that better satisfy consumers' demands depending on the consumption information provided by the human resources and marketing network and the rich category and high quality rendered by the product and R&D network. In this way, the misallocation cost of products can also be reduced. The cost saved in the model of consolidation of three networks can be swapped for the producer profit or consumer surplus, which is exactly the ultimate goal of enterprises.

4. Consolidation of Three Networks and Risk Swap
   In the model of consolidation of three networks, the human resources and marketing network extends all over the globe, suggesting that the market is also global. Though each market is exposed to certain risks, systematic risks have been significantly reduced. Meanwhile, in this model, the product and R&D network develops more varied products, and the finance and capital network effectively promotes customer stickiness and avoids the risk of customer loss with its interest distribution mechanism and the corresponding incentive effect. Based on the global market, diverse products and customer stickiness, consolidation of three networks effectively swaps and spreads risks, reduces the uncertainties in enterprise operations and lays a solid foundation for its long-term stable development.

5. Consolidation of Three Networks and Corporate Culture Swap
   Consolidation of three networks swaps the corporate culture in traditional market models. Corporate culture exerts profound influence on the enterprise's production and operations as well as employees' working state and mental attitude. In the model of consolidation of three networks, corporate culture attaches more importance to the cultural elements such as sentiments and humanity. For instance, adhering to the aim of "promoting human health and serving the community" and the development of comprehensive health, Tiens deeply explores and refines the essence of traditional culture and makes it the core culture for Tiens to organize and rally the team. Depending on consolidation of three networks, particularly the human resources network, Tiens emphasizes customers' product experience and also service experience through interpersonal communication and face-to-face exchange, and enables customers to really identify Tiens products and the health culture added to the products.

6. Consolidation of Three Networks and Governance Mechanism Swap
   The model of consolidation of three networks paves the way for the swap of the traditional governance mechanism and the establishment of a new governance mechanism. The consolidation of three networks closely integrates

the human resources and marketing network and the finance and capital network, combines distributors and sellers into one and draws up the capital distribution plan based on the direct and indirect sales of products. As a result of these measures, distributors pay attention to not only their own performance but also the performance of the whole team and even the whole enterprise, which significantly promotes the enterprise's cohesion and competitiveness. Moreover, with the advent of a new development stage, the consolidation of three networks model will supply the access for distributors to be promoted to be enterprise partners. The partnership introduced will inspire the enthusiasm of thousands of distributors. Based on the accounting of indirect performance and the promotion system from distributors to partners in this model, Tiens has successfully swapped the traditional corporate governance mechanism and enhances the extendibility, sustainability and stability of enterprise development.

II. Core Values of Consolidation of Three Networks

Consolidation of three networks achieves great success because of its core values, which endow consolidation of three networks with competitiveness in terms of production, research, development and marketing of the enterprise that is not seen in traditional market models.

1. Core Element

The core element in the core values of consolidation of three networks that significantly distinguishes this new model from any other market model lies in that it has created a human resource team of high loyalty, extendibility and interest relevance. The human resource team is considered as the core element of consolidation of three networks for two reasons. First, this team, showing high loyalty, extendibility and interest relevance, cannot be found in enterprises of other market models. Second, this team plays a guiding role in enterprise development and assures the market expansion of the enterprise with its great stability. By comparison, the enterprises adopting other market models are faced with uncertain market consumer teams and unstable relationships with distributors. In the model of consolidation of three networks, the human resource team is the core element as well as the subjective factor that gives full play to the core values of consolidation of three networks.

2. Core Benefits

The consolidation of three networks model creates a human resource team of high loyalty, which conversely enables this model to evolve into a new market model of new production relationships, new circulation relationships and new supply-demand relationships and helps the enterprise acquire greater benefits. The core benefits of consolidation of three networks are embodied in four aspects, in that it: (1) assists in lowering the transaction cost; (2) improves the efficiency of resource allocation; (3) assures the stability and extendibility of the market; and (4) motivates distributors and even consumers. Though the human resources network constitutes the core element and the major carrier of consolidation of three networks, it still requires the close cooperation of the product and R&D network and the finance and capital network. The core element of the human resource team is merely a static factor that cannot acquire any benefit independently. The core benefits can only be realized through the cooperation and interaction with the other two networks in multiple aspects and the perfect integration of the three networks.

3. Core Requirements
   The core element and core benefits make up the most fundamental characteristics of consolidation of three networks and the major carrier to realize the model's core values. However, some basic conditions must be fulfilled to give full play to the core values of consolidation of three networks to the maximum. These conditions are considered as the core requirements of consolidation of three networks. There are three core requirements. First, the space will be enlarged. It means that consolidation of three networks will extend its presence to different countries or regions around the world and expand the boundary to avoid any growth constraint that may arise. Second, the depth will be improved. In other words, consolidation of three networks needs to constantly attract more human resources at different spatial dimensions and increase the replication frequency of the multi-level marketing system. Third, the scope will be expanded. The product category will be enriched to include diverse and high-quality products in the consolidation of three networks model, thus to attain the best possible coverage of consumers' consumption menu.

CHAPTER 5

CONSOLIDATION OF THREE NETWORKS: PREREQUISITES AND IMPLEMENTATION APPROACHES

SECTION 1
EVOLUTION OF COMPETITIVE ENVIRONMENT AND CONSOLIDATION OF THREE NETWORKS

I. Evolution of Competitive Environment and Innovation of Market Models

Why can the model of consolidation of three networks achieve great success after its sudden emergence? In the final analysis, this is because this model adapts to the laws of economic and social development and embraces more competitive advantages in the fierce market competition due to its unique attributes. The current evolution of competitive environment mainly embodies the following characteristics:

First, market competition becomes increasingly fierce. New business formats are constantly emerging based on the popularization of the internet, and fierce competition is extending to a broader space as driven by globalization, informatization and urbanization. Ultra-large enterprises are occupying a bigger market share by seizing the market shares of medium and small-sized enterprises, which intensifies the competition among enterprises for survival and development.

Second, the marketing cost and circulation cost are rising. Enterprises are organizing marketing activities in various ways to occupy a bigger market share. Meanwhile, the circulation cost is growing due to the multiple links in the process of circulation including transportation, distribution and sales exhibition.

Third, repeat sales are decreasing, while customer stickiness is weakening. The constantly emerging new products and new models have reduced the repeat sales of products. Customer stickiness to many products other than some branded products apparently weakens. This situation forces enterprises to carry out advertising and promotion activities more frequently and extensively, raising senseless costs.

Fourth, supply and demand are still subject to serious disconnection. Though enterprises depend more on the terminal sales data in production organization based on the application and development of information technology, the disconnection between supply and demand has not been effectively improved. This is mainly because production can hardly be adjusted according to the changes, as customer stickiness has been falling due to the increasing diversity of products.

The evolution of the competitive environment of market calls for the innovation of the enterprises' market models so as to reply to the new pressures brought by market changes. This new market model will contribute to enhancing customer stickiness, lowering the transaction cost and reducing the supply-demand disconnection, thus improving the core competitiveness of the enterprise and acquiring competitive advantages in constant market competition.

II. Limitations of Traditional Marketing Models and the Rise of the Direct-Selling Model

In the competitive environment exposed to drastic changes, traditional marketing models have no way to solve the above issues. First, traditional marketing models cannot reduce any marketing process, so they cannot effectively lower the circulation cost. Second, traditional marketing models can hardly promote repeat sales or customer stickiness. Third, in traditional marketing models, sales are still determined by production, which inevitably results in supply-demand disconnection. In general, as to traditional marketing models, enterprises adopt the homogeneous competition model, where the characteristics of customer stickiness and consumers' consumption amount make no difference and interpersonal connections have not been made full use of. Therefore, these models cannot effectively respond to the changes of market competition.

Being a new marketing model, the Direct-Selling model is fundamentally characterized by the increased return of proceeds from consumption or sales of products; and it also expands the scope of repeat sales of products and distributes the returns from these repeat sales. With regard to the recognition of repeat sales of products, the product purchases of the lower-level consumers recommended or introduced by consumers are recognized as the repeat sales of the higher-level consumers, and a part of the return from these repeat sales are paid to the higher-level consumers. Therefore, this model motivates customers to promote repeat sales of products, closely connects consumers and enterprises, and thus reduces circulation processes and corresponding costs, and avoids the supply-demand disconnection of products. With the higher consumption amount and the higher repeat sales, consumers can acquire bigger benefits, which may even cover consumers' actual expenditures and provide them with consumer surplus and net profit. In this way, it considerably encourages consumers to make full use of their connections to extend the sales chain of products, expands the scale of enterprises' production and sales and earns a market share much greater than that of traditional marketing models.

III. Competitive Advantages of the Direct-Selling Model of Consolidation of Three Networks

Consolidation of three networks of Direct-Selling enterprises is the new market model evolved from the Direct-Selling model. Compared to commonly seen Direct-Selling models, it presents significant competitive advantages and assures the market dominance of an enterprise in the competition with traditional enterprises and other Direct-Selling enterprises.

1. Market Characteristics of Consolidation of Three Networks

First, consolidation of three networks proposes new concepts of human resources relations and services. In the model of consolidation of three networks, human resources have built up the interest chain among each other through product sales or consumption, which increases human resources' enthusiasm to help and promote each other and drives the internal expansion of the human resources scale. Moreover, when carrying out marketing activities, human resources attach greater importance to interpersonal emotional communication and first-hand experience. They adhere to the same enterprise spirit and gradually cultivate new consumption and service concepts, such as 'consumption is wealth,' 'promote human health' and 'serve the community.'

Second, consolidation of three networks closely integrates production, consumption and distribution. As the terminal market of sales or consumption, the human resources and marketing network delivers the market information it collects to the product and R&D network to help the product and R&D departments produce an appropriate quantity of high-quality products adapting to market demand. In the meantime, the human resources and marketing network conveys the sales or consumption information to the finance and capital network, which conducts redistribution of product revenues based on relevant information. In this way, production, consumption and distribution are closely integrated, lowering the marketing cost and circulation cost, alleviating and even eliminating the imbalance between supply and demand.

Third, consolidation of three networks makes the best use of the incentive effect of the bonus system. This model scales up the incentive effect of the bonus system of Direct-Selling models. With the global market space, diversified products, high product quality and rationally designed bonus system, consolidation of three networks constantly expands the market extension, increases the amount of bonus, produces the greatest incentive effect, and thus wins a more evident competitive advantage over other Direct-Selling enterprises.

2. Competitive Advantages of Consolidation of Three Networks

The market characteristics of consolidation of three networks determine its unique competitive advantages.

The first is the market advantage. In the model of consolidation of three networks, repeat sales of products increase and customer stickiness is improved. In particular, customer stickiness shows a dynamic trend, where 'the old brings the new' becomes the ordinary state, suggesting the self-reproduction feature of customer stickiness in this model. The global development of consolidation of three networks further highlights this market advantage.

The second is the product advantage. In the model of consolidation of three networks, the product and R&D network has production bases and R&D teams distributed all around the world, assures the diversity of products, improves product quality and speeds up the release of products.

The third is the cost advantage. In the model of consolidation of three networks, in view of greater customer stickiness and consumption stability, enterprises can determine their production and supply by the sales amount, thus reducing the waste of overproduction and meanwhile lowering the inventory cost.

The fourth is the brand advantage. Enterprises adopting the model of consolidation of three networks also obtain the brand advantage. The brand advantage is essentially the result, consolidation and continuance of the competitive advantages of consolidation of three networks. The model of consolidation of three networks successfully increases enterprises' market shares and improves consumers' loyalty. The human resource team's oral advertising of the enterprises and their products will further enhance social cognition and recognition of the enterprise and gradually build and strengthen the brand image.

The fifth is the operational advantage. In the model of consolidation of three networks, all the links of production, consumption and circulation are closely connected to and support each other. In the meantime, this model orients on market demand, assures smooth operations through precise accounting, has all links of the operations perfectly integrated with each other and avoids unnecessary formalities,. This facilitates the supervision and management by executives, improves enterprises' operational efficiency and helps them to acquire operational advantages.

SECTION 2
ESSENTIAL CONDITIONS AND MAIN TACTICS OF CONSOLIDATION OF THREE NETWORKS

I. Essential Conditions of Consolidation of Three Networks

Enterprises that execute consolidation of three networks must adopt a Direct-Selling operation and the persistent incentive mechanism and must show a strong ability in resource swapping.

1. A Direct-Selling Operation is the Prerequisite for Consolidation of Three Networks
As a matter of fact, a Direct-Selling operation contains the basic core of the consolidation of three networks model, the reduced processes of circulation, introduction of multi-level sales and the reward point system and interpersonal connection network derived therefrom. Without the essential conditions of a Direct-Selling operation, the 'three networks' may exist in varying degrees but they cannot be consolidated. In this case, the market characteristics and competitive advantages of consolidation of three networks will be gone, and the market value will significantly decline or even vanish.

2. Persistent Incentives Constitute the Important Support to cConsolidation of Three Networks
To make full use of the competitive advantages of consolidation of three networks, the human resource team's initiative will be brought into full play. This is the subjective factor that contributes to the success of enterprise operations. However, to achieve this goal, a persistent incentive mechanism is required. While a Direct-Selling operation makes it possible to achieve consolidation of three networks, persistent incentives help give full play to the competitive advantages of consolidation of three networks and constitute an important support to activate the model of consolidation of three networks. By 'persistent' incentives we mean that the enterprises adopting consolidation of three networks will timely adjust the incentive plan pursuant to the development stage and the changes of market environment, to maintain and constantly strengthen the incentive effect and avoid the decline of the incentive effect.

3. Swap Ability is the Basic Guarantee for Consolidation of Three Networks
To adopt the model of consolidation of three networks, the domestic market will be swapped for the global market; old management models will be swapped for the new; traditional marketing channels will be swapped for the human resources marketing channel; independent research, development

and production will be swapped for joint research, development and production; and the financial management of simple recording and accounting will be swapped for the financial management of the incentive effect. We can imagine how difficult it is to perform the resource or model swap that involves products, talents, management and operations and all other factors. These swaps can hardly be completed without a leader who takes charge of the whole situation and looks forward or without determined and resolute executors. Hence, a strong swap ability is regarded as the basic guarantee for the establishment and smooth operation of consolidation of three networks.

II. Main Tactics of Consolidation of Three Networks

In addition to the essential conditions for the establishment and improvement of the model of consolidation of three networks, corresponding tactics will be formulated during the performance of the model to adapt the model to the demand of enterprise development and make use of the model's powerful driving force to the extreme.

1. Model Swap

Model swap is considered as the main strategy of the establishment and expansion of consolidation of three networks. The process by which the model of consolidation of three networks replaces traditional market models or traditional Direct-Selling models is actually a complete swap of the market model. This kind of swap is a strategy rather than a tactic. However, the model swap is not only about strategies. In addition to the strategic swap of original factors with the core factors of consolidation of three networks, other models of the enterprise including the governance model, management model, operations model, production model, R&D model and accounting model will also be swapped corresponding to the new model of consolidation of three networks. In this way, these new models can assure the smooth operation of consolidation of three networks and achieve better results than original traditional market models do.

2. Resource Integration

Another prerequisite to the successful swap and operation of the model of consolidation of three networks is to integrate resources of different types at different levels, which include the integration of both internal and external resources. Integration is mainly performed in two manners: the reintegration of existing resources and the integration of new resources. The construction and expansion of the production and R&D network is a typical instance of resource integration.

3. Regional Cooperation
An important support to the application and implementation of consolidation of three networks rests in regional cooperation, including the cooperation of major regions in China as well as the cooperation of regions overseas. Why is regional cooperation needed? It can spread risks, enhance the extendibility and improve the co-movements. Regional cooperation can maintain order and unification of the market, facilitate rapid expansion of the market, enable consolidation of three networks to give full play to its advantages in geographical positions or economic space and effectively control the enterprise's operating risks.

4. Network Expansion
Network expansion here has two meanings: first, the constant and independent development of the breadth and depth of the three networks; second, the simultaneous online and offline expansion. The expansion of 'three networks' refers to the expansion of market space and product category and the corresponding expansion of financial information and capital flow. At the initial stage of development, expansion of the three networks is mainly carried out offline. However, with the popularization of the internet, the new three networks online gradually usher in a historical opportunity for development, where the human resources and marketing network, product and R&D networks and finance and capital network can be perfectly integrated through the internet platform by means of modern internet technologies.

5. Integration of Distributors and Sellers
One of the important tactics to expand consolidation of three networks is to integrate distributors and sellers to the greatest extent. Since the three networks are extendible, a large number of pure consumers still exist at a certain static time. It is the existence of these pure consumers that make Direct-Selling models more attractive. However, dynamically, it would be better if all consumers at each point of time can be successfully converted to be distributors who purchase products repeatedly. Only on this basis can the three networks expand at a higher rate. Therefore, it is of great significance to reduce the loss of pure consumers and promote the change of their roles for the sake of giving full play to consolidation of three networks.

6. Interconnection and Sharing
Interconnection and sharing here contain three meanings: first, the interconnection and sharing among the three networks; second, the interconnection and sharing among different regions and business segments; and third, the interconnection and sharing between the online and the offline.

The interconnection and sharing among the three networks make up the core requirement of consolidation of three networks. In other words, to achieve the 'consolidation,' the three networks must interconnect and share. The human resources and marketing network, product and R&D network, and finance and capital network must be interconnected through a mechanism and share information, which will finally promote the integration of the three networks.

SECTION 3 IMPLEMENTATION PATH OF CONSOLIDATION OF THREE NETWORKS

Only by taking the initiative to propose the strategy of consolidation of three networks and adopting corresponding measures to implement the strategy can the three networks be truly consolidated and the competitive advantages of the consolidation be brought into full play.

I. Outline and Expansion of Three Networks

1. Human Resources and Marketing Network

Interpersonal relations make up the core power to drive the expansion of the human resources and marketing network. The Direct-Selling model focuses on the interaction among people and shows multi-level relationships like one-to-many or higher level-to-lower level, where interpersonal relations function as the catalyst for constant market expansion.

The independent product exhibition store is the platform foundation for the development of the human resources and marketing network. Different from the traditional shopping mall sales model, the independent product exhibition store places emphasis on its individual characteristics, reveals its own connotation and taste and better attracts consumers' attention.

Globalization is considered as the fundamental prerequisite to the spatial expansion of the human resources and marketing network. The success of Direct-Selling enterprises necessarily depends on the spatial expansion of the network, so openness is the soul. The less-open human resources and marketing network will inevitably shrink.

A complete appraisal and position rank system is an important guarantee for the constant spiritual development of the human resources and marketing network. Only when the network operates orderly and energetically can it continue its expansion. Meanwhile, it is of great significance to correctly appraise the performance of the human resource team and assign proper positions and ranks.

2. Product and R&D Network

The basic requirement for the expansion of the product and R&D network is the focus on product quality. Only with sound product quality the expansion of the product and R&D network makes sense; otherwise, the enterprise will fall into a business dilemma during the expansion.

The product and R&D network adheres to the fundamental principle of product relevance during expansion. The products of Direct-Selling enterprises must see a high rate of repeat sales and be easy to preserve and display. Hence the products must show certain relevance. When the product and R&D network has expanded to a certain scale, the relevance enables products to present their same connotation and attribute, which is favourable for the construction and communication of the image of the enterprise's products.

The inevitable course to promote the density of the product and R&D network is the further detailed classification of products. Consumers have different requirements on the same category of products. By constantly enriching the product category and effectively satisfying consumers' different demands, it can facilitate the market expansion and improve the market share of the enterprise's products.

An effective approach to improve the development ability of the product and R&D network is to borrow external wisdom. In addition to its own R&D team, the enterprise will make use of research forces from the institutions of higher learning in various forms. Also, it can apply OEM production to rapidly enrich the product category and improve product quality.

International investment is an important measure to assure the expansion of the product and R&D network. To avoid policy barriers of some countries on market and production, or to further promote the ability to assure supply, the enterprise can invest on product production in some foreign regions, which is a necessary strategic move for the enterprise.

3. Finance and Capital Network

Information-based management is an important approach to improve the efficiency of the finance and capital network. By installing finance software, training finance personnel, connecting the financial system with the human resources and marketing system and the product and R&D system through the internet and realizing the orderly management and rapid transmission of information, the efficiency of the finance and capital network can be improved.

The improvement of the ability of fund allocation can constitute a guarantee for the finance and capital network to perform its management function. Fund, which has no function itself, is the basic guarantee for the survival and development of an enterprise. The finance and capital network is endowed with the power to raise and distribute the fund based on operations demand, so it is necessary to improve its ability to effectively mobilize funds for the sake of the efficient operations of the enterprise.

To bring the finance and capital network into full play, an important measure is to formulate the distribution incentive plan. The finance and capital network will draw up the proper distribution incentive plan according to the management and operations information obtained, thus to encourage personnel of all departments to work hard. This is one of the functions of the finance and capital network.

II. Implementation Path of Consolidation of Three Networks

The three networks are consolidated through the interaction among the value flow, information flow and the logistics and capital flow, while the smooth interaction among them depends on the enterprise's efforts in strategies, management, organization, platform and information.

The basic prerequisite to the realization of consolidation of three networks is to determine the strategic goal of constant market exploration. The strategic goal varies in each enterprise. However, Direct-Selling enterprises adopting the model of consolidation of three networks need to constantly develop the breadth and depth of market, as they can only maintain a sound momentum of growth by continuously exploring the market. This strategic goal makes the consolidation of the three networks necessary.

The fundamental means to achieve consolidation of three networks is to conduct resource swaps in good time. While all enterprises have their three networks, only a few of them that enjoy the ability of resource integration and swap have realized the consolidation. To achieve consolidation of three networks and maintain its flexibility and effectiveness, it is necessary to make and implement decisions resolutely according to the development goals in different periods and swap some impeding factors for more active factors.

An effective organizational structure will institutionally guarantee the realization of consolidation of three networks. Corresponding organizations will be established and their operational efficiency will be improved to consolidate the three networks and promote its effective operation. The departments directly associated with the three networks, including branch offices, special stores, R&D departments, production departments and financial departments, will play their role, and the departments of global management such as the training department and human resources department will also actively promote the consolidation of three networks.

Platform construction is also an important method to adapt consolidation of three networks to ever-changing circumstances. These platforms may involve tourism, medical care, education, e-commerce and logistics. Though not directly related to the three networks, these platforms play an important part in upgrading certain functions of the three networks and effectively promoting the consolidation. For example, the logistics network, education network and tourism network facilitate the exploration of the human resources and marketing network and the expansion of the product and R&D network, and also interact with the finance and capital network.

Information-based management is regarded as a magic weapon to improve the operations efficiency of consolidation of three networks. By making use of the internet to gather, organize and analyse the massive information obtained in the enterprise's daily operations and regulate the interactions among the three networks, it will significantly advance the timely, accurate and well-coordinated operation of consolidation of three networks and greatly promote its operations efficiency.

III. Periodic Features of Consolidation of Three Networks

The implementation path of consolidation of three networks is theoretically discussed above. Here, with Tiens, we will study the features of consolidation of three networks in different development stages as well as some associated requirements.

1. The First Start-up Period: the Expansion of the Human Resources and Marketing Network based on Superior Products

In the early days, Tiens had successfully developed a high-tech biological product, the high-calcium supplement, after having gone through a lot of difficulties and setbacks. This product had been welcomed by consumers for its magical effects. In this period, Tiens had trained and cultivated a batch of business elites and was relatively successful. However, the real success of an enterprise is to maintain sustainable development and earn corresponding profit. In this sense, the newly born Tiens had not gone far enough. Hence, it was an urgent task for Tiens to swap the market model and turn the product advantage into the market advantage and finally into the enterprise advantage.

At the critical moment of Tiens, the founders of the enterprise decided to adopt network-based direct selling to sell the high-calcium supplement. By the end of November 1995, branch offices had been established in all provinces and regions other than Tibet (of China) and Taiwan. Within only one year after the founding of Baojinfa Trading Company, the number of sellers for the high-calcium supplement and other healthcare products had reached as high as 600,000, with an annual sales volume exceeding 2 billion yuan. On this basis, it achieved a big leap since the founding of Tiens.

Despite all the difficulties and setbacks during the first start-up, Tiens had finally won great success by perfectly combining a superior product and the Direct-Selling model.

The experience of Tiens mentioned above demonstrates that for Direct-Selling enterprises at the initial stage, the basic feature rests in the rapid expansion of the human resources and marketing network as supported by superior products. In this period, the product and R&D network was still underdeveloped, and there was no consciousness to consolidate the three networks.

2. Second Start-up: Consolidation of Three Networks Upon the Full Development of the Three Networks
On April 18, 1998, the State Council issued a circular on prohibiting pyramid selling. Against this difficult situation, Tiens initiated its international network and marched into the world. It transformed its original marketing method in the Chinese market to a new marketing model with Chinese characteristics, retail chain store and international network-based direct selling. It established branch offices and a retail chain store network for traditional marketing and adopted the modern network-based direct selling model derived from developed countries. In 2001, Tiens opened its global website. By then, Tiens had integrated the three networks, the business personnel network, special store network and global website, which were known as the old three networks. After that, the product category of Tiens had been increasingly enriched along with the rapid expansion of its global network.

The process by which Tiens marched into the world and played a part in the world market depending on network-based direct selling is called the second start-up of Tiens. In this period, the human resources and marketing network had expanded swiftly, which drove the full development of the product and R&D network and the finance and capital network and made it necessary to consolidate the three networks at a higher level. The concept of three networks at that time had already covered all the links of marketing, research, development, production, sales and distribution, and the consolidation referred to sorting out the responsibilities and relations of the three networks, establishing a smooth system and mechanism and thus assuring the integration of the three networks at a higher level. With the full development of these networks and the consolidation of three networks at a higher level, the enterprise could expand its market influence, enrich its product category, provide highly effective incentives to the human resource team through financial distribution and bonus accounting and maintain its market vitality.

3. Third Start-up: Consolidation of Three Networks Based on the Externalization of Functions

With the third start-up, Tiens aims to better adapt to the ever-changing market competition and rise up to the challenge brought by the internet and globalization. It also aims to seize the opportunity in the 'Belt and Road Strategy,' embrace the rise of Internet+ and comprehensive health industry, reform its own management system, governance structure and corporate culture and, as guided by the new enterprise strategy, build Tiens into a century-old enterprise full of energy and responsible for human health with the spirit of enterprising and innovation.

To achieve success in the third start-up, Tiens cooperates with the national Belt and Road strategy by formulating the strategic development planning of 'one body with multiple wings' and putting forward a series of theoretical innovation and strategic measures including 'consolidation of three networks,' 'multi-network interaction' and 'household consumption creates wealth while the management of household consumption creates more wealth.' The core of the third start-up of Tiens lies in the innovation and implementation of terminal modes. Tiens will construct seven terminal modes simultaneously (direct selling, comprehensive health, new e-commerce, tourism and resort, education and training, barter, and points and e-wallet), and create added value through interaction.

In this period, consolidation of three networks still plays an important role in the third start-up. It is not only the main part of the 'one body,' but also the most fundamental platform and the most important support for the seven terminal modes. Consolidation of three networks enriches the 'one body,' lays the foundation for the existence of 'multiple wings' and enables the seven terminal modes to interact and support each other. Therefore, consolidation of three networks is the main body, a sharing platform and also an operations mechanism.

Throughout the three start-ups, consolidation of three networks has been exposed to certain changes according to circumstances. First, it bears heavier and clearer responsibilities as a main body, and the core status of direct selling has become more prominent. Second, the space and market of consolidation of three networks are developing in a three-dimensional way, and the enterprise businesses centring on consolidation of three networks are becoming diversified and integrated. Third, the contents of the three networks are more abundant, since various business forms have been incorporated or integrated into the human resources and marketing network, the product and R&D network, and the finance and capital network to varying degrees, and are combined and integrated with each other in new forms, producing the more advanced and complicated model of consolidation of three networks, which plays a key role in the new journey of the enterprise.

In general, in the new development stage, many internal functions of the consolidation of three networks have been externalized. These externalized functions can operate independently and be strengthened, and also promote the consolidation of the three networks and the efficiency of the model.

CHAPTER 6

CONSOLIDATION OF THREE NETWORKS AND TRANSCENDENCE PRACTICE: EFFECTS AND EXPERIENCE

SECTION 1
PRACTICAL EFFECTS AND EXPERIENCE IN CONSOLIDATION OF THREE NETWORKS

I. Practical Effect of Consolidation of Three Networks

By adopting and gradually improving the consolidation of three networks model, the enterprise can acquire continuous internal competitiveness and become more competitive than ordinary enterprises in terms of customer stability, marketing, risk sharing, cost control and cultural communication.

1. Consolidation of Three Networks Improves the Enterprise's Ability and Efficiency of Human Resources Exploration

With regard to customers, Tiens has perfectly integrated distributors and consumers through consolidation of three networks, significantly enhanced customers' stickiness by advocating wealth creation by consumption and attracted approximately 40 million families as its customers. Undoubtedly, customer stability constitutes an important support to the constant expansion of customer size. Through over two decades of development, Tiens has made a great leap from an enterprise with merely seven young entrepreneurs to a large group with over 10,000 international managers.

2. Consolidation of Three Networks Improves the Enterprise's Ability and Efficiency of Product R&D and Market Supply

The product and R&D network plays an important part in consolidation of three networks. With the continuous growth of customer size, the increasingly diverse product category and the deepening global market layout, Tiens has maintained a high rate of market expansion. By the end of 2016, Tiens had been dedicated to exploring the essence of Chinese traditional medicine and health preservation culture depending on advanced biotechnology; developed over 1,000 kinds of products under five major categories including health food, personal care, household items, beauty and cosmetics, and health equipment in the world; established production bases and OEM plants in China, Vietnam, Spain, Russia, Indonesia and India and some other countries and regions; and spread its products to over 190 countries and approximately 40 million families. Tiens products are also changing. For example, the luxury brand Richy One has been cultivated.

3. Consolidation of Three Networks Improves the Enterprise's Ability and Efficiency of the Integration of Global Resources
The market model of consolidation of three networks also facilitates the exploration of the global human resource team and marketing network. Expanding the global presence of Tiens products of low consumption and high added value can prevent the market risk and policy risk of a single market, and also advance the ability of Tiens to earn foreign exchange and acquire more resources worldwide. In this way, Tiens will become a national enterprise exerting worldwide influence.

4. Consolidation of Three Networks Improves the Enterprise's Ability and Efficiency to Flexibly Adapt to Market Demand Changes
While the human resource team and interpersonal connections play an important part in direct selling, the enterprises that have consolidated three networks attach greater importance to market means. They adhere to market orientation to design the layout of product research, development and production lines, provide the market with products that better satisfy market demand at a lower production cost and through a more convenient supply chain, raise the consumption welfare and operations benefits of the existing human resource team and attract more potential consumers to join the team. Only by emphasizing the guiding role of market in the enterprise's product production and operations can Tiens maintain its enterprise vitality and constant growth.

It is exactly these practical effects of consolidation of three networks that help the enterprise achieve transcendence. Tiens was selected as one of the Top 500 Chinese Enterprises of 2017 and ranked the 420th with an operating income of 33.5 billion yuan, making it the only Direct-Selling enterprise among the Top 500 Chinese Enterprises of 2017. The name of Tiens has already been heard throughout the world.

II. Successful Experience of Consolidation of Three Networks

Consolidation of three networks only achieves the above effects based on its competitive advantages in terms of market, product, cost, brand and operations. However, these competitive advantages can only be turned into practical advantages when some conditions are satisfied. What the enterprises adopting consolidation of three networks must do is to create these conditions.

1. Flexibly Draw up a Points-based System and Strengthen Market Advantage through Wealth Creation by Consumption
The implementation of a points-based system makes it possible to create wealth through consumption. This system will greatly mobilize the enthusiasm of the human resource team, urge them to change from consumers to distributors, increase repeat sales of products and further promote the development and expansion of product consumers and distributors.

2. Widely Apply OEM and Customized Production, Rapidly Upgrade Product Quality and Enrich Product Categories
With the expansion of the human resource team, the consumption demand is increasingly diversified; and as time goes on, increasing demand is proposed on new products. Under these circumstances, the enterprise partners with enterprises that embrace a strong ability of product research, development and production but lack the ability of marketing, lowers the product cost by means of OEM and customized production and uses the products to meet the consumption demand of the human resource team themselves. In this way, the market share will ceaselessly grow.

3. Supply Goods Directly Based on Demand and Determine Production Based on Sales, to Lower the Circulation and Inventory Cost of Products
In the model of consolidation of three networks, the human resources and marketing network and the product and R&D network are closely connected with each other through the information chain and logistics chain. The enterprise can make full use of the information, R&D, produce and supply products according to market demand, reduce the intermediate distribution and circulation links, lower the inventory cost of products, match supply and demand more accurately and thus minimize resource wastage.

4. Make the Best of the Human Resources Advantage and Build the Enterprise Image and Product Brand by Organizing Large-scale Conferences
The large-scale and widely distributed human resources constitute the advantageous resources of enterprises adopting consolidation of three networks. Based on these resources, the enterprise is capable of organizing large-scale conferences. Though the contents of conferences are confined to internal circulation, these conferences are open to society in form and therefore show great influence. They play an important role in cultivating the enterprise image and product brand.

5. Promote Information Construction, Assure Information Interconnection, and Make Information the Important Carrier for the Consolidation of all Networks
   Though the connections among networks are mainly realized through institutional arrangements, the role of information exchange will not be neglected. To assure the smooth exchange of the networks, it is necessary to construct information-based platforms and apply financial software and enterprise management software in the enterprise. Warehousing, logistics and e-commerce platforms are all important parts of information construction.

6. Think Highly of Resource Swap and Adapt Consolidation of Three Networks to Ever-changing Circumstances
   To assure the model of consolidation of three networks is more adaptive to future development, resource swaps will be carried out at the right time according to the enterprise's development period and market conditions. The core of resource swaps is the interest. In other words, the swap in any form is essentially the swap of interest, which aims to sacrifice the smaller short-term interest for the bigger long-term interest. The resource swap is always accompanied by the swap of the human resource team, so it is undoubtedly difficult to complete the swaps. However, the enterprise must spare no effort to obtain the swapping ability, since it is considered as the fundamental guarantee that assures the model consolidation of three networks can be flexibly adjusted according to development demand.

SECTION 2
POTENTIAL ADVANTAGES AND DIRECT-SELLING MARKETS IN CONSOLIDATION OF THREE NETWORKS

I. Inherent Contradictions of Consolidation of Three Networks

In view of the inherent defects of consolidation of three networks, the enterprise will not merely rely on the model of consolidation of three networks to acquire persistent competitiveness, but will make breakthroughs and innovations.

1. The Increasingly Intensified Market Competition Compresses Network Expansion
   Along with increasingly fierce competition in the Direct-Selling market, some latecomers have also constructed their own human resources and marketing network and launched direct competition with and compressed the expansion of the human resources and marketing network of Tiens.

Hence, it becomes difficult for Tiens to sustain a high growth rate. At present, more than 80 enterprises have acquired the license for direct selling in China, challenging the model of consolidation of three networks.

2. Products Cannot Effectively Satisfy Market Demand due to Insufficient Diversity
The product and R&D network in the consolidation of three networks is an important factor that attracts distributors and consumers. The human resource and marketing team can only constantly develop and expand based on the high quality and rich categories of products. When no competitor is around, distributors or consumers pay more attention to the bonus rewards from product consumption. However, when competitors are increasing, the competitors may attract distributors or consumers by their substitutable products. Hence, how to promote product diversity and improve the brand image becomes an important question to be solved by the product and R&D network.

3. Modern Internet Renders Weak Support to Relationship Marketing
In the consolidation of three networks, the human resources and marketing network centres on interpersonal connections, so relationship marketing is regarded as the fundamental characteristic. However, though the internet still supports interpersonal connections to a certain degree, the effect falls far behind that of interpersonal face-to-face communication. In this case, the internet can hardly be perfectly combined in the consolidation of three networks. Therefore, it is still one of the enterprise's goals to incorporate the internet in the three networks.

4. Consolidation of Three Networks Faces Complicated and Volatile Market and Legal Environment during Global Expansion
When the enterprise is developing its market based on consolidation of three networks, it necessarily encounters a complicated and volatile market and legal environment, which not only increases the communication cost and product design cost during the expansion of the human resources and marketing network, but also raises the cost to make adjustments according to different policies and laws. Cultural concepts and consumption principles vary significantly in different countries, and administrative policies and legal requirements on Direct-Selling enterprises also differ greatly. Therefore, when promoting the development of the human resources and marketing network, product and R&D network, and finance and capital network, the enterprise needs to make more investments to adapt to these differences. In this way, the operating cost of consolidation of three networks increases imperceptibly.

5. The Product Price that is Deviated From the Market Value Raises Questions
   In the model of consolidation of three networks, the points-based system and bonus system provide consumers and distributors with more returns, which constitutes the driving force for the self-expansion of the human resources and marketing network. In this case, the product price has to be deviated from its market value. The loss of surplus incurred by the deviation between the product price and the market value is mainly borne by the newest consumers. Therefore, this structural deviation leads to the redistribution of surplus. The market often questions the fairness of the redistribution, which causes stress on the enterprise operations, impedes some consumers from joining its production and marketing network and restricts its enterprise.

II. Potential Advantages of Consolidation of Three Networks

As a matter of fact, in addition to helping the enterprise coordinate the relations among production, circulation and marketing and lowering its operating cost, consolidation of three networks also embraces many other potential advantages. These potential advantages will be turned into practical advantages when the enterprise has reached a certain stage of development, and then promote the higher-level development of the enterprise.

1. The Networks in Consolidation of Three Networks Cover Extensive Areas
   Consolidation of three networks emphasizes the extensive areas of these networks. Some enterprises have their networks spread over the whole world, which bring more opportunities for their development. The global network facilitates the expansion of global trading and logistics activities, enhances market competitiveness and lowers the business cost of the enterprise by means of information exchange, platform sharing and foreign exchange activities.

2. The Networks in Consolidation of Three Networks Present the Attributes of Economies of Scale
   The human resources network in the consolidation of three networks generally shows a large scale, where human resources are very loyal to the enterprise and agree with its development path and strategies. With a large-scale human resource team, the enterprise will naturally acquire its customer base when exploring other businesses. In this way, it can start from a higher ground, and lower or even avoid the huge risk at the initial stage of investment.

3. The Networks in Consolidation of Three Networks Function as Display Platforms
The human resources and marketing network in the consolidation of three networks includes the special stores opened in every corner of the world as the platforms for product display and interpersonal exchange. These platforms that display products play an important role in the e-commerce expansion and online and offline integration of the enterprise.

4. The Networks in Consolidation of Three Networks are Diverse and Expandable
Since the consolidation of three networks is open to the outside, the breadth and depth of products and businesses can be further developed. The expandability of products and businesses assures constant growth of the enterprise's operating income, helps distributors and consumers earn more surpluses and reduce the loss of internal consumption to the minimum.

III. Coordination of Potential Advantages and Inherent Contradictions of Consolidation of Three Networks

Consolidation of three networks has some problems and inherent contradictions. However, it also enjoys potential advantages, which can resolve or relieve these questions or contradictions only if these potential advantages are fully utilized.

1. The Existing Human Resource Team Makes it Favourable for the Horizontal Expansion of Businesses
As the unique advantageous resource of the enterprise, the existing large-scale human resource team plays an important role in the horizontal expansion of businesses, and therefore shows great potential competitive advantages. For example, if the enterprise transfers the human resource team to business sectors other than direct selling through a certain form of incentive, then this newly opened business sector will develop rapidly. Other new Direct-Selling enterprises can only compete with it in Direct-Selling businesses, but fall far behind it in the new business sectors. Therefore, compared to new enterprises, it enjoys greater market competitiveness on the whole.

2. Global Layout of Networks Enables the Enterprise to Produce, Research, Develop and Trade Products in a Larger Area
With the improvement of a global network layout and the stable growth of the human resource team, the enterprise can invest more time and space in demand investigation, research, development and production of products, and even produce products against a certain market or spread products to

other markets. By doing this, the enterprise can assure product diversity while getting returns from mass production. Moreover, with a global network layout, the enterprise can regulate surplus and deficiency of products worldwide and trade local specialties to further enrich production lines. Meanwhile, part of trade goods are introduced into the product network, so the product network is able to break through the constraints of the research, development and production capacity, maximize the product diversity and earn returns from regional price differentials.

3. The Integration of the Human Resources and Marketing Network and Online Shopping Facilitates the Expansion of the Human Resource Team
   Though a pure online display can hardly develop the human resources and marketing network, the existing human resource team can promote the rapid construction and expansion of online shops. As an open port, online shops help online consumers understand the Direct-Selling businesses of the enterprise and impel them to voluntarily join direct selling. In this way, the online and the offline are perfectly integrated, constantly promoting the expansion of the human resources and marketing network. In this sense, the internet is helping the enterprise develop its Direct-Selling businesses in another way. This new model of consolidation of four networks is favourable for maintaining and even improving the enterprise's market competitiveness.

4. The Deviation Between Product Price and Market Value is Gradually Reduced along with Product and Business Diversification
   The increasing categories of products and the constant emergence of new Direct-Selling business sectors based on the Direct-Selling human resource team will gradually reduce the deviation between product price and market value. On this condition, not only can most consumers and distributors acquire greater surplus returns, but also the newest consumers will suffer from fewer losses and even obtain part of the surplus returns. By doing this, every individual consumer and distributor can expect and realize incomes from the Direct-Selling businesses, which will considerably make the enterprise's human resource team more attractive to consumers and enhance the overall competitiveness of the enterprise.

IV. Transcend Direct-Selling – Crossover Integration and New Consolidation of Three Networks

To promote the coordination of potential advantages and inherent contradictions of consolidation of three networks, it is necessary to transcend direct selling depending on internet platforms, crossover integration of various resources and re-swapping of resources, develop the depth and breadth of the content and connections of consolidation of three networks and thus construct a new consolidation of three networks. The practice of Tiens is combined here to discuss the connotation and operations mechanism of the new consolidation of three networks. We will emphasize the powerful connection function of the internet, build a crossover social e-commerce platform, and cultivate Linkers of a large number and various types, which will promote the evolution of consolidation of three networks.

1. Expansion of the Content of Consolidation of Three Networks

(1) Human Resources and Marketing Network

The original human resources and marketing network is centred on human resources and special stores all around the world. After the global crossover social e-commerce platform is introduced, the platform breaks through the C2C or B2C service models of traditional e-commerce, and combines the online and the offline by serving C or B. In the meantime, consumers, entrepreneurs and managers have all become Linkers, and the global crossover social e-commerce platform and Linkers constitute the new human resources and marketing network. Distinguished from traditional e-commerce, the global crossover social e-commerce platform is in a private domain, and therefore maintains the customer stickiness of the original human resources and marketing network and lowers the cost to acquire customers. Meanwhile, compared to original Direct-Selling models that have only depth but no breadth, the new network achieves explosive spatial expansion.

(2) Product and R&D Network

The original product and R&D network mainly includes the products of high repeat sales, small size and high value. After the global crossover social e-commerce platform is introduced, the scope of products has expanded from the five major categories to daily necessities worldwide. In other words, instead of being confined to the products of high repeat sales, small size and high value, the new product and R&D network incorporates all products of large demand, high value, great utility and good experience. In this way, traditional direct selling has been transcended and replaced, and a new business segmentation has been gradually formed. The business sectors other than healthcare will usher in greater development opportunities.

(3) Finance and Capital Network

The original finance and capital network mainly refers to the incentive mechanisms associated with the interest distribution between the enterprise and distributors and among distributors, as well as the corresponding finance and capital settlement network. After the global crossover social e-commerce platform was introduced, PointsWin Wallet has become the point platform that attracts users and gathers resources and the bridge connects users and the resources of the 'one-body multiple-wings comprehensive health ecosystem.' Embedded with the functions of winning, using, exchanging and circulating points, this platform enables users to buy from and sell to the whole world through the points. Moreover, PointsWin Wallet also provides financial products and services including money management, instalment plans for consumption, insurance and nondeposit microcredit. Therefore, the finance and capital network is no longer confined to the exchange of internal information and capital, but has its denotation and connotation further expanded.

2. Development of the Linking Method of Consolidation of Three Networks
   After the global crossover social e-commerce platform is introduced, the linking method of consolidation of three networks is exposed to further development. Since the global crossover social e-commerce platform features the function to link products, people and information, all networks are linked to each other more closely. In the meantime, the exhibition function of the internet will strengthen the brand effect of the enterprise's product marketing; and Linker and PointsWin will further promote the incentives to and stickiness of the human resource team. The core value of consolidation of three networks will grow. Moreover, as the global crossover social e-commerce platform is in the public and private domains at the same time, information flow becomes smoother among the three networks and thus plays a bigger role in coordinating the operations of all networks and guiding their future development.

PART III

SWAP PROCESS AND TRANSCENDENCE PRACTICE II: 'MULTI-NETWORK INTERACTION'

GUO QINGFANG

'Multi-network interaction' is a business form to realize swap and transcendence as well as an important manifestation of new retailing, which transcends both direct selling and traditional retailing. A realistic and important instance for multi-network interaction is the 'seven-network interaction of Tiens,' consisting of a global human resources and marketing network, global education and training network, global barter network, global membership points network, global tourism network, global health network and 'JTMM' global 'Linker' network. Multi-network interaction that shows the scope economy effect, economic synergy effect and economic integration effect and embraces both direct and indirect values created by various subnets, lays the solid foundation for the realization of swap and transcendence. To attain better economic results of swap and transcendence, multi-network interaction also requires scientific and effective institutional design, including the structure of divisional organization and the rational estimate, monitoring and distribution of the economic benefits in various subnets.

CHAPTER 7

BASIC CONNOTATIONS, CHARACTERISTICS AND TRANSCENDING PERFORMANCE OF MULTI-NETWORK INTERACTION

SECTION 1
BASIC CONNOTATION OF MULTI-NETWORK INTERACTION

I. Definition of Multi-network Interaction

Multi-network interaction is a way to integrate traditional Direct-Selling models and nonDirect-Selling models under the technology and market conditions in the new period. It is also a special operations model that achieves the great effect of benefit overlay by perfectly integrating the active and effective factors in various business models such as traditional direct selling, traditional diversification, e-commerce and third-party payment.

With the ongoing business model innovation led by the internet, Internet+ and +Internet have become popular, based on which an innovation paradigm is formed, industrial integration or crossover. From the perspective of the form, multi-network interaction is the typical 'n+x' or 'x+n' model. No matter whether n+x or x+n and whether integration or crossover, the networks have priorities in the interaction, and can be divided into the leading force and the accessory force. However, based on the connotation of multi-network interaction and the differences between multi-network interaction and traditional diversification, it can be seen that multi-network interaction is grounded in consolidation of three networks; multi-network interaction is neither n+x nor x+n; and there is no absolutely leading and accessory status among the subnets, as the leading force will flexibly change according to specific conditions. As a matter of fact, what leads multi-network interaction is a system instead of individual subnets. This leading system is the consolidation of three networks of product sales and benefit distribution, personnel connection and capital settlement (***sw***). The so-called multi-network interaction is essentially the integration of networks under the leading system of consolidation of three networks,$^{sw\Lambda<n,x>}$.

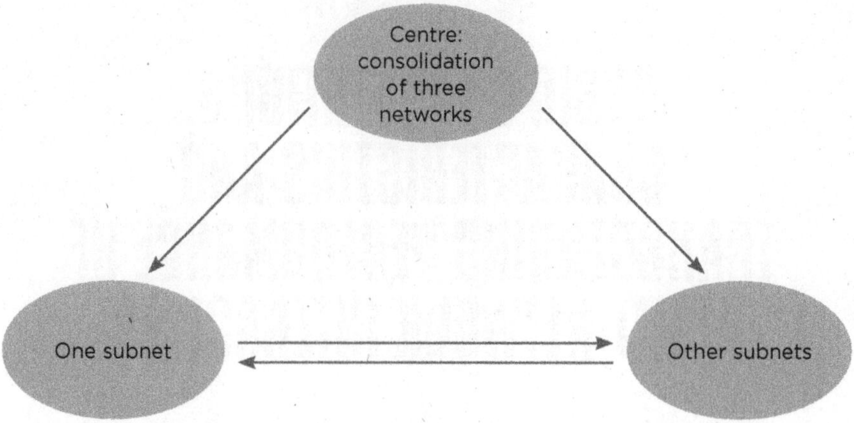

Figure 7-1 Basic Form of Multi-network Interaction

II. Comparison between Multi-network Interaction and Traditional Diversification

1. Similarities

The diversification of traditional enterprises is an operations model by which an enterprise runs multiple businesses and industries or covers several links of a certain industrial chain. Multi-network interaction also extends across multiple businesses and industries and covers several links in a certain industrial chain. Therefore, the two are similar in form.

2. Differences

There may or may not be a connection among the multiple business modules of traditional enterprises. Connection is often found between the typical upstream and downstream businesses, which is called the linear train mode; and if no connection, it can be called the loose graphite mode. Subnets of multi-network interaction are mostly connected with each other, but the network nodes are relatively independent; and in the meantime, the network nodes also promote and support each other. This situation constitutes a typical diamond model. Diversification is essentially a process where the enterprise involves multiple aspects of business activities or industries while multi-network interaction unifies and internalizes subnets by means of the leading system of consolidation of three networks; all subnets are exposed to mutual swaps and close connections of personnel, capital, materials, information and affections, which is an integration that mixes all nets and factors. See the comparison between multi-network interaction and traditional diversification in Table 7-1 below.

	Train-mode diversification	Graphite-mode diversification	Multi-network interaction
Crossover	Actually no	Yes	Yes
Connection	Strong	Weak	Strong or relatively strong
Integration	Linear upstream-downstream integration	Weak	Nets within nets, strong
Risk and performance	Short board	Capital dissipation	Low

Table 7-1 Comparison between Multi-network Interaction and Traditional Diversification

III. Differences and Connections between Multi-network Interaction and Traditional Direct Selling

1. Differences

   Multi-network interaction and traditional direct selling show significant differences. Though with various products, traditional direct selling has strict constraints on the selling model. Selling is mainly performed based on interpersonal connections and products are similar to each other. Contrarily, the sales model of multi-network interaction is very flexible. In addition to traditional direct selling, multi-network interaction sells things through traditional sales, internet platforms or other channels. The products and services in this model can involve many industries flexibly.

2. Connections

   Despite the great difference with traditional direct selling, multi-network interaction is essentially the result of the development of traditional direct selling's sales models and scope. While the root and soul of multi-network interaction is still traditional direct selling, it has transcended traditional direct selling.

SECTION 2
CHARACTERISTICS AND SCOPE OF APPLICATION OF MULTI-NETWORK INTERACTION

I. Characteristics of Multi-network Interaction

1. Networked
   Multi-network interaction and traditional diversification are essentially divided by the consolidation of three networks in traditional direct selling. Rather than being simply diversified, multi-network interaction is conducted based on networks. Consolidation of three networks constitutes the foundation for the realization of swap and transcendence through multi-network interaction. It is exactly because multi-network interaction is built on the Direct-Selling foundation of consolidation of three networks that multi-network interaction can be distinguished from traditional diversification. Each subnet in multi-network interaction embodies the inner attribute and operations structure of consolidation of three networks. Therefore, different business modules of traditional diversity have formed the 'network.'

2. Diversified
   Multi-network interaction is conducted in a form of crossover, so it embraces the commercial diversity naturally. For example, multi-network interaction of Tiens may include traditional direct selling and traditional education and training, or may include different sectors such as tourism, hotels, health and e-transaction platforms.

3. Coordinated
   Multi-network interaction requires good cooperation and a seamless connection of businesses as well as interest coordination. It typically presents the three factors of Marx's Concept of Production Relations: who controls the operations resources, the status and relations of different subnets, and how to distribute interests. All these need overall coordination based on the top-level design.

4. Open
   Any rational factor in effective business models and any feasible and valuable commercial activities can be incorporated in the system of multi-network interaction. Inclusiveness is the prerequisite to this open process.

5. Innovative
   Multi-network interaction is a process exposed to constant innovation and transcendence. It unceasingly absorbs the positive factors in new business models or expands new business or markets. Considering the uncertainties

of innovation (particularly the innovation 'from 0 to 1' that shows the characteristic of 'unknown unknowns'), a rational fault-tolerant mechanism will be established for the innovation of multi-network interaction.

6. Sharing
   Each subnet in multi-network interaction has its relatively independent status and interest. However, since multi-network interaction is an overall system, all subnets can share the common business factors or infrastructure (such as the brand and platform), and meanwhile will adhere to the basic concept of sharing, thus to make up a big harmonious family.

II. Applicability of Multi-network Interaction

Multi-network interaction is a kind of important strategic transformation and innovation that cannot be implemented by all enterprises because certain restraint conditions need to be satisfied. Multi-network interaction proposes special requirements on and sets a threshold for enterprises, making it difficult to imitate. Enterprises that adopt multi-network interaction must meet some key conditions. Only for the enterprises meeting these key conditions can the multi-network interaction satisfy the necessary (but not sufficient) conditions.

1. Scale
   Multi-network interaction can only play its scale economy effect, synergistic effect and integrated effect upon a common condition, the business scale. The scale here includes the enterprise's marketing income, assets and manpower.

2. Experience and History
   As the initiator and practitioner that promotes multi-network interaction, Tiens has unparalleled advantages in this aspect. Tiens correctly chose the Direct-Selling model in 1995, since it had successively completed the construction of a joint venture model, the cultivation of a market system and capital accumulation.

3. Brand
   The interaction of multiple networks has a common attribution, the enterprise's brand. The brand is an intangible asset that is essential to multi-network interaction and functions as the link shared by these networks during interaction. Multi-network interaction proposes a high requirement on the brand. For many enterprises that intend to implement the strategy of multi-network interaction, the brand is needed as a key 'catalyser.' The great brand awareness of Tiens helps the group vigorously promote multi-network interaction.

SECTION 3
TRANSCENDING PRACTICE DEMONSTRATED IN MULTI-NETWORK INTERACTION

Multi-network interaction contains double swap and double transcendence. Double swap means: the internal swap of Direct Selling (nonDirect-Selling) among the subnets of multi-network interaction; and the swap of Direct Selling and nonDirect-Selling business activities in the subnets of multi-network interaction. Multi-network interaction also embodies double transcendence: transcending direct selling by introducing traditional nonDirect-Selling businesses; and embedding the spirit and DNA of direct selling in traditional nonDirect-Selling businesses.

Multi-network interaction, the synthesis and transcendence of traditional selling models, is a new retailing model constructed upon the combination of internet technologies and direct selling. The marketing mix theory develops from '4P,' '4C' and '4R' to the '4S' of multi-network interaction. See the comparison of '4P,' new '4P,' '4C,' '4R' and '4S' in Table 7-2. Seen from this table, it is apparent that the '4S' system of multi-network interaction is more vital, more human, and more open.

	4P	New 4P	4C	4R	4S
Components	Product	People	Customer	Relevancy	Stockholder
	Price	Process	Cost	Reaction	Service
	Place	Program	Convenience	Relation	Shared
	Promotion	Performance	Communication	Reward	Society
Transaction object	Goods and 'things' of service	Goods and 'things' of service	Goods and 'things' of service	Goods and 'things' of service and social relations	Community of interests
Leading force	Enterprise	Enterprise	Consumer	Consumer	Enterprise and consumer
Relationship direction	One-way	One-way	One-way	Two-way	Integrated

Table 7-2 Comparison of 4P, New 4P, 4C, 4R and 4S

CHAPTER 8

SPECIFIC COMPOSITION OF MULTI-NETWORK INTERACTION

Multi-network interaction is essentially a system, while each subnet is the subsystem of this system. The subnets' effective operations as well as their vitality and competitiveness constitute the foundation of multi-network interaction, so it is important to fully understand each subnet in multi-network interaction. With the recent years of innovative development, Tiens has become a typical representative of multi-network interaction. Multi-network interaction of Tiens consists of seven networks: the global human resources and marketing network, global education and training network, global barter network, global membership points network, global tourism network, global health network and JTMM's global Linker network. This study will introduce the basic composition and operations of multi-network interaction with the multi-network interaction of Tiens as an example. However, as an operations model, multi-network interaction's specific content and scope are diversified, and not limited to that of Tiens.

Multiple networks in the multi-network interaction are relatively independent and meanwhile interconnected. On the basis of favourable products, they will constitute an organic operations system where they promote (restrict) each other. In the multi-network interaction system, subnets vary from each other in their status or function. If the multi-network interaction system is compared to a running car, the good product is like the high-quality power steering oil of the car; the global human resources and marketing network and global education and training network are like the engine as they play the core role; the global barter network, global membership points system, global tourism network and global health network are the propeller and supercharger, which promote and enhance the system operations; and JTMM's global Linker network is like the conveyor and sensor of the car, showing the integration and focus function.

It is noteworthy that though multi-network interaction is an open system, the global human resources and marketing network, global education and training network, and global Linker network are always the core and key subnets, from which other subnets are derived. We will give full play to the expandability and openness of multi-network interaction during the derivation of subnets, and meanwhile consider the coordination difficulties and costs caused by the excessive expansion. We will be cautious about the quantity and types of subnets derived.

SECTION 1
GLOBAL HUMAN RESOURCES AND MARKETING NETWORK

I. Status of Global Human Resources and Marketing Network

Direct selling adheres to three major principles: personalization, openness and expandability. In the business models centring on direct selling, the human resources and marketing network is an indivisible unity. The human resources comprising the direct-seller team constitute the foundation of the marketing network, while the marketing network is essentially the platform and results of the direct-seller team's construction, expansion and performance. Without the human resource team made up by direct sellers, the stable, dense and expanding marketing network can hardly be constructed. Conversely, if there is no marketing network, there will be no interest basis and platform to support the construction, connection and maintenance of the direct-seller team.

The human resources and marketing network is a cell of the enterprise's centring on direct selling. Direct sellers may be ordinary families or individuals that work part-time or full-time. According to the time they join the team, they will form a 'multi-level' supervisor-subordinate relationship. Each direct seller has their own consumer group. Certainly, consumers can also purchase products from stores or other direct sellers on their own initiative. Direct sellers are the 'walking' advertisement of enterprises and products. Being a leading Direct-Selling enterprise in China and around the world, Tiens is connected to over 40 million families worldwide, demonstrating its large scale. Compared to the large sales volume of Tiens, its cost of marketing (through the human resources and marketing network) is not high mainly for three reasons: (1) Direct sellers are independent wholesale sellers but not official employees of the enterprise, so Tiens does not need to pay them any base salary or provide them any welfare. Direct sellers are consumers, and consumers are direct sellers. In Tiens, people are all free entrepreneurs. They cooperate with each other equally, and no one works for others. They just help people to help themselves; (2) The investment threshold is low. In direct selling, sellers do not need any fixed sales office, so they can save the rent and decoration investment; and (3) The sharing mechanism is applied. In the human resources and marketing network, sharing is superior to sales promotion, since promotion is trying to sell the product that the seller has never used to others, but sharing is to recommend the good product that the seller is using to others. Sharing has been listed as one of the five development concepts – innovation, coordination, green, openness and sharing – put forward in the Fifth Plenary Session of the Central Committee of the 18th CPC National Congress in October 2015.

II. Advantages of the Global Human Resources and Marketing Network

The human resources and marketing network presents many advantages: (1) It provides ordinary groups with the platform for individual entrepreneurship. Direct selling renders a platform for ordinary people to start-up businesses in an easier way. Since no large amount of funds is needed, individuals do not need to undertake too much capital risk. Compared to traditional investment and entrepreneurship, anyone joining direct selling will receive systematic guidance. This is a huge appeal to people who want to start a business; (2) It provides consumers with better products and services. Since direct selling cuts down many intermediate links in sales channels and reduces many expenses, it supplies products of better-cost performance to consumers. Moreover, direct selling is performed one to one, so consumers can buy things beyond any doubt, which can hardly be achieved by traditional selling; and (3) It promotes the development of manufacturing enterprises and facilitates social progress. Direct selling realizes significant cost savings, so the funds saved can be applied to the R&D of products or talent introduction, which increases the competitiveness of the products and facilitates enterprise development. In addition, the simplification of sales channels also reduces the time for consumers to acquire the products. In this way, sales efficiency is improved and the possibility of fake and inferior products is lowered.

SECTION 2
GLOBAL EDUCATION AND TRAINING NETWORK

I. Status of Global Education and Training Network

Since it is a great challenge to sell products, explore markets and expand the team, direct sellers and their teams and families must enjoy the capability to believe in and challenge themselves to win success. For instance,

Tiens never treats the families and people involved in the sales and consumption of Tiens products as the 'bloodless' interest machine, but regards them as flesh and blood. Enterprises should think highly of the moral quality, knowledge, experience and talent of these families and people, attach importance to their affinity and communication ability, and also advocate service awareness and teamwork. Therefore, an increasing number of Direct-Selling enterprises place emphasis on a high-quality corporate culture. They are willing to put great efforts and investments in proper education and training, to cultivate direct sellers' correct concepts of direct selling and improve their specialization, but not for the sole purpose of making money. By doing this, it not only directly advances the personality growth of direct sellers, but also improves their image among consumers, which greatly facilitates the development of Direct-Selling undertakings.

In addition to the centralized and comprehensive education network of Direct-Selling enterprise headquarters, the education network of Direct-Selling enterprises can also be divided into the education and training tasks of different groups. Many direct-seller teams have their own clubs for dinner parties or gatherings, where they can explain, recommend and display products to their friends or strangers. The education and training of different levels includes successful experience, psychology, nutrition, cosmetology, how to demonstrate products, how to sell products, how to use new products featuring certain new technologies, how to follow up with customers, how to share Apps, how to make friends with strangers, how to lead a team, how to cultivate a rookie into a leader and the new policies of the enterprise.

Many domestic and foreign Direct-Selling enterprises are communicating products essentially depending on interpersonal relations. However, the Direct-Selling enterprise and its products are the common wealth as well as common responsibilities of all relevant personnel and families. The enterprise can carry out large-scale public education to penetrate potential consumers and direct sellers. This is also an important manifestation of the education and training network.

II. Innovation of the Global Education and Training Network of Tiens

Tiens undertakings involve a great number of active direct sellers, consumers and families, and over 40 million families worldwide are taking part in it. In addition to incentive systems such as a salary, Tiens provides a complete set of training to the families and individuals engaged in direct selling and consumption of Tiens, aiming to systematically train those who participate in Tiens undertakings through formal or informal approaches.

Family is a cell of society. Tiens mainly runs the business of household commodities and focuses on health preservation, making it extremely suitable for family operations and consumption. Family is the main carrier of living consumption as well as the main force of production and operations. Families run many small- and medium-sized enterprises in Europe and Japan. Similar to workshops, they do not expand their scale. Economically, despite no scale merit, they can produce high-quality products and survive for a long term.

Consumer goods and health are always key topics for a family. Each family seeks the common development of its material wealth and spiritual wealth. Tiens offers products for a healthy body enriching the whole family, which requires a better relationship between direct sellers and their families. The concept of family consumption and business entities has broken the limit of simple understandings of family consumption, which develops the moral quality cultivation and technology training of direct selling to family education that covers health, wealth creation and social relations.

Tiens has organized a global education committee, with a senior direct seller serving as the chairman. Large-scale education or training activities are held regularly or irregularly, where some experienced direct sellers go up onto the stage in stirring music and tell stories of how they became successful men with annual incomes of over several million yuan from 'an ordinary person' or 'a screw of the society,' or how they gave up their original jobs of good incomes after they 'understood Tiens.' To spread the influence of direct sellers or consumers to their families, Tiens puts great importance on family education. In this case, education is not only an undertaking itself, but also a business with high commercial values. Tiens breaks the constraints of traditional Direct-Selling enterprises that only provide internal training for the Direct-Selling team, but regards education as a business module of certain market potential and profitability, and opens and shares the internal training and external education service for the enterprise's Direct-Selling team.

SECTION 3
GLOBAL BARTER NETWORK

Globalization is the general trend of the current world economy, and multinational enterprises have become the main carriers. However, with the global economy and industry reengineering, it costs to use external markets. An important part of the transaction cost in external markets is the time and expense for the buyer and seller to seek and reach a favourable price, in addition to the risk costs including international political risks, economic risks such as the exchange rate fluctuation and the contractual risks of the transaction.

As a response to this situation, global multinational enterprises adopt anti-marketization measures and create a so-called theory of internalization. Since both parties to the transaction are internal members of a unified economic interest subject, a multinational enterprise, during the internal trade, the costs of external market transactions mentioned above can be avoided. To save the cost is an important approach to maximize economic interests. Moreover, internal trade can also reduce the risk of operations uncertainties in the external market.

The global barter network proposed by Tiens reflects this trend. It makes use of Tiens Direct-Selling teams and sales channels distributed in over 190 countries worldwide to creatively integrate the multinational enterprise's internal transactions and external markets. The global barter network of Tiens gives full play to the advantage of the multinational enterprise in global resource allocation, and also opens to all potential direct sellers or consumers worldwide, suggesting the perfect combination of openness and sharing.

SECTION 4
GLOBAL MEMBERSHIP POINTS NETWORK

Three fields are associated with the global membership points network: third-party payment, internal fund management of large global multinational enterprises and the points reward system.

I. Third-party Payment

Being an emerging economic activity integrating trade, payment and finance, third-party payment is developing by leaps and bounds along with the development of the computer's computing and storage system as well as the development of the internet, particularly the intelligent mobile system. Third-party payment refers to the transaction support platform offered by a third-party independent institution that has contracted with major banks in the country of products and foreign countries and embraces a certain strength and reputation. When making a transaction on the third-party payment platform, the buyer will use the account provided by the third-party platform to pay for the commodities they chose; then the third party will notify the seller of the arrival of the payment and urge the seller to deliver the goods; the buyer will inform the third party, after having examined the goods received, and then the third party will transfer the payment to the seller's account.

As supported by the intelligent mobile system, many independent third-party payment systems have acquired rapid development, represented by WeChat, Alipay, Lakala and Reapal. These third-party payment platforms show evident characteristics. For example, the third-party payment platform provides a series of application interface programs that integrate the payments of different kinds of bank cards in the same interface to link up with banks during a transaction settlement, which makes online shopping quicker and more convenient. Moreover, consumers and merchants do not need to open different accounts in different banks, lowering the cost of consumers' online shopping. Third-party payment constitutes an important part of the modern financial service industry and supports and boosts the rapid development of China's internet economy. As an emerging industry of new technology, new business form and new model, third-party payment has a vast market demand in the future.

II. Internal Fund Management of Group Enterprises

Since many large group enterprises have reached a certain scale of transaction volume and assets, they have special needs on a centralized management of funds. As to group enterprises, who controls the funds controls the rules. Only by controlling the financial revenue and expenditure as well as capital flow of subsidiaries can the parent enterprise guide the subsidiaries' production and operations activities in accordance with the development strategies formulated by the parent enterprise. This is quite essential for Direct-Selling enterprises. To manage internal funds, group enterprises generally establish the capital settlement centre at headquarters or have their member enterprises make investments to jointly establish a finance enterprise.

By performing financial management through the capital settlement centre, the enterprise group's monitoring over subsidiaries has been vigorously strengthened: (1) The capital settlement centre controls the first-hand financial information of the group enterprise. With the right of settlement, the centre is responsible for all capital operations of the group enterprise. Decision makers can know the financial position of subsidiaries and conduct real-time monitoring based on data from the centre; and (2) The capital settlement centre enjoys the right to allocate funds. It can understand the revenue and expenditure conditions of subsidiaries through financial information and judge whether any abnormal circumstance occurs or whether the fund use conforms to the group's development strategy, thus to realize financial in-process control.

Generally, the financial enterprise or capital settlement centre features three functions. The first function is settlement. All member enterprises of the group (the Direct-Selling teams or direct sellers of Direct-Selling enterprises) open accounts at the financial enterprise or capital settlement centre on a unified basis, while the financial enterprise or capital settlement centre handles capital settlement businesses at the bank with only one account. The second function is internal control. After the financial enterprise or settlement centre is established, all incomes of subsidiaries (the Direct-Selling teams or direct sellers of Direct-Selling enterprises) will flow to the financial enterprise or capital settlement centre, which can monitor revenue and expenditure and the use of funds.

In the context of financial liberalization and mixed operations, the financial enterprise or financial service enterprise, as the nonbanking financial institution of mixed operation, plays the role of the treasury of the group enterprise. It carries out overall management over the funds of the group and subsidiaries, activates idle funds of the group through flexible use of funds and diversified investment, and provides comprehensive financial services to support the development strategies of the group enterprise.

III. Points Reward System

The points reward system manages customers with points. In an enterprise adopting this system, points are used to measure people's values, reflect and assess people's comprehensive performance, and determine the welfare and material treatment of employees. Employees with high points enjoy greater benefits and the enterprise's promises for a better future. In this way, employees' subjective initiative and enthusiasm are fully mobilized. The real corporate culture must turn employees' behaviours into habits, while the points management system links employees' behaviours to their points, being very beneficial for the construction of a healthy corporate culture. The points system is also applied to overcome equalitarianism in distribution. As the points represent an employee's comprehensive performance, their ranking can be clearly determined according to their points. The bonuses are also associated with employees' rankings according to points. The bonuses for everyone are distributed unevenly, while the bonuses for a small part of people can be openly offered on the stage, which completely solves the issue of equalitarianism in distribution. The points system can also be adopted to retain talents. Where the points management system is applied, employees with a longer time of direct selling or consumption and better performance will have higher points and a stronger sense of achievement. Meanwhile, they can acquire greater benefits and may even be rewarded with equity.

The bonus points system can be considered as the soul of the Direct-Selling industry because it directly decides whether direct sellers can obtain reasonable returns, whether they can do this work for a long time, whether they have the power to summon and unite others, whether they have a sense of achievement and whether most of them can realize their dreams. On the whole, Direct-Selling enterprises are always improving their institutions. As a manifestation of the improvement, with regard to the responsibilities and rights of Direct-Selling enterprises and direct sellers, Direct-Selling enterprises are doing more and more, though originally they were only responsible for goods supply but now they also take on the tasks of website publicity and international logistics; and direct sellers are doing less and less but earning more bonuses. However, it becomes more difficult for direct sellers to build and maintain the huge self-consumption group. The bonus points system is functioning as leverage in the interest game between Direct-Selling enterprises and direct sellers.

IV. E-wallet

On the grounds of globalization, the three fields associated with the global membership points system – third-party payment, internal fund management and the points reward system – integrate with each other and develop together. On this basis and considering the cooperative role of the global barter network and the internet, a Direct-Selling-extended ecosystem that integrates direct selling, trade, incentives, finance and foreign exchange is formed. E-wallet is the core of this ecosystem.

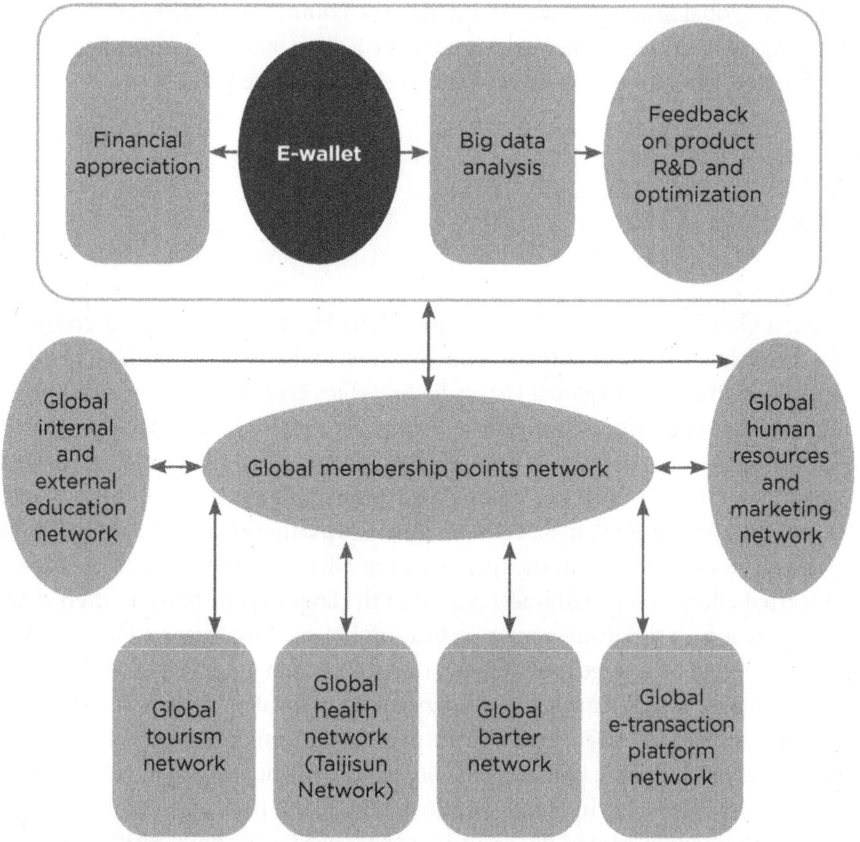

Figure 8-1 Direct-Selling-extended Ecosystem and the Role of E-wallet

Tiens put forward an innovative idea: e-wallet. E-wallet is a data key characterized by the following functions. First, the function of internal electronic currency. Transcending the country border, this internal electronic currency matches with the global barter network. It can be used as currency of equal value among the enterprise's direct sellers or consumers to make a purchase, payment or calculation and obtain a corresponding income. The income from direct selling or other sales models can also be settled through e-wallet. Second is the data function. E-wallet can store important data on direct selling or consumption for points and rewards computation. Also, through e-wallet, the enterprise can implement big data management to dynamically manage, monitor and optimize product sales, R&D, and realize iterative production, R&D. While running direct selling as the core business, Tiens also transcends and breaks the limit of direct selling that excessively relies on connections and face-to-face interactions and integrates direct selling with e-commerce and combines Direct-Selling products with ordinary consumer goods. In addition, Tiens also runs businesses of comprehensive health and comprehensive life. It has established the global health network, global tourism network and global e-commerce JTMM and thus built a commercial ecosystem derived from Direct-Selling businesses. E-wallet plays a crucial and essential role in this system, as shown in Figure 8-1.

SECTION 5
GLOBAL TOURISM NETWORK

Being a global Direct-Selling enterprise, Tiens has direct sellers and consumers distributed in 190 countries and involves more than 40 million families worldwide. It organizes global Direct-Selling elites exchange and incentive plans regularly or irregularly, where global tourism plays an important part. For example, the success of the August 3 Celebration and Russian International Annual Meeting of China Tiens 2014 astonished China and even the rest of the world. On May 8, 2015, more than 6,500 Tiens business partners from all over the world gathered along the coast of the blue ocean at Nice, France, where they made a concerted effort to set a Guinness record of the largest-scale body-written characters, creating a beautiful scenery in beautiful Nice. This event had become the new highlight of the large international cultural exchange activity 'Tiens Dreams Bloom in Nice – 20th Anniversary Celebration Carnival of Tiens in Nice France.' Also at this carnival, a sea, land and air parade of a grand scale was successfully held. As certified by the Guinness Record official on site, a total of 6,262 people jointly participated in this event within the specified time and at the specified place. Tiens people created the record for the largest-scale body-written characters of the world.

More importantly, Tiens has become a comprehensive group that is engaged in biotechnology, health management, hotel and tourism, education and training, e-commerce, financial investment and real estate, and integrates industrial capital, commercial capital and finance, laying a solid industrial foundation for the development of the global tourism network.

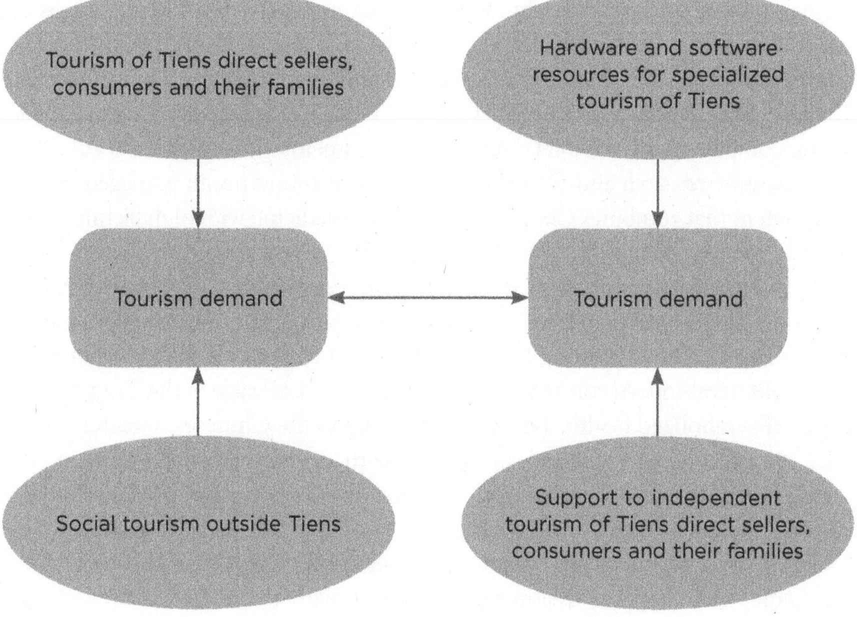

Figure 8-2 Positive Interaction between Supply and Demand of the Global Tourism Network of Tiens

The global tourism network of Tiens sees a positive interaction between supply and demand. The tourism demand of Tiens is proposed by both internal customers and social groups outside the company. The large number of Tiens direct sellers, consumers and their families are naturally the high-quality clients of its global tourism network. The fast growing per-capita income of Chinese people makes up the foundation of the social expansion of tourism. Direct sellers and consumers of Tiens, who are distributed in every corner of the world, provide the channels and methods to organize personalized, centralized or other forms of tourism. The positive interaction between the supply and demand of the global tourism network of Tiens is shown in Figure 8-2.

SECTION 6
GLOBAL HEALTH NETWORK

The global health network of Tiens is an important process for the realization of comprehensive health. Taijisun Hospital is a medical institution established upon Tiens' idea of developing a comprehensive health industry, and it provides high-end, high-quality medical care services. Based on a respect for life sciences and an infinite pursuit for human health, with the 'comprehensive health industry' as the focus, 'preventive treatment of diseases' as the goal and the latest health management concepts as the support, Tiens invested and established the Taijisun Hospital International Health Management Centre. The centre integrates health management, comprehensive rehabilitation, medical cosmetology, and medical education and scientific research and is constructed on an all-round health management service system that combines Chinese and Western medicine with high technologies.

The two characters 'Tai' (泰) and 'Ji' (济) in the word Taijisun (泰济生) stem from two divinatory symbols in the ancient Chinese classical, *The Book of Changes*. Tai is the Qiankun Hexagram, indicating auspiciousness and prosperity, and Ji is the Jiji Hexagram, suggesting the success of great things and the noble ambition to benefit mankind. According to Sun Simiao, a medical sage in the Tang dynasty, Jiji itself symbolized health. 'Sun' here, referring to the Chinese character 'Sheng' (生), means 'life,' 'growth' and 'life and growth in nature.' Thus, the name Taijisun implies "a balance of yin and yang and the coordination of water and fire result in people's health." Originating from the Chinese cultural essence of 'Taiji creates everything,' Taijisun Hospital adheres to the traditional idea of Chinese medicines that "replace treatment of diseases with preventive treatment; and prevent diseases from exacerbating," combines it with modern science and technology perfectly, and creates a brand new health model integrating Chinese and Western medicine. Embracing internationally advanced equipment, specialized expert teams, advanced service concepts and a complete service process, Taijisun provides the ultra-early, precise, systematic, comprehensive and safe screening of tumours that leads the country or even the rest of the world and provides a reliable basis for the prevention, diagnosis, early intervention and therapy of cancer.

The global health network constitutes an important part in the layout of the comprehensive health industry, but its development depends on certain conditions. Tiens provides over 40 million families distributed in 190 countries with medical care and health services through the global health network. This network realizes the comprehensive health concept of Tiens by means of social medical services, advances the brand recognition of the Group, and improves consumer trust and stickiness against health products, Direct-Selling businesses and even the sales of other products. In view of the powerful strategies, excellent medical team and large direct-selling team and customer base of Tiens, its global health network enjoys great development potential as long as it is well coordinated and operated.

SECTION 7
JTMM GLOBAL LINKER NETWORK

I. Definition of the JTMM Global Linker Network Business Model

The business model of JTMM's (Just To Make More) global Linker network is the integrated innovation of the two important internet-based transaction modes, B2C and O2O, supported by the other six subnets, as driven by the rapid development of internet technologies and We-media social models. B2C is a retail business model that sells products and services directly to consumers. JTMM of Tiens shows the characteristics of a B2C comprehensive shopping centre, which, like a traditional shopping centre, has a large consumer base, a stable website platform, a complete payment system, a reliable safety system and a convenient transaction process. In the event of a large customer base, diverse products and convenient logistics, a B2C comprehensive shopping centre enjoys a cost advantage as well as advantages in 24-hour opening, no regional restrictions and richer product categories. This is of great significance for Tiens and the 40 million families in 190 countries of the world, since it provides more choices of consumer goods for people involved in Tiens undertakings.

O2O (Online to Offline) means to combine offline business opportunities with the internet and make the internet the platform for offline transactions. Any enterprise that runs online shopping stores and offline stores at the same time where the product prices are completely consistent can be called O2O. The advantage of O2O lies in the perfect integration of the online and the offline. It not only makes full use of the advantages of the internet in cross-region and cross-border operations, massive information and mass users, but also fully explores offline resources and promotes online users' transactions of offline commodities and services. Hence, it is of great significance for the global enterprise Tiens that extends its presence to over 190 countries. The transaction activities of the other six subnets assure a great market capacity as support to O2O.

Tiens embraces unique advantages in developing JTMM's global Linker network. First, over 40 million direct sellers, consumers and their families involved in Tiens undertakings are distributed in 190 countries worldwide, laying a solid foundation for the customer base development of JTMM and avoiding the difficulties in early promotion of e-commerce. Instead of 0 to 1, it is a process from 100 to 10,000, which is much easier. Second, the global barter network supplies special and attractive products in a large quantity to JTMM. Finally, the core of the O2O marketing model is online payment, and Tiens e-wallet can meet the requirements of the online payment of global electronic transaction platforms.

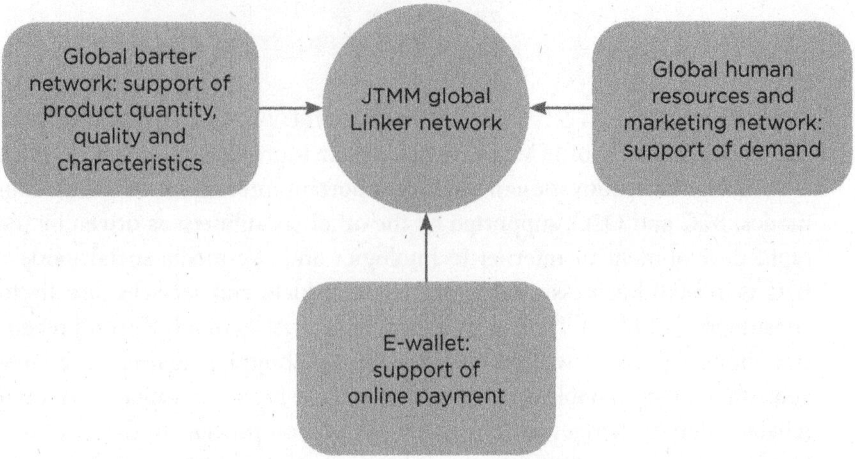

Figure 8-3 Supports to the Global Electronic Transaction Platform of Tiens

II. JTMM's Global Linker Network Is an Important Focus of the Strategic Transformation of Tiens

JTMM's global Linker network that combines B2C and O2O plays an important role in the strategic transformation of Tiens. First, it is of great significance for Tiens to set foot in e-commerce. By means of e-commerce, it can fully make use of the internet's great advantage of transcending time and space, break the limit of face-to-face communication based on interpersonal connections, and see great potential and room for the multiplication of the market share. The online invitation to Tiens Direct-Selling businesses will be more attractive through the online experience.

Second, by running e-commerce, Tiens will enrich product categories. The combination of JTMM's global Linker network and the global barter network, which is excellent, unique and innovative, will extend Direct-Selling businesses to many other business sectors and turn Tiens into a comprehensive production, trade and finance enterprise with direct selling as the core.

III. Solid Technology Foundation for the Innovation of JTMM's Global Linker Network

1. Rapid Development of the Internet of Things

The Internet of Things means to collect information on the object or process that should be monitored, connected and interacted with in real time through various kinds of information sensors and constitutes a huge network jointly with the internet. It is established for the purpose of realizing the connection among things, and people and among all the things in the network for convenient identification, management and control.

The Internet of Things consists of five layers: the support layer, perception layer, transmission layer, platform layer and application layer, which respectively account for 2.7%, 22.0%, 33.1%, 37.5% and 4.7% of the whole Internet of Things. Most merchants are located at the perception and transmission layer, making the two the areas of the fiercest competition.

The products of the Internet of Things cover all applications ranging from sensor controllers to cloud computing. With the products serving the smart home, traffic and logistics, environmental protection, public security, intelligent fire control, industrial monitoring, and personal health sector, the Internet of Things has become one of the strategic high grounds for economic and technological development of the current world. It is understood that the scale of the Internet of Things exceeded 250 billion yuan in 2011 and was expected to exceed 500 billion yuan by 2015.

2. Personal Mobile Terminals of the Internet

The smartphone is a general term for all the mobile phones that feature an independent operating system and an independent running space by which users can install programs provided by third-party service providers such as software, games and navigation programs and can access the internet wirelessly through the mobile communication network. Smartphones are widely used all around the world but are not known to and used by everyone. They have completely replaced the keyboard phones popular in previous years for three major characteristics: excellent operating systems, free installation of all types of software (only in Android systems) and touch screen operations on a large screen.

With the technology development and the reduction of the production cost of mobile phones, more and more people have started using smartphones. Smartphones start to guide or dominate all aspects of people's work and life, alter people's lifestyles and even result in the transformation of social development. As driven by numerous innovative Apps, Alipay and WeChat, smartphones, the hardware of the mobile internet, are exerting significant influence on people's lives and changing the business content and pattern. Smartphones not only solve people's basic necessities of life but also transform the traditional way of people's economic exchanges, social information and personal emotions. In economic exchanges, traditional transfer and remittance have been substituted by online banking, WeChat transfer and Alipay; people bring mobile phones with them instead of wallets when going to the supermarket; and people purchase financial products and manage family wealth through mobile phones. One day physical currency will disappear perhaps, and money will only be a number in mobile phones. The wide application of smartphones has been a great shock to traditional business models. Since factories can directly contact terminal consumers through mobile phones, middlemen and channel distributors are disappearing. In the future, the business winning more clicks will win in the end.

CHAPTER 9

ECONOMIC SPILLOVER EFFECTS FROM MULTI-NETWORK INTERACTION PROVIDE A POWERFUL DRIVING FORCE

SECTION 1
ECONOMIC SPILLOVER PERFORMANCE OF MULTI-NETWORK INTERACTION

I. Scope Economic Effect of Multi-network Interaction and the Corresponding Mechanism

The market competitiveness of multi-network interaction is largely derived from the scope economic effect. Scale economy refers to the phenomenon that the economic benefits increase with the expansion of the product or service categories of the enterprise, which provides more categories of products or services at a lower cost. In terms of the enterprise strategy, the scale economy is mainly manifested as diversified operations and multi-product operations. This economy supplies differentiated products and services through business integration, realizes market integration by guiding consumers' consumption habits and contents, and finally leads to industrial integration.

Since the development of direct sellers and consumers, particularly the business model innovation of the family consumption operation, is the starting point and objective of a multi-network interaction, its scope economic effect is mainly reflected as the consumption performance effect, which means to improve the consumption attraction of the enterprise's products and services through industrial integration under multi-network interaction. To be specific: (1) Industrial integration has produced many new products and services, satisfying people's demands of higher-level consumer goods after improvements in people's incomes and living standards; and (2) Industrial integration has compelled more people to join and explore the market, intensified market competition, and promoted the construction of a new market structure. The extension of the industrial chain and the integration of industries reduce costs (including the cost of large-scale production, enterprise governance cost and transaction cost), adding to the values of multi-network interaction.

II. Economic Synergistic Effect of Multi-network Interaction and the Corresponding Mechanism

From the perspective of enterprise operations, the favourable results of multi-network interaction depend on the synergistic effect of all links or factors inside the enterprise. Simply put, the so-called synergistic effect means '1 + 1 > 2,' the overall effect obtained when different links, different stages and different aspects of enterprise production, marketing and management make joint use of the same resources. In this way, the overall benefits obtained by the enterprise are greater than the sum of benefits acquired by independent departments. The synergistic effect of Tiens multi-network interaction depends on the use of visible resources as complements and the use of intangible assets (the enterprise brand and its promotion).

Multi-network interaction is essentially the synergistic effect of the diversification strategy. This effect is embodied in the process of how to share the resources of labour, products, services, capital, knowledge, skills, relations and brands to lower costs, spread market risks and achieve scale effects.

III. Economic Integrated Effect of Multi-network Interaction and the Corresponding Mechanism

As the overall strategic transformation and design of enterprise swap and transcendence, multi-network interaction is planned and implemented from top to bottom, showing a strong synergistic effect. Synergy refers to gathering some isolated things or elements that were originally decentralized and connecting them, thus to make an organic whole. Integrated management stresses on the integrated thought, by which all elements penetrate and absorb each other to form a new 'organism.' Synergy not only improves personal ability, but also integrates many independent labour forces through an integrated design and a platform to form a new force. The effect of this new force is much greater than the sum of the effects of individual elements.

SECTION 2 VALUE CREATION MECHANISM ANALYSIS OF MULTI-NETWORK INTERACTION

I. Multi-network Interaction Features a Special Value Creation Mechanism

The special value creation mechanism of multi-network interaction manifests in three aspects. First, distinguished from the ordinary value chain that shows a simple vertical relation, the superior and the inferior, the subnets in multi-network interaction are in a horizontal relation, where each net is the upstream of another network (other networks) and in the meantime the downstream of another network (other networks). Second, the seven networks of Tiens have no main business (revenue) or service business (cost), as every network is making a profit and also improving the profits of other networks. The value-creation mechanism of multi-network interaction differs from the classical idea of 'value chain.' According to the basic concepts of value chain theory, not every link within the enterprise's numerous 'value activities' creates values; the operating activities that truly create value are those called the 'strategic links' in the enterprise's value chain. Finally, subnets are parallel and equal to each other, and support and serve each other.

II. Direct and Indirect Value Creation in Multi-network Interaction and their Manifestations with Tiens as an Example

The global human resources and marketing network, global education and training network, global barter network, global membership points system, global tourism network, global health network and global electronic transaction platform network of Tiens are all main businesses that make profits, as well as secondary businesses that promote and increase the benefits of other networks, which respectively manifest as direct and indirect value creation. The process that the seven networks mentioned above create value through their own businesses is called direct value creation; and the process that the seven networks improve the benefits of other nets is called indirect value creation.

1. Manifestations of Direct and Indirect Value Creation of the Global Human Resources and Marketing Network

Direct value creation of the global human resources and marketing network includes the sales and consumption of Direct-Selling products, as well as the consumption of nonDirect-Selling products of Tiens. As a result of the transformation and transcendence of Tiens, the global human resources and marketing network is no longer confined to the sales and consumption of Direct-Selling products, but the consumption of nonDirect-Selling products is also included.

Indirect value creation of the global human resources and marketing network is mainly manifested by how it promotes and supports the global education and training network, global barter network, global membership points network, global tourism network, global health network and global electronic transaction platform network.

(1) Indirect value creation of the global human resources and marketing network in the global education and training network. The global human resources and marketing network proposes great demand on the education or training of product functions, health, interpersonal relations, soul,

marketing technologies and some other aspects, assuring stable demand of the global education and training network. Consisting of direct sellers or consumers from over 40 million families in 190 countries worldwide, Tiens can promote the brand recognition of its global education network. More importantly, the feedback from the global human resources and marketing network on education activities and demand will enrich and optimize the global education and training network and make it more targeted. In this way, the global human resources and marketing network renders great support for the global education and training network to design, launch and promote education services and products for a globalized society.

(2) Indirect value creation of the global human resources and marketing network in the global barter network. The global human resources and marketing network indirectly creates value in the global barter network mainly on two major grounds. First, the large global human resources and marketing network involving over 40 million families from 190 countries worldwide proposes a great demand on the global barter network itself. Second, all these families find products, and some direct sellers or families can provide the barter network with supply information on special and high-quality products. Some of them will even become the direct suppliers or distributors of some products.

(3) Indirect value creation of the global human resources and marketing network in the global membership points network. The sales rewards and consumption rewards for the more than 40 million families from 190 countries worldwide in Tiens global human resources and marketing network constitute the basis and core of the global membership points network.

(4) Indirect value creation of the global human resources and marketing network in the global tourism network. On one hand, the sales rewards and consumption rewards for the more than 40 million families from 190 countries worldwide in Tiens global human resources and marketing network can be realized by centralized or decentralized tourism, which constitutes the important customer base of the global tourism network. Moreover, these families may also spontaneously propose tourism demand, making them important customer resources of the global tourism network. On the other hand, these families can make up a tourism sharing club and invite others to their own country or city for travel and exchange, where the global tourism network functions as the tourism platform. As expected, the global tourism network will do well in product development, supervision, and service to provide featured, warm and exchange-oriented products.

(5) Indirect value creation of the global human resources and marketing network in the global health network. On one hand, the sales rewards and consumption rewards for the more than 40 million families from 190 countries

worldwide in Tiens global human resources and marketing network can be realized by centralized or decentralized medical services of the global health network, which constitutes the important customer base of the global health network. Moreover, these families may also spontaneously propose demand on Taijisun medical services, making them important customer resources of the global health network.

(6)Indirect value creation of the global human resources and marketing network in the global electronic transaction platform network. On one hand, the large global human resources and marketing network involving over 40 million families from 190 countries worldwide proposes great demand on the global electronic transaction platform network itself. On the other hand, all these 40 million families from 190 countries worldwide of Tiens find products, and some direct sellers or families can provide the global electronic transaction platform network with supply information on special and high-quality products. Some of them will even become the direct suppliers or distributors of some products, the shop in shops, and adhere to the principles of openness, specialty, interconnection, exchange, health and sharing.

2. Manifestations of Direct and Indirect Value Creation of the Global Education and Training Network

Direct value creation of the global education and training network is derived from the service incomes from education and training, which consist of two parts: (1) the education services of the global education and training network for the global human resources and marketing network on sales, consumption, society and soul; (2) and the social education services and products supplied by the global education and training network to the whole world.

Indirect value creation of the global education and training network is mainly manifested by how it promotes and supports the global human resources and marketing network, global barter network, global membership points network, global tourism network, global health network and global electronic transaction platform network. (1) Indirect value creation of the global education and training network in the global human resources and marketing network. By improving the quality, technology, knowledge and wisdom of the global human resources and marketing network, the global education and training network not only consolidates and improves the effect and quantity of product sales and consumption of the global human resources and marketing network, but also increases the appeal of Tiens by providing effective education products and services and attracts more people to join Tiens undertakings. (2) Indirect value creation of the global education and training network in the global barter network.

The global education and training network creates limited indirect value for the global barter network. (3) Indirect value creation of the global education and training network in the global membership points network. The education services and products supplied by the global education and training network are included in the points, and therefore constitute a part of the global membership points network. (4) Indirect value creation of the global education and training network in the global tourism network. The global education and training network creates limited indirect value for the global tourism network. (5) Indirect value creation of the global education and training network in the global health network. The global education and training network creates limited indirect value for the global health network. (6) Indirect value creation of the global education and training network in the global electronic transaction platform network. The global education and training network creates limited indirect value for the global electronic transaction platform network.

3. Manifestations of Direct and Indirect Value Creation of the Global Barter Network

The direct value created by the global barter network refers to the gains from the trade of global featured products inside and outside the enterprise. These gains can be divided into two parts: (1) price gains, the part by which the sales price of the product exceeds its purchase cost and circulation cost; and (2) foreign exchange gains, the exchange loss incurred by the fluctuation (particularly the substantial change) of the foreign exchange rate avoided due to the global barter activities.

Indirect value creation of the global barter network is mainly manifested by how it promotes and supports the global human resources and marketing network, global education and training network, global membership points network, global tourism network, global health network and global electronic transaction platform network. (1) Indirect value creation of the global barter network in the global human resources and marketing network. The global barter network provides more choices of product sales and consumption to the global human resources and marketing network, betters its sales and consumption conditions and improves its sales, consumption results and utility. (2) Indirect value creation of the global barter network in the global education and training network. The global barter network creates limited indirect value for the global education and training network. (3) Indirect value creation of the global barter network in the global membership points network. The product purchases in the global barter network contribute certain purchase points to the global membership points network. (4) Indirect value creation of the global barter network in the global tourism network. The global barter network creates limited indirect value for the global tourism network. (5) Indirect value creation of the global barter network in the global health network. The global barter network creates limited indirect value for the global health network. (6) Indirect value creation of the global barter network in the global electronic transaction platform network. The global barter network increases the number and diversifies the features of the global electronic transaction platform network and meanwhile enhances the appeal of the global electronic transaction platform network.

4. Manifestations of Direct and Indirect Value Creation of the Global Membership Points Network

Direct value creation of the global membership points network is essentially the process by which Tiens manages and invests its capital to acquire financial incomes.

Indirect value creation of the global membership points network is mainly manifested by how it promotes and supports the global human resources and marketing network, global education and training network, global barter network, global tourism network, global health network and global electronic transaction platform network. (1) Indirect value creation of the global membership points network in the global human resources and marketing network. Favourable points design and accumulation effectively encourage the stability and expansion of the global human resources and marketing network and promote its appeal. (2) Indirect value creation of the global membership points network in the global education and training network. Favourable points design and accumulation increase the added value of the global education and training network, make it more attractive and develop its expanding strength. (3) Indirect value creation of the global membership points network in the global barter network. Favourable points design and accumulation increase the added value of the global barter network, make it more attractive and develop its expanding strength. (4) Indirect value creation of the global membership points network in the global tourism network. Favourable points design and accumulation increase the added value of the global tourism network, make it more attractive and develop its expanding strength. (5) Indirect value creation of the global membership points network in the global health network. Favourable points design and accumulation increase the added value of the global health network, make it more attractive and develop its expanding strength. (6) Indirect value creation of the global membership points network in the global electronic transaction platform network. Favourable points design and accumulation increase the added value of the global electronic transaction platform network, make it more attractive and develop its expanding strength.

5. Manifestations of Direct and Indirect Value Creation of the Global Tourism Network
The direct value created by the global tourism network is mainly derived from the tourism revenue, which comprises two parts: (1) the centralized or decentralized tourism services purchased by Tiens as rewards; and (2) the social tourism services open to the whole world.

Indirect value creation of the global tourism network is mainly manifested by how it promotes and supports the global human resources and marketing network, global education and training network, global barter network, global membership points network, global health network and global electronic transaction platform network. (1) Indirect value creation of the global tourism network in the global human resources and marketing network. Favourable design of tourism products of the global tourism network improves the incentive effect of tourism rewards given by the global human resources and marketing network and plays a positive role in its stability and expansion. (2) Indirect value creation of the global tourism network in the global education and training network. The global tourism network creates limited indirect value for the global education and training network. (3) Indirect value creation of the global tourism network in the global barter network. The global tourism network creates limited indirect value for the global barter network. (4) Indirect value creation of the global tourism network in the global membership points network. The product purchases in the global tourism network contribute certain purchase points to the global membership points network. (5) Indirect value creation of the global tourism network in the global health network. The global tourism network creates limited indirect value for the global health network. (6) Indirect value creation of the global tourism network in the global electronic transaction platform network. The global tourism network creates limited indirect value for the global electronic transaction platform network.

6. Manifestations of Direct and Indirect Value Creation of the Global Health Network
The direct value created by the global health network mainly come from medical service revenue, which comprises two parts: (1) the centralized or decentralized medical services purchased by Tiens as rewards; and (2) the social medical services open to the whole world.

Indirect value creation of the global health network is mainly manifested by how it promotes and supports the global human resources and marketing network, global education and training network, global barter network, global membership points network, global tourism network and global electronic transaction platform network. (1) Indirect value creation of the global health network in the global human resources and marketing network. Favourable and effective medical service results of the global health network improve the incentive effect of the medical service rewards given by the global human resources and marketing network and play a positive role in its stability and expansion. (2) Indirect value creation of the global health network in the global education and training network. The global health network mainly creates indirect value for the global education and training network by adding the course design of medical care. (3) Indirect value creation of the global health network in the global barter network. The global health network creates limited indirect value for the global barter network. (4) Indirect value creation of the global health network in the global membership points network. The medical service purchases in the global health network contribute certain purchase points to the global membership points network. (5) Indirect value creation of the global health network in the global tourism network. The global health network creates limited indirect value for the global tourism network. (6) Indirect value creation of the global health network in the global electronic transaction platform network. The global health network creates limited indirect value for the global electronic transaction platform network.

7. Manifestations of Direct and Indirect Value Creation of the Global Electronic Transaction Platform Network

Direct value created by the global electronic transaction platform network refers to product sales in online stores of the global electronic transaction platform network, including both Direct Selling and nonDirect-Selling products.

Indirect value creation of the global electronic transaction platform network is mainly manifested by how it promotes and supports the global human resources and marketing network, global education and training network, global barter network, global membership points network, global tourism network and global health network. (1) Indirect value creation of the global electronic transaction platform network in the global human resources and marketing network. With diversified, high-quality and special products and convenient and good-experience shopping conditions, the global electronic transaction platform network betters the sales and consumption conditions of the global human resources and marketing network, improves its sales and consumption results and utility, enhances its appeal based on the network effect and increases the stickiness of direct sellers and consumers. (2) Indirect value creation of the global electronic transaction platform network in the global education and training network. The global electronic transaction platform network creates limited indirect value for the global education and training network. (3) Indirect value creation of the global electronic transaction platform network in the global barter network. The global electronic transaction platform network can be used as the transaction platform for the global barter network, to expand and facilitate its operations. (4) Indirect value creation of the global electronic transaction platform network in the global membership points network. Product purchases in the global electronic transaction platform network contribute certain purchase points to the global membership points network. (5) Indirect value creation of the global electronic transaction platform network in the global tourism network. The global electronic transaction platform network creates limited indirect value for the global tourism network. (6) Indirect value creation of the global electronic transaction platform network in the global health network. The global electronic transaction platform network creates limited indirect value for the global health network.

SECTION 3
MULTIPLIER ANALYSIS OF BENEFIT OVERLAY EFFECT IN MULTI-NETWORK INTERACTION

I. Benefit Overlay Effect of Multi-network Interaction

As the prerequisite to multi-network interaction, all subnets must have their own competitive products and services; otherwise, multi-network interaction may result in a negative influence on or create obstacles for each subnet. Therefore, direct value creation is not independent from indirect value creation in the multi-network interaction, since direct value creation is the basis and premise for indirect value creation.

In multi-network interaction, the subnets significantly vary from each other in terms of their business nature and profit model. No unified formula can be provided for profit accounting. Moreover, these subnets are also exposed to unbalanced development, so it is inappropriate to apply the same model of value accounting. Though the specific quantity of scale of value can be hardly calculated, their ability to create value can be briefly described with the potential energy of value creation. The essence of multi-network interaction is the potential energies of value creation, mutually promoting, strengthening, and enhancing each other, while the increase of the income and profit of each subnet is merely the manifestation and the result.

Among various subnets of Tiens multi-network interaction, their potential energies of value creation propose special requirements and present different manifestations, as shown in Table 9-1.

Subnet name	Manifestations of value creating potential energy
Global human resources and marketing network	Scale expansion of individual and family participants (particularly the families); stability and loyalty of personnel (families)
Global education and training network	Expansion of internal and external students (particularly the external); high popularity and recognition
Global barter network	Category, quality and features of products, improvement of customer stickiness
Global membership points network	Fund pool scale
Global tourism network	Quantity of tourism customers, satisfaction, special tourism resources
Global Taijisun	A large number of medical customers, high satisfaction
Global "JTMM" network	Category, quality and features of products, improvement of customer stickiness

Table 9-1 Manifestations of the Value Creating Potential Energy of Each Subnet in Tiens Multi-network Interaction

II. Direct Multiplier Analysis of Benefit Overlay Effect in Multi-network Interaction

The benefit overlay effect in multi-network interaction can be expressed by the mutual enhancement of value creating potential energies of different subnets. As multi-network interaction is a dynamic organic system, the benefit overlay effect of multi-network interaction is essentially the manifestation and result of the operations of this system. Being an organic system, the benefit overlay effect in multi-network interaction consists of three key links: (1) The state or level of value creating potential energy of the subnet in multi-network interaction is the state variable of the benefit overlay effect of multi-network interaction. The state or level of value creating potential energy of the subnet in multi-network interaction is denoted by the variable L_i (which refers to the subnet in multi-network interaction); and (2) The level of transmission of value creating potential energy among the subnets in multi-network interaction, how the value creation in one subnet promotes the value increase of another subnet, is mathematically denoted by $\beta_{ij}=\frac{\partial L_j}{\partial L_i}$; (3) The external variable θ_i that affects the value creating potential energy of each subnet in multi-network interaction includes the changes of the subjective efforts, policies and plans of Tiens and external market conditions. θ_i is the logical start of value creation in multi-network interaction.

The benefit overlay effect of multi-network interaction can be represented by the sensitivity of the value creating potential energy of each subnet to the external variable θ_i in the dynamic and organic system of multi-network interaction. The sensitivity is the multiplier. The multiplier can be divided into the direct multiplier and complete multiplier by the number of interactions. The direct multiplier merely calculates only the sensitivity of the value creating potential energy of each subnet in the dynamic organic system of multi-network interaction to a certain external variable θ_i, while the complete multiplier also considers the feedback mechanism of multi-network interaction on the basis of the direct multiplier. Theoretically, the feedback times of multi-network interaction are infinity.

It is assumed that if the value creating potential energy of each subnet adheres to simple inertia, the value creating potential energy of each subnet of multi-network interaction remains unchanged if there is no influence from other subnets, policies and external market environment, and the development potential energy of the current period is equal to that in the previous period. Then, the direct multiplier of the benefit overlay effect of multi-network interaction can be represented by the following set of simultaneous equations.

$$\begin{cases} L_{1t}=L_{1t-1}+0\cdot L_{1t}+\beta_{21}L_{2t}+\beta_{31}L_{3t}+\beta_{41}L_{4t}+\beta_{51}L_{5t}+\beta_{61}L_{6t}+\beta_{71}L_{7t}+\theta_{1t} \\ L_{2t}=L_{2t-1}+\beta_{12}\cdot L_{1t}+0\cdot L_{2t}+\beta_{32}L_{3t}+\beta_{42}L_{4t}+\beta_{52}L_{5t}+\beta_{62}L_{6t}+\beta_{72}L_{7t}+\theta_{2t} \\ L_{3t}=L_{3t-1}+\beta_{13}\cdot L_{1t}+\beta_{23}L_{2t}+0\cdot L_{3t}+\beta_{43}L_{4t}+\beta_{53}L_{5t}+\beta_{63}L_{6t}+\beta_{73}L_{7t}+\theta_{3t} \\ L_{4t}=L_{4t-1}+\beta_{14}\cdot L_{1t}+\beta_{24}L_{2t}+\beta_{34}L_{3t}+0\cdot L_{4t}+\beta_{54}L_{5t}+\beta_{64}L_{6t}+\beta_{74}L_{7t}+\theta_{4t} \\ L_{5t}=L_{5t-1}+\beta_{15}\cdot L_{1t}+\beta_{25}L_{2t}+\beta_{35}L_{3t}+\beta_{45}L_{4t}+0\cdot L_{5t}+\beta_{65}L_{6t}+\beta_{75}L_{7t}+\theta_{5t} \\ L_{6t}=L_{6t-1}+\beta_{16}\cdot L_{1t}+\beta_{26}L_{2t}+\beta_{36}L_{3t}+\beta_{46}L_{4t}+\beta_{56}L_{5t}+0\cdot L_{6t}+\beta_{76}L_{7t}+\theta_{6t} \\ L_{7t}=L_{7t-1}+\beta_{17}\cdot L_{1t}+\beta_{27}L_{2t}+\beta_{37}L_{3t}+\beta_{47}L_{4t}+\beta_{57}L_{5t}+\beta_{67}L_{6t}+0\cdot L_{7t}+\theta_{7t} \end{cases} \quad (1)$$

Let the identity matrix be:

$$I=\begin{pmatrix}1&0&0&0&0&0&0\\0&1&0&0&0&0&0\\0&0&1&0&0&0&0\\0&0&0&1&0&0&0\\0&0&0&0&1&0&0\\0&0&0&0&0&1&0\\0&0&0&0&0&0&1\end{pmatrix}$$

Then, the value creation transfer matrix of multi-network interaction will be:

$$A=\begin{pmatrix}0&\beta_{21}&\beta_{31}&\beta_{41}&\beta_{51}&\beta_{61}&\beta_{71}\\\beta_{12}&0&\beta_{32}&\beta_{42}&\beta_{52}&\beta_{62}&\beta_{72}\\\beta_{13}&\beta_{23}&0&\beta_{43}&\beta_{53}&\beta_{63}&\beta_{73}\\\beta_{14}&\beta_{24}&\beta_{34}&0&\beta_{54}&\beta_{64}&\beta_{74}\\\beta_{15}&\beta_{25}&\beta_{35}&\beta_{45}&0&\beta_{65}&\beta_{75}\\\beta_{16}&\beta_{26}&\beta_{36}&\beta_{46}&\beta_{56}&0&\beta_{76}\\\beta_{17}&\beta_{27}&\beta_{37}&\beta_{47}&\beta_{57}&\beta_{67}&0\end{pmatrix}$$

Equation (1) can be converted into the matrix and vector direction

$$I\bullet\begin{pmatrix}L_{1t}\\L_{2t}\\L_{3t}\\L_{4t}\\L_{5t}\\L_{6t}\\L_{7t}\end{pmatrix}=\begin{pmatrix}L_{1t-1}+\theta_{1t}\\L_{2t-1}+\theta_{2t}\\L_{3t-1}+\theta_{3t}\\L_{4t-1}+\theta_{4t}\\L_{5t-1}+\theta_{5t}\\L_{6t-1}+\theta_{6t}\\L_{7t-1}+\theta_{7t}\end{pmatrix}+A\begin{pmatrix}L_{1t}\\L_{2t}\\L_{3t}\\L_{4t}\\L_{5t}\\L_{6t}\\L_{7t}\end{pmatrix}\qquad(2)$$

By transforming Equation (2), we obtain:

$$\begin{pmatrix}L_{1t}\\L_{2t}\\L_{3t}\\L_{4t}\\L_{5t}\\L_{6t}\\L_{7t}\end{pmatrix}=(I-A)^{-1}\begin{pmatrix}L_{1t-1}+\theta_{1t}\\L_{2t-1}+\theta_{2t}\\L_{3t-1}+\theta_{3t}\\L_{4t-1}+\theta_{4t}\\L_{5t-1}+\theta_{5t}\\L_{6t-1}+\theta_{6t}\\L_{7t-1}+\theta_{7t}\end{pmatrix}\qquad(3)$$

Where,

$$B=(I-A)^{-1}=\begin{pmatrix} 1 & -\beta_{21} & -\beta_{31} & -\beta_{41} & -\beta_{51} & -\beta_{61} & -\beta_{71} \\ -\beta_{12} & 1 & -\beta_{32} & -\beta_{42} & -\beta_{52} & -\beta_{62} & -\beta_{72} \\ -\beta_{13} & -\beta_{23} & 1 & -\beta_{43} & -\beta_{53} & -\beta_{63} & -\beta_{73} \\ -\beta_{14} & -\beta_{24} & -\beta_{34} & 1 & -\beta_{54} & -\beta_{64} & -\beta_{74} \\ -\beta_{15} & -\beta_{25} & -\beta_{35} & -\beta_{45} & 1 & -\beta_{65} & -\beta_{75} \\ -\beta_{16} & -\beta_{26} & -\beta_{36} & -\beta_{46} & -\beta_{56} & 1 & -\beta_{76} \\ -\beta_{17} & -\beta_{27} & -\beta_{37} & -\beta_{47} & -\beta_{57} & -\beta_{67} & 1 \end{pmatrix}^{-1}$$

From Equation (3), we can see that the direct multiplier analysis of the benefit overlay effect of multi-network interaction is associated with three points. (1) The early potential energy of value creation of the subnet in multi-network interaction. The higher early potential energy of value creation of the subnet in multi-network interaction suggests the greater ability of the subnet to directly create value and is favourable for improving the indirect value creation of other relevant subnets in multi-network interaction. (2) The performance and innovation of core businesses of the subnet against the changes to the current policies, innovation and market environment. The more effective the performance and innovation of core businesses of the subnet against changes to current policies and innovation and market environment, the greater the ability of the subnet to directly create value and improve the indirect value creation of other relevant subnets in multi-network interaction. (3) Effectiveness of the connections among the subnets of multi-network interaction. The closer connections among the subnets of multi-network interaction improve these subnets' direct value creation ability, as well as the indirect value creation ability of other relevant subnets.

The specific value of the direct multiplier of the benefit overlay effect in multi-network interaction can be simulated and optimized by setting a rational value of , the direct multiplier of the benefit overlay effect in multi-network interaction and rationally making use of the function MINVERSE ( ) and MMULT ( ).

III. Complete Multiplier Analysis of Benefit Overlay Effect in Multi-network Interaction

On the basis of the direct multiplier, the complete multiplier analysis of the benefit overlay effect in multi-network interaction considers the cumulative reinforcement effect resulting from infinite back-and-forth feedback of multi-network interaction and transmission. Here and subsequently, C denotes the complete multiplier of the benefit overlay effect of multi-network interaction. The calculation process of the complete multiplier is as follows:

$$C=B+B\cdot B+B\cdot B\cdot B+\cdots\cdots+B\cdot B\cdots B \qquad (4)$$

Let's multiply both sides by B^{-1}:

$$B^{-1} \cdot C = I + B + B \cdot B + B \cdot B \cdot B + \cdots\cdots + B \cdot B \cdots B = I + C \qquad (5)$$

From further calculation we obtain:

$$(B^{-1} - I) \cdot C = I \qquad (6)$$

We thus get that the complete multiplier of the benefit overlay effect of multi-network interaction is: $C = (B^{-1} - I)^{-1}$

CHAPTER 10

INSTITUTIONAL FRAMEWORK THAT GUARANTEES EFFECTIVE OPERATION OF MULTI-NETWORK INTERACTION

SECTION 1
MECHANISM FOUNDATION OF MULTI-NETWORK INTERACTION

I. Multi-network Interaction from Three Perspectives: Productivity, Production Relations and Superstructure

Multi-network interaction is a comprehensive, complex, coordinated and open system that attaches importance to innovation, specialization and coordination. As an all-round and profound reform of swap and transcendence, multi-network interaction will be analysed from three perspectives: productivity, production relations and superstructure. Multi-network interaction and its corresponding productivity, production relations and superstructure constitute the '$n\wedge3$' pattern. The basic mechanism for the swap and transcendence results of a global seven-network interaction in terms of productivity, production relations and superstructure is shown in Figure 10-1.

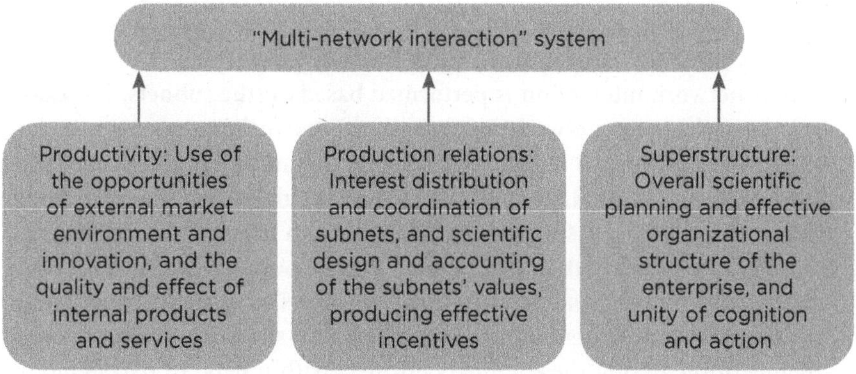

Figure 10-1 "$n\wedge3$" Pattern of the Swap and Transcendence Results of Multi-network Interaction

II. Productivity Problems of Multi-network Interaction

Multi-network interaction demands great competitiveness and market appeal of the core products and services (research, development and production) for the interaction, as well as the full utilization and innovation of changes in the market environment.

III. Production Relations Problems of Multi-network Interaction

Multi-network production relations involve the problems of delimitation of property rights, status of interest of relevant subjects and interest distribution. Therefore, interests will be rationally distributed and coordinated among various subnets and the value realization and value distribution of subnets' value chains in multi-network interaction will be designed and settled scientifically, to produce effective incentives and constraints. The above three problems will be fully, rationally and fairly dealt with to bring multi-network interaction into full play; otherwise, internal conflicts of interest may arise and severely affect the multi-network interaction.

IV. Superstructure Problems of Multi-network Interaction

Multi-network interaction is implemented from top to bottom, which requires vigorous support, overall scientific planning and an effective organizational structure, as well as the unity of cognition and awareness among all subnets and their stakeholders.

SECTION 2
ORGANIZATIONAL STRUCTURE OF MULTI-NETWORK INTERACTION

I. Basic Principles for the Organizational Structure Design

1. Specification of the Business Scope of the Networks

Multi-network interaction is performed based on the subnets. For example, as to the seven networks of Tiens multi-network interaction – including the global human resources and marketing network, global education and training network, global barter network, global membership points network, global tourism network, global health network and global electronic transaction platform network – despite overlapping business operations and mutual connections, these networks have their own business scope that is quite distinct from others. There should be neither vicious competition among these subnets nor nets within nets. In particular, the global barter network and the global electronic transaction platform network will be well coordinated.

2. Flat Management and Light Assets
Multi-network interaction will give full play to the advantages of the scale economy and sharing economy and avoid repetitive construction by sharing software and hardware infrastructures, making the best of social resources, and lightening the assets. From the management perspective, some management functions of the subnets of multi-network interaction will be centralized at the enterprise to reduce management levels, enable flat management and avoid organizational overlapping and overstaffing.

3. Make the Subnet of Multi-network Interaction an Entity and a Legal Person
Though multi-network interaction shows the characteristics of an enterprise when 'planning' for resource allocation, the subnets in multi-network interaction are running independent businesses. Business connections among the subnets are clearly settled through the internal 'transactions' of the enterprise. In addition to the businesses associated with other subnets of the enterprise, subnets of multi-network interaction also independently explore their social businesses. To achieve this, these subnets of multi-network interaction will be made the professional operations and management entity and the legal person.

II. Selection of Organizational Structure of Multi-network Interaction

Multi-network interaction is a typical industrial integration and crossover. The industrial integration promotes the development of the organizational structure from vertical integration to horizontal integration, hybrid integration and virtual integration. Three representative management structures have been gradually formed in the practices of modern enterprises: the line organization, line-function organization and divisional organization. The line organization is the simplest centralized organization, where the leadership relationship is established vertically and no special functional division is established. It looks like a straight line from top to bottom. The line-function organization is established on the basis of the line organization; corresponding functional divisions are set up under the leadership of top leaders, who are responsible for unified command and functional divisions provide advice and instructions. It is essentially a variety of the linear organization, as both are consistent in nature. The divisional organization adheres to the overall principle of 'centralized decision making and decentralized operations.' In this organization, the enterprise is divided into several relatively independent operations units by product, region and customer; and these divisions can set up the functional departments they need.

In consideration of the basic operations mechanism and management system of multi-network operations, the divisional organization is more appropriate, and the sharing function of these subnets should be better transferred to the enterprise group.

SECTION 3
BENEFIT ASSESSMENT AND ALLOCATION OF MULTI-NETWORK INTERACTION

I. Attach Importance to the Development Paths and Mutual Benefit Assessment and Allocation of the Subnets of Multi-network Interaction Against their Unbalanced Development

There are four imbalances in the value creation and spillover ability of the subnets of multi-network interaction. The first is the imbalance in the direct value creation ability. All subnets vary considerably in their direct value creation. For instance, the direct value creation ability of the global education network may be weaker than that of the global barter network. The second is the imbalance in the indirect value creation ability. Though the global education networks direct value-creation ability may be weaker than that of the global barter network, its ability of indirect value creation exceeds the latter as it significantly increases the businesses of other subnets. The third is the imbalance in the expansion rate. The expansion of the global education network may be faster than the expansion of the global Taijisun network because it takes a long time for traditional Chinese medicine and health preservation to take effect and be recognized by others. The fourth is the imbalance of the sensitivity to the macro business cycle. The global tourism network is more sensitive to the macro business cycle than the global education network.

These development imbalances require the subnets implementing different road maps. The focus of each subnet will be determined according to the development basis and market opportunities of different networks. Meanwhile, multi-network interaction will coordinate the benefit assessment and allocation among subnets and guarantee fairness and justice.

II. Technical Innovation such as the Internet Provides Key and Fundamental Support to the Benefit Assessment and Allocation of Multi-network Interaction

In addition to logistics, capital flow and interest flow, effective information communication, exchange and data mining also constitute the key factors that contribute to the effective operation of multi-network interaction. Seeing the rise and maturity of the block chain, cloud computing, big data and artificial intelligence, multi-network interaction will make the best of these latest technologies. It will also depend on these technologies to achieve the network effect of multi-network interaction, find the law of economic behaviours, discover important consumption characteristics and effectively launch many derivative activities, and thus realize the real 'interaction' of these networks. We can measure and dynamically monitor the multi-network interaction effect of Tiens by using the multiplier model of the benefit overlay effect of multi-network interaction, which will help Tiens to find out reasons for any issues and make timely adjustments.

III. Parameter Estimation for the Measurement and Monitoring of the Benefit Overlay Effect of Multi-network Interaction

The key to measure and monitor the benefit overlay effect multiplier model of multi-network interaction is to obtain the interaction quantities between every two subnets. Hence, $\beta_{ij}=\frac{\partial L_i}{\partial L_j}$. In practice, the value of β_{ij} can be acquired by calculating the related coefficients of the annual (monthly, quarterly) changes of business indicators between every two subnets of multi-network interaction. These business indicators may be the sales income growth rate, the customer base expansion rate, or profit growth rate of the subnets. We can get related coefficients through self-programming, but simple calculations can be done with the formula CORREL ( ) in EXCEL.

IV. Measurement and Monitoring of the Transmission Direction of the Benefit Overlay Effect of Multi-network Interaction

Though the parameters of the benefit overlay effect of multi-network interaction can be acquired by the calculation of related coefficients of the annual (monthly, quarterly) changes of business indicators between every two subnets of multi-network interaction, the related coefficients fail to suggest the transmission direction of the interaction between every two subnets. It is necessary to determine the transmission direction of interaction between every two subnets in addition to the quantity of interaction. Logically, the transmission direction of the interaction between every two subnets in multi-network interaction has four possibilities: Subnet A causes the change of Subnet B; Subnet B is the reason for the change of Subnet A; both subnets contribute to the changes of each other; and both subnets have no connection to the changes of each other (the higher coefficient suggests that the change is caused by other factors, particularly the factor that both subnets are exposed to).

As the foundation and premise, empirical and logical analysis will be conducted for the transmission direction of the interaction between every two subnets. Based on qualitative analysis, the Granger Causality test can be adopted to make a prudent and detailed quantitative analysis and definition.

V. System Architecture for the Measurement and Monitoring of the Benefit Overlay Effect of Multi-network Interaction

The measurement and monitoring of the benefit overlay effect of multi-network interaction can be considered as an important part of the daily management of Tiens. The Tiens measurement and monitoring system of interactive effect of seven nets interaction (TMSIESNI) is constructed by applying information and data processing technology and adhering to the above ideas.

The operations architecture of the TMSIESNI is shown in Figure 10-2.

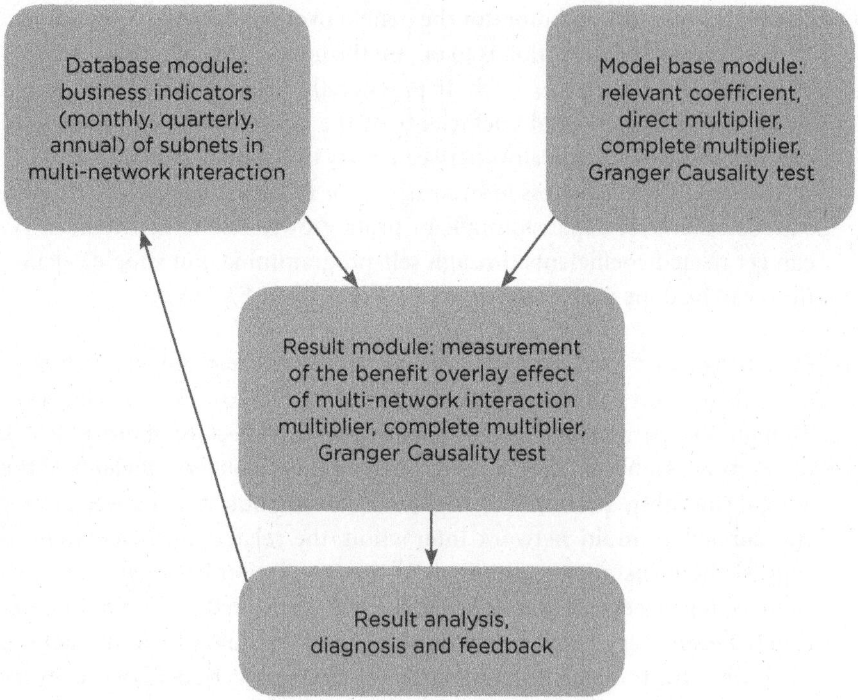

Figure 10-2 Operations Architecture of the TMSIESNI

SECTION 4
GLOBAL COORDINATION OF MULTI-NETWORK INTERACTION

Tiens has spread its businesses to over 190 countries worldwide and involved more than 40 million direct sellers and consumers' families. Therefore, the seven-network interaction of Tiens must be planned and coordinated from a global perspective. Attention will be paid to both the opportunities, the challenges and special demands of globalization.

I. Global Coordination of the Global Human Resources and Marketing Network

In the global human resources and marketing network of Tiens, direct sellers and consumers come from different countries, which vary significantly in economic and cultural levels. Therefore, during operations, the global human resources and marketing network will appropriately adjust its business content and focus of products and services according to the different economic levels and cultural characteristics in different countries and attempt to be as local as possible.

II. Global Coordination of the Global Education and Training Network

The global education and training network of Tiens provides education and training businesses to the global human resources and marketing network and also other specialized education and training businesses. When supplying education and training to the global human resources and marketing network, the global education and training network will improve the contents and methods of education and training. When providing education and training services to any party other than the global human resources and marketing network, the global education and training network will absorb the essence from the services to the global human resources and marketing network, attempt to deviate from the latter and design new education and training products. The global education and training services provided to any party other than the global human resources and marketing network can be implemented in a form of Chinese traditional culture including traditional Chinese medicine.

III. Global Coordination of the Global Barter Network

The global coordination of Tiens global barter network is of great potential and is exposed to certain risks. For overall coordination, it is necessary to make full use of the special role of over 40 million families of direct sellers and consumers from over 190 countries worldwide in acquiring and selling products. Meanwhile, the global barter network will complete the supporting constructions of the supply chain in advance before operation.

IV. Global Coordination of the Global Membership Points Network

The global membership points network and e-wallet of Tiens plays a very essential role in the seven-network interaction of Tiens. E-wallet is the virtual currency inside the enterprise. To achieve global coordination, the global membership points network will link up electronic currency with exchange rates to avoid excessive exchange rate risks.

V. Global Coordination of the Global Tourism Network

Tourism internationalization is the overall planning of the global tourism network of Tiens. Adhering to internationalization and high-end tourism resources, this network spares no effort to develop e-commerce, converts traditional 'pure tourism' into resort or journey experiences, develops the open e-commerce platform for tourism services and connects consumers and merchants in real time based on the big data from the global business of Tiens to better satisfy tourists' demands. Meanwhile, it also strives to develop the overseas-travel market of China, attract more international tourism enterprises to join the global tourism network and strengthen the cooperation with international airlines and world-famous hotels.

VI. Global Coordination of Global Taijisun Network

The global coordination of the global Taijisun network aims to spread Taijisun medical services with the soul of traditional Chinese medicine to the rest of the world. To achieve this, it needs to explore and discover masters of traditional Chinese medicine and promote and demonstrate the magical effect of traditional Chinese medicine to foreign consumers and their families and have them experience the magic personally.

VII. Global Coordination of JTMM Linker Network

The global coordination of JTMM's Linker network needs to accomplish several tasks. First, make it convenient, intuitive and fast to browse the website, to improve consumers' online shopping experiences. Second, promote the website to the whole world, pay attention to optimizing the product content and improve website traffic and conversion rates, where the global human resources and marketing network can be used as a great way to attract traffic, stabilize fans, improve conversion rates and increase the exposure of products. Third, overcome the language barrier and invest more in minority languages (such as Latin and Russian) services.

Finally, provide flexible and convenient cross-border payment and settlement services, improve the risk-control system, and conform to the payment habits of direct sellers and consumers (and their families) distributed worldwide.

PART IV

SWAP PROCESS AND TRANSCENDENCE PRACTICE III: ‘ONE BODY WITH MULTIPLE WINGS’ MODEL

ZHAO QILAN

'One body with multiple wings' is a development model of an enterprise that is based on the effective integration and sharing of multi-network resources, forms the primary-secondary relationship among different business sectors through constant swap and transcendence and has the primary lead the coordinated development of other business sectors.

The development of one body with multiple wings model is more or less influenced by many different factors, including the external environment such as the economic environment, market environment and legal environment and internal factors such as effective incentives and product lines. The one body with multiple wings model aims to realize the long-term development of an enterprise and develops different business sectors through effective swap and integration of internal and external resources of the enterprise based on diversified superimposition (demand, product and market superimposition) and resource sharing. From the value chain, swap chain to ecological chain, one body with multiple wings continuously improves the enterprise's core competitiveness.

CHAPTER 11

'ONE BODY WITH MULTIPLE WINGS' AND ITS BASIC STRUCTURE

Being a development model of Direct-Selling enterprises, one body with multiple wings is a development of the enterprise management theory. This chapter will mainly define one body with multiple wings, explain its basic frame and structural elements and theoretically prepare for the analysis of the conditions, mechanism and competitiveness of one body with multiple wings in the practice of swap and transcendence.

SECTION 1
THE MEANING OF ONE BODY WITH MULTIPLE WINGS

I. One Body with Multiple Wings

1. Definition of One Body with Multiple Wings

When the hawk flies in the sky, the wings are supporting it. The body and the wings constitute a well-coordinated organic whole. One body with multiple wings is a development model innovatively created when the Direct-Selling enterprise reaches a certain stage of development. For instance, Tiens has depended on its Direct-Selling businesses for development, and now it is exploring global comprehensive health, global tourism, global e-commerce Direct-Selling platform (JTMM), global education training and innovative business forms under the Internet+ background such as social e-commerce and Linker in addition to its primary business of direct selling. Tiens has evolved its development pattern from the consolidation of three networks, multi-network interaction to one body with multiple wings.

One body with multiple wings is a development model of an enterprise, which is based on the effective integration and sharing of multi-network resources acquired throughout the enterprise's development, forms the primary-secondary relationship among different business sectors and has the 'primary' lead the coordinated development of other business sectors. 'One body' here means to integrate all resources and abilities needed for the development of primary businesses to achieve enterprise development; and 'multiple wings' refers to constructing a diversified, pluralistic and stereoscopic resource network and providing personalized, differentiated and customized products and services to customers. The collaboration and coexistence of one body and multiple wings jointly promote the enterprise's development.

The composition and characteristics of consolidation of three networks, multi-network interaction and one body with multiple wings are listed in Table 11-1.

	Composition	Business sector	Characteristics
Consolidation of three networks	Human resources and marketing network Product and R&D network Financial and capital network	Direct selling (health products) Education (training)	Form resultant force
Multi-network interaction	Global human resources and marketing network Global education and training network Global barter network Global membership points network Global tourism network Global health network Global e-commerce direct selling platform	Direct selling (health products) Education (training) Tourism service Health service E-commerce platform	Interdependence and interactivity (interaction), making the best use of resources
One body with multiple wings	When direct selling as the one body, education (training), tourism, health service and e-commerce as the multiple wings; When education (training) as the one body, direct selling, tourism, health service and e-commerce as the multiple wings	Direct selling (health products) Education (training) Tourism service Health service E-commerce platform	Interdependence and interactivity, conversion of the primary and secondary status, coexistence, and development of one body and multiple wings

Table 11-1 Composition and Characteristics of Consolidation of Three Networks, Multi-network Interaction and One Body with Multiple Wings

As a matter of fact, the body and wings are interrelated. Since both the body and wings are open to the outside, they exert mutual influence and share resources to some extent. The one body and multiple wings can be interconverted, and the composition and role of the body and wings vary when seen from different perspectives.

2. Characteristics of One Body with Multiple Wings

(1) The one body with multiple wings is open to the outside. While both the primary and secondary status are changeable, the principle is immutable.

Openness means to exchange energy and materials with the outside, by which the enterprise develops through the constant exchanges with the outside and is continuously and dynamically optimized from the lower level to the higher level, from the simplicity to the complexity and from the disorder to the order. The model of one body with multiple wings being open means that as a development model of the enterprise, it is exchanging resources, energy, and information with other systems in the same environment and achieves development through constant exchanges.

Literally, one body with multiple wings shows a primary-secondary relationship, with the one body as the primary and the multiple wings as the secondary. The relation between the body and the wings may change in different perspectives. The model of one body with multiple wings features a characteristic similar to that of transformers. Under a given condition, a wing in the multiple wings may become the one body, while others will be the wings. Interaction, interconnection and mutual support are seen between the one body and multiple wings and among the multiple wings, and all these wings are cooperating with the one body. In other words, from the perspective of direct selling, direct selling is the one body, with tourism, comprehensive health and education as the wings. If from the tourism perspective, various tourism resources that are efficiently operating centring on tourism businesses form the one body, with direct selling, comprehensive health and education as the wings. Therefore, the composition of the body and the wings will be different if viewed from different perspectives. However, regardless of the changes, the principle of one body with multiple wings never changes.

(2) The core tie of one body with multiple wings still rests in the interests.

The core tie between the body and wings is still the interests. When there are two or more groups of interest subjects, their interest relationship will drive their behaviours and cause the interaction, laying the foundation for the realization of the interest relationship. Moreover, as long as a group is formed, it will become an independent interest subject, and the group interest is essentially its self-interest. The interest relationship is a new resource allocation relationship generated under the guidance of resources and behaviours. In the model of one body with multiple wings, the interest is the tie.

(3) The body and wings in one body with multiple wings are all independent legal people.
Either the body or the wings in one body with multiple wings are independent legal people. As independent legal people, on one hand, they constitute the one body with multiple wings with other independent legal people, and on the other hand, each independent legal person must safeguard its own interest during operations and different legal people have a consistent goal despite different business methods. It is the interests that connect these independent legal people. Different independent legal people run different business sectors and form the development model of one body with multiple wing with interests as the tie during the development. The coexistence and coordinated development of different business sectors are realized through the sharing of resources.

II. One Body and Multiple Wings

Since the founding of Tiens, it has always been adhering to one clear aim that is to focus on the health industry and seek the method and road leading to "health, wealth, peace and development" of human beings. On these grounds, it chose R&D of health food. Through over two decades of development, Tiens has developed its catalogue of Direct-Selling products from the key product of a high-calcium supplement at the early stage to now over a thousand types of products, and has promoted these health products to the whole world. To date, Tiens' main businesses span direct selling, education, tourism, Taijisun (comprehensive health) and the social e-commerce platform JTMM.

On the business side, one body and multiple wings reveal the primary-secondary relationship generated among different business sectors of the enterprise during its development, which is relative and changeable.

On the social e-commerce side, with direct selling, education, tourism and Taijisun, Tiens has made up the one body with multiple wings structure. The resources that support the operation and development of social e-commerce form an organic whole, the one body; while direct selling, education, tourism and Taijisun (comprehensive health) are the multiple wings that boost the development of social e-commerce. In this case, social e-commerce is the one body, the primary (business), and education, tourism and Taijisun (comprehensive health) are the secondary (businesses), the multiple wings. The one body and multiple wings share resources and promote the development of each other. One body decides the development direction of the system, and the multiple wings influence the development path and rate of the system.

For example, the tourism business is not only promoting traditional tourism products in the market to attract customers, since tourism customers may be transferred to social e-commerce and other businesses. Similarly, the customers of the tourism business may come from two sources: attracted by tourism marketing channels or transferred from the social e-commerce business.

In this event, the social e-commerce business has assured a certain customer base for the tourism business. Conversely, tourism customers may propose certain demands on social e-commerce, making themselves the customers of social e-commerce in the meantime. The working resources of the one body, social e-commerce, are shared with the tourism business, which promotes the development of tourism businesses; and conversely, the resources of the wing, the tourism business, are also shared with social e-commerce, further enabling the primary business of social e-commerce to expand its consumer group and promoting the development of social e-commerce.

III. The Body and Wings from Different Perspectives

Viewed from different perspectives, the body and wings show different compositions. If from the perspective of tourism, the resources supporting the operation and development of tourism constitute an organic whole, the one body, and social e-commerce, education and comprehensive health are the multiple wings that promote the development of the body.

1. One Body and Multiple Wings from the Perspective of Tourism

Anything in nature or human society that attracts tourists is the tourist resource that can be developed and utilized to generate economic benefits, social benefits and environmental benefits. By means of the rational integration of tourist resources and operations planning, travel agencies provide high-end tourists with personalized and customized tourism services and supply middle and low-end tourists with standard and competitive tourist products and services of multiple combinations.

From the perspective of tourism, tourism is the one body and other business sectors are the multiple wings in the one body with multiple wings model. In this case, tourism is the primary, and other businesses are the secondary businesses. Take Tiens as an example; the tourism business is independent while making up the structure of one body with multiple wings with other business sectors. Social e-commerce resources can be considered as a wing for tourism, since social e-commerce customers may have tourism demands, which may be derived from their own love for travel or business reward. Regardless of the nature, potential tourism demands may be converted to real demand that can be satisfied by the travel agencies. In this way, the potential tourism demands in social e-commerce businesses are transformed to real market demands in tourism businesses. The social e-commerce businesses assure the demand market of travel agencies to a certain extent, and the market will develop along with the growth of social e-commerce. Hence, social e-commerce has become a wing that drives the development of tourism. It is the same case with direct selling and comprehensive health businesses where the customers' potential demands on tourist products may be transferred to the practical market demand on tourism. During the development of the one body with multiple wings, seeing the better coordination between the primary and secondary businesses, greater contributions will be made by the multiple wings to the one body. Thus, as promoted by the multiple wings of social e-commerce, direct selling, comprehensive health, and the e-commerce Direct-Selling platform, tourism businesses will usher in healthy development.

2. One Body and Multiple Wings from the Perspective of the Social E-commerce Platform

In the context of Internet+, Tiens has launched a social e-commerce platform. Being an important part of one body with multiple wings, the social e-commerce platform is fully open to the whole world, with social intercourse, people and traffic as the core. The platform not only enables consumers to socialize with others and shop at the same time, but also saves consumers money as long as they buy a lot based on corresponding incentive measures. The merchant can expand its businesses and earn stable commissions through this platform.

From the perspective of the social e-commerce platform, it has become the one body. The primary business of the platform is to construct and operate the social e-commerce platform in the shared economy in the age of the internet. It outsources the investment promotion to regional agencies, creates a platform perfectly integrating social intercourse and boutique shopping for consumers by building its own brand, introducing famous brands and third-party suppliers, and drawing into foreign specialized products through branches overseas, and provides a business platform for merchants.

The social e-commerce platform shares active customers of other business sectors. Before the social e-commerce platform was built, direct sellers acquired benefits by selling and consuming Direct-Selling products but had to purchase their daily consumer goods elsewhere. However, after the establishment of the social e-commerce platform, direct sellers can satisfy their living consumption demand directly through the social e-commerce platform; and meanwhile obtain certain refunds or benefits according to their consumption amount at the social e-commerce platform. Thus, Direct-Selling resources have become a vigorous wing that promotes the development of the social e-commerce platform. Moreover, customers of the comprehensive health, tourism and education (training) sector also propose demand on daily consumer goods like distributors do in Direct-Selling businesses; and the social e-commerce platform can attract direct social consumers through various channels and turn potential customers into direct consumers with the incentive mechanism. In this way, the comprehensive health, tourism and education (training) sector function as the multiple wings to the social e-commerce platform and promote its development and expansion.

The social e-commerce platform is constantly accumulating and expanding the enterprise's partner resources, customer resources, customer resources and brand resources. The coexistence and coordination of one body and multiple wings further promote the enterprise's market competitiveness and benefit multiple parties.

3. One Body and Multiple Wings from the Perspective of Comprehensive Health
From the perspective of comprehensive health, comprehensive health itself is the one body, while other business sectors including social e-commerce, tourism, and education (training) have become the multiple wings. The body and the wings depend on each other for coordinated development. The comprehensive health sector is also an open medical service platform, providing comprehensive health medical care to ordinary customers as well as customers from other business sectors such as social e-commerce, tourism and education (training).

Special Column 11-1: One Body and Multiple Wings from the Perspective of Tiens Comprehensive Health

By 2011, Tiens products had spanned over 190 countries and regions of the world. Tiens people are consuming or running the business of Tiens products, significantly driving the value flow of labour, logistics, funds, R&D, quality inspection and production as a great engine and impeller. On these grounds, Tiens planned and constructed Taijisun Hospital International Health Management Centre.

It is the official foundation of Taijisun that brings Tiens the real comprehensive health industry. The first move of Taijisun was to communicate and cooperate with the Direct-Selling sector in China to develop a genetic testing program. This program would be the key to a new market for Taijisun in the future. As a special marketing tool, Taijisun's genetic testing program helped Tiens upgrade the level of customers in the market and improved the demand and quality of customers.

To further better its comprehensive health service, Tiens has established the "comprehensive health technology innovation system" relying on its international standard R&D centre and quality inspection centre, the "comprehensive health production and logistics system" based on modern production workshops and automatic warehouses, the "comprehensive health service system" with the support of Taijisun Hospital International Health Management Centre, All-Legend Hotel and Tiens international conference centre and the "comprehensive education system" based on Tiens College, and has perfectly mixed and integrated several business forms of Tiens. Depending on integrated comprehensive health management system, Taijisun has started to improve the life quality of the targeted social e-commerce platform consumers by means of health management and has provided partners with a more solid and orderly marketing fund source. The body and the wings promote each other and achieve a coordinated development.

SECTION 2
BASIC ELEMENTS AND STRUCTURE OF ONE BODY WITH MULTIPLE WINGS

I. Basic Elements of One Body with Multiple Wings

An element is the minimum unit essential for the existence and movement of an objective entity, an indispensable factor that constitutes an entity and a basic unit for the composition of a system. The constituent elements of one body with multiple wings refer to the fundamental resources needed for Tiens to carry out social production (service) operations activities with the model of one body with multiple wings, and the basic elements demanded to maintain the operation of one body with multiple wings. One body with multiple wings can be considered as a system. In this system, the basic components of the one body and the basic components of the multiple wings are the constituent elements of one body with multiple wings.

One body with multiple wings is a collaborative system with a specific goal. According to the studies of Chester I. Barnard, Fremont E. Kast and James E. Rosenzweig on organizational elements, the elements of one body with multiple wings consist of the internal and external environments, the goal, members and essential material conditions.

1. Internal and External Environments

The external environment is the environment observed outside the one body or multiple wings. Any system exists in a certain external environment and always exchanges materials, energy or information with the external environment. For one body with multiple wings, the macro external environment includes the political environment, economic environment, social environment and cultural environment; the meso environment refers to the market environment, production environment and scientific research and technology environment for the industry; and the micro environment is the environment made by stakeholders, such as the local government, customers, suppliers and competitors.

The internal environment indicates the model of relationships among internal members or groups of one body with multiple wings, such as the structural environment, institutional environment and cultural environment. The development of the internal environment will be consistent with that of the external environment. In view of the great uncertainties in the development of the external environment, the internal environment will be adjusted to the changes of the external environment, to assure the coordination between internal and external elements.

2. Goal
   The goal is the common aspiration recognized by all members. One body with multiple wings is established as long as two or more groups collaborate with each other for the same goal. The goal unifies the one body with multiple wings; and without a common goal, one body with multiple wings can never be established and has no reason to exist. When determining the goal, Tiens will be fully aware that it will represent the goal of the one body as well as the common goal of multiple wings. Without a clear goal, the structure of Tiens' one body with multiple wings will no longer exist. The goal is the intended purpose of one body with multiple wings and points out the development direction of this model.

3. Members
   Members here suggest the business sectors covered by one body with multiple wings. To achieve the goal of one body with multiple wings, a certain number of members must join this model; but to become the members, certain access procedures or formalities must be completed. During the development of one body with multiple wings, the business sectors will be exposed to adjustments from time to time according to the changes of the internal and external environments. The new business sectors will be introduced in due time, and the declining business sectors will be eliminated in a timely manner.

4. Material conditions
   Certain material conditions must be satisfied to assure the operation of one body with multiple wings. From the perspective of social e-commerce, social e-commerce is the one body and other relevant independent business sectors including tourism, comprehensive health and education constitute the multiple wings to social e-commerce. The roles of the body and wings

are changeable. If from the perspective of tourism, tourism is the one body, while social e-commerce and other businesses become the multiple wings. However, regardless of different perspectives, the basic material elements for one body with multiple wings are constant, including human resources, capital and products (and services).

(1) Human Resources

At a macro level, human resources refer to the population at the working age or enjoying the labour capability though younger or older than the labour age in a certain country or region. At the micro level, human resources are the resources possessed by the people in an organization within a certain period that can be used by the enterprise and make contributions to value creation, including education, capability, skill, experience and physical strength and so on.

The current connotation of human resources known to people was firstly defined by Peter F. Drucker, the master of management, in *The Practice of Management*, who argued that human resources had certain qualities that were never seen in other resources, namely coordination, integration, judgment and imagination. Coordination here refers to the coordinating and directing of talent during decision making. Decision makers will not only know and utilize various organizational forms well, but also be skilful in exercising the power to orderly direct and control others and coordinate human, material and financial resources for optimum results. The coordinating ability consists of two parts, the coordination of interpersonal relations and the coordination of work. Integration here refers to the talent to integrate into a team. Judgment means the personality-embodied ability that applies values to certain events in forms of selections. Imagination is an ability by which people create a new image based on an existing image and can only be realized upon certain knowledge.

The human resource is a special resource, which can only be developed by an effective incentive mechanism before it brings visible economic value to the enterprise. Therefore, in one body with multiple wings, the capabilities of human resources or talents mainly show as follows. (1) Effective communication ability. In the operation and management of one body with multiple wings, it is essential to timely communicate information to subordinates, peers, superiors or other personnel. (2) Great employee motivation ability. Adopt various measures to motivate employees and inspire their enthusiasm, initiative and creativity. (3) Favourable interpersonal ability. Interpersonal skills constitute a premise to effective operations and management, which mean to make use of various skills to establish favourable interpersonal relations and "let others help me." Managers (or distributors) will have the following important interpersonal skills: active listening, effective feedback, instructions, conflict resolution and negotiation.

(2) Capital

Capital refers to the social relations of material wealth or the production of economic values. According to the enterprise accounting theory, capital is the fund that the owner invests in production and operations to generate benefits. It is a basic element for the enterprise's operating activities as well as an essential condition for the founding, existence and development of enterprises. Capital must be provided to create one body with multiple wings, as this model requires certain capital scale for existence and needs to raise capital constantly for development.

(3) Products (and services)

A product is anything that can be supplied to the market for people's use and consumption and satisfy people's certain demands, including tangible goods, intangible services, organizations, concepts, or a combination of the above. In general, there are five levels of products: the core product, basic product, expected product, attached product and potential product. The core product is a complete product supplied to the buyer for direct interests and utility; the basic product is the macro concept of the core product; the expected product is the product featuring certain characteristics or conditions that the buyer expects to see; the attached product means the product beyond customers' expectations; and the potential product refers to the product or thing under development that may be improved or changed in the future.

An enterprise needs to constantly launch products and services that meet targeted consumers' demands for the sake of development. For example, Tiens mainly focused on the production of health food right after its founding in 1995; but only three years later, Tiens had been registered and applied for inspection of products in 37 countries. By now, Tiens has developed over 1,000 kinds of products under five major categories including health food, personal care, household items, beauty and cosmetics, and health equipment, has a stable consumer group from 40 million families and spreads its businesses to more than 190 countries. As Tiens continuously provides new products to meet different consumers' demands and explores multi-industry businesses, the model of one body with multiple wings is developing rapidly.

II. Relations among the Elements of One Body with Multiple Wings

The elements of one body with multiple wings include the internal and external environments, the goal (target), members and essential material conditions. These elements show the following relations: the goal (target) determines the development direction of one body with multiple wings; the common goal enables the integration of the members of one body with multiple wings and makes it a whole of dynamic development; the internal and external environments offer a condition for the establishment of one body with multiple wings; the composition of members (business sectors) determines the structure of one body with multiple wings; and the essential material conditions lay the foundation for the development of one body with multiple wings.

These different business sectors that constitute one body with multiple wings are independent to each other and jointly make up the structure based on a certain proportion, which largely decides the nature of one body with multiple wings. From a different perspective, the same element in one body with multiple wings shows different characters, positions and roles. The members of one body with multiple wings are exposed to a dynamic development, as they are constantly adjusted to the changes of the internal and external environments.

III. One Body with Multiple Wings Structure Diagram

The multiple business sectors of the Direct-Selling enterprise constitute the structure of one body with multiple wings through mutual dependence and promotion. The body and wings are different from different perspectives, but their interaction mechanism remains unchanged. The structure diagram of one body with multiple wings is shown in Figure 11-1.

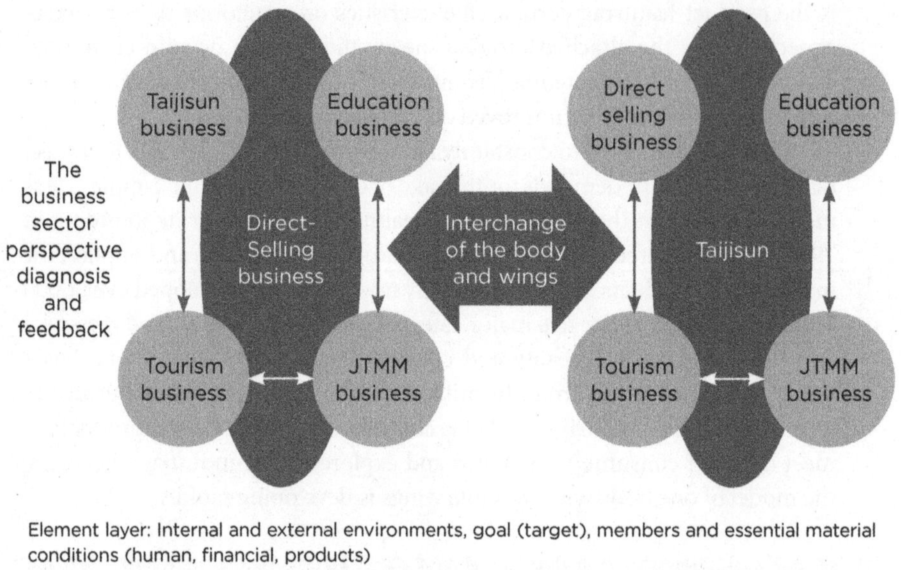

Figure 11-1 One Body with Multiple Wings Structure Diagram

As seen from Figure 11-1, different business sectors constitute the structure of one body with multiple wings, with one business as the one body and other businesses as the multiple wings. The body and wings may have their positions interchanged if the business perspective changes. In this case, a certain wing in multiple wings turns into the body. and the original body will become a wing in multiple wings.

However, regardless of the changes of the body and wings, the internal and external environments, the goal (target), members (business sectors) and essential material conditions (human, financial, product) are always the basic elements of one body with multiple wings. The only difference lies in the different manifestations of these elements in the case of different business sectors that make up the body or wings. The relations among resource networks, business entities and customers in the business sectors of one body with multiple wings are listed in Table 11-2.

Business sectors		Direct selling	Comprehensive health	Education & training	Tourism	Social e-commerce platform
Special resource networks		Global human resources and marketing network Global barter network Global membership points network Global training network	Global comprehensive health network	Global education and training network	Global tourism network	Social e-commerce network
Business entities		Direct-Selling enterprises Distributors	Comprehensive health enterprise of the Direct-Selling group	Education and training enterprise of the Direct-Selling group	Tourism enterprise of the Direct-Selling group	Platform operator Partners (merchants)
Customers	One's own	Director sellers Pure consumers	Comprehensive health demand customers Direct sellers	Operators	Ordinary tourists	Ordinary consumers
	Sharing	Comprehensive health Tourism E-commerce platform Education and training	Direct selling Tourism E-commerce Direct-Selling platform	Direct-Selling training Tourism training E-commerce Direct-Selling platform Education training	Direct selling Taijisun E-commerce Direct-Selling platform Education training	Direct selling Taijisun E-commerce Direct-Selling platform Education training

It can be seen from Table 11-2 that different business sectors have their own resource networks. Business entities vary in different business sectors. Some effective resources (such as effective customer resources) of one business sector may be shared in other business sectors.

Table 11-2 Resource Networks, Business Entities and Customers in One Body with Multiple Wings

SECTION 3
SELECTION OF STRUCTURAL ELEMENTS OF ONE BODY WITH MULTIPLE WINGS

I. Principles for the Selection of One Body with Multiple Wings Structural Elements

Structural elements of one body with multiple wings are the business sectors that constitute one body with multiple wings. When choosing the business sectors for one body with multiple wings, the following principles will be observed.

1. Evident Competitive Advantage

The business sectors as a part of the one body or multiple wings will embrace a stronger ability to acquire resources compared with other business sectors, enjoy an evident advantage in resource allocation and have a stronger value creating ability. Therefore, they can constantly convert resources into competitiveness and turn potential advantages into competitive edges, so as to develop and grow despite fierce competition.

2. Great Demand Elasticity

Market demand is regarded as one of the essential conditions for the existence, development and prosperity of the business sectors of one body with multiple wings. The business sectors as a part of one body with multiple wings must enjoy a large and stable market capacity at home and abroad. They will adhere to the basic principle of 'maximum income elasticity' of demand. In other words, the income elasticity of demand of products will be no lower than one.

3. Advanced Technologies

The business sectors as a part of one body with multiple wings must place special emphasis on the role of technological progress. The business sectors selected will reflect the major development direction and trend of technological progress and absorb advanced technologies rapidly, thus to improve the labour efficiency of these sectors, increase the technology added value of the products and win advantages in market competition.

4. Strong Relevance

The selected business sectors as either the body or the wing will be closely associated with other sectors and will drive their development. In this way, the body and wings in this model can mutually promote the development of each other. The relevance among the body and wings is essentially a structural status in terms of technological structure, product demand structure and resource structure among different business sectors. The relevance among the body and wings refers to the degree of diffusion of the technological structure, product demand structure and resource structure among different business sectors as well as the intensity of their mutual dependence and mutual promotion.

II. Selection of Business Sectors in One Body with Multiple Wings by Means of the BCG Matrix

The BCG Matrix can be applied to the selection of business sectors of one body with multiple wings. Generally, the product structure is decided by two basic factors: the market attraction and enterprise strength. The market attraction includes the growth rate of the enterprise's sales volume (amount), the strength of competitors and the profit level. Among them, the sales growth rate is the most important comprehensive indicator and reflects the market attraction. The enterprise strength manifests as the market share, technology, equipment and capital utilization capability, among which the market share is the internal element that determines the enterprise's product structure and directly reveals its competitiveness.

As shown in Figure 11-2, the interaction of the above two elements results in four different product (business sector) types that sees different prospects: (1) the business sector of high sales growth rate and high market share (stars); (2) the business sector of low sales growth rate and low market share (dogs); (3) the business sector of high sales growth rate and low market share (question marks); and (4) the business sector of low sales growth rate and high market share (cash cows).

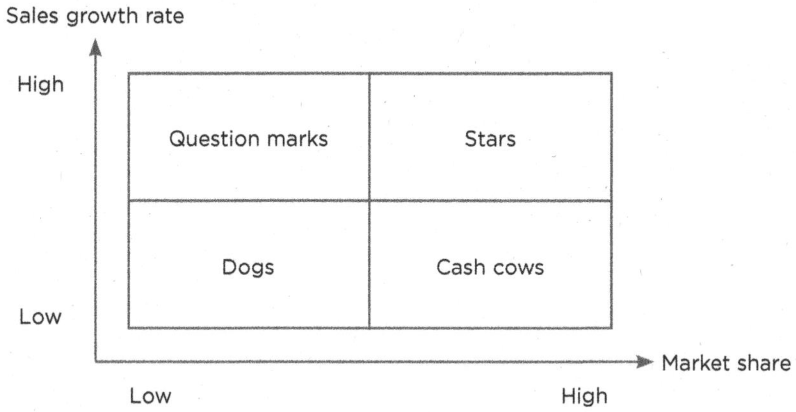

Figure 11-2 Matrix for Business Sector Selection of One Body with Multiple Wings

III. Selection of Business Sectors of One Body with Multiple Wings

Different measures will be adopted for different sectors.

1. Stars. They are located in the quadrant of high growth rate and high market share. These businesses may become the cash cows in the one body with multiple wings, so investment will be increased to support their rapid development.

2. Cash cows. Also known as the substantial-profit businesses, they are in a quadrant of low growth rate and high market share, suggesting that they have entered a maturation period. They are the source of the enterprise's cash, and investment increase is not needed due to their low growth rate.

3. Question marks. They are in a quadrant of high growth rate and low market share. The high growth rate suggests great market potential and good prospects, while the low market share points to problems of marketing. Hence, the improvement program of question marks is generally incorporated in the long-term plan.

4. Dogs. Also known as the declining businesses, they are in a quadrant of low growth rate and low market share. As the first measure, these businesses will be reduced and then be withdrawn. The businesses of extremely low sales growth rate and market share will be immediately eliminated. Second, the surplus resources will be transferred to other business sectors.

CHAPTER 12

INTERNAL AND EXTERNAL ENVIRONMENTS FOR THE DEVELOPMENT OF ONE BODY WITH MULTIPLE WINGS

The development model of one body with multiple wings is created in certain internal and external environments. By analysing the external environment such as the economic environment, market environment and legal environment, this chapter will explain the influence of direct selling, effective incentives and product lines inside the enterprise on the emergence and development of the model of one body with multiple wings and offer a theoretical basis for the enterprise's selection of development models.

SECTION 1
EXTERNAL ENVIRONMENT FOR THE DEVELOPMENT OF ONE BODY WITH MULTIPLE WINGS

I. The Belt and Road and E-commerce Development

1. The Belt and Road has Brought Development Opportunities

With the implementation and development of the Belt and Road Initiative, Chinese enterprises are increasing their investments in the countries along the Belt and Road at a high speed. The countries along the Belt and Road have a large population reaching 4.521 billion, accounting for approximately 62.3% of the world population. Though most of them fall under the middle- and low-income countries, the sustained progress of the Belt and Road strategy will necessarily boost the economic and social development in these areas and improve their living and consumption standards. Hence, these countries see unlimited market opportunities, making it a great chance for Chinese enterprises to go global. Chinese enterprises can seize these opportunities to attain great development. Drawing support from the Belt and Road policy, Tiens has further explored its overseas market, strengthened the construction of its overseas production bases in Vietnam and Spain, optimized the construction layout of its global supply chain and actively promoted exchange and cooperation with international excellent enterprises.

2. E-commerce has Altered People's Shopping Habits
As China's GDP has maintained a growth rate ranging between 6% and 7% in recent years, people's living standards are improving and consumption is increasing, driving the steady growth of the e-commerce market. E-commerce has changed people's shopping habits and brought enterprises with the new business (e-commerce). The O2O model has transformed people's consumption habits, led online consumers to physical stores and enabled customers to experience services offline after purchasing commodities and services online. In this way, it integrates the online and the offline, realizes resource sharing and all-round interaction, and constantly enhances users' stickiness to network consumption.

The internet can expand consumers' social range, and e-commerce can break through the temporal and spatial limits. Compared to direct selling that depends on interpersonal direct sales and is therefore subject to temporal and spatial limits, e-commerce runs 24 hours a day. E-commerce can make basic marketing decisions more precisely based on the database, which not only lowers the distributor's costs, but also broadens the channels for business exploration of distributors (partners) and does business online and offline at the same time. Social e-commerce also expands the enterprise's scope of business, leads to performance improvement and profit rise, and increases the development space and incomes. In this condition, the team of distributors (partners) will be more stable.

Special Column 12-1 Tiens E-commerce Platform

In the context of Internet+, Tiens developed its social e-commerce platform. Compared to traditional e-commerce platforms, Tiens' social e-commerce platform is characterized by its interaction and sharing system. In this platform, users can not only do e-commerce shopping, but can also enjoy the opportunity to share the platform profits after their consumption. The platform adopts the incentive mechanism, by which users can acquire more rewards by means of consumption, sharing and communication, such as social media sharing and WeChat Moments communications. In addition to these incentives, the platform also organizes all kinds of theme activities. In this platform, consumers can buy high-quality commodities and acquire the rewards provided by the platform; and the partners of the platform can share common resources.

Social e-commerce can also be considered as the tool of a new concept culture and new media marketing. It advertises on various new media to provide customers with information on product characteristics and sales volume, and meanwhile leads customers to practical experiences and interactions offline. Also, it pushes product information according to user preferences based on big data, to increase the page views and users' stickiness of the platform. It provides high-quality products to consumers including the partners, satisfies member customers' daily demands, thus activates members who are not active and meanwhile attracts more nonmember customers. Social e-commerce makes full use of the network expansion capability of e-commerce and shares resources to expand the market share.

II. Population, Income and Values

1. Population Structure and Size

Population environment refers to the total influence of demographic characteristics of a country or region including the population size, distribution, composition and education level on marketing activities. Where there are people, there are consumer demands. With a given level of income, the population size directly determines the potential capacity of a market. By the end of 2016, the total population in mainland China was 1.38271 billion, having increased by 8.09 million compared to the end of the previous year, where the urban permanent population was 792.98 million, accounting for 57.35% of the total population (urbanization rate of permanent population), 1.25% higher than that by the end of the previous year.

The ageing of a population considerably increases the market demand for health products through direct selling. According to statistics, by the end of 2015, the population aged 65 or above in China accounted for 10.5% of the total population. It is expected that the elderly population will increase by 260 million by 2020 and the ageing problem will reach its peak by 2050, with the elderly population keeping stable at around 400 million for a long period. The increasingly intensified ageing trend will constantly enlarge the demand for health products.

People now eat for health instead of to be full. The rapid economic development has promoted the consumption. People are no longer content with having enough to eat but start to pursue nutrition and health. This transformation of food demand pushes forward the development of healthy and high-quality products.

Social e-commerce consumers are becoming younger. Young people have gradually become the newly emerging force of social e-commerce. In the next few years, two new consumer groups, the post-90s and post-00s, will gradually rise and occupy an increasing proportion in industrial consumption. Moreover, social e-commerce workers (partners) will also be younger with a higher educational level. More and more post-80s, post-90s and post-00s consumers will play a dominant role in the partner group.

In the opinion of the post-90s and post-00s consumers, cost performance and product quality are no longer their primary concerns. What drive their consumption are personalization, consumption experience, freshness and fashion. They are keen on network and social consumption, like entertainment and fashion, pursue personalization and diversity and satisfy their own personalized consumption aspirations. Friends' recommendations and internet word of mouth exert greater influence on them. In the context of Internet+, the younger generation of consumers has become the main force. The products and marketing methods of one body and multiple wings will adapt to this trend.

2. Per Capita Income
The residents' income has sustained a rapid growth. The national per-capita disposable income was 23,821 yuan in 2016, having grown by 44.3% compared to 2012. After allowing for inflation, the actual growth has reached 33.3%, with an annual real growth rate of 7.4%. It is 0.2% higher than the annual growth rate of GDP of the same period, and 0.8% higher than the average annual growth rate of per capita GDP of the same period.

Income disparity has been narrowed and the Gini coefficient has slightly dropped. The per capita disposable income ratio of urban and rural residents was 2.72 in 2016 (rural residents' income = 1), 0.16 lower than that in 2012, suggesting the increasingly small income gap between urban and rural residents from 2012 to 2016. By 2016, the national per capita disposable income Gini coefficient was 0.465, 0.009 lower compared to the number of 0.474 in 2012. The total income gap is narrowing.

3. Consumption Values
Consumption values are considered an important part of the consumer value system. With the constant increase of residents' income and the transformation of consumption concepts, the consumption structure is constantly improved, consumers' emphasis is transferred from quantity to quality and many tangible material commodities are replaced by service consumption. Service consumptions such as food and beverage, culture and entertainment, leisure and tourism, education and training, medical care and hygiene, and healthcare have become the consumer focus. Personalized and diversified consumptions have gradually become mainstream.

III. Competition of Direct-Selling Market

According to the *Regulations on Administration of Direct Sales*, direct selling is defined as "the distribution mode by which the Direct-Selling enterprise recruits direct sellers who directly promote products to end consumers at any place other than a fixed business office." Direct-Selling enterprises adopt the multi-level channel structure, team pay method and personal sales skill training as the support to the sales system and generally hit the market with rapid consumer goods such as health products and personal care products. These expendable products require repeat purchases and are easy to carry and store. However, these are also the main products of traditional selling enterprises, indicating the fierce market competition that Direct-Selling enterprises face.

Enterprise		**Infinitus**	**Amway**	**Perfect**	**Mary Kay**	**Nu Skin**	**Avon**	**Tiens**
Performance rank in 2016		1	2	3	6	10	71	14
Founding year		1992	1959	1994	1963	1984	1886	1996
Product composition		Health food, personal care, household items, skincare	Health products, cosmetics, personal care, home care, household items	Personal care, nutrition and health products	Skincare, cosmetics, personal care, sun protection products, fragrance	Personal care, nutrition and health products	Cosmetics, personal care, fragrance, jewellery, underwear	Nutrition and health, beauty and personal care, household cleaning, fashion and light luxury, home technology
Direct-Selling method		Multi-level	Store + employed sellers	Store + employed sellers	Multi-level	Store + employed sellers	Single level	Franchise, interaction, experience, adviser
Performance (100 million yuan)	2016	270	230	220	95	49	0.5	30
	2015	260	244	225	100	44.5	2	60
	2014	165	287	223	100	44.4	3.5	73
	2013	120	293	174	77	64	5	68
	2012	105	271	135	63.5	26.7	8	26

Seen from this table, most major Direct-Selling enterprises have seen a performance growth in China in general. Amway had maintained high performance but has seen a decline since 2013. Infinitus and Perfect had shown a rapid increase of performance respectively in 2007 and 2010. Compared to other Direct-Selling enterprises of stable growth, Infinitus, Perfect and Amway form a tripartite confrontation pattern and are exposed to fierce competition.

Table 12-1 Some Direct-Selling Enterprises and Their Performance in China

SECTION 2
INTERNAL CONDITIONS FOR THE DEVELOPMENT OF ONE BODY WITH MULTIPLE WINGS

I. Direct Selling Is the Foundation of One Body with Multiple Wings

One body with multiple wings is a development model created when the Direct-Selling enterprise reaches a certain stage of development. To develop this model, the enterprise will become a platform to provide an internal environment for the model.

Along with the rapid development of the information network technology and wide application of the internet, the platform economy of high stickiness has become a new engine that drives economic development as well as the focus of investments and start-ups in the internet industry worldwide. The core of platform economy is to build an intermediate platform to connect suppliers and consumers, match supply and demand more perfectly, and solve the pain points of consumers and suppliers. Direct selling is a platform based on a huge interpersonal sales network. Only with these interpersonal resources can product transactions and service transactions including the basic necessities of life be realized, which is the foundation of the development of one body with multiple wings. In the age of Internet+, this model growing based on direct selling will be innovated, upgraded and optimized.

One body with multiple wings is more targeted after being integrated on the internet. The social e-commerce platform introduced to the model of one body with multiple wings constitutes an important part of the model and plays the role of a new platform for social e-commerce within the model. Being highly targeted and goal-oriented, the platform can recommend products to members and partners, adjust prices and arrange for the website layout to be precisely pursuant to consumers' demands based on big data, and finally attain the goal of social consumption. By applying the internet, it can also strengthen the exchanges between the merchants (partners) and consumers and improve users' stickiness.

Combine virtuality and reality and achieve common and synergetic development of multiple industries. One body with multiple wings consists of both real businesses and virtual businesses. Virtuality and reality will be combined to achieve the superimposed development of one body with multiple wings and realize the synergetic development of multiple business forms in different business sectors, with the Direct-Selling sector's R&D, production, sales, logistics, customer service and after-service departments as the support. Within a single business sector, these departments will be coordinated as an organic whole to provide competitive products and services to the market and satisfy customers' demands. Meanwhile, different business sectors in one body with multiple wings will depend on and promote each other for synergetic development. Other business sectors can make use of the effective integration and sharing of online and offline resources of the social e-commerce platform to construct a market operation model that combines the online and offline.

Share resources and effectively increase the value of social connections. The greatest feature of social e-commerce lies in the fact that it is not only a business model that shares products but also an industry that shares business opportunities. Therefore, the model of one body with multiple wings can make the best of this feature, launch the internet-based incentive mechanism to attract ordinary consumers and turn them into members or partners. Various resources in different business sectors of this model such as human resources, education resources and customer resources can be integrated and shared under different conditions, which can improve the effective use or resources, benefit multiple parties, and realize the coexistence and development of different business sectors. This constantly innovated marketing model has promoted the reform of the consumption model and service method, becoming the engine that creates new profit points and drives economic growth.

II. Effective Incentives and Fractal Structure Are the Core of One Body with Multiple Wings

1. Effective Incentives

The coexistence and synergetic development of different business sectors of the one body with multiple wings model depend on the incentive mechanism of the model. The effective incentive mechanism will promote the coordinated and superimposed development of different business sectors with interests as the bond.

(1) Adhere to Human Orientation and Establish the Salary Incentive System

When formulating the salary incentive system, the enterprise will adopt Maslow's Theory and Two-factor Theory, both of which centre on the personal demand of employees. To satisfy the most fundamental physiological demands and safety demands of merchants (partners), the enterprise will provide attractive incentives and render material assurance for their life.

The broad social connections lay the foundation for business success. With the development of the Direct-Selling enterprise, merchants (partners) can depend on the social e-commerce platform of a high position worldwide to contact more customers of a higher level, satisfy their social and emotional demands, and pursue their careers.

The enterprise has formulated the promotion standards to afford an opportunity for the self-actualization of merchants (partners). They can obtain greater development space if their causes and incomes constantly rise with the promotion. The enterprise has also established the education and training organization to render technological support during the growth of merchants (partners), improve their personal skills and indirectly satisfy their demand for self-actualization.

(2) Scientific Goal-setting

To scientifically set goals, the enterprise has developed a salary incentive system consisting of different levels. It quantifies the rewards and sets each common target with a precise amount, and the reward corresponding to each level is also in a precise amount. There is no ceiling or floor. The merchants (partners) can expressly set their own performance goals based on their own capabilities, which conform to their own requirements and meanwhile satisfy the enterprise's goals.

The difficulty to achieve the goal will be considered for goal setting. If it is too easy to reach the goal, employees will get slack at work; and if it is too difficult, they cannot reach the goal no matter how hard they work as restricted by their abilities, so the incentive mechanism fails.

2. Fractal Structure

The fractal can be considered as a collection where the constituent elements show similarities to a certain degree. By applying the fractal theory in enterprise management, the enterprise essentially regards each sub-system or organ in the enterprise system as a fractal unit, and then simply divides complex systems by the fractal unit.

Organization structure fractal. The enterprise fractal is a kind of self-organization. The enterprise can generate new fractal units based on its overall development strategy and then transform itself to achieve the strategic goal. The fractal of the enterprise means to establish the enterprise's organizational centring on the process, observe the condition based on its logistics, information flow and capital flow, set up the fractal units, emphasize team organizations and parallel work, and realize a flat structure.

Operations process fractal. The operations process fractal is mainly determined by the enterprise's organizational structure fractal. The operations results of the structure fractal are obtained when all fractal units play their roles and are embodied in all organizational levels of the enterprise. Therefore, the structure fractal is related to all aspects of the enterprise. One body with multiple wings of the Direct-Selling enterprise comprises multiple different business sectors, which run different businesses, demand different resources and capabilities, and explore the market in different ways. However, their operating mechanisms show the fractal characteristic and they stick to the same operations goal. All business sectors can adjust their own operations process, to finally reach the goal of the optimum performance, discover the best operations mode and realize coexistence and development of these sectors.

Function fractal. Based on the mutual relation between the one body with multiple wings system and the external environment, the fractal units of different business sectors enjoy their special authorities as intelligent autonomous organizations and attach great importance to autonomy and coordination. In case of any change to the external environment of one body with multiple wings, all fractal units (business sectors) will rapidly respond to the change depending on the enterprise organizations and the coordination of these organizations. They will allocate all the internal resources based on the market rules. Therefore, all organizations of the enterprise show similar systematic functions, and the functions of different business sectors are also similar to the overall functions of the one body with multiple wings system.

III. Product Lines Are the Fundamental of One Body with Multiple Wings

One body with multiple wings is a development model created according to the changes of the internal and external environments when the enterprise reaches a certain development stage. The model is not the ultimate goal. The ultimate goal of an enterprise is to supply rich products through the market to satisfy different groups' demands and thus to attain enterprise development. Hence, product lines constitute the fundamental of one body with multiple wings.

Special Column 12-2 Diversified Product Lines of Tiens

Tiens runs diversified product lines for target markets and target customers. These products are repeatedly and regularly consumed and may lead to chain consumption behaviours for the connections among products. Meanwhile, the enterprise also stimulates its sales performance by increasing the categories of commodities. Tiens product lines are mainly divided into five categories: nutrition and health food, personal care, beauty and cosmetics, household items and health equipment.

Nutrition and health food. Tiens' nutrition and health food consists of two types: functional food and nutrition supplement food. The functional nutrition and health food mainly centres on the core product high-calcium supplement series, including: high-calcium chongji (medicine to be taken after being mixed with boiling water, wine) for the middle and old aged that supplements calcium; low-sugar high-calcium chongji that supplements calcium for diabetics; high-calcium chongji for children that supplements calcium for children; and high-calcium milk powder for infants that supplements calcium for infants. In addition, it also supplies commodities such as a zinc-supplement crystal and Weikang vitamin supplement that helps the body's absorption of calcium.

Beauty and skincare products. Targeting female consumers, that occupy over half of total consumers, Tiens has developed a beauty and skincare product series that meets women's needs, including: the whitening series of cosmetics for professional women; moisturizing premium series and aloe series for young women; and ginseng series for older women.

Household items. To meet consumer demands for daily use household items, Tiens has developed household products including: toothpaste, perfumed soap, shower gels and lotions for personal care; Tiens wool cleaner and Tiens underwear cleaner for clothes cleaning; and fruit, vegetable and tableware cleaner, oil cleaner and porcelain cleaner for household cleaning.

Health equipment. To satisfy the demands of consumers who pursue a high-quality life, Tiens has developed a health equipment series, including a hypotension apparatus that regulates blood pressure, a sleeping pillow that helps consumers sleep well, a multi-functional leg massager and a breast care apparatus.

Consumer-oriented Tiens' products attach extremely great importance to the quality and technological content of products. They have been widely recognized by consumers with their high quality in the market (Li Yan: *Case Study of Tiens Marketing Strategies*, Harbin Engineering University dissertation, 2009).

SECTION 3
SUFFICIENT AND NECESSARY CONDITIONS FOR THE DEVELOPMENT OF ONE BODY WITH MULTIPLE WINGS

I. External Sufficient and Necessary Conditions for the Development of One Body with Multiple Wings

The external sufficient and necessary conditions for the development of one body with multiple wings include sufficient consumer demand, the integration of business sectors into the age of "Internet +" and the innovation of the business model.

1. Consumer Demand

   As analysed above, population is an important factor that influences market demand and market size. With a given level of income, the population directly determines the potential capacity of a market. In general, the ageing population is increasing year by year, and is estimated to reach 260 million in 2020. The ageing trend and increasingly evident 'sub-health' of young people propose a huge market demand for direct selling's health products. In addition, with rapid economic development and a constant improvement of per capita income, people's consumption concepts are changing, transferring their focus from the price to the product quality and nutrition. People now eat for the goodness of food instead of to be full and pay more attention to health, so the demand for nonnecessities is growing rapidly, which stimulates the market demand for health products.

   The change of the marketing method has attracted potential consumers. By analysing the changes of consumers' consumption habits in the current market environment, it can be concluded that individual consumers show their increasing independent consciousness in terms of demand awareness, purchase awareness, brand image, product selection, product performance, cost performance and satisfaction. Nowadays, what consumers need is no longer the product itself, but the products of functional values, brand values, aesthetic values and safety guarantee, as well as the supporting after-sales, customer care, complaints system and consumption incentives. Compared to the traditional marketing model that can no longer satisfy current consumers' demands, social e-commerce focuses on "providing consumers with satisfactory consumption experiences," promotes the interaction between potential consumers and brand products to satisfy them, shortens the process for consumers to decide on the purchase, creates new market opportunities and improves customers' loyalty and recognition to enhance consumption.

2. E-commerce

   The online and the offline can be well combined through the social e-commerce platform of one body with multiple wings. To be specific, consumers can purchase the products they need directly by online order, and then the products will be delivered to the consumer's door. In this way, customers can experience the products personally without going out, and can ask questions to professional consultants face to face. The combination of social intercourse and e-commerce will effectively superimpose social and e-commerce marketing measures to improve the success rate of sales.

   The perfect combination of social intercourse and e-commerce brings new opportunities to one body with multiple wings and promotes the comprehensive development of enterprise businesses.

3. Business Model
   As a comprehensive concept, the business model mainly describes the holistic and systematic character of an enterprise. A business model includes value creation, value acquisition and value protection, rather than only the profit model. Instead of giving up the content of value acquisition, it perfectly integrates value sources, value creation and value acquisition, comprehensively coordinates with the value networks involved in value delivery and value protection and balances the two mechanisms, value creation and value acquisition.

   The connotation of the business model is extended from an economic and operating level to a strategic level. The business model generally concerns the enterprise's products, marketing, profit and process in the early stage, and later shifts its focus to customer relations, value provision and even market segmentation, strategic goals and value propositions.

   Being a brand-new model, one body with multiple wings views things from the perspective of customers and is more open to the outside. The innovative changes of the service contents, methods and organizational forms produce strategic competitive advantages.

II. Internal Sufficient and Necessary Conditions for the Development of One Body with Multiple Wings

1. Stability and Expansion of Merchant (Partner) Resources
   How to effectively improve merchants (partners) and customers' loyalty and retain merchants (partners) and customers is the necessary question that must be answered for the development of one body with multiple wings. The social e-commerce adopting one-to-one or one-to-many marketing stresses on the lifetime value of customers, advocates long-term interaction and communication with customers and builds a relationship with each customer, to understand and satisfy customers' demands to the maximum extent and finally improve customers' loyalty. In the meantime, the superimposed development of one body with multiple wings can only be achieved by establishing an effective incentive mechanism, stabilizing the resources of merchants (partners) and constantly expanding the group of distributors.

   Customer resources constitute the important strategic resource of the enterprise. Therefore, for the goal of developing businesses, it is necessary to stabilize the current customer group, continuously expand the consumer group and redefine the scope of customers. The enterprise can satisfy the demands of customers at different levels with diversified products and more accurately position diversified products with a multi-brand strategy, which is also favourable for marketing. In this way, merchants (partners) can conduct targeted publicity when promoting different products, while customers can easily distinguish products of different categories based on the brand, thus to enhance customers' loyalty.

2. Enhancement of Competitiveness
   By analysing the market competition faced by Direct-Selling enterprises, it can be seen that the core competitiveness of one body with multiple wings is mainly embodied in the products, human resource network, reward system and training.

   Products: Provide customers with better products and services to improve the enterprise's technological competitiveness to a level and assure that the enterprise's technological level meets the demand of product or service innovation. Take the initiative to carry out scientific research activities, improve the technological content of products and raise product prices.

   Human resource network (partner network): The human resource network is the key to enterprise success. One body with multiple wings cannot survive without a human resource network all over China and even the world. Only with the constant development and penetration of the human resource network in different markets of the whole world can one body with multiple wings continuously promote the coexistence and coordinated development of different business sectors.

   Reward system and training: The development of the enterprise relies on the development of each partner. To achieve a win-win goal, this system combines the interests of partners with the enterprise interests and has each partner strive for a common goal, thus to stimulate people's motivation. Meanwhile, the distributors' ability to explore the market is constantly improved through training.

3. Customer Stickiness and its Multiple Identities
   Customer stickiness was firstly applied to describe the financial cost and opportunity cost incurred by the change to other alternatives in traditional marketing. However, along with the rapid development of internet consumption, customer stickiness is more frequently used to describe the relation between consumers and websites and the characteristics of consumers' behaviours. To be specific, it refers to the condition where users constantly and repeatedly consume certain products/services or visit certain consumption platforms, and, even influenced by the pressure to change or other factors, still choose to constantly and repeatedly consume certain products/services or visit certain consumption platforms without any change. This is actually consumers' psychological dependence formed based on continued use, as well as consumers' aspiration to repeatedly consume the product or visit the platform in the future.

   The formation of customer stickiness is essentially the formation of customers' consumption habits, while customer satisfaction is an important factor that influences consumption habits. With a better website or product satisfaction, customers will be more likely to visit the website or purchase the product repeatedly, which is favourable for the establishment of customer stickiness.

Multiple identities constitute one of the most important factors that distinguish social e-commerce from traditional retailing. More concretely, partners enjoy the following multiple identities: (1) Customer: They can consume enterprise products as a customer; (2) Merchant: Customers identify the enterprise's products, system and culture after several experiences of product consumption, become the merchants after training and promote products for the enterprise; and (3) Partner: Simultaneously with product sales, they attract some customers as members and can become partners after having attracted a certain number of members at different levels, who will start to take charge of team management and seek common development with the enterprise.

Customer stickiness and multiple identities are more complex in the model of one body with multiple wings, mainly because multiple identities may manifest themselves in different ways in different enterprises. In this model, consumers may purchase the product or service of only one business sector, or purchase products or services from several business sectors; and consumers buying products or services from multiple business sectors may show different manifestations of identities in different business sectors.

It is necessary to maintain customer stickiness and their multiple identities to sustain the healthy development of one body with multiple wings. On one hand, for customers presenting a weaker connection to the businesses of the enterprise, it is important to sustain and enhance their stickiness, understand their other consumption demands, direct them to other business sectors of the enterprise and promote their connections with the enterprise, thus to increase their identities and improve their stickiness. On the other hand, for customers with a stronger connection to the enterprise, it is important to be aware of their importance to the enterprise, maintain their stickiness, understand their development demand and attract them to be partners, to facilitate the development of one body with multiple wings.

CHAPTER 13

OPERATION MECHANISM OF ONE BODY WITH MULTIPLE WINGS

With its own operations mechanism and development direction, one body with multiple wings depends on diversified superimposition including demand superimposition, product superimposition and market superimposition, and the mutual interaction and promotion of one body and multiple wings for its healthy development.

SECTION 1
DIVERSIFIED SUPERIMPOSITION IN THE DEVELOPMENT OF ONE BODY WITH MULTIPLE WINGS

I. Demand Superimposition

Either the Direct-Selling enterprise or the traditional retailing enterprise must have products that satisfy consumers' demands for the sake of better development. According to Maslow's Hierarchy of Needs, people's needs can be divided into five levels by the order of occurrence and strength, respectively, physiological needs, security needs, love and belonging needs, esteem needs and self-actualization needs. Instead of proposing single needs, consumers always make demands at a higher level after the low-level needs are satisfied to a certain degree.

As in the evolution of Maslow's Hierarchy of Needs, consumers' needs can also be divided into personal needs, family needs, and family and friends' circle needs by the object of consumption demand. Personal needs are mainly the needs of individual consumers themselves, including physiological needs and security needs. Family needs are the superimposition of personal needs. In addition to the personal needs of family members, it is necessary to satisfy the needs for maintaining family relations and carrying out family activities, such as love and belonging needs. The family and friends' circle needs refer to the needs of the small circles consisting of several families, which are a further superimposition of family needs. In addition to meeting the internal needs of families, it is also necessary to satisfy the needs of different families during their communication, such as the esteem needs. Sales enterprises can meet consumers' personal needs through personal products and health products.

In general, if enterprises can satisfy more levels of consumer needs, consumers will have greater confidence in and dependence on the enterprise. Therefore, to realize healthy development, general retailing enterprises will study the superimposition of personal needs, family needs and family and friends' circle needs, to develop products oriented on consumer demands and satisfy the demands of the consumer market. Direct-Selling enterprises can involve consumers in businesses by making them direct sellers and even distributors and provide them with career opportunities while supplying products, thus to satisfy consumers' self-actualization needs. Hence Direct-Selling enterprises will not only produce products that meet the demands of the consumer market, but will also build a complete Direct-Selling system to fulfil consumers' needs at multiple levels.

II. Product Superimposition

Products are superimposed based on the superimposition of consumers' needs. In the model of one body with multiple wings, product superimposition is realized by adding single products up to be a series of products and adding single series of products up to multi-series products. Generally, enterprises only supply relatively simple and similar products with a limited life cycle at the early stage. Enterprises must develop new products against the constantly increasing needs of consumers and enrich their product lines and series, to sustain the development of enterprises, expand consumer markets, improve customer stickiness, avoid customer loss, and then acquire greater economic benefits and social reputations. In the development model of one body with multiple wings, Direct-Selling enterprises constantly expand and superimpose their product catalogue and product series according to customer demand and market competition. For instance, starting with the single product of a high-calcium supplement, Tiens is now supplying a wide range of health products of multiple functions, cosmetics, daily necessities and instruments, leading the path of product superimposition during the development of one body with multiple wings.

Special Column 13-1 Path of Product Superimposition of Tiens

1. From a Single Product to a Series of Products
   In the early development period of Tiens, its product superimposition was mainly represented by the superimposition of health products. In 1993, when Tianjin Tiens Bioengineering Company was founded, Tiens' high-calcium supplement was considered as the only product; and it became Tiens' long-standing star product after it was launched in 1995. In 1997, on the basis of the high-calcium supplement, Tiens gradually expanded its product catalogue to other calcium supplements including hypoglycemic high-calcium chongji, a high-calcium supplement for children, brain-strengthening high-calcium capsules, high-calcium milk powder and sea-buckthorn calcium soft capsules. With the further development of health food, this series was extended to cover a fat-reducing tea, spirulina tablets, cordyceps mycelium capsules, iron-supplement crystals, zinc-supplement crystals, chitin capsules and double-fibre tablets, which can reduce blood fat, retard the ageing process, relax the bowels or regulate immunity.

2. From a Single Series to Multiple Series
   Tiens regards the series of health products as its leading product line and puts forward the idea to maintain the balanced development of health products, cosmetics, daily necessities and instruments. This is the superimposition of the single series of health products to acquire multiple series of products.

   In the instruments area, Tiens launched the 'Xuebao' acupoint applicator as early as in the 1990s, and afterwards, has successively released health equipment such as the Qi and blood circulation machine, hypotension apparatus, healthy mattress, fruit and vegetable cleaning machine and air purifier. In the cosmetics field, Tiens initially launched the 'Poem' series, then released three series of cosmetics (including the ginseng multi-vitamin series) at the end of 2004 and beginning of 2005. Tiens later launched 10 series of cosmetics, including the Magic Gold series as well as cosmetics products with Frenchic and Aprotie as the theme in 2006. Nowadays, the Group is mainly selling the Time Shadow and Celles Tiane Hydra series, as shown in Figure 13-1.

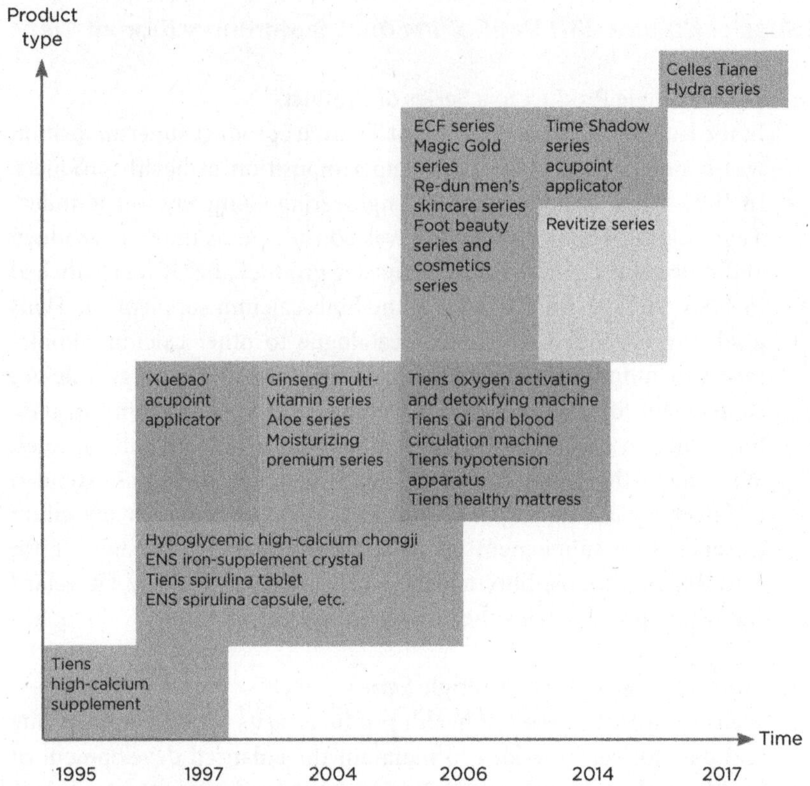

Figure 13-1 Diagram of Product Superimposition of Tiens

Nowadays, Tiens supplies products in the following categories and series:

1) Nutrition and health: three series, respectively, removing excess materials, adjusting the balance of the human body and supplementing nutrition;
2) Beauty and personal care: Time Shadow skincare products, personal care products (woman's personal care, oral care and body care) and Time Shadow fragrance and cosmetics;
3) Easy home: household cleaning supplies including washing powder for clothes and household cleaning products;
4) Fashion and light luxury: five series, respectively, wrist watches, silk scarves, leather goods, jewellery, and scarves;
5) Health equipment: two series, respectively, healthy bedding and household technologies (e.g. rheumatism plasters, air purifiers, energy bracelets and health instruments); and
6) Publicity and sales support: product added value and travel.

The development path of product superimposition above reveals the progressive development of Tiens from a single product of a high-calcium supplement to a complete series of health products, and then to cosmetics, daily necessities and instruments. The process of superimposing single products, including the superimposition of products of different forms and of different functions, and making a series of products is essentially the expansion of original single products. Hence, this series of products can satisfy consumers' different demands on a certain field, such as health products. The superimposition of a single series to provide multiple series of products are expanding the original single series and enlarging the consumer market. For example, instruments, daily necessities and cosmetics are the results of superimposition of the series of health products. In particular, the health equipment series and the health products series complement each other. In the meantime, daily necessities and cosmetics are superimposed to develop the consumer market, spread products to a larger consumer group, satisfy more consumer demands and compete with other Direct-Selling enterprises mainly engaged in cosmetics.

In addition, the superimposition of single products up to a series of products and the superimposition of a single series up to multiple series are not arranged according to an order. Instead, they develop together and jointly promote the expansion of the product lines and markets of the enterprise. Seen from the development path of its product superimposition, after Tiens' high-calcium supplement acquired a certain market for Tiens, the health equipment series was launched. Later, simultaneously with the expansion of the nutrition and health products series, the cosmetics and daily necessities were successively released. Apparently, the product superimposition is guided by market demand and the enterprise's development strategy. After the single series are superimposed up to multiple series, all these series develop together and continue to superimpose products within their own series, thus constantly enriching the product lines of the enterprise and sustaining and pursuing the growth of the consumer market.

III. Market Superimposition

Market superimposition is the way to expand consumption. The market superimposition of one body with multiple wings manifests itself as a development from the domestic market to the international market. Market superimposition is of particular significance for the internationalization of the enterprise. On one hand, after the long-term development of an enterprise, the original market is gradually saturated and market competition becomes increasingly intensified, so the enterprise urgently needs a new market, especially an overseas market, to achieve sustainable development. On the other hand, the enterprise's development is subject to the influence of various factors, and the Direct-Selling industry is not understood by most people. Direct-Selling enterprises are exposed to opportunities and risks at the same time. By expanding to an overseas market, it can reduce the impact of drastic changes of the market on the enterprise and maintain the healthy development of the enterprise. Therefore, after having developed to a certain degree, the enterprise often seeks market superimposition by developing from the domestic market to the international market, to expand market demand and realize the enterprise's development and growth.

SECTION 2
THE GROWTH PATH AND DIRECTION OF ONE BODY WITH MULTIPLE WINGS

I. Growth Path of One Body with Multiple Wings

The process by which a Direct-Selling enterprise sees the superimposition of consumer demand, products and markets is essentially the process by which it grows. The global enterprise in China always leads the growth path of market seeking, resource seeking, strategic asset seeking and a 3L-3E growth path. Among them, the 3L-3E growth path has summarized the motive and process of enterprise growth completely. Based on the LLL analysis framework (linkage, leverage and localization) put forward by Professor John Mathews at Macquarie University, Australia in 2006, 3L-3E contends that the multinational enterprise must put great efforts to globalization, to win more market opportunities and acquire advantages; then leverage its self-owned resources and the resources of market leaders or partners; and finally improve its own learning ability through the interconnection with international partners and leverage. On the basis of this 3L analysis model, Professor Fan Libo, Director of Multinational Company Research Centre, University of International Business and Economics, proposed embeddedness, equipoise and endogenous as the key points for the enterprise's interconnection, leverage and study. In this way, the 3L-3E growth path was created.

According to the 3L-3E growth path, interconnection refers to the process by which the multinational enterprise acquires the most essential and complementary strategic resources for it to integrate into the whole globe. Since strategic assets are generally placed at the high-end link of the value chain, the embeddedness of the multinational enterprise into the global value chain becomes the key point for interconnection. Leverage means that the multinational enterprise integrates with associated parts overseas and has free resources to play as the leverage, to make resources of both parties flowable, transferable and sustainable.

The key to this rests in the balance, the will of both parties to cooperate and their confidence and cooperation attitude. Localization is the process where the multinational enterprise constantly accumulates its experience and finally integrates itself into the local market overseas. The enterprise can accumulate its advantages by means of interconnection and leverage, transform explicit knowledge to tacit knowledge and finally achieve a qualitative change and establish the endogenous advantage. Therefore, the key to the enterprise's localization is the development of its endogenous ability.

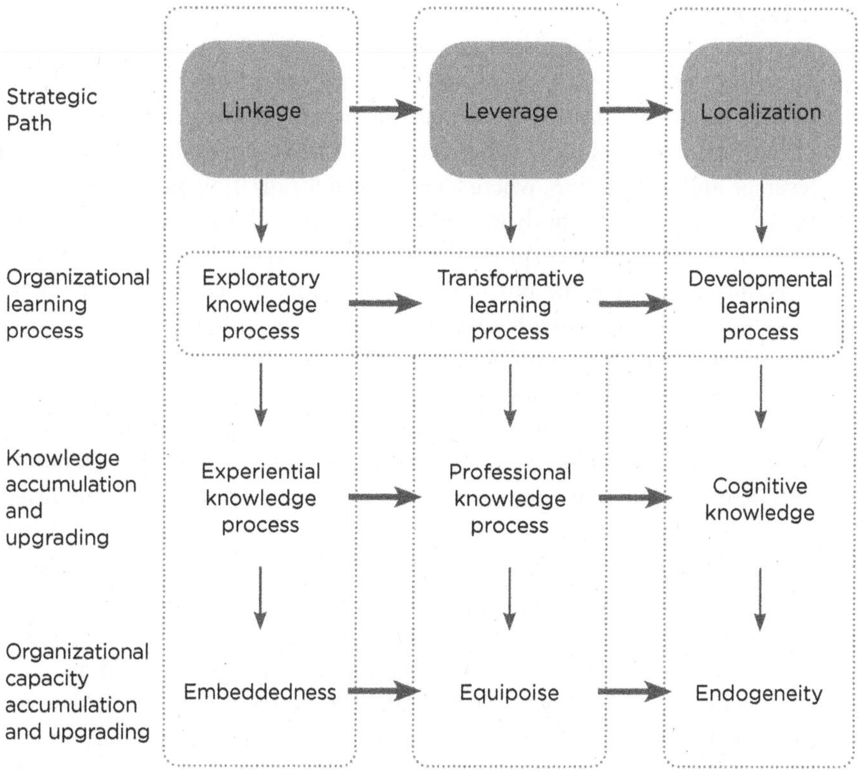

Figure 13-2 Strategic Growth Path of One Body with Multiple Wings from the Perspective of Organizational Learning

As shown in the figure above, the core of the growth path of one body with multiple wings is the learning process. The superimposition of consumer demand, products and markets is the object as well as the result of learning, which results in the constant development of the superimposition. Direct-Selling enterprises study consumer demand and, based on the study results, superimpose products and markets, and achieve interconnection and resource swapping among different product series and different businesses. Meanwhile, the enterprise will perform a new round of learning based on the feedback on products from consumers of different markets, thus adjusting the product strategy and market strategy and starting new superimpositions. This process will repeat itself endlessly. Through constant superimpositions in the one body with multiple wings model, Direct-Selling enterprises will learn more complete and abundant market information, convert their understanding of the market and consumers to their endogenous advantages and finally localize themselves in overseas markets.

II. Growth Direction of One Body with Multiple Wings

According to the 3L-3E growth path mentioned above, the growth path of one body with multiple wings consists of three stages: interconnection, leverage and localization, where leverage and localization are considered as the key. Therefore, one body with multiple wings will regard the localization of the Direct-Selling enterprise in different markets as the ultimate growth direction. To achieve the purpose of localization, the Direct-Selling enterprise will choose the growth direction of one body with multiple wings and determine product positioning based on the superimposition of consumer demand, products and markets.

First, product positioning will give consideration to consumer demand. As the basic demand has been satisfied along with the social and economic development, consumer demand will be superimposed up to a higher level. Whether a product can occupy a large market share mainly depends on whether it satisfies consumers' demands, especially the consumer demand that has not been met by market products. Hence, product positioning will be oriented on consumers' demands, or the product will stimulate the emergence of new demand and will be exposed to further superimposition.

Second, it is necessary to consider other products of the enterprise when product positioning is determined. To meet greater market demand and sustain development and operations, the enterprise must continuously launch new products for product superimposition within a series or among multiple series. When determining the positioning of new products, the enterprise will avoid its conflict with existing products' positioning and prevent any substitution or competition between the two. Instead, the new product will be a supplement to existing products and satisfy the consumer demand that has not been met by existing products. In this way, the new product and existing products can promote each other. Therefore, the product superimposition of the enterprise, including existing products and the products to be launched, will be considered when product positioning is determined. Product positioning will be clarified based on product superimposition, while it will further advance the progress of product superimposition, which will promote the development of all the products of the enterprise.

Third, product positioning will also take the enterprise's different markets into consideration. With the market superimposition of the enterprise from domestic to foreign markets, the variations among different markets will be more evident. In this case, the enterprise can adopt the differentiation strategy for product positioning to adapt to different markets. By analysing the superimposed markets and making different positions for the products of different characteristics, the enterprise can adapt itself and the products to different market conditions and lower the market risk.

Generally speaking, one body with multiple wings is growing and developing toward the ultimate direction of globalization and localization. To achieve this goal, product positioning will be determined based on the superimposition of demand, products and markets. Direct-Selling enterprises can acquire further development by comprehensively considering the characteristics of different markets and consumer demands as well as the enterprise's existing product lines and finding the rational product positioning. When the group of stable end consumers reaches a certain scale through accumulation (superimposition), the enterprise can go beyond in-channel consumption, create new demand, explore new markets, cultivate new wings and then realize model innovation.

SECTION 3
DEVELOPMENT EXPERIENCE OF ONE BODY WITH MULTIPLE WINGS FROM TIENS

I. One Body with Multiple Wings Practice of Tiens

In the one body with two wings of Tiens, Taijisun Hospital International Health Management Centre plays an important part. Taijisun is mainly engaged in in-depth physical examinations, health preservation of traditional Chinese medicine, exercise rehabilitation, VIP private health management proposals and after-care services. It has established an anti-ageing research centre; launched special medical care programs including biological healthcare, biological cosmetology and immunocyte therapy; provided patients with intervention programs; and attracted global network members with its special businesses such as ultra-early screening of tumours, susceptibility gene detection and immunocyte therapy. The other 'wing' is the overseas retail online shopping e-commerce platform, which mainly runs a WeChat business e-commerce platform, overseas online shopping and international trade, supplies services of zero inventory, zero investment and zero risk to offline distributors and meanwhile uses offline physical stores to provide experience platforms for online e-commerce. Besides, when practicing one body with two wings, Tiens also regards education and training as an important support to the strategic development of one body with two wings. Oriented on social demand, Tiens' education and training sector cultivates interdisciplinary entrepreneurial talents who enjoy an international vision and professional ability, combine knowledge learning with practice ability, and have both civilization qualifications and an innovation ability.

To implement the strategy of one body with two wings, Tiens announced nine business measures in 2016: (1) Respond to the government's call of the Belt and Road and carry forward the Tiens culture; (2) Make it easy to acquire promotion rewards, which are in forms of both cash and tourism; (3) Set up special rewards for constant incentives to create rich men; (4) Adhere to new concepts of health and fashion and provide new product experiences; (5) Hold six conferences as needed and present wonderful stage performances; (6) Optimize the image of stores and explore the blank market; (7) Adopt automatic delivery that is free and upgrade the interest protection of the current month; (8) Perform Taijisun precise detection and comprehensively upgrade susceptibility gene detection; (9) Make wealth from family consumption with the Tianle e-commerce platform.

In 2017, on the basis of the one body with two wings strategy, Tiens further put forward the new development strategy of one body with multiple wings. In this strategy, the 'wings' have extended from the original comprehensive health and e-commerce Direct-Selling platform to global comprehensive health, global tourism, e-commerce global Direct-Selling platform (JTMM and the internet), global education and training, and global barter. With health products of the comprehensive health industry as the primary business, Tiens has integrated comprehensive health, direct selling, retailing, e-commerce, healthcare services, education, hotel, tourism, financial investment, real estate and the fashion industry. Various business forms and the primary business of Tiens have made up the pattern of stores-within-nets and nets-within-stores that feature crossover integration, interconnection and innovative development. In the meantime, the change from one body with two wings to one body with multiple wings further clarifies the interconnection and interaction between the 'one body' and 'multiple wings' and makes different business sectors of Tiens more active and flexible.

II. Innovation Characteristics of One Body with Multiple Wings

1. Innovation of Business Concept

Breaking the traditional business concept of low risk, low return and high risk, high return, one body and multiple wings has achieved the swapping of profit points among different business sectors, maximized the interests of Tiens and lowered the operations risk. In this way, Tiens earns profits from one business sector, and earns even more profits from multiple business sectors, realizing the goal of low risk, high return.

2. Innovation of Consumption Model
   The model of one body with multiple wings perfectly integrates direct selling, cloud microbusiness and comprehensive health businesses. All these businesses have established their own consumption incentive mechanisms, which let consumers enjoy economical and high-quality products, reduce consumers' consumption risks and significantly lower consumers' consumption costs through the points and invitation incentive policies. In this way, direct sellers become more confident and assured of self-consumption and invitation consumption.

3. Innovation of Invitation Model
   The model of one body with multiple wings has significantly improved the enterprise's invitation ability, realized the barrier-free invitations among direct selling, cloud microbusiness and comprehensive health businesses and developed emerging markets for direct sellers to help them succeed. Moreover, the interconnection, interaction and mutual benefits among multiple businesses have also significantly increased the contact between potential consumers and the Direct-Selling enterprise's brands and enhanced the brand stickiness.

4. Innovation of Marketing Model
   The model of one body with multiple wings adopts experiential marketing, which orients on the market and direct sellers, adopts the means of product experience and demonstration, and combines education, training, interpretation and experience to encourage consumers and direct sellers to participate in the experience and recommend these products to their friends. This marketing model of high participation is favourable for career-oriented sales and promotion.

5. Innovation of Wealth Creation Model
   Through one body and multiple wings, the Direct-Selling enterprise has achieved the mutual connection, mutual benefit and mutual swapping of various business sectors. It suggests that the universal conversion mechanism can be used for profit points of these business sectors. Moreover, according to the consumption conditions of customers in each sector, this model will retain customers within the enterprise and achieve an income superimposition.

6. Innovation of Organizational Structure
To implement the model of one body with multiple wings, business sectors will connect, benefit and swap with each other, which requires these business sectors coordinating with each other at the organizational structure level by means of business connection, financial settlement and personnel matching, to assure the smooth flow of products, customers, information and capital.

III. Experiences and Enlightenment of One Body with Multiple Wings

The following experiences and enlightenment can be obtained from the practice of one body with two wings and one body with multiple wings by Tiens:

1. One Body and Multiple Wings Will Respond to the Call of National Policies
The changes of macro policies generally exert a deep influence on an enterprise's development. During the development of one body with multiple wings, the enterprise will answer the call of the Belt and Road, closely link its development with the implementation of national policies, attempt to achieve lead-forward development with the aid of national policies and further expand its market and influence.

2. Actively Apply New Technologies
An important characteristic of one body with multiple wings is the application of new technologies. With direct selling as the body, the e-commerce platform and comprehensive health were the original two wings and still constitute an important part in the current model.

Comprehensive health here refers to the high-end healthcare service organization that integrates testing, prevention, treatment and recovery. It depends on high-end equipment and advanced technologies to provide customers with health management services including basic physical examinations, accurate detection, early prevention and chronic disease intervention, as well as medical care services such as emergency treatment, hospitalization, remote diagnosis and referral. For example, the health service program of gene testing is developed with the latest technologies. The application of new technologies in the products or services in different business sectors has significantly supported the practice and development of one body with multiple wings. During the further implementation of one body with multiple wings in the future, emerging technologies will be continuously introduced and applied to attract more customers and collect and analyse customer data to connect with and serve customers better.

3. Linkage of Multiple Wings
   The development model of one body with multiple wings determines the mutual conversion and mutual support among different business sectors of the Direct-Selling enterprise. Through multi-network interaction and interconnection of different business sectors, it can constantly explore potential demand, realize the common development of different business sectors, and enable these business sectors to support each other more vigorously and interchange with each other more flexibly. Since the ties among different business sectors are strengthened, these businesses can direct customers to each other more effectively and be linked with each other more closely. The mutual support among these businesses will boost the more balanced development of the enterprise and bring big profits to it.

CHAPTER 14

MARKET COMPETITIVENESS OF ONE BODY WITH MULTIPLE WINGS

An enterprise participates in market competition and grows and develops during the competition. The enterprises adopting different development models show different characteristics in their sources of competitiveness. This chapter starts with enterprise competitiveness and core competitiveness to analyse the sources of the competitiveness of one body with multiple wings, and then explains its market competitiveness from the perspectives of the value chain, swap chain and ecological chain.

SECTION 1
ENTERPRISE COMPETITIVENESS AND CORE COMPETITIVENESS

I. Enterprise Competitiveness

1. Concept of Enterprise Competitiveness

   American scholar Philip Selznick was the first to propose the concept of competitiveness overseas. He described an enterprise's relevant skills to implement strategies with the term 'distinctive competence.' Professor Spence from the Enterprise and Government Research Centre, Kennedy School of Government, Harvard University, believed that enterprise competitiveness referred to an enterprise's ability to trade in the international market. According to the World Economic Forum, enterprise competitiveness was defined as "an enterprise's ability to create more wealth in a balanced manner in the world market compared to other competitors." George. M. C. Fish, Chairman of US Council on Competitiveness, argued that enterprise competitiveness was essentially an enterprise's stronger capability to acquire, create and apply knowledge compared to other competitors. The President Committee's Report on Industrial Competitiveness of the US considered that enterprise competitiveness meant "an enterprise's ability to provide good products and services to international markets and improve people's living standards in the country in a free and favourable market."

In China, Professor Jin Bei from Chinese Academy of Social Sciences is one of the earliest scholars studying competitiveness. He held that "enterprise competitiveness is an enterprise's comprehensive quality to constantly provide products or services to market (consumers, including productive consumers) more effectively than other enterprises do and acquire profit and development."

2. Content of Enterprise Competitiveness
Enterprise competitiveness as a concept only exists in a market economy. Since enterprise competitiveness involves industries in a competitive and open market, there is no so-called enterprise competitiveness in a monopolistic and closed market. The essence of enterprise competitiveness is the productivity (or working efficiency) of an enterprise compared to other enterprises. It manifests itself in two ways: the consumer value (market share and consumer satisfaction) and the enterprise's self-interest (profit and development). These two points are indispensable to each other. From a dynamic and long-term perspective, these two share great similarities. Enterprise competitiveness determines the long-term state of the enterprise, so the competitiveness is sustainable and nonaccidental. Some short-term and accidental factors that influence the enterprise's operations status may show no direct relation with enterprise competitiveness, though these factors may exert influence on the basis of enterprise competitiveness. As a comprehensive quality of an enterprise, enterprise competitiveness is determined and affected by many different factors which often interact with each other. Therefore, the factors influencing enterprise competitiveness are not independent, but influence on the enterprise's status as a whole. It can be seen from the definition of enterprise competitiveness, which is a long-term determinant for the survival and development of an enterprise.

3. Levels of Enterprise Competitiveness
Enterprise competitiveness is embodied in three levels. The first is the product level, referring to the enterprise's abilities of product production and quality control, service provision, cost control, marketing and product R&D. The second is the institutional level, including the structure platform made up by operations and management elements, internal and external environments, resource relations, operations mechanisms, enterprise scale and brand and the property rights system. The third is the core level, comprising the corporate culture centring on the corporate philosophy and values, internal and external enterprise image, innovation ability, differentiated

and special enterprise characteristics, steady financial position, excellent vision and long-term goal of global development. The first level is the superficial competitiveness; the second level is about the competitiveness of the supporting platform; and the third level is the really core competitiveness.

II. Enterprise Core Competitiveness

1. Concept of Enterprise Core Competitiveness

The core competitiveness of an enterprise is the enterprise's decision-making abilities, including correctly judging the overall situation, making breakthroughs and blazing new trails for competition, learning widely from others, forging ahead without hesitation, and assuring quality and being faithful. It is a comprehensive system made up of knowledge and special skills (technological and managerial skills) and relevant resources (such as human resources, financial resources, brand resources and corporate culture) acquired during the enterprise's long-term production and operations, the unique ability of the enterprise, as well as the combination of a series of skills and knowledge deeply rooted in the team. Depending on this ability, the enterprise can implement one or several core processes in alignment with world-class standards. The core competitiveness of an enterprise is essentially the core competence that is formed by its long-term accumulation and embodied in its essence, supports its previous, present and future competitive advantages, and enables it to gain the upper hand in competition.

The enterprise's core competitiveness can be summarized as the five points below: employees' knowledge and skills; the enterprise's technological development and innovation ability; the enterprise's management, production and operations ability; the enterprise's ability of brand building and brand utilization; and the enterprise's unique culture and values. The core competitiveness is what the competitors can hardly surpass in a long period, suggesting a long life cycle and great stability. Thus, it helps the enterprise acquire long-term and stable competitive advantages and stable super-profits.

2. Categories of Enterprise Core Competitiveness

The first category is core competence based on the view of integration and coordination. The integration view, coordination view, network view and combination view fall into this category. This core competence is the ability of the organization to integrate the enterprise's resources, skills and knowledge, and the accumulation of knowledge. This process of accumulation involves the coordination of different production skills of the enterprise, the combination of different technologies and the transmission of values. By accumulating the core competence, the organization will soon find opportunities in products and markets and acquire more big profits.

The second category is the core competence based on the cultural view, including the knowledge view. Patton, et al. believed that the valuable organizational culture of an enterprise that could not be completely imitated by others constituted the most important core competitiveness of an enterprise; and they also emphasized that the core competitiveness was included in the enterprise's culture and was embodied in several aspects of the enterprise including the skills and technology, technical values and the management system. Kevin Coyne and Steven Hall from McKinsey also put forward that the core competence rested in the combination of a series of complementary technologies and knowledge inside a certain organization, which enabled one or several key businesses of the enterprise to lead the industry. This idea stressed that the core competence was manifested in different abilities of the enterprise in a form of knowledge.

The third category is the core competence based on the resource view. Jay Barney emphasized that the foundation to enterprise success was to obtain the resources of potential rental value, since these resources constituted the most fundamental conditions for the enterprise to constantly gain excess profits. Olivier Furrer considered that the core competitiveness of an enterprise lay in the different decisions and processes adopted by different enterprises to acquire strategic resources. Only by acquiring strategic resources can an enterprise have a unique position in the industry; and an enterprise gains status depending on its special abilities in identifying, accumulating, storing and activating the resources.

The fourth category is the core competence based on the technology view. Patel and Pavitt held that the difference in enterprises' innovation abilities and technological levels was the fundamental cause for heterogeneity of enterprises. M. H. Meyer and J. M. Utterback put forward the idea that core competitiveness was the enterprise's ability of product R&D, production and manufacturing, and marketing, which would directly affect enterprise performance.

The fifth category is the core competence based on the system view. This school argued that the core competence was the organic combination of multiple skills, complementary assets and operations mechanisms that supported the enterprise's competitiveness and competition advantages in businesses. This competence is cultivated upon the enterprise's strategy and structure, depends on people with special skills as the carrier and involves multiple levels of people and all functions of the organization. Thus, communication, participation and cross-organizational vision and identity are required. The real core competence of an enterprise is the combination of the its technological competence, core organizational competence and core cultural competence.

3. Relations between Enterprise Competitiveness and Enterprise Core Competitiveness
Enterprise competitiveness and core competitiveness are two different but related concepts. With regard to competitiveness, most factors that decide and influence enterprise competitiveness are comparable among different enterprises and measurable to a great extent. Therefore, the study of enterprise competitiveness attempts to quantify the factors of enterprise competitiveness to compare the enterprises. Furthermore, competitiveness factors are tradable (or contestable) to a certain degree. It means that many factors of enterprise competitiveness can be acquired by trading in the market or imitating other enterprises. By comparison, the core competitiveness refers to the unique strengths of an enterprise that cannot be traded or imitated.

The core competitiveness of an enterprise is considered as the internal factor that exerts the most long-term and decisive influence, generally hidden in the innermost layer of 'knowledge.' The core competence and enterprise competitiveness of an enterprise may have the same manifestations, like gaining upper hands over other competitors, providing products or services to markets more efficiently, and gaining economic benefits. However, competitiveness factors see a wider scope, and core competitiveness factors are more centralized.

III. One Body with Multiple Wings Improves Enterprise Core Competitiveness

Instead of pursuing merely the short-term profits, the one body with multiple wings model bears the goal to achieve the long-term development of the enterprise. This model achieves effective swap and integration of the enterprise's internal and external resources through multi-network interaction, assures a stable market for the Direct-Selling products and guarantees a high reputation of the products at home and abroad.

One body with multiple wings promotes the core competitiveness of Direct-Selling enterprises, not only demonstrated by the final performance of enterprise competitiveness, such as the ability to explore and occupy the market, but also proved by how the one body with multiple wings model promotes the acquisition of human resources (labour forces), capital, sales networks and various soft resources, which constitute the fundamental elements of the enterprise's competitiveness. By means of resource sharing, swap and integration among the one body and multiple wings, the fundamental elements in various business sectors (multiple wings) of Direct-Selling enterprises are upgraded, further advancing the enterprise's competitiveness.

Competition is full of changes and challenges. With market development, the focus of competition is changing. To adapt to ever-changing demands, the one body and multiple wings model must dynamically adjust its competition strategy to seek new sources of competitiveness. Meanwhile, enterprises must keep making innovations to assure the competitive advantages of the model. For example, responding to the dynamic changes of market competition, the enterprise not only joins market competition based on its own resources, but also establishes extensive partnership through multi-network interaction; removes the barriers among enterprises; carries out cross-department, cross-function and cross-enterprise cooperation; develops steady, favourable and friendly cooperation between the enterprise and suppliers and customers; and shares risks and interests to achieve a win-win situation. Moreover, to satisfy users' personalized needs, the Direct-Selling enterprise will adjust its existing organizational structure, coordinate the commodity flow, capital flow and information flow, comprehensively analyse the market, create new ideas, enter the new field and develop the new market. In the meantime, the Direct-Selling enterprise also realizes network-based marketing, electronic-based transactions, information-based trade and a paperless and automatic office to improve the quality and efficiency of the operation of one body with multiple wings and to establish itself in an invincible position in the fierce market competition.

In the development model of one body with multiple wings, Direct-Selling enterprises constantly advance theoretical, institutional, technological and cultural innovation to guide enterprise development with theoretical innovation, safeguard distributors' and sellers' interests with institutional innovation, protect consumers' health with technological innovation and create the enterprise brand with cultural innovation. In this way, it can improve the core competitiveness of Direct-Selling enterprises and achieve their rapid growth and transcendental development.

SECTION 2
SOURCES OF COMPETITIVENESS OF ONE BODY WITH MULTIPLE WINGS

I. Fundamental Internal Sources of Competitiveness

Enterprise competitiveness refers to an enterprise's power to compete in the market. The competition among enterprises is essentially the battle for consumers and market share, the result of which is determined by consumers' selections of products and services. Therefore, the internal source for enterprise competitiveness is the competitive power of products and services, including the price, cost and quality of the products, the product brand, the differences in product structures and how the services satisfy customers.

1. Price and Cost
   Since a consumer is an economically rational person, price is an important factor that influences on consumers' selection of products. Commodities show price elasticity of demand. For the same product in the same market, the product of the lower price enjoys a higher competitive power if all other factors are consistent. Microeconomics assume that the sales of commodities rise along with the drop of the price, which is concluded from general facts in real life. Therefore, when the enterprises of the same business sell the same products in the same market, the sales price makes up one source for the difference of enterprise competitiveness.

   The cost is the foundation to the price, and meanwhile determines whether the product enjoys a competitive price and profitability. From the perspective of either the consumers' selection or the enterprise's profit, the cost advantage has always been the fundamental source for enterprise competitiveness. The enterprise of a lower cost will attract more consumers and earn more than the industrial average level even without other competitive advantages.

   In the model of one body with multiple wings, the enterprise shares resources through multi-network interaction, improves the efficiency of resource integration by new swapping, shortens the development cycle of technologies and new products, has advantages of elements complement each other, rapidly forms a scale economy, lowers the operating cost and improves its comprehensive competitiveness.

2. Product Quality
   Quality is a functional element of the enterprise competitive sources. Quality is the fundamental premise of the market exchange of commodities as well as the decisive factor of the enterprise's value realization. The commodities produced under the worst conditions, the inferior products, can only adjust the market value when demand exceeds supply; while the commodities produced under the best conditions, the superior products, can adjust the market value even when supply exceeds demand. Since the markets of most countries of the world, including China, are exposed to oversupply, the production price of the commodity is determined by the high-quality commodity. In other words, the enterprises failing to provide high-quality commodities to markets are not competitive at all.

   Nowadays, excellent enterprises at home and abroad place one of their important strategies on improving the quality of products and services. Japanese enterprises have achieved success globally for their high-quality products. In the meantime, most consumers can no longer tolerate products of medium quality but become pickier. To win and maintain advantages in competition, enterprises must implement total quality control (TQC). TQC refers to the enterprise's extensive and organizational management over the whole process of reproduction and over products and services, thus constantly improving the quality. For example, Tiens has won the trust of over 40 million families from more than 190 countries and regions of the world by means of the strict control of raw materials and the application of several food safety and quality control system certifications, supplying customers with a green, healthy, natural, high-tech and high-quality fashion life.

3. Product Differentiation
   In an economic sense, differentiation is to create scarcity, the scarcity in terms of the enterprise's product manufacturing or management in a market structure of supply-demand balance or oversupply that distinguishes an enterprise from other competitors. In this way, it produces 'local short supply' that enables products to enjoy a competitive advantage and win innovative excess value. The enterprises with competitive advantages generally show strong differentiation capabilities, or we can say that the differentiation capabilities make the enterprises stick out from all competitors. While assuring the low cost, high quality, and good brand and service, the enterprise will work hard to create differentiation. To be specific, the enterprise will realize differentiation through product differentiation, service differentiation, personnel differentiation, channel differentiation, image differentiation and some other ways.

   Adopting multi-network interaction, one body with multiple wings and new swap, Direct-Selling enterprises can not only acquire new technologies and new products more rapidly, but also integrate resources and markets at a lower cost in a wider range and further optimize and integrate the corporate culture and business operations models. By doing this, they can provide more differentiated products or services to market and cultivate new differentiation advantages quickly.

4. Brand
   The brand is an important source of enterprise competitiveness. Good enterprises around the world, in addition to product manufacturing, own the ability to create, maintain, protect and develop their brands. The American Marketing Association defines brand as: "Brand is a name, term, sign, symbol or design, or their combination, which is used to identify the product or service of a single seller or a group of sellers and to distinguish the product or service from that of competitors." Excellent brands will bring the enterprise with competitive advantages: (1) The enterprise can reduce the marketing cost based on high brand awareness and customers' loyalty to the brand; (2) As customers expect distributors to run the brand, the enterprise can bargain with distributors better; (3) The product of the brand can be sold at a higher price due to the high brand awareness; (4) The brand can

be more easily developed considering the great brand reputation; and (5) In fierce price competition, the brand can somehow protect the enterprise. Therefore, as an intangible asset, the brand assures the competitive advantages of suppliers, consumers and competitors.

Through multi-network interaction, one body with multiple wings and new swap, Direct-Selling enterprises will seize the market first, increase the brand value and enhance customers' loyalty. For example, Tiens has carried out the exploration of 'reverse branding,' by which Tiens swaps its brand for high-quality products produced by other enterprises that comply with the technological and quality requirements of Tiens, puts the Tiens brand on these products and releases them to the market for unified sales through the domestic and international marketing network of Tiens. Reverse branding assists the enterprise in rapidly increasing its product varieties and seizing the market. Meanwhile, Tiens has built a favourable brand image by charity activities and honest operations.

5. Core Competence

Core competence is the minimum unit for the analysis of an enterprise. It is neither a single person, nor organizational unit (or team) consisting of two or more people organized based on certain rules for a certain purpose, nor other 'material' or 'social' factors, but reflects the essential capability of an enterprise. Though the competence difference is an abstract concept, it helps the in-depth analysis of an enterprise. The enterprise's competences can be divided into different types, such as the general competence and special competence, organizational competence and social competence, technology competence, market expansion competence and management competence, while each competence can be further sub-divided. Secondly, the core competence is the most important resource or asset of an enterprise. The enterprise competence can clearly define the activities that an enterprise can undertake and handle internally, and the core competence determines the business scope of an enterprise, especially the breadth and depth of the enterprise's diversified businesses. The excessive pursuit of nonrelated diversity may result in the lack of the core competence. Thirdly, the difference in the enterprise's core competence decides the difference in the enterprise's efficiency. The difference in the efficiency determines the difference of the enterprise's income.

As the foundation for the long-term competitive advantage of an enterprise, the core competence will feature the following characteristics: (1) Value superiority. The core competence will improve enterprise efficiency and make the enterprise more excellent than competitors in value creation and cost reduction. (2) Heterogeneity. The core competence of an enterprise will be unique and the key to the enterprise's success. The heterogeneity of core competences determines the heterogeneity among enterprises as well as their differences in efficiency. (3) Nonreplicability. The core competence is generated upon accumulation during the long-term production and operations of an enterprise and deeply integrates the special composition and experience of the enterprise, making it nonreplicable. (4) Nontradability. The core competence accompanies special enterprises. It can be perceived but cannot be traded in the market like other production factors. (5) Hard to replace. Compared to other enterprise resources, the core competence is less threatened by substitutes.

An enterprise adheres to the long-term fundamental strategy of accumulating, maintaining and applying the core competence. The enterprise's strategies can be divided into the market strategy, product strategy and technology strategy. Those functional strategies are merely the extrinsic and dominant strategies. In the age of information explosion, the enterprise can only acquire temporary advantages relying on one or few functional strategies. Only by pursuing the core competence can an enterprise remain invincible. Therefore, enterprises set up the dynamic pursuit of core competence as the long-term strategic goal. To accumulate the core competence, the key lies in establishing the learning organization, and increasing the enterprise's special assets and recessive inimitable knowledge in practice.

II. Major External Sources of Competitiveness

1. Economic Environment

   A steady economic growth facilitates the improvement of enterprise performance. A long-term steady economic growth demonstrates the steady business environment of the enterprise, where the enterprise can make a long-term investment plan. The enterprise can avoid the loss incurred by inventory adjustment and risk preparation responding to the adverse impact, lower the transaction cost resulting from incomplete information and thus improve the production and operations efficiency. More importantly, seeding a steady growth, the enterprise will rely less on policies and rent-seeking space, but invest more financial and human resources in technology research, development and innovation, which will advance its long-term competitiveness.

2. Policy Environment

   A steady or even tight fiscal policy and a prudent monetary policy will enhance the enterprise's rational management and improve its profitability and competitiveness. In a booming economy, an expansionary fiscal policy works against the enterprise performance and competitiveness improvement due to two reasons. First, it will lead to the enterprise's excessive dependence on government policies; and second, enterprises may pay more attention to production capacity but ignore quality and efficiency under expansionary fiscal policies. When a steady or even tight fiscal policy is implemented, the enterprises faced with a greater budget constraint are more motivated to improve production efficiency and improve product quality under the pressure to reduce the cost and increase the profit, which will enhance the enterprise's competitiveness. A prudent monetary policy is favourable for stabilizing the financing environment of an enterprise and helps it make long-term strategic planning and fund arrangement more appropriately and implement the investment plan that improves the core competitiveness more patiently.

3. Market Environment
Fair market competition is one of the sources of enterprise competitiveness. Therefore, in an economy more oriented on the market, micro-economic subjects will be more active in orderly competition, and the enterprise competitiveness and performance will be more evidently improved. In the mature market mechanism, resources will flow to the enterprises of higher production efficiency and competitiveness considering the principle of survival of the fittest in the market, which boosts the development of enterprises with higher efficiency and thus promotes the benign development of the whole industry. When adjusting the industrial structure and implementing a strategy of transformation and upgrading, there is a need to not only attach importance to increasing the proportion of hi-tech industries, but also focus on all-round industrial technology upgrading, to narrow the gap with the frontier technologies of developed countries in all industries and comprehensively improve the quality and international competitiveness of Chinese industries.

4. Industrial Environment
The external environment for a micro-enterprise is relatively permanent. An enterprise cannot change its external environment but has to adapt to it. All enterprises in the same industry in the same country are exposed to a similar economic environment. Therefore, the variation of the industrial environment as the external source of competitiveness leads to greatly varied competitiveness.

With economic development, technological progress and intensification of market competition, the industrial structure is of increasing significance for the enterprise's profitability. In a sense, choosing a good industry is far more important than choosing a good product. American strategist Michael E. Porter once pointed out that even slight overproduction would cause a price war and lower profitability in some industries where structural pressure was put on powerful purchasers of fierce competition. In other industries, overproduction exerts only minor influence on profitability considering the ideal structure. According to Michael E. Porter, if in a hopeless industry, the enterprise may produce very little benefit no matter how talented and hard-working the entrepreneur is, not to mention creating a bright future. Therefore, the enterprise will first decide on the industry where it competes. It will choose the industry that is growing and is able to provide long-term profit to the enterprise. The risk will rise if a declining industry is chosen. The important and fundamental factor that determines the enterprise's profitability lies in the attraction of the industry. An enterprise may be more likely to succeed and enjoy greater competitive advantages in a more attractive industry, and vice versa.

An enterprise will correctly select the industry not only when it starts a business, but also when the enterprise runs into a crisis. Even if the enterprise is in the ascendant, it will be prepared for danger by considering how to maintain and improve enterprise competitiveness and maintain the status within the industry and what industry to choose in the future. Theoretically, each industry has its own life cycle, and any industry that the enterprise joins will gradually decline in the future. The existing competitive advantages of an enterprise may be constantly reduced due to imitation by competitors and the changes of market demand and may even be fundamentally eliminated due to new market demand. Therefore, the enterprise will be clearly aware of which stage of the life cycle its industry is in, make strategic adjustments and transfer timely, change its industry, and reconstruct its competitiveness when seeing the changes to the enterprise's external environment and internal conditions. In this way, it can take the initiative in market competition and become the market leader. If only thinking about winning over competitors in the same track without long-term planning, the enterprise will be ephemeral.

In short, in a stable external environment, the Direct-Selling enterprise can acquire a more favourable environment by advancing its internal competitiveness during the development of one body with multiple wings. First, it can help the Direct-Selling enterprise keep a stable mood of operation, perform technological innovation more patiently and cultivate and reinforce its core competitiveness. Second, it assures the Direct-Selling enterprise's sound financial performance and enables the enterprise to avoid speculation and excessive debts and maintain stable cash flow to resist market risks. Third, with a steady external environment, the Direct-Selling enterprise will adopt a business strategy of legal stability, which means to stick to the compliance of business conducts, reduce the legal and policy risk, lower the investment in government relations and prevent policy dependence by which the enterprise will ignore its practical conditions and blindly follow the policies.

III. Interaction of the Internal and External Sources of Competitiveness

A stable economic growth creates a favourable business environment for enterprise operations and management, helps the enterprise with long-term development planning and investment decision-making, enables the enterprise to arrange for technology innovation programs with stable expectations and offers a condition for the cultivation of the enterprise's core competitiveness. More importantly, in a stable economic environment and policy environment, the enterprise can invest more capital and energy in the R&D activities for technological innovation, which technologically supports the long-term development of the enterprise and constantly improves its long-term market competitiveness.

With the advent of the 21st century, human beings usher in a new age of knowledge economy and e-commerce. In this new era, the sources of enterprise competitiveness are rapidly changing and make up new combinations. The R&D of a single factor, the traditional enterprise learning capability and after service capability can no longer satisfy the needs for development. Innovation, particularly the innovation of the supply chain and its management characterized by the win-win principle, has become the new source of enterprise competitiveness. Faced with economic globalization, the enterprise finds it more difficult to increase the investment gains only depending on its own efforts. An important channel to improve enterprise competitiveness is to participate in the supply chain and innovate the management of the supply chain.

Numerous Direct-Selling enterprises have established the supply-chain partnership with first-class enterprises and formed strategic alliances to share risks and interests and achieve a win-win situation. These alliances promise to respond to customer demands more quickly and provide services of higher quality while assuring the same product cost and quality.

Simultaneously, Direct-Selling enterprises can seize the development opportunities afforded by the Belt and Road development strategy of the Internet+ age, lower their operating costs, improve product quality, and supply differentiated products and services to cultivate a good brand image and raise the brand value. For example, by means of a series of model innovations including new swap theory, consolidation of three networks, multi-network interaction, one body with multiple wings, and household consumption creates wealth, Tiens has perfectly combined the internal and external sources and constantly improves its competitiveness, to keep an invincible position in the fierce market competition.

SECTION 3
FROM THE VALUE CHAIN, SWAP CHAIN TO THE ECOLOGICAL CHAIN

I. Value Chain and Supply Chain

1. Basic Theory of Value Chain

Michael E. Porter writes: "Every enterprise is an aggregation of design, production, sales, delivery and all other activities that support its products, and all these activities can be concluded with a value chain." The value creation of an enterprise is realized through a series of activities, which can be divided into basic activities and supporting activities. Basic activities include feed logistics, production work, delivery logistics, marketing and sales, and services; and supporting activities consist of procurement, technology development, human resources management and enterprise infrastructure. These different but interrelated production and operations activities constitute a dynamic process of value creation, which is called the value chain.

As required by the value chain theory, the enterprise will coordinate and control all the links in the value chain instead of optimizing merely one link, thus enhancing the enterprise's competitiveness. The basic value chain model proposed by Michael E. Porter is shown in Figure 14-1. According to this figure, basic activities include feed logistics, production, delivery logistics, marketing and sales, and services. Feed logistics refers to all activities associated with the product input such as purchase, warehousing, and distribution, which specifically includes raw material transportation, inventory control, vehicle dispatch and return to suppliers. Production here refers to all the activities associated with the conversion from the input to final products, such as machining, packageing, assembling, equipment maintenance and inspection, printing, and management of facilities. Delivery logistics (delivery of finished products) are all the activities related to the product concentration, storage and shipment to the buyer, such as finished product inventory management, raw material transportation, vehicle dispatch, order handling and production scheduling. Marketing and sales are all activities that offer the buyer a way and guide them to purchase products, such as advertising, promotion, sales teams, quotations, channel selection, channel relations and pricing. The service here refers to any activity that increases or maintains the product value by providing services, such as installation, maintenance, training, parts and components supply, and product adjustment.

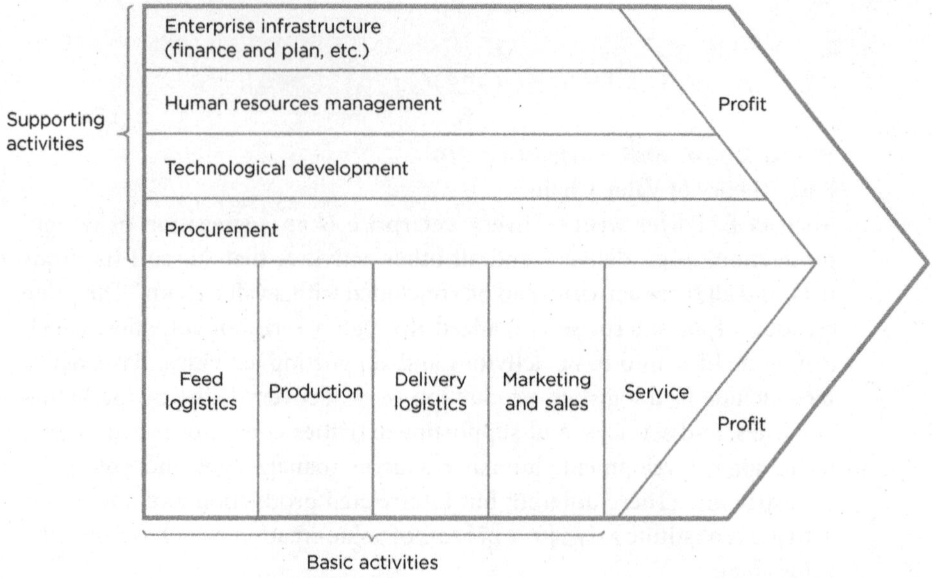

Figure 14-1 Model of Basic Value Chain

Among the supporting activities, procurement is any activity to purchase the inputs for the enterprise's value chain. It comprises the procurement of raw materials and the procurement related to supporting activities such as R&D equipment. Technology development refers to the development of the technological content in each valuable activity, including the technologies manifested as know-hows, processes and process equipment. Human resources management means the recruitment, employment, training, development and remuneration of all personnel involved, which not only supports the basic and supporting activities, but also sustains the whole value chain. Enterprise infrastructure consists of many activities, including overall management, planning, finance, accounting, law, government affairs and quality control. Distinguished from other supporting activities, the enterprise infrastructure plays its supporting role through the whole value chain rather than through single activities.

2. Value Chain in One Body with Multiple Wings

   Most Direct-Selling enterprises are international, supplying varieties of products to and running businesses in many countries and regions. For example, Tiens has established a modern production base in Wuqing Economic-Technological Development Zone, which accommodated multiple modern production lines and several warehouses for raw materials and packageing materials, to produce and sell over a hundred varieties of products including nutrition and health food, beauty cosmetics, personal care products and household items.

The value chain theory of Michael E. Porter divides the enterprise's value-creating activities into basic activities and supporting activities. Basic activities refer to the essential links in value creation by the enterprise, while supporting activities are carried out in each basic activity to support the whole value chain or basic activities. In accordance with Michael E. Porter's value chain theory, we will discuss the value chain of one body with multiple wings from the perspectives of five basic activities and the supporting activities.

(1) Feed Logistics

As with other nonDirect-Selling enterprises, Direct-Selling enterprises have two channels to supply the raw materials and subsidiary materials of products. The first is the backward integration channel. In this channel, the raw materials are supplied by the company's headquarters to assure the 'naturalness' of products. However, the raw materials for other products are purchased from suppliers. To assure the excellent quality of products in the one body with multiple wings model, it is necessary to strictly control the raw materials of health products and strictly assess and manage suppliers of other products' raw materials. The enterprises will propose uniform and clear requirements on the supplier qualification appraisal, testing and assessment of raw material samples, examination of suppliers' production environments, quality inspection of raw materials and regular preventive monitoring and review to assure the high quality of suppliers and guarantee the quality of raw materials supplied.

(2) Production

In the development model of one body with multiple wings, Direct-Selling enterprises establish production bases at home and abroad to satisfy market demands. In regard to production management, Direct-Selling enterprises always adhere to the principle of advanced technologies and excellent quality, adopt automatic production and management computer programs, and cooperate with the data exchange system of headquarters to realize automation, thus significantly improving production efficiency. The enterprises also endeavour to better production quality management, constantly strengthen the philosophy of reinforcing quality management, and assure quality management and supervision in every link of production. Quality control is the foundation of quality management, but the enterprises do much more than that. They stress on the control of the whole production process, strictly control every link of production, and implement total quality management (TQM) for the whole process of product research, development and production activities and relevant supporting processes. With TQM, quality supervision is performed in the whole process of production, which can effectively prevent product problems and provide safe and reliable products to consumers based on the production bases of the multiple wings.

(3) Delivery Logistics

To quickly respond to the market, the development model of one body with multiple wings gives consideration to the importance of logistics. To cooperate with global operations strategies, the enterprise has established corresponding production and logistics bases in different countries or regions, to allocate and replenish goods to the nearest stores. Relying on the perfect warehousing system and powerful logistics centre, it takes only two to 10 days to deliver the products to distributors. Most enterprises use a third-party supplier for logistics, to give better play to their own advantages and have the third-party logistics supplier cover their deficiency. In this way, the products can be delivered to customers more quickly and conveniently. If the customer's purchase reaches a certain amount, the customer can order goods through the internet, telephone or fax. Within two to three days after the order is placed, the enterprise will entrust a third-party logistics supplier to deliver goods to the customer or distributor. Modern communication measures are fully utilized here. As supported by logistics and information flow, consumers can get the products without going out, which significantly saves the customers' purchase cost.

(4) Marketing and Sales

Seen from the above analysis, the marketing network of a Direct-Selling enterprise is of great significance for its competitiveness. In the development model of one body with multiple wings, the interconnection and resource sharing among the one body and multiple wings enable the coexistence and common development of different business sectors of the Direct-Selling enterprise. Customers of direct selling are generally divided into three types: A. Pure consumers. This kind of customer only purchases and recognizes the products, and they are pure consumers of Tiens; B. Companion. They are direct sellers of the enterprise, who not only use the products, but also recommend products to some friends occasionally. They are just between the full-time direct sellers and pure consumers; C. Full-time distributors. They are only responsible for selling products. The latter two groups of customers constitute the most important and the largest customer group of the Direct-Selling enterprise. Recognizing both the enterprise's products and sales model, they are the most faithful customers.

For example, Tiens currently adopts the sales channel of 'store + employed direct sellers.' To date, Tiens has opened hundreds of special stores in 34 provinces, municipalities and autonomous regions, making up a large-scale national service network. Special service ambassadors are assigned to each store to sell products to customers directly. In addition to stores, the large number of direct sellers are also the main sales channel of Tiens. An important responsibility of stores is to serve direct sellers and help direct sellers sell products or recommend new sales companions.

(5) Service

Direct-Selling enterprises and other enterprises vary significantly in their services for customers. Direct-Selling enterprises supply consumers with high-quality products and pre-sale and after-sale services through stores and sellers, and constantly create and optimize customer services. Compared to traditional selling enterprises, which seldom perform product demonstrations for target customers, Direct-Selling enterprises often provide some products to target customers for introduction and demonstration. Moreover, all direct sellers accept quite a few training sessions before the sales of products to improve their ability to demonstrate products, thus to have the target customers clearly see the performance and appearance of products and stimulate customers' desire to buy products. In addition, in direct selling, the best product demonstration is the direct seller themself, as the direct seller also uses the products, shares the experience with others and shows the improvement effect of the product to others.

Based on the analysis of the five points above, we can acquire the value chain model of one body with multiple wings as shown in Figure 14-2.

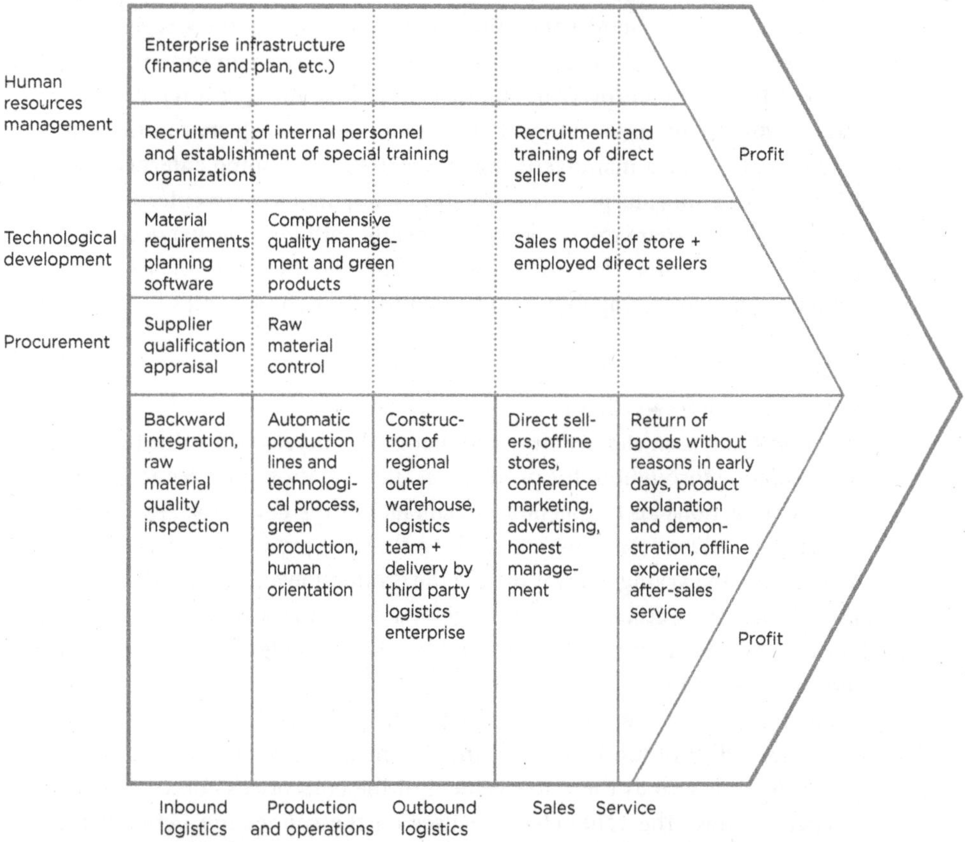

Figure 14-2 Value Chain Model of "One Body with Multiple Wings"

In a word, Direct-Selling enterprises make full use of their special abilities in raw materials, production, product distribution, marketing and services, and effectively implement value chain management inside the enterprise, and thus have acquired consecutive competitive advantages and economic performance higher than the average.

3. Basic Theory of Supply Chain

The national standard Logistics Terms (GB/T 18354-2006) defines the supply chain as follows: "The supply chain is a network-chain structure that is formed in the process of supplying products or services to end users during product production and circulation." Professor Ma Shihua argued that the supply chain was a functional network-chain structure that integrated the supplier, manufacturer, distributor, retailer and end user in the whole process from the procurement of raw materials, production of intermediate products and finished products, and delivery of products to consumers through the sales network by means of the control of information flow, logistics and capital flow.

Pursuant to the practical operations of the supply chain, there is generally an enterprise placed at the core position of the supply chain system, which is called the core enterprise in supply chain. This enterprise regulates on and coordinates the information flow, capital flow and logistics in the supply chain. It can be a manufacturing enterprise or a retailing enterprise. As driven by the core enterprise's information on demand, other enterprises in the supply chain share the work and cooperate with one another according to their business functions and constantly increase the value of the whole supply chain through capital flow, information flow and logistics.

II. Swap Chain

1. Basic Theory of Swap Chain

The swap chain is an effective way and method to increase the value through new swapping throughout the production and operations process according to the endogenous and exogenous advantages of the enterprise. Every link that creates values from raw materials to finished products may see value appreciation in varying degrees during the production and operations activities. If integrating certain links through new swapping, a value-added chain based on new swapping may be formed (as shown in Figure 14-3), which is known as the swap chain.

In the same way as the value chain, the swap chain also stresses on the overall effect of the enterprise, the optimization of total resources and their values, as well as the improvement of the enterprise's comprehensive competitiveness. The value chain focuses on the connection between the enterprise's internal factors and the production and operations activities and emphasizes the optimized combination and coordination among internal activities, to create greater value for the enterprise. In contrast, the swap chain, based on the value chain, pays much more attention to the connection between the internal and external markets and various resources, attaches importance to the influence of market demand on internal links of the enterprise, and advocates integrating the internal and external resources and connections of the enterprise through the swap chain oriented on market demand, thus to achieve rapid development of the enterprise.

The swap chain is created to adapt to modern market economy development and the new requirements of enterprise management. Two principles will be adhered to when giving full play to the active role of the swap chain. The first is the open loop principle. It means we will not consider the swap chain as a closed, linear and single chain, but will be aware of its openness and connection to the world. New swapping can be performed in every link of production and sales. The second is the optimization principle. It means to apply swapping based on the enterprise's advantages, increase enterprise value through swapping and create new competitive advantages of the enterprise. This is the essential content and requirement of the swap chain.

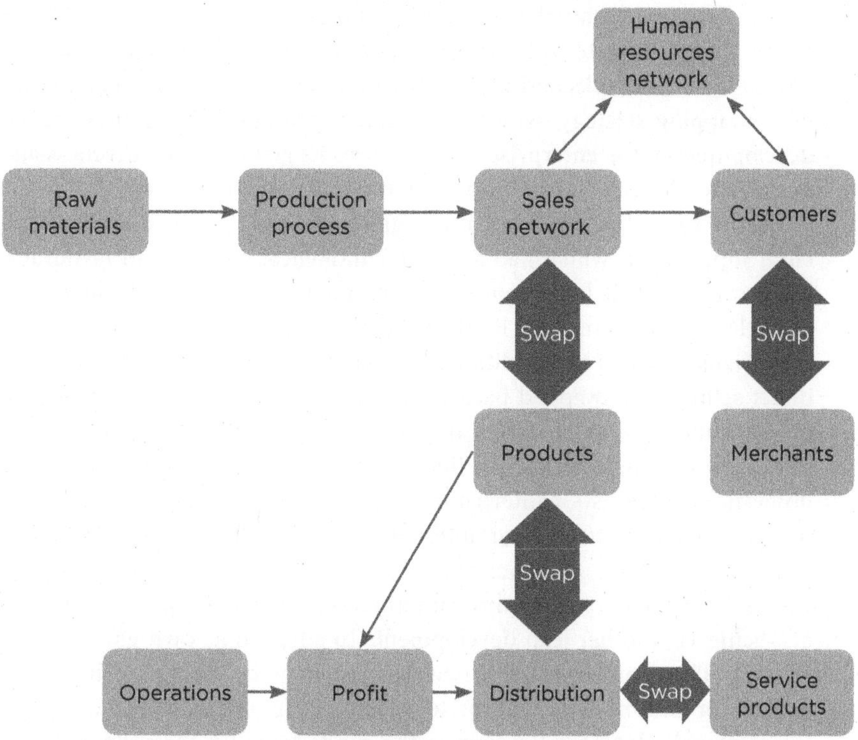

Figure 14-3 Diagram of Swap Chain

2. The Practice of New Swap Chain

As is commonly known, the development of any enterprise depends on the production factors including land, labour, capital, technology, management, information, brand and reputation. The key to an enterprise's success in fierce market competition, and also the smart move for the enterprise to realize leapfrog development, rests on whether the enterprise can effectively utilize its production factors and available resources, perform necessary swaps in a timely manner and according to its development status, and break the constraints of undersupply of production factors and resources through swapping.

Enterprises in different development stages propose different demands on production factors and other resources. In the early period of development, capital and management are often the scarcest and most important factors to enterprise development. Therefore, it is particularly critical to exercise all means to get more disposable funds and management talents for the enterprise. With the growth and development of an enterprise, it will increase its demand on new technologies and new processes. Hence, new and high technologies will be introduced, and advanced processes will be applied to replace the backward technologies and processes. This is of great significance for the development and growth of an enterprise.

For example, during the development process of one body with multiple wings, Tiens integrates internal and external resources through consolidation of three networks and multi-network interaction and implements the new swapping strategy, which significantly promotes the transcendental development of the enterprise and improves its global competitiveness and expansion. This is a typical instance of the practice of new swap.

In the early days of Tiens, it put great efforts to produce its high-calcium supplement, which had a high technological content and favourable healthcare effect. It had been widely accepted by consumers right after it was released to the market. By then the Tiens brand was established. After that, Tiens swapped the traditional model of store sales for network-based direct selling and swapped backward equipment for advanced equipment overseas and achieved its first leap development. With the expansion of the sales network, Tiens pushed the limits of the market and coverage, swapped domestic operations for international operations, swapped domestic business management talents for international network-based Direct-Selling management talents, and constantly developed new products for swapping. In this way, the enterprise realized multinational operations in a short period and achieved another leap development. To adapt to its own globalization strategy, Tiens implemented a new swap strategy by swapping the family system for the modern enterprise system, swapping existing talents for international talents, and swapping the goods trade for the services trade, and has achieved a leap development again.

III. Ecological Chain

The ecological chain refers to the ecological environment where enterprises interact with and influence each other. Like living things, no enterprise or organization can survive for a long time in isolation from the world. Instead, the enterprise depends on other enterprises or organizations directly or indirectly for survival and becomes a combination that shows certain laws. For an individual enterprise, other enterprises or organizations, the whole social and economic environment constitute its external environment. As the enterprise exchanges materials, energy and information with the external environment, it and the external environment constitute a whole process of interaction, mutual dependence and common development. The enterprise can achieve its sustainable development by influencing and changing the external environment.

The view of system and the view of sustainable development are important parts of the ecological concept. The view of system emphasizes that the enterprise will consider itself as a part embedded in the enterprise's ecological system, be aware of its common future with the system members and the whole system, and have a holistic view during the formulation and implementation of strategies. The enterprise's ecological chain reflects on and connects all factors of the system based on holism and the view of system and underlines that the enterprise will give due consideration to the interests of other members and the whole system when formulating and implementing strategies. The ecological chain of the enterprise not only solves existing problems, but also attaches greater importance to the future. In other words, its fundamental goal is to maintain the sustainable growth and development of the enterprise's ecological system.

Special Column 14-1 Ecological Chain of Tiens

Tiens has seized the development opportunities brought by the national Belt and Road development strategy and the age of Internet+ to create its own ecological chain. Through two decades of development, Tiens has built a strategic alliance with first-class enterprises worldwide, expanded its global consumption network to approximately 40 million families, extended its businesses to over 190 countries and regions, and established its branch offices in 110 countries and regions.

Tiens has integrated global resources, realized the interconnection, integration and interaction of multiple businesses through big data and cloud computing, combined the upgrading of technological innovation ability with the improvement of the modern industrial system, achieved crossover integration and innovation development, and built the ecological chain of the enterprise. The global comprehensive health platform constructed by Tiens adheres to the principle of ecological operations and advocates a green, healthy, natural, hi-tech and high-quality life. It has built a top health management organization integrating inspection, prevention and treatment, Taijisun, which makes full use of its advantages in technology, equipment and an expert team, as well as world first-class health management and medical care resources to provide customized services and supply global high-end customers with all-round, one-stop, personalized and high-quality health management services. In the meantime, Tiens has also launched overseas online shopping, swapped for featured high-quality products in foreign countries through Tiens' global network, collected them in the e-commerce Direct-Selling platform, and supplied global partners with carefree one-stop entrepreneurship supporting activities.

With regard to ecological operations, in the path to internationalization, Tiens pursues not only the international output of products but also the international output of excellent Chinese culture. Tiens is dedicated to spreading the oriental health culture, based on China's traditional healthcare theory of "removing toxins from the body, regulating body functions, supplementing supplements and preventing diseases." Tiens also promotes the 'new nourishing' theory that requires nourishing the body, the face and the environment, combines the latest findings and research results of the world in terms of life sciences, nutrition and health preservation and medicine, adopts modern high technologies and sticks to the health concept of "preventing diseases, retarding the ageing process and caring for the environment." Simultaneously, Tiens is popularizing the new nourishing idea to all countries in forms of product exhibitions, community heath concept training and traditional health preservation knowledge classes. The voice of health and healthy travel conveys Tiens' positive energy of health and undertakes the responsibilities of healthy culture communication.

Also, Tiens managers adopt delicacy management to adjust products, services and the operations process. With professional knowledge and skills as the premise, advanced technology as the guarantee, data as the standards and information as the means, Tiens managers place the service providers' focus on satisfying customers' demands to acquire higher efficiency, greater benefit and stronger competitiveness, and control the key links in the operations and management process. They set up and implement precise management standards to examine and supervise employees, apply strict measures to regulate employees' behaviours, assure the fulfilment of responsibilities and cultivate a fine culture for implementation. According to a popular saying in Tiens, "Even when 99.99% of products are of high quality, the mistakes of 0.01% will damage the image of all products. Greater importance will be attached to the 0.01% in a larger production scale." Upholding this idea, Tiens has become the first large-scale health food manufacturer in China that has passed the HACCP food safety certification. In addition, it has also passed the ISO 9001 quality certification, ISO 22000 food safety certification, ISO 17025 international laboratory certification, ISO 14001 environment certification and OHSAS 18001 occupational health and safety certification. It also conforms to the requirements of *Good Manufacturing Practices*. Furthermore, Tiens also respects the different religions and cultures of consumers. It has acquired the Halal certification of Islam and the Shariah certificate issued by Indonesia MUI. Part of its products have met the product standards of the EU and the Ministry of Health and Wealth of Japan as well as green requirements and are approved to enter the markets of over a hundred countries.

As to customized services, in addition to experiential marketing and one-on-one product consulting services, Tiens also provides precise physical examinations, precise diagnosis, precise treatment, precise rehabilitation and precise services to customers through Taijisun, where common people can enjoy the medical care services of specialist departments, the care services of a sanatorium, the concierge services of a five-star hotel and the health preservation services of private clubs.

PART V

SWAP PROMOTES TRANSCENDENCE: CORPORATE GOVERNANCE MODEL INNOVATION IN DIRECT-SELLING ENTERPRISES

JU JINWEN

With the expansion of the enterprise, the changes of the external institutional environment and technological progress, the corporate governance and management model will also constantly evolve. Therefore, Tiens has been exposed to a violent and fundamental swap of the model, which assures the self-transcendence of Tiens.

At the critical moment soon after its founding, Tiens chose to apply the Direct-Selling model in the middle and later 1990s. Since the centralized model where “major power is centralized in one man’s hands and minor powers are not decentralized” works against business expansion in a wider scope, Tiens started to explore the modern corporate governance and management model with centralization as the core and decentralization as the support, which supported Tiens to successfully complete its second start-up. With the wide application of the internet and internationalization, Tiens is faced with great challenges to the corporate governance and management model again. To accomplish the goal of the third start-up, Tiens resolutely gives up the single enterprise ownership model and starts to explore the partnership system to build Tiens into a century-old firm. The partnership system, accompanied by an effective Direct-Selling system, is promoting the new transcendence of Tiens.

CHAPTER 15

CORPORATE GOVERNANCE, MANAGEMENT MODEL AND SWAP

Since the date when enterprise was founded, its governance and management model had been selected. However, from a historical perspective, any corporate governance and management model is not immutable but, instead, is gradually evolving along with the size expansion and the constant changes of the external institutional environment and technological progress. Under the influence of information orientation, wide application of network and globalization, the reform of the corporate governance and management model becomes an urgent task again. The key to the survival of the enterprise lies in how to adapt to changing times and take the initiative to choose the more flexible and effective model. This chapter will summarize the general rules of the corporate governance and management model and its future trend, to provide a fundamental basis for the transcendence of the governance and management model of Tiens in its third stage.

SECTION 1
GENERAL RULES OF THE EVOLUTION OF CORPORATE GOVERNANCE AND MANAGEMENT MODEL

The corporate governance and management models vary in different countries. Even in the same country or region, the models may differ from each other in different historical periods. In view of the evolution of corporate models worldwide, they have gone through three stages, respectively represented by the classical proprietorship model, shareholder model and stakeholder model.

I. Evolution of the Corporate Governance and Management Model

It can be seen from the evolution of corporate models worldwide that most enterprises integrate the ownership and controlling power at the initial stage, then transform to the equity-oriented model where the ownership and power are separated, and finally transfer to the sharing model led by stakeholders. The corporate governance and management models and their evolution models represented by developed countries including the US and Japan have reflected the basic trends of world corporate governance and management models and their changes. Generally, different governance and management models correspond to different development stages of the enterprise. In other words, the corporate governance and management models will adapt to the different development stages of the organizations and new goals and advance with the times.

1. Dictatorship at the Initial Stage of the Enterprise
   In the initial stage, enterprises mostly adopt the 'dictatorial' governance and management model. In this period, the major decisions of the enterprise are decided by the owner. This dictatorial model is highly effective for small-sized enterprises and has a favourable effect. However, as the enterprise grows, with its strength developing and its size expanding, it becomes less effective since the enterprise leader may be the best in a certain industry but is not proficient in all businesses. If the enterprise owner still exercises the sole decision-making power in the new situation, the enterprise may tumble down. Thus, in the later first stage, the enterprise will necessarily transform its model from benefiting from speculation in the chaotic market to benefiting from the standard market, which is essentially the transition of the enterprise from individualistic heroism to collectivism. The enterprise will exercise the decentralization of authority and separate part of the decision-making power from the owner, to establish an owner-centred decision-making team. As an essential requirement on the reform of the corporate governance and management model, the key decisions will be made through team discussion to guide the development of the enterprise in a correct strategic direction.

2. Normalization and Lean Management in the Middle Stage of the Enterprise
   After the ownership and management of the enterprise were separated in the initial stage of the enterprise, the major content of corporate governance and management has become how to give full play to the role of the board of directors and management, how to carry out strategic management, and how to motivate and constrain the agents. In this process, in addition to the introduction of some market-oriented mechanisms and management methods, it is of great significance to offer standard processes and uniform regulations on the fundamental operations and management of the enterprise. Senior managers and ordinary employees from either the board of directors, the management or the functional departments, and production

lines, mostly follow certain processes and standards. Their performances are measured with scientific indicators. Though people's creativity is restricted in this case, the blindness and chaos of employees' work can be effectively avoided. Meanwhile, the standard processes and normalization guarantee the quality improvement of products, services and management.

Normalization will inevitably influence on individual creativity. Therefore, the contradiction between normalization and creativity must be solved by innovation of the corporate governance and management model, which is to transform extensive management to lean management, transferring the focus from institutions to humanity. In this stage, the major content of enterprise management comprises: the standard process of organizational operations; lean manufacturing; construction of cultural and autonomous organizations; creation of the enterprise's core competitiveness; building of the flat organization; and knowledge management and so on.

3. Networking in the Late Stage of the Enterprise
As driven by the American economy, all countries of the world have successively ushered in the age of the internet since 2000. Economic networking is embodied in the mobile connection between people and the internet, as well as the connection between things and the internet, the 'Internet of Things.' Networking and digitization start to show their great influence on the corporate governance and management model.

First, there is an emphasis on the strategic change of business ecosystem construction. The so-called business ecosystem refers to the economic union made up by different types of organizations (including suppliers, sellers, customers, competitors and scientific research institutes) that are interrelated and changing. Under the background of the internet, business competition increasingly manifests itself as competition among the whole ecosystem. While expanding the platform and upgrading the monopolistic position, large enterprises will also simplify themselves and support the platform's efficiency and users' stickiness with more external extensions. Mobile internet technologies can be applied to help enterprises build their business ecosystems, since the networks and intelligence will further lower the governance cost, operations cost and management cost of the ecosystem.

Second, there is the rise of the network-based corporate governance model. An increasing number of enterprises adjust their governance and management models depending on the application of networks and intelligence. The traditional corporate governance model is in a vertical and linear structure, by which the board of directors is responsible for the supervision. By comparison, the emergence of the mobile internet helps the enterprise deliver the internal information to each minority shareholder and even each stakeholder at an extremely low cost. The information asymmetry between major shareholders and minority shareholders, and between managers and stakeholders is considerably reduced, making it more possible for minority shareholders and different stakeholders to participate in decision-making. In the meantime, based on the application of networks and intelligence in the mobile internet, communities of online shareholders and online stakeholders emerge and interact with each other in real time. The mobile internet that breaks through regional constraints directly promotes the modernization of corporate governance. By making use of the technologies in the mobile internet age, modern corporate governance can reduce the cost for minority shareholders to participate in corporate governance and inspire their great enthusiasm to join corporate governance.

Third, we have the platform-based management model. As driven by the rapid development of information technology in recent years, the wide application of networks and digital technologies enable enterprises to realize a network connection, which eliminates information asymmetry and breaks spatial and temporal restrictions. In this way, many enterprises can easily communicate and share information, negotiate, trade, and discuss and carry out cooperation on the industrial platforms. More and more enterprises transform their own organizational structures and management models based on the application of networks and intelligence. They mostly adopt the organizational design of 'large platform + small front end' to assure a scale effect, satisfy customers' diverse demands and reach a new balance between scale and personalization of the enterprise.

SECTION 2
EVOLUTION OF CHINESE PRIVATE ENTERPRISE GOVERNANCE AND MANAGEMENT MODEL

Under the impact of informatization, networking, digitalization and globalization, the operation models of Chinese private enterprises have encountered huge challenges, but have also seen a rare opportunity to surpass Western enterprises. Chinese private enterprises must plan for and adapt to the changing circumstances of the world.

I. Governance Model in the Initial Stage

For a long time, Chinese private enterprises of sole proprietorship generally adopted a family governance model. With a complete integration of ownership and management, the family system is mainly established based on blood ties. This model, with the head of the family as the core and family members as the leadership, depends on personal authority and experience for enterprise governance and management. Occasionally, the enterprise owner may assign other family members to manage the enterprise, and build a network-based model integrating funds, information and management. The participation of family members is necessary in this stage, not only because it overcomes the shortage of funds, but also because family members can set up common interests and goals and cooperate more easily. In this model, the enterprises show greater cohesion due to the blood ties. In the tough time at the beginning of the start-up, family members manage and work at the same time, and can even continue to support enterprise growth without pay. The personal trust built upon blood ties makes up for the lack of institutional trust, simplifies the enterprise's supervision and incentive system, and effectively remedies the insufficient technology and management level of private enterprises. The relatively simple organizational structure is favourable for resisting risks. In case of an imperfect market, incomplete rules and insufficient information, the enterprise can be more flexible in operations and resist risks to a certain degree based on its simple organizational structure, fewer management levels and great trust and cooperation among members. In a sense, the family-system management model is competitive for private enterprises in this stage.

The enterprises founded on partnership generally adopt the governance and management model of division and cooperation. These enterprises often have higher efficiency than sole proprietorship does based on the financial union, integration of the connections and technologies of partners, and division and cooperation in financial management, promotion and all other links. However, with the further size expansion of private enterprises, family members and partners can no longer meet the development demands of modern enterprises with their existing knowledge and management ability. In other words, these traditional management models of private enterprises fail to support the enterprises' development.

II. Transformation to Modern Management Models

As the number of employees increases and management affairs become increasingly complex with the size expansion of private enterprises, the original sole proprietorship and partnership models can no longer adapt to the new demands in new conditions, which urges their transformation to the enterprise system. Hence, most private enterprises in China have chosen the modern corporate governance model of a joint stock system at the beginning of the 21st century.

The joint stock reform of private enterprises mainly follows employee stock ownership, a future stock system and an option system. Most of them distribute shares to enterprise employees, especially the technical and managerial personnel. Moreover, to retain talents and motive employees' enthusiasm, some enterprises innovatively create the so-called 'future stock,' which means to provide some enterprise cadres with some 'performance shares' (gratuitous shares) and pay the share money with dividends from performance shares. These performance shares will turn into real shares after a few years. Another choice is the option system, also known as the stock option system. It means that the owners can purchase some enterprise shares at an agreed price under agreed conditions.

By adopting the joint stock system, it means that the enterprise accepts the internal governance structure as enterprises, so it will draw up the articles of association of the enterprise and determine the power balance system among the shareholders' meeting, board of directors and board of supervisors. In the joint stock system, the investors have their role directly changed to professional managers. A professional manager system will be constructed for the private enterprise to optimize its internal governance structure, carry out professional management and transit itself from 'manageing an enterprise with people' to 'manageing an enterprise with institutions.' It is characterized by the separation of ownership and management, the special principal-agent system in modern enterprises. As to decision-making, the original individual decision-making is replaced by collective decision-making. Compared to small enterprises that stress the leadership of the owner, large enterprises depend more on institutions for enterprise management. Thus, as the enterprise size is expanding, owner-led management will be replaced by institutional management. When institutional management is adopted, the enterprise will operate following regulations and rules and settle specific affairs of the enterprise in a democratic and scientific manner, which reflects the separation and balance of powers in the corporate governance structure. The separation of powers embodies the separation of the enterprise's ownership and management. In view of the further development of social labour division and differentiation of social roles, the operations and management of the enterprise become increasingly professional.

III. Private Enterprises' Selection of the Governance and Management Model under the Impact of the Internet

Since the beginning of the 21st century, especially after 2010, a new social and economic environment has been formed based on the rapid development of the internet. Traditional enterprises may be in great danger of elimination if they cannot transform themselves to adapt to the new environment. In the age of the internet, capital is not the sole factor that creates value, but such factors as knowledge, capability and other internal and external resources can all create value.

The internet was merely a means of communication in its early days, by which information was disseminated through Weibo, WeChat and other websites on the internet. When the internet became associated with sales channels, e-commerce emerged. Later, the internet extended its influence to the supply chain and became 'Internet+,' which refers to the in-depth integration between the internet and the enterprise's business value chain. This idea has made full use of the internet, and it can also be applied to the governance and management of the whole enterprise. The internet can be applied to research, development, production, supply chain and every link in pre-sales and after-sales services. In this situation, with the support of big data, big traffic and a big platform, the internet can be used to optimize the whole value chain and all processes of enterprise governance and management.

In the current Internet+ age, Chinese private enterprises have innovated many new governance and management models. For example, the Internet+ value-creating model is "spending other people's money to do one's own business." However, other people are not paying for nothing, but require the constant innovation of the enterprise's governance, management and technology. In other words, enterprises will utilize new technologies to search for the innovation points in businesses with commercial value and will innovate the channels and products adapting to the internet age. Meanwhile, they will assure the corresponding institutional support by innovating the governance and management model to adapt to the internet age and establish the performance system as a support.

Businesses are always dynamic in the age of Internet+. In particular, the businesses of internet enterprises change very frequently, as new products and new services are consecutively launched. Dynamic businesses will be done with flexible business processes, which will also sustain business stability. Then what corporate governance and management model will be applied in this special business environment? The current models are characterized by multiple levels and modularity, transverse stratification and longitudinal decoupling. The transverse stratification is divided into a foreground level or environment, then a flexible intermediate level and business logic and processing service, then a stable background environment and data and resources. Longitudinal decoupling means the functional modules or the small, cellular and decoupled modules of the system, which are connected by information interaction through standard interfaces. Each module and each level can be arranged in a different software and hardware environment to assure flexibility, elasticity and expansibility.

CHAPTER 16
EVOLUTION AND TRANSCENDENCE OF THE TIENS MODEL

In the early 1990s, Tiens was officially founded in Tianjin. Shortly after two decades of hard struggle, Tiens developed into a large diversified multinational enterprise that leads the hi-tech biological industry. With assets valuing several billion yuan, branch offices established in more than 90 countries, products sold to 168 countries and regions and 8 million employees at home and abroad, Tiens has undoubtedly become one of the best among Chinese private enterprises. Then, how does Tiens achieve transcendental development? What corporate governance and management model does Tiens apply? How will Tiens make correct choices in the age of information and globalization and lead the enterprise to an even brighter future? We will offer some suggestions for the future development of Tiens based on its previous history and the studies above.

SECTION 1
FIRST START-UP AND THE TIENS MODEL

In early 1993, Li Jinyuan, the founder of Tiens, came to Tianjin and registered Tianjin Tiens Economic Development Company with his own funds accumulated from his previous businesses. The first start-up of Tiens officially commenced. At that time, Tiens selected the red sage root and its manufacturing process as its primary business. On July 13 1993, Tiens Economic Development Company signed a *Technology Transfer Contract* with a biotechnology research department of the Chinese Academy of Sciences and decided to give up the red sage root and its manufacturing process. It transferred its business to the production of health products. Tiens' main product was a high-calcium supplement, which was manufactured by extracting calcium and other supplements from animals' bones. On this basis, Tiens further developed a series of products by launching seven high-calcium supplement products, including Tiens' high-calcium supplement, hypoglycemic high-calcium chongji (medicine to be taken after being mixed with boiling water or wine), a high-calcium chongji for children, brain-strengthening high-calcium capsules, high-calcium capsules, high-calcium low-fat milk powder and high-calcium milk powder for infants. In addition, it also produced chewable tablets of a good taste suitable for all ages and a high-calcium gourmet powder as a condiment. So far, Tiens' primary goods were in good shape.

Despite these excellent products, their sales volume was low due to Tiens' traditional distribution and sales method. The monthly return was smaller than 20,000 yuan, compared to the monthly advertising cost of 600,000 yuan, which suggested that Tiens had to spend 20,000 yuan each day.

Tiens suffered from great pressure due to the poor sales. At this critical moment, Li Jinyuan received a letter of recommendation, which suggested Tiens adopt the modern network-based direct selling method for Tiens' high-calcium supplements. Li Jinyuan immediately decided to adopt this unfamiliar method to sell Tiens' high-calcium supplements. On August 3 1995, Baojinfa Trading Company, founded by Tiens, acquired approval for operations. The company attached great importance to the economic benefits of sellers and especially designed the bonus system to enhance the vitality of the enterprise. Compared to the international practice that the enterprise's sales occupy 54% of total sales and sellers occupy 46%, right after direct selling was adopted, the enterprise's sales in Tiens accounted for 52.5% and sellers made up 47.5%, 1.5% higher than that in the international practice. This bold innovation helped Tiens' high-calcium supplement quickly open the Chinese market. Its sales volume was only 94,000 yuan in July 1995, which sharply rose to 1.6 million yuan by September. Since then, Li Jinyuan led Tiens to establish branches in various provinces, municipalities and autonomous regions. In merely 20 days from September 28 to mid-October 1995, nine branch offices had been built up in China. In the first anniversary celebration meeting on August 3 1996, Li Jinyuan issued a call for "stepping out of China and walking up to the world" and advocated spreading network-based direct selling overseas and bringing Chinese health products to all of humanity. This slogan essentially bred the great idea of Tiens' second start-up.

SECTION 2
THE SECOND START-UP AND TRANSCENDENCE OF THE TIENS MODEL

For a variety of reasons, especially policy constraints, Tiens had to build up branch offices and special stores in 1997, attempting to transform its marketing method. However, the sales volume declined considerably since Tiens started store-based operations. The sales volume of Tiens products reached 2 billion yuan in 1997, which drastically dropped to 100 million in 1998.

Encountered with this difficult situation, Tiens officially offered the slogan of 'the second start-up.' On the basis of its original networks of sellers and special stores, Tiens initiated its international network and started marching into the world market. Since then, the marketing model in the Chinese market has been changed to the model of special stores + international network-based direct selling, a marketing model with Chinese characteristics. It varies from the traditional model of store selling that mainly depended on branch offices and the network of special stores, and also differs from modern network-based direct selling in developed countries.

Tiens officially entered the international market in 1998 and had established subsidiaries and branch offices in 86 countries and regions and spread its businesses to 168 countries and regions shortly in three or four years. The sales volume had been rapidly rising year by year. From that time, Tiens had stepped into a new stage to occupy the international market. Tiens has set up its organizations in Asia, Europe, America and Australia, and, it has developed its market in Southeast Asia and Europe maturely. The Asian market is divided into the East Asian region and Southeast Asian region, respectively, with China and Indonesia as the centre. The European market consists of three parts: Eastern Europe, Western Europe and the Middle East; and Eastern Europe is the centre. The market exploration of Asian and European markets focuses on Indonesia and Eastern Europe, which are the two major platforms for Tiens' international market development in the future.

In regard to the corporate governance and management model, despite the rapid scale expansion of Tiens in the second start-up and its entry to the world market, it had not extricated itself from the centralization model favoured by Chinese people where "major power is centralized in one man's hands and minor powers are not decentralized." However, Tiens' decision makers had realized the weaknesses and problems of this model, taken the initiative to accept expert opinions and had started to explore the modern corporate governance and management model with centralization as the core and decentralization as the support according to the practical conditions of Tiens.

First, it reorganized the functions of the group headquarters. The group headquarters should consist of four centres bearing four functions: the strategic planning and decision-making centre, leadership centre, capital operations centre and information centre, leaving all other businesses to lower levels, such as the production centre, supply centre and marketing centre. It followed the method of 'small headquarters in a big enterprise.'

Second, decision-making of the group was classified into four levels, respectively, strategic decision-making, major operations decision-making, general operations decision-making and business decision-making. Strategic decision-making was conducted by a committee convened by Li Jinyuan; the major operations decisions were made by the deputy general managers of the group; the general operations decision-making was completed by the middle level of the group; and business decisions were made by the grassroots.

Third, it strengthened the strategic goal management. Since 2002, Tiens had increased its support to the goal management system as demanded by internationalization. The senior managers of the organization should determine the annual business objectives including the development objective, income objective and management objective in accordance with the strategic goals of Tiens. This objective would be determined upon demonstration and optimum selection. Then, the annual objective of the company would be broken down by the senior managers. All centres, departments, overseas regional platforms, logistics supply centres and domestic and foreign branch offices would formulate their own working objectives based on the annual objectives of the group. The objectives system was subject to a three-level management, which helped in strengthening standardization, consolidating the foundation for qualification, and performing assessment. Meanwhile, Tiens also determined the human resources department as an important support to the enterprise's development strategy.

Fourth, it determined the strategic business departments. The financial and human resources departments were positioned as the strategic business departments of the enterprise, which should participate in relevant strategic decision-making and implementations and support strategic goals.

Fifth, it adopted the 'six-network interaction' model. With the advent of the 21st century, the information technology revolution has brought forth earth-shaking changes worldwide. The internet has reduced the world into a small global village. Any enterprise failing to apply high technologies and advanced marketing ideas adapting to the times can hardly survive. Tiens restructured the essential factors and relaxed control over minor ones based on market positioning, attached greater importance to the international market and kept with the times by constructing the operations model of six-network interaction. The six networks here refer to the human resources network, international education network, international logistics network, international internet, international capital operations network and international tourism network. Six-network interaction was the marketing strategy of Tiens that was practically adopted in domestic and foreign enterprise operations. Six-network interaction involved six networks, which all went beyond the connotations in a traditional sense and interacted with and promoted each other, making up a whole serving for the same goals. Undoubtedly, the model of six-network interaction was a great creation of Tiens.

SECTION 3
THE THIRD START-UP AND RE-TRANSCENDENCE OF THE TIENS MODEL

Seeing the wide application of the internet and globalization, Tiens was faced with huge challenges in the selection of the corporate governance and management model, like most private enterprises do. As early as 2012 to 2013, Tiens had put forward the slogan of the third start-up. Then, what exactly were the challenges in terms of corporate governance and management that Tiens was facing? What countermeasures would Tiens adopt in the third start-up?

Tiens' previous two start-ups were definitely successful, but success did not necessarily mean perfection. If observing from the perspective of corporate governance, we can see that Tiens' enterprise ownership structure had never been exposed to huge changes since its birth. Until now, Tiens was still adopting individual ownership.

According to the analysis above, individual ownership of the enterprises is a commonly seen governance and management model among enterprises in their initial stage, which has its own advantages. However, the reform of this model was an urgent task for Tiens on such a large scale.

First, the enterprise of individual ownership can hardly raise large amounts of funds. Even though Tiens had developed to the current scale, it still needed large investment for the sake of the further expansion of businesses. However, individual ownership is confined to the personal funds of the owners. Meanwhile, this ownership makes it difficult for the enterprise to apply for a loan. Hence, individual ownership undoubtedly restricts the enterprise's expansion and large-scale operations.

Second, investors undertake huge risks. In individual ownership, the owner bears unlimited liability for the enterprise. Though the enterprise will constantly intensify the budget constraint, the owner must undertake all risks. Considering this, it will hinder the enterprise from making investments in the sector or area of greater risks and prevent the enterprise from developing the emerging hi-tech industries.

Third, the effective incentive and supervision mechanism can hardly be established in individual ownership. Though these enterprises also adopt the enterprise system, their basic relations inside are essentially labour relations, so the labour and management have completely different objectives. The enterprise pursues a maximum profit, while employees seek maximum personal benefits. In this case, employees have no motive to work hard actively for the enterprise, show no interest in major decisions and never take the initiative to supervise others. Therefore, with individual ownership, the enterprise cannot implement effective incentives or maximize the efficiency of corporate governance and management.

Fourth, individual ownership influences the continuity of the enterprise. Tiens, born in the 1990s, is only 30 years old now. Li Jinyuan expects Tiens to be a century-old firm. However, with individual ownership, the enterprise belongs to a natural person. Any accident to the owner or to enterprise operations may endanger the survival of the enterprise.

Special Column 16-1 Jack Ma's Venture Partnership

Alibaba firstly proposed the concept of 'partner' in 2009, when Jack Ma announced that the 18 founders of the enterprise would become partners. Since then, Alibaba has officially stepped from the age of founders to the age of partners.

In the final analysis, Alibaba refused to give up the partnership system and claimed that it was an 'institutional innovation' for the simple reason that Jack Ma did not want to lose his control over the enterprise at that point. Why did Jack Ma pay so much attention to the power of control? This could be traced back to Jack Ma's previous experience. In 1995, Jack Ma founded 'China Pages' and put in great efforts. However, soon after he broke the ice, competitors had sprung up. In particular, a similar business under Hangzhou Telecom emerged, also naming itself China Pages. Hangzhou Telecom had abundant money and resources compared to Jack Ma, so Jack Ma decided to cooperate with Hangzhou Telecom. Jack Ma and his team took up 30% of shares, while Hangzhou Telecom took 70%. However, the cooperation soon went wrong. As a result, Jack Ma left China Pages and gave his shares to the employees whom he started the business with as a present.

In 1997, the Ministry of Foreign Trade and Economic Cooperation (MOFTEC) established China International Electronic Commerce Centre, which was managed by Jack Ma and his own team. Jack Ma had 30% of the shares and MOFTEC held 70%. Though Jack Ma was practically running the business, the final control belonged to the government based on the share proportion. After that, Jack Ma led his team back to Hangzhou and found Alibaba.

The controlling power has always been a secret worry for Alibaba. Controlling power is important to all enterprises and seems more important to Jack Ma. By comparison, in Tencent, Pony Ma seems to have no fear of losing controlling power. If Jack Ma loses controlling power, the synergistic effect among finance (Ant financial services group), logistics (Cainiao Network) and Taobao will disappear. Ali Finance, which is the main hope for the future of Jack Ma, will suffer a serious blow.

CHAPTER 17

DIRECT-SELLING MODEL AND ITS INCENTIVE MECHANISM

According to *Marketing Management*, by the marketing master Philip Kotler, direct selling falls in the category of the nonstore-selling model. Compared to store selling, the nonstore-selling model that sells commodities and services saves the consumer opportunity costs to adopt traditional information receiving means and traditional procurement channels to purchase products and services, and enables consumers to purchase commodities timely, effectively, economically and conveniently. Also, producers can directly sell products to consumers without any middleman or retail store, which enormously reduces the transaction cost, shortens the commodity circulation cycle and improves the enterprise's competitive advantages.

In mainland China, direct selling was first adopted by Avon, founded in January 23 1990. Later, Amway entered China in 1992, and Sunrider, the third largest Direct-Selling enterprise in America, joined the Chinese market in 1993, which symbolized the start of the Direct-Selling age in China. Direct-Selling undertakings and enterprises in China have suddenly risen in these few decades. In 1993, approximately 20 Direct-Selling enterprises emerged in China, with more than 1 million employees, and their presence extended to over 30 cities. Through over a decade of development, direct selling has become a new force that cannot be ignored in commodity sales. As is widely known to all, Tiens started direct selling in 1996. Driven by the Direct-Selling model, Tiens has risen rapidly and has become one of the best among Chinese private enterprises and one of the leaders in the Direct-Selling industry. Then, what is the magic of direct selling as a marketing mechanism?

SECTION 1
DIRECT SELLING AND BONUS SYSTEM

There are multiple methods of incentives that the enterprise can adopt. Among them, the bonus incentive that is directly associated with marketing is considered as the most effective in the economic circle. In multi-level direct selling, the sellers earn profits in two ways. First, they obtain returns from the sales of products. Second, they acquire the incentive bonuses of 'organizational development and management' if they recommend and introduce other sellers.

In general, multi-level Direct-Selling enterprises may offer different bonus systems, and direct sellers can choose the system they like and consider appropriate according to the actual situation.

There are a number of bonus systems used by Direct-Selling enterprises. They can be divided into zeroing and accumulation by the discount rate calculation method, represented by America Amway and Taiwan Hsin Ten; or divided into the American, Japanese and Taiwan style by having bonus system characteristics, such as America Amway, Japan Nibbo and Taiwan Carnation; or divided into the points system, generation system, matrix and dual-track system by their design structure. Moreover, based on the cycle of bonus payment, it can be divided into annual pay, monthly pay, weekly pay and daily pay; and based on accumulation, it can be divided into limited accumulation (part of performance bonus) and unlimited accumulation (the whole performance bonus).

Here we will focus on the analysis of the stairstep system, mixed system, uni-level system, matrix system, dual-track system, generation dividend system and T90 system.

I. Stairstep System

This is the earliest and the most commonly used mainstream system among Direct-Selling enterprises. This system sets up many 'steps' for distributors to motivate them to climb up step by step. The better sales performance they achieve, the more stairs they climb and the more remunerations they obtain. The bonuses in the system mainly consist of two parts: the sales bonus, which is the profit from sales of products and varies based on different sales volumes; and the leadership bonus, which is calculated by the 'number of generation' (the performance of the generation refers to the team performance instead of individual performance) and is given to leaders for their organization, management and guidance. Therefore, the latter is also known as the organization and guidance reward. The stairstep system encourages the sales of products, so the liability amounts for individuals and teams are set high. To acquire high income in this system, distributors have to constantly increase the sales volume. As a great characteristic, the stairstep system allows detachment and zeroing and the floating calculation of bonuses.

II. Mixed System

Derived from the stairstep system, the mixed system has kept the promotion and generation bonus system. The bonuses in this system can be divided into four types. The first is the sales bonus. The sales level is associated with the bonus percentage. With a higher sales level, the higher proportion of bonus can be obtained. The second is the difference bonus, which is designed to encourage the recommendation of new distributors. This difference bonus is calculated by subtracting the bonus percentage of the lower-level distributors from the distributor's percentage. It is also known as the unlimited generation bonus. The third is the generation bonus. When the distributor reaches a certain level, they can obtain a certain proportion of the lower level's bonus. The distributors in the organization who have not reached this level will be excluded. The fourth is the dividend bonus. Both the mixed system and the improved stairstep system have designed the special reward that motivate distributors to improve sales. The mixed system is mainly characterized by the infinite whole-team accumulation of performance, coexistence of the difference and generation bonus, and the special dividend bonus.

III. Uni-level System

The uni-level system attaches importance to consumption. It motivates distributors to constantly sell products and recommend other distributors during their promotion, but they only acquire the generation bonus after they leave the level. The uni-level system advocates "equal stress on consumption and sales," so it does not set a high 'team liability amount' like the stairstep system does. Self-consumption is also easier to achieve. Generally, the uni-level system is a mixed system, or combines the infinite generation bonus, quick activation bonus or special dividend bonus, or sets a lower liability amount. The uni-level system shows the following characteristics: more grades, special rewards and relevant rewards to encourage those who have not reached this level.

IV. Matrix System

According to research, this system firstly emerged in the 1980s. Its basic concepts include stabilizing loyal consumers; acquiring higher income from the deeper organizational network; obtaining stable income from the fixed repeated consumption in the organizational network; and emphasizing the mutual help among consumers and having the strong help the weak. The matrix system places the focus on the whole organizational structure and advocates a completely consumption-guided organizational network. Main bonuses in the matrix system include the consumer refund bonus, which refunds consumers to encourage consumers to join in the undertaking (instead of relying on the distributors' sales); and the generation bonus of the organizational network. The matrix system is built on the basis of consumers and sets no team liability amount and a very low individual liability amount. Therefore, to make big money, distributors will constantly develop the consumer market.

V. Dual-track System

Created in the 1990s, this system aims to "develop the organization in two lines" and attempts to make the system easier to follow and copy. To lower the operations difficulty, the dual-track system excludes the individual and team liability amount commonly used in the stairstep system. Instead, it applies the concept of 'infinite generation' and calculates the bonus based on the performance of the whole organization. The dual-track system upholds the concept of 'consumption is wealth' and sets up a direct recommendation reward, which is considered as a trick to encourage distributors to simply attract more distributors. Hence, it is the most controversial bonus system by now. In the dual system, bonuses are calculated weekly in most cases. When the distributors reach certain performance requirements in both lines, they can get the reward. After the reward is received, their performances will return to zero. It shows the following characteristics: infinite-generation accumulation of the whole team; no detachment from the organizational network; infinite accumulation of performance; balanced dual-track system; liability amount and regeneration system.

VI. Generation Dividend System

Distributors get their rewards based on their performance and acquire the corresponding generation bonus in view of their levels. However, in this bonus system, part of the bonuses will be deposited in the enterprise. However, the bonuses are partly deposited in all systems to different degrees other than the grading system.

It can be seen that the Direct-Selling bonus system in China has experienced four stages. The first stage showed the typical pyramid characteristics, by which the earlier participants collected membership fees from later participants. In this period, direct selling was in chaos. The second stage was the zeroing bonus system, which was characterized by the fair and rational income distribution among direct sellers but proposed a high requirement on talents. The third stage was the network-based selling system, which adopted network-based selling and the better of the zeroing system and accumulation system. The fourth was the uni-level Direct-Selling system, which is a Direct-Selling system with Chinese characteristics that suits the national conditions of China.

SECTION 2
BONUS SYSTEMS AND THEIR STRUCTURE

Now we will discuss the basic elements and mechanisms of bonus systems in direct selling below.

I. Allocation Ratio

The allocation ratio is the percentage of the performance bonuses paid by the Direct-Selling enterprise to the direct seller in the total business volume. Once determined, the allocation ratio will remain unchanged despite the different distribution methods in different parts and levels. The performance bonuses can be generally divided into the 'performance bonus' that encourages new distributors to develop the sales network and promote sales; the 'leadership bonus' that is used to strengthen the system training and management and enhance individual and organizational performance; and the 'welfare system' that unites direct sellers and associates their future with the enterprise's future.

There are two opposite theoretical opinions about the allocation ratio. One holds that the higher the allocation ratio the better, since it has a greater appeal to distributors; and the other argues that the lower allocation ratio is more rational, since it will lower the product price to be accepted by the market. When determining the bonus system, the enterprise will firstly consider the allocation ratio. According to statistics, the practical allocation ratio of Agel is 35–37% and Amway is 30%. Like many other enterprises, Forever Living permanently sets different points volume (PV) values for different products, and the specific allocation ratio depends on the product portfolio, but its average allocation ratio is 40%. The allocation ratio of Herbalife is 33.8%, compared to 44.9% of Mannatech, around 32% of Monavie and approximately 60% of Sunrider and Nu Skin.

II. Price and Junior Bonuses

As to the performance bonus, the bonus amount allocated by the enterprise is calculated by multiplying the bonus base of the performance of the current month by the bonus rate reached in the current month. For example, if the bonus base is USD 200, and the bonus rate is 3%, the bonus amount is $6. The bonus base is the business volume (BV), the price of the products sold by the enterprise. Defined as the value or price of the products sold, the price here may be the retail price, the direct-seller price (preferential price for customers), or the 'net business volume' after the tax and management cost are deducted. It may be flexibly adjusted along with the fluctuation of prices. The total amount is in proportion to the sales. When the retail price is adopted as the bonus base, the enterprise will combine the retail profit and discount and release it to the direct seller in the following month. However, the enterprise needs to pay more business taxes in this case, so this method is seldom used. The retail price includes the retail profit and the direct seller's purchasing price, while the direct seller's purchasing price also comprises the enterprise's taxes and incidental expenses. Therefore, many enterprises rationally choose 'net business volume' as the bonus base, which is generally calculated as 85% of the direct seller's price, or even 80% or over 60% in a few enterprises.

Prices fluctuate frequently in the global market economy, varying from time to time. When the price index goes up or down, the sales amount will necessarily change, particularly in international Direct-Selling enterprises, even if the sales quantity remains unchanged. Therefore, attention will be paid to not only the inflation in a country but also the unstable international foreign exchange rate. In this case, the pure business volume cannot truly reflect the practical sales capability in a dynamic market. To solve this problem, the concept of 'points volume' (PV) is introduced. The PV will not change with the fluctuation of prices and can truly represent the sales capability. Another advantage to introduce this concept lies in that the enterprise does not need to alter its commission system when exploring the market of a new country (or region) and only needs to adjust the price and point of the commodity to adapt to local conditions.

This system brings two major benefits. First, it avoids and controls the foreign exchange rate risk in different countries. Second, it motivates direct sellers to participate in the exploration of emerging markets. Tiens is now using this concept but adopts some different measures specifically.

III. Accumulation and Zeroing

'Accumulation' and 'zeroing' are two essential concepts in the direct-selling incentive system.

Accumulation means that the performance bonus of a direct seller is determined by their performance and bonus rate. Direct sellers can depend on the accumulative sales of individuals and the team to acquire the highest discount rate for the performance bonus. With a given sales volume, by increasing the bonus rate of new sellers, they can improve their bonuses and encourage them to be more active. The accumulation system is designed for this sake.

Zeroing suggests that direct sellers can only acquire the corresponding rate when reaching a certain performance level in the current month. In the zeroing system, the profit ratio is directly proportional to the sales capability of an individual or a system. The calculation of direct sellers' bonuses is made based on a certain time span (generally a month). In other words, when the sales volume and profit ratio of a distributor is calculated, the sales volume only includes the total quantity of the current month, and the profit ratio is determined based on this quantity. The calculation in the next month will be based on the sales volume of the next month. The consumption market and profit created by a direct seller in the Direct-Selling model will return to zero after the end of each time span, when everything starts over again.

Through a comparison between the two incentive mechanisms, accumulation and zeroing, we can see that with a given sales volume, the direct seller in the accumulation system may acquire more bonuses than that in the zeroing system in the early stage. However, in a later stage, the situation is just the opposite, since the direct seller in the zeroing system acquires a considerably large level difference and, in the accumulation system, sellers are at the same level and have no level difference. In the accumulation system, the leader at a higher level may earn less money when the lower level reaches better performance, since the bonuses are accumulated by the lower level. In this case, for the sake of more bonuses, the higher-level leader must explore the new market or have the system develop downward and be detached from the leader themselves. By doing this, the leader can acquire the leadership bonus of this system. Therefore, if the accumulation system is adopted, the enterprise will not set a too high proportion of performance business when designing the system and determining the allocation rate, otherwise a large group of people will be of the highest rank but make no money.

In the zeroing system, anyone depending on accumulation for a high rate will find this method works for only the current month. Therefore, based on the advantage of the zeroing system, any consumer newly joining the Direct-Selling model can compete fairly with earlier consumers. Therefore, the major enterprises in this industry such as Amway, Sunrider, Nu Skin and Unicity all adopt the zeroing system.

CHAPTER 18

THE TIENS DIRECT-SELLING MODEL AND ITS SELF-TRANSCENDENCE

Since the mid and late 1990s, Tiens has become a typical Direct-Selling enterprise. We do not deny that as a latecomer, Tiens has learned valuable experiences from other excellent Direct-Selling enterprises such as Amway. However, Tiens is never fettered by old conventions, and always blazes new trails. Hence, it has cultivated a Direct-Selling model with distinctive Tiens characteristics.

SECTION 1
FROM CONSOLIDATION OF THREE NETWORKS, SIX-NETWORK INTERACTION TO SEVEN-NETWORK INTERACTION

'Seven-network interaction' has become a popular phrase among Tiens nowadays. Seven-network interaction was directly derived from six-network interaction, which developed from the consolidation of three networks. This model of network interaction, distinguished from the Direct-Selling models of any other Direct-Selling enterprise of the world, including Amway, constitutes the essence of Tiens' direct selling and makes great contributions to Tiens' undertakings.

I. Consolidation of Three Networks

The so-called consolidation of three networks refers to a Direct-Selling system that integrates the business personnel network, special store network and global website.

In the mid and late 1990s, Tiens officially initiated direct selling to solve its issue in product sales. Vigorously supported by Li Jinyuan, a Direct-Selling network of Tiens was rapidly constructed all over China. This was exactly the 'business personnel network' of Tiens, suggesting that Tiens took its first step in developing the network interaction Direct-Selling model.

Later, Tiens transformed its operations model as required by the government and therefore put vigorous efforts to build a huge 'special store network' in China. Before the construction of special stores, the number of branch offices of Tiens in all provinces had been incomparable for general Direct-Selling enterprises. In just 20 days from September 28 to mid-October, 1995, Tiens established nine subsidiaries in China; and by the end of November, branch offices had been established in all provinces in China other than Tibet and Taiwan. In the age of chain store sales, these branch offices distributed at every corner of China laid the foundation for the formation of Tiens' model of 'nets-outside-nets and network interconnection.' When the enterprise invested in the construction of the first batch of special stores, enterprise sellers followed the example and also opened special stores, which were endorsed and supported by the enterprise. Therefore, a large-scale special store network was rapidly built. By then, the second network of Tiens had been cultivated.

However, Tiens did not stop. Being aware that the current world had ushered in the internet age, Tiens started the construction of a global website in 2001. The completion of the global network symbolized the establishment of the consolidation of three networks in early Tiens. In this network system comprising the physical business personnel network and special store network, as well as a virtual global website, the combination of the online and the offline began to take shape.

The special store network and the internet had been introduced to the international network-based direct selling of Tiens, which eliminated the shortages of network-based direct selling through hardware construction, carried forward the advantages of word-of-mouth sales and thus developed the strong points and avoided the weak points. By means of three-network interaction, Tiens' marketing model improved the integration of humanity, rationality and sociality to a new level. With three-network interaction, the Tiens enterprise progressed by leaps and bounds, and the business personnel could develop the team and sell products online. The combination of the global internet and logistics network made the sales of Tiens' health products very transparent, open and modern, and Tiens' sales methods more standard and scientific.

Direct selling had emerged and developed for a century by that time, but it had always adopted word-of-mouth marketing without a store. Compared to that, Tiens created a new model that combined networks with stores. The mutual support between networks and stores pushed forward the rapid development of Tiens. The stores played the role of branch offices and supported the rapid development of the networks.

Consolidation of three networks became highly recognized in academic circles. Jin Yuan believed that this was a contribution and innovation of

Tiens to human marketing undertakings, a product of the rapid development of high technologies in the new age and a crystal of management innovation. As a premise to this model, every Tiens person is a consumer, seller, capital owner, wealth creator and wealth distributor at the same time. Based on high-quality products and driven by an excellent system, Tiens has rapidly built itself into a powerful multinational group and has captured the attention of the world.

II. Six-network Interaction

Consolidation of three networks is merely the embryo of Tiens' network interaction Direct-Selling model. After the Tiens international annual meeting was held in Jakarta in June 2002, Li Jinyuan made a special report on six-network interaction for sellers in Shenyang and officially put forward the idea to develop the Tiens consolidation of three networks to six-network interaction. The six networks here include the human resources network, education network, the internet, logistics network, capital operations network and tourism network. Moreover, each network name is preceded by 'international,' which shows the special characteristic of the second start-up by which Tiens has marched into the world market.

1. International human resources network: It means to rationally cultivate and comprehensively utilize social human resources according to the development of international society. In a modern sense, the human resources network gathers individuals from different social categories to be a group or a network, explores the dynamic role and the maximum value of talents, and accumulates resources. Tiens makes use of advanced and blood ties-based network marketing to attract a large number of far-sighted people and create great achievements together. This is the foundation for the business miracle of Tiens.

2. International education network: During the network development, Tiens adheres to educating people with correct business principles, cultivating people with a noble corporate culture, and encourageing people with a positive team spirit. The group actively builds a healthy sales network system, attempts to perform talent education in a local, hierarchical, institutional and network-based manner, and has constructed an education team of pioneering spirit and cultivated a batch of talents of junior, middle and senior-levels of education. The enterprise facilitates the industrialization and specialization of international education, practically implements the management, examination and reward systems for lecturers, and strives to build an international lecturer team of high quality, vitality, rich experience and great influence.

3. International logistics network: It explores multiple channels with modern technologies and improves logistics efficiency. To establish the global logistics system, Tiens produces featured, life-oriented, diversified, local and branded products, and in the meantime sells some featured high-quality products by purchasing patents or acquiring general distribution rights in local markets after thorough investigations on international markets, thus to enrich the network and increase the product categories. By cooperating with local production and processing enterprises in the international market, which will complete the processing, quality inspection and packageing of Tiens products, it can shorten the lead time, lower the cost and improve competitiveness. Based on the sharing of existing product resources, Tiens will further establish a more extensive and dynamic resources sharing channel, build a complete mechanism for information gathering, follow-up, feedback and decision-making and make full use of information technology to improve the initiative, focus and efficiency of product development and promotion.

4. International tourism network: The international tourism network offers a huge space for people's development and communication, and the branch offices all over the world make up the Tiens' biggest advantage compared to other travel agencies. This network aims to have every consumer understand global tourism resources, select the travel routes they like and enjoy the fun of travel. Tiens organizes large-scale travel seminars, travel annual meetings and travel training every year, when consumers can free themselves from the travel agencies, tourist guides and translators and independently choose their own food, accommodation, transportation, shopping and entertainment activities.

5. International capital operations network: The construction of the capital operations network is an embodiment of Tiens' economic strength as well as the motive force for enterprise development. It mainly integrates the funds and capital from different regions and prepares for the listing of Tiens.

6. International internet: It is an optimum choice for a multinational enterprise to make full use of information technology, promote the comprehensive market development, build the information superhighway with high technologies, and create a website for online shopping, shopping mall displays and information feedback. The successful establishment of Tiens' website helps the group achieve effective global information communication, realize online marketing, improve the sales of Tiens' products and supply convenient and high-quality services worldwide. Tiens spares no effort to: give full play to the advantages and roles of the internet in information flow, talent flow, online shopping, online previews, logistics, sales network management, education and training and capital operations; timely master the latest market and international

dynamics through the internet; enable flat management of global interactions and resources sharing that saves time and reduces distance; implement institutional, scientific, information based and systematic management; and further explore sales channels and improve its market shares.

The six networks here show interactive relations. The international internet connects the human resources network, international education network, international logistics network, international tourism network and international capital operations network. The international education network gives training to the human resources network. The human resources network sends information on input, delivery and demand to the international logistics network, supplies customers to the international tourism network which will organize trips, and invests in and holds shares of the international capital operations network which conversely promotes and explores the human resources network. The international education network technologically guides the international logistics network and tourism network. In the meantime, the international capital operations network financially supports the international logistics network and tourism network.

As a unique creation of Tiens, six-network interaction is a rarely seen modern enterprise organization in China. It is regarded as a miracle of marketing and a great leap of the distribution system. Harmoni, the President of Indonesia Direct Marketing Association, called six-network interaction "a miracle of direct selling which will be promoted and learned from worldwide." Being a newly emerging development in the marketing and distribution system, six-network interaction has laid the foundations for the creation of the advanced Tiens' culture by perfectly combining theory and practice for the long-term and the orderly development of Tiens.

III. Seven-network Interaction

In January 2017, Li Jinyuan put forward the idea of seven-network interaction on the basis of six-network interaction. In addition to the basic connotations of the six networks mentioned above, the 'international procurement and trade network' is added. Meanwhile, this new concept is included in the greater blueprint 'one body with multiple wings, seven-network interaction and terminal mode' and further develops the theories of network interaction and new swap of Tiens in depth and breadth.

The international procurement and trade network was established to meet the demands of Tiens expanding international businesses. As Tiens is extending its businesses to more countries, it has become a regular international enterprise. Thus, Tiens needs to sell its products to more countries and is exposed to increasing risks brought by the exchanges of different currencies, the foreign exchange risk. Moreover, this problem will be more prominent with more countries or regions involved. The international procurement and trade network can hedge a part of the risk, and meanwhile understand more about the local markets when selling products. For example, through the international procurement and trade network, Tiens will get to know the advantageous industries and featured products of a country and make some international trades. Therefore, it is a necessary choice for Tiens to expand its business scope and avoid the Direct-Selling risks.

As we can see from the evolution of the Tiens model, consolidation of three networks in the early stage mainly served for direct selling. Six-network interaction also mainly served for direct selling but was not confined to traditional businesses, while the tourism network and capital operations network started independent operations, suggesting the beginning of diversified operations in Tiens. The recent seven-network interaction further strengthens the strategy of diversified operations.

SECTION 2
DIRECT-SELLING INCENTIVE SYSTEM OF TIENS

The Direct-Selling incentive system of Tiens, specifically including the reward and bonus mechanisms, is largely identical with the models in most other Direct-Selling enterprises, including Amway. In consideration of commercial privacy, we will mainly review the incentive system for Tiens' overseas Direct-Selling businesses.

I. Rank System

Like any other Direct-Selling enterprise, Tiens ranks its direct sellers based on their performance. The whole system consists of three types of ranks: basic ranks, exploration ranks and honorary ranks.

1. Basic Ranks

According to Tiens' rules, a distributor with personal performance accumulated up to 200PV is rated as four-star. The personal performances corresponding to five-star, six-star, seven-star and eight-star are listed in the table below. This table suggests that Tiens encourages newcomers, as demonstrated by the low performance requirements for four-star and five-star (<200PV or 200PV). However, the performance requirements for higher ranks such as six-star, seven-star and eight-star show a geometric growth. The higher, the harder. Tiens also requires that four-star distributors purchase an initiation package before joining in, which depends on the laws of different countries. To ascend to six-star or above, a distributor must satisfy the requirement of 200PV personal consumption.

Direct seller's rank	four-star	five-star	six-star	seven-star	eight-star
Personal accumulated performance	<200PV	200 PV	5,000 PV	25,000 PV	100,000 PV

Table 18-1 Basic Ranks and Performance Requirements

2. Exploration Ranks
   Exploration ranks are one level above the basic ranks. As shown in the table below, the setting of these ranks also encourages newcomers and makes it harder for the higher levels. The corresponding performance requirements for the higher levels also show a geometric growth.

Exploration rank	Bronze card	Silver card	Gold card	Platinum card
Exploration performance	100BV	200BV	400BV	800BV

Table 18-2 Exploration Ranks and Performance Requirements

Direct sellers of exploration ranks can enjoy the product discount of retailing. The same rate of discount is given to the product price and the distributor's PV and BV. The PV and BV after discount will be included in the calculation of the bonus for retailing performance.

Exploration rank	Bronze card	Silver card	Gold card	Platinum card
Exploration performance	100BV	200BV	400BV	800BV
Discount	-	5%	8%	15%

Table 18-3 Exploration Ranks and Discount

3. Honorary Ranks
   Honorary ranks are the highest ranks for distributors set up by Tiens, which consist of six grades. Similarly, the performance requirements increase dramatically for higher levels (see Table 18-4).

Bronze lion	Silver lion	Gold lion	Gold star	Director	Honorary director
Cultivate two eight-star	Cultivate three eight-star	Cultivate four eight-star	Cultivate five eight-star	Cultivate four gold-lion	Cultivate four directors

Table 18-4 Honorary Ranks

II. Eight Major Reward and Distribution Principles

Based on the rank system, Tiens also formulates the reward and distribution principle corresponding to the distributor's performance. In general, the rewards can be divided into Type A and Type B.

1. Type A Reward

The Type A reward is defined as the exploration and business reward, comprising three parts: the service reward, exploration reward and cultivation reward. The bonus distribution is as follows:

(1) Service Reward

It varies by the rank. The bonus proportion for the lowest bronze card is 8%, compared to 15% for the highest platinum card. See Table 18-5.

Rank	Bronze card	Silver card	Gold card	Platinum card
% of service reward	8%	10%	12%	15%

Table 18-5 Service Reward

(2) Exploration Reward

The distribution principles of the exploration reward: one input, multilateral calculation; one exploration reward for one party and several exploration rewards for several parties; no zeroing of regional performance; and no deposit, to maximize the benefits of direct sellers. See Table 18-6.

	Exploration performance	Proportion	Weekly cap/ department
Bronze card	100BV	8%, 9%	$800
Silver card	200BV	9%, 10%	$1,600
Gold card	400BV	10%, 11%	$3,000
Platinum card	800BV	11%, 12%	$5,000

Table 18-6 Exploration Reward

As ruled by Tiens, the direct sellers newly ascending to the exploration ranks do not need to buy personal performance within four weeks. The purchase of personal performance of 50PV takes effect since the current week (effective for four weeks) and will be made again in the fifth week. Since when there is retained performance, distributors can win one exploration reward every 12 weeks and the retained performance can be continuously retained without an infinite amount.

(3) Cultivation Reward

This is a reward based on the reward. The higher-level card shows a higher generation for reward allocation. See Table 18-7.

Rank	Bronze card	Silver card	Gold card	Platinum card
Examination	1. The individual must win the exploration reward in the same week; 2. Generation of cultivation reward = the number of direct sellers of exploration rank directly recommended.			
1st generation	-	5%	5%	5%
2nd generation		5%	5%	5%
3rd generation			5%	5%
4th generation				5%

Table 18-7 Cultivation Reward

According to Tiens' rules, the cultivation reward is calculated based on the network of recommended sellers. Any direct recommendation will be counted as the first generation. The base for the cultivation reward is associated with the exploration rewards of the lower level; and the unqualified generation will be reduced.

2. Type B Reward

The Type B reward is defined as the retail performance. Specific rules for reward allocation are listed below:

(4) Sales Reward

The sales reward accounts for 35% of the total bonus and is divided into the direct and indirect reward. See specific conditions in Table 18-8.

Rank		four-star	five-star	six-star	seven-star	eight-star	Bronze lion	Silver lion	Gold lion	Star gold	Director	Honorary director
% of reward		-	10%	15%	20%	25%	28%	30%	32%	33%	34%	35%
Upgrade requirements	Personal accumulative performance	<200	200	200	200	200	200	200	200	200	200	200
	Network accumulative performance	-	200	5,000	25,000	100,000	Two eight-star	Three eight-star	Four eight-star	Five eight-star	Four gold-lion	Four directors
Reward requirements	Personal performance	-	20	20	100	200						
	Team performance						1,000					
	Network performance						Two eight-star, 5,000PV	Three eight-star, 5,000PV	Four eight-star, 5,000PV	Five eight-star, 5,000PV	Four active gold-lion	Four active directors

Table 18-8 Sales Reward

(5) Leadership Reward

This accounts for 12.5% of the total bonus. The principles for the bonus distribution include: direct sllers get rewards if surpassing the same level or the lower level. See Table 18-9.

Generation	eight-star	Bronze lion	Silver lion	Gold lion	Star gold	Director	Honorary director
Exam requirements	Personal performance 200 Team performance 200	Meet the honorary active requirements of the corresponding rank					
1st generation	2%	2%	2%	2%	2%	2%	2%
2nd generation	1.5%	1.5%	1.5%	1.5%	1.5%	1.5%	1.5%
3rd generation	1%	1%	1%	1%	1%	1%	1%
4th generation	1%	1%	1%	1%	1%	1%	1%
5th generation		1%	1%	1%	1%	1%	1%
6th generation		1%	1%	1%	1%	1%	1%
7th generation			1%	1%	1%	1%	1%
8th generation				1%	1%	1%	1%
9th generation					1%	1%	1%
10th generation						1%	1%
11th generation							1%

Table 18-9 Leadership Reward

According to Tiens' rules, direct sellers of eight-star and above will get a team performance of the eight-star rank. The unqualified generation will be reduced.

(6) Excellence Reward

This accounts for 2% of the total bonus. The allocation principles are: get direct sellers promoted based on their specific ranks; increase the promotion depth; transcend the promotion requirements; star gold gets the performance of star gold, director gets the performance of directors, and honorary director gets the performance of honorary directors. See Table 18-10.

Active rank generation	Star gold	Director	Honorary director
1st generation	0.2%	0.2%	0.2%
2nd generation	0.2%	0.2%	0.2%
3rd generation	0.2%	0.2%	0.2%
4th generation	0.2%		

Table 18-10 Excellence Reward

This rule is applicable for sellers of the ranks between active star gold and honorary director. The unqualified generation will be reduced. Then the direct seller gets the team performance of the lower level with the same honorary rank. One-star gold lion to five-star gold lion are all deemed as star gold. For example, the star gold team's performance will be the whole network performance (retailing) of the lower level at a rank of star gold or below, adding to the individual performance.

(7) Honorary Reward

This accounts for 4% of the total bonus. Allocation principles are: reducing the small market; lowering the consumption pressure; input from one country to benefit the whole world; reward can be superimposed. See Table 18-11.

Rank	Bronze lion	Silver lion	Gold lion	Star gold	Director	Honorary director
% of bonus	1%	0.75%	0.5%	0.2% x 5	0.5%	0.25%
Personal performance	200PV					
Team performance	1,000PV	1,000PV	1,000PV	1,000PV	1,000PV	1,000PV
Lower level and network performance	Two eight-star, 5,000PV	Three eight-star, 5,000PV	Four eight-star, 5,000PV	Five to ten eight-star, 5,000PV	Four active gold-lion	Four active director

Table 18-11 Honorary Reward

According to Tiens' rules, the exploration performance and retailing performance are all incorporated in the examination of the honorary rewards; and both are involved in the allocation of the honorary reward.

(8) Special Rewards

This sales reward accounts for 2% of the total bonus. Its allocation principles are: points system; more winners; setting a positive example.

To be specific, special rewards include an international travel seminar reward; high-end car fund; and luxury housing fund.

Rules for the international travel seminar reward are as follows: Tiens rules the qualification and content of the reward. Tiens will publish the travel reward proposals every year. Any direct seller that meets the examination requirements in the proposal can participate in the international travel seminar organized by the enterprise.

For the high-end car fund and luxury housing fund the reward qualification is: any direct seller of bronze lion or above who meets corresponding activity conditions will have the opportunity to win the high-end car fund and luxury housing fund. Meanwhile, the high-end car fund and luxury housing fund is a one-time cash reward, with a value of $195,000 US.

Tiens further specifies the reward requirements:

1. Promotion Activity Reward
   Direct sellers who reach the promotion activity requirements for the bronze lion, silver lion, gold lion, director or honorary director can acquire the corresponding special reward fund. See Table 18-12.

Rank	High-end car fund			Luxury housing fund	
	Bronze lion	Silver lion	Gold lion	Director	Honorary director
Activity examination condition	Be active for three consecutive months within six months after promotion (including the month of promotion)				
Interim reward (USD)	5,000	5,000	5,000	20,000	80,000

Table 18-12 Promotion Activity Reward

2. Activity Continuity Reward
   Direct sellers who have reached the activity requirements for 12 consecutive months and 10 accumulated months of gold lion, director and honorary director will obtain the corresponding special accumulated reward fund (subtracting the reward already obtained earlier). See Table 18-13.

Rank	High-end car fund			Luxury housing fund			
	Gold lion			Director			Honorary director
Activity examination condition	Active for 12 consecutive months, 10 accumulative months	Active for 12 consecutive months, 10 accumulative months (excluding the active months of the previous reward)	Active for 12 consecutive months, 10 accumulative months (excluding the active months of the previous reward)	Active for 12 consecutive months, 10 accumulative months	Active for 12 consecutive months, 10 accumulative months (excluding the active months of the previous reward)	Active for 12 consecutive months, 10 accumulative months (excluding the active months of the previous reward)	Active for 12 consecutive months, 10 accumulated months accumulative months
Accumulated reward (USD)	**15,000**	20,000	25,000	**45,000**	75,000	115,000	**195,000**

Table 18-13 Activity Continuity Reward

In addition to the above rules, Tiens gives the following specific explanations for each reward to assure the implementation:

A. Activity requirement for direct sellers of the honorary ranks: fulfil the requirements on the personal performance, team performance and lower-level requirements of this rank.

B. The number of active months for gold lion and director in each stage excludes the active months of the previous stage.

C. Exploration performance is considered in these rewards: service reward, exploration reward, cultivation reward, honorary reward, special reward.

D. Retail performance is considered in these rewards: sales reward, leadership reward, excellence reward, honorary reward, special reward.

E. The exploration ranks are determined based on personal exploration performance.

F. Exploration performance and retail performance jointly support the rank promotion of direct sellers.

G. Exploration performance is not included in the examination of personal performance and team performance.

H. Exploration reward is calculated based on the placement network, and other rewards are calculated based on the recommendation network.

I. The activity whole-network examination of honorary ranks includes the exploration performance and retail performance. The first-year preferential is 3,000PV of the whole network for eight-star.

J. When the total bonus corresponding to the exploration performance accounts for over 70% of exploration performance BV, the bonus will be allocated at a rate of 70%.

CHAPTER 19

THE TIENS MODEL AND ITS EFFICIENCY

Tiens was founded in the early 1990s. After three start-ups, Tiens is completely different today. What Tiens has achieved in just three decades can be considered as a miracle of private enterprises. This great result proves that Tiens must have done something right along the way. We believe that the success of Tiens started from the early 1990s. Its first right move was choosing the correct product, Tiens' calcium powder; the second right decision was choosing the correct sales model, direct selling; and the third right decision was choosing the correct market, the international market. These three major strategic decisions corresponded to the previous two start-ups of Tiens. The selection of calcium powder and direct selling was completed in the first start-up; and marching into the international market was the theme of the second start-up. At present, Tiens is going to make a big choice. Can it make the right choice again? The only standard by which to judge this choice is efficiency.

SECTION 1 FIRST START-UP AND BUSINESS PERFORMANCE

The first start-up of Tiens lasted from 1992 to 1998, which could be further divided into two small stages, respectively between 1992 and 1995, and between 1995 and 1998.

From 1992 to 1995, Tiens was dedicated to infrastructure construction, including financing, civil engineering, technology development and application, and market choice. In those four years, Tiens relied on its own strength to independently accomplish many things, introduced several technologies from the laboratory to the market and finally decided to produce calcium powder.

In the second small stage from 1995 to 1998, Tiens was officially established and generated benefits rapidly. In this stage, Tiens had correctly chosen the Direct-Selling model and completed the construction of the joint venture model, market system and capital accumulation. In this embryonic stage, Tiens adopted the customer-model development strategy to concentrate consumers' individual needs and behaviours as well as distribution channels. By adopting the customer-based strategy, Tiens took the lead in the transformation from the seller's market to the buyer's market in China at that time. Therefore, Tiens had achieved rapid growth and development. During this period, Tiens successfully released new products to the Chinese market. For example, it released health products including Tiens' iron-supplement crystals, Tiens' spirulina tablets and Tiens' spirulina capsules to the Chinese market in 1997. In 1998, it further released health products such as Tiens' cordyceps mycelium capsules, chitin capsules, zinc-supplement crystals, fat-reducing tea and Weikang soft capsules to the Chinese market. From 1999 to 2001, more health products were launched, including Tiens' three-highs capsules, Tiens' diet tea, Tiens' beauty capsules and Tiens' hypotensive tea. To date, multiple series of Tiens' health products are popular in the market. With regard to the health functions of Tiens' products certified by the Ministry of Health of the PRC, they respectively supplement calcium, regulate immune functions, relax the bowels, supplement zinc or iron, regulate blood fat, eliminate toxins and nourish the skin, fight against tumours, support hypoxia and fatigue resistance, resist oxidation and retard ageing, regulate blood sugar, regulate blood pressure, regulate gastrointestinal functions, and reduce fat and weight. They provide a total of 15 functions, over 70% of the 22 functions supplied by all health products in China.

By now, Tiens has launched over 20 health products in the Chinese market, which are currently popular, and has released 197 kinds of products in total to the Chinese and international market. Tiens is regarded as a vigorous enterprise worldwide for its many varieties of products, large scale of production and wide market coverage.

This embryonic period laid a solid foundation for the further development of Tiens and enabled it to take the initiative to respond to national policy adjustments and resist operating risks and accumulate strength. It ended the operation of 'developing before standardizing' of Tiens and started the operations model of 'developing while standardizing.'

SECTION 2 SECOND START-UP AND BUSINESS PERFORMANCE

As influenced by the operating environment, Tiens started to enter overseas markets and has actively participated in other industries since 1998 to spread operating risks, which marked the start of Tiens' channel development strategy. In just four years, Tiens established branch offices in the five continents and avoided the decline of operating income resulting from market contraction. By 2002, the domestic net assets of Tiens had developed from the original 20 million yuan to 1.6 billion yuan (excluding overseas assets), and the group had paid taxes of 640 million to the government.

As to business development, the profit of Tiens had grown by around 16% and the sales volume had increased by 31% in 2008. In regard to production and logistics, Tiens had actively advanced the construction of overseas production bases and the initiation of OEM programs, constantly strengthened its production management function, continued to push on delicacy management of production and continuously improved global production planning and management. For R&D, Tiens had constantly strengthened the construction of the infrastructure for R&D based on the business development demand of the group, developed products fulfilling market demands and acquired outstanding achievements. The quality department had not only assured product quality, but also actively supplied quality inspection and training services in these regions, having effectively guaranteed the quantity and quality of Tiens products. Based on the work above, Tiens successfully passed many certifications in 2008, including the Halal assurance system, ISO 9001 quality management system, ISO 10012:2003 measurement management system, ISO 14001 environment management system and OHSAS 18001 occupational health and safety management system. Therefore, the global quality management centre, global production management centre, planning and dispatch department, and the president office jointly won the excellent project prize of food safety program development. The global production management centre won the excellent comprehensive project prize of delicacy management. The global R&D centre won the excellent project prize of national enterprise technology centre project and global R&D centre skin care series. The global marketing centre won the excellence prize for the Tiens' direct-seller information management platform project and TS promotion project. The global management centre and global production centre won the delicacy management model practice model.

The year 2011 was when Tiens advanced by leaps and bounds. In this year, the global Direct-Selling volume had reached an annual growth rate of 25.5%, and the global profit had increased by 63.2% compared to the previous year.

All-Legend Hotel had earned an operating income over 120 million yuan in 2011, with the income from primary businesses exceeding 40% of the annual budget income.

In 2011, Tiens International Health Industrial Park was fully put into use. It established the comprehensive health technology innovation system relying on the international standard R&D centre and quality inspection centre; the comprehensive health production and logistics system based on modern production shops and automatic warehouses; the comprehensive health service system with the support of Taijisun Health Management Centre; All-Legend Hotel and Tiens' international conference centre; and the comprehensive education system based on Tiens College. All of these laid a solid hardware foundation for Tiens' third leap forward.

Also, in 2011, Tiens improved its business division control and strengthened its management. In this year, Tiens officially implemented the business division management system, constantly improved it in practice and built a business system mainly depending on the global Direct-Selling division, product supply division, All-Legend division, Taijisun division, real estate division and Tiens College. In this way, Tiens constructed a functional system supported by the global human resources management centre, global law and audit centre, global administration centre, engineering division and group planning system; cultivated a performance examination and incentive system that linked the salary to performance and combined short-term incentives with long-term incentives; and laid the management foundation for the future development of the group.

In 2011, the production centre achieved an output of 633,000 boxes, with an annual growth rate of 58%; and the output value created that year was 4.89 billion yuan, having increased by 89%. The production cost per box had dropped by 16.7% on average compared to 2010, and the output value per man hour had risen by 150% on average compared to 2010. The procurement of raw materials, package materials and imported items made by the procurement centre had grown by 130% annually. The shipment businesses at the domestic, import and export warehouses of the logistics centre increased by 37% compared to 2010. To deliver goods to the destination in a timely, safe and accurate manner, the logistics centre had strengthened the regulation and management of third-party logistics providers and the general warehouse and had improved the processes and management; it further refined customer service standards to enhance customer satisfaction; planned for and adjusted transportation routes in a timely manner, improved delivery efficiency and placed focus on the supply to key countries; and, seeing the rise of OEM/ODM businesses, successfully initiated off-site clearance/shipment businesses. It also had remote manufacturers directly deliver goods to branch offices overseas, which involved businesses in Shenzhen, Dalian and

Shanghai, and would save a week's time for delivery and the unloading and loading cost at headquarters.

In 2011, the research institute made great achievements. For example, Tiens' Life Science and Technology Research Institute was founded in May as officially approved by Tianjin Science and Technology Commission and the Civil Affairs Department, making the development of Tiens' products advance a further step. It laid the organizational foundation for the rapid development of the enterprise in terms of technology. In 2011, the Institute launched eight products to the market. In particular, the L-carnitine diet tablet, which had previously failed to meet the qualifications for health food approval, was released to market within 10 months after complicated legal procedures including entrusted processing and renaming. This new product went on to perform well. Air purifiers from the equipment category, were launched by the end of the year after about one year of research and sold well right after release. The Research Institute and Taijisun had cooperated to found the biological products research department, laying a solid foundation for both parties' work associated with bioengineering products and stem cells.

In accordance with to Li Jinyuan's overall strategy for Tiens, All-Legend Division was founded in the first half of 2011. It symbolized that Tiens would vigorously develop hotels, conferences, exhibitions, hotel management, tourism, property management and cultural media as new businesses. All-Legend Division realized an operating income of over 120 million yuan in 2011, where the operating income from primary businesses, the conference centre, was approximately 85 million yuan, accounting for over 40% of the annual budget income. It had signed agreements with 716 enterprises and received more than 30 large groups comprising over 1,500 people and more than 65 groups of over 500 people. All-Legend Hotel Management Company had signed a consignment agreement with seven hotels in 2011. All-Legend International travel agency earned a sales income of over 16 million yuan in 2011.

SECTION 3
THIRD START-UP AND BUSINESS PERFORMANCE

Tiens conducted demand and market research in all major regions of the world between 2011 and 2012 and determined the necessity to launch the third start-up based on the investigation results. In the future, Tiens will lead the international path, adopt an equity system, orient on businesses, become listed and develop partnerships. Only by replacing heavy assets with light assets and by acquisition and merger can Tiens grow bigger and stronger, stand longer and be better. Tiens has become a multinational enterprise group that integrates industrial capital, commercial capital and financial capital and covers biotechnology, health management, hotel tourism, education and training, e-commerce and financial investment. Tiens has extended its businesses to more than 190 countries, established branch offices in 110 countries and regions and formed a strategic alliance with numerous first-class enterprises in different countries worldwide. In the meantime, it has innovatively developed diversified products including nutrition and health food, healthcare products, beauty and skin care products and household items, including products under the high-quality fashion brand Richy One. Tiens is assuring a high-quality life for stable consumers and partners from approximately 40 million families worldwide and makes them healthy, happy, beautiful and wealthy.

Adhering to the development strategy of a comprehensive health industry, Tiens has invested more than 7 billion yuan in the construction of Tiens International Health Industrial Park that covers an area of 1 square kilometre. This is a comprehensive industrial park that integrates product R&D, pilot testing and incubation, production, medicine and health research, and hotel and conference facilities. It consists of the comprehensive health technology innovation system relying on the international standard R&D centre and quality inspection centre; the comprehensive health production and logistics system based on modern production shops and automatic warehouses; the comprehensive health service system with the support of Taijisun Health Management Centre; All-Legend Hotel and Tiens international conference centre; and the comprehensive education system based on Tiens College. By building a health industrial chain integrating talent flow, logistics, capital flow and information flow, Tiens has built Tiens International Health Industrial Park into a real comprehensive health industrial cluster base, which is constructed on a solid platform and assures Tiens' broader development.

Tiens' internationalization bears the strategic goal of a high-quality talent team and local and international management. Tiens possesses an invincible international team that studies, innovates and has good manners consisting of over 10,000 international managers. Among specialized talents, 35% or more employees have a Master's degree or above.

	Operating income (10,000 yuan)	Net profit (10,000 yuan)	Asset (10,000 yuan)	Owner's equity (10,000 yuan)	Number of employees
2010	2,789,021	285,112	1,159,199	849,427	2,475
2013	2,960,033	328,153	1,194,124	895,468	2,404
2014	3,048,834	338,982	1,206,065	925,018	2,099
2015	3,219,568	369,124	1,220,968	958,023	4,101
2016	3,320,985	339,736	1,237,939	980,157	8,313

Table 19-1 Changes of Tiens' Business Status

Source: Data of 2010, 2013, 2014, 2015, 2016 from China Enterprise Confederation, China Enterprise Directors Association, Development Report of China's Top 500 Enterprises (2010, 2013, 2014, 2015, 2016), Enterprise Management Publishing House.

PART VI

SELF-TRANSCENDENCE CREATES GLORY: FROM HOUSEHOLD CONSUMPTION TO HOUSEHOLD BUSINESS CONSUMPTION

FENG LEI

Consumption is always the key point of direct selling and the global cross-border social e-commerce platform. The development from consumption to household consumption and finally to household business consumption, as well as the practice of the consumption ecological chain and business circle, have promoted the upgrading of the development concepts of the Direct-Selling model, returned to the idea of household consumption, broken the constraints of products and consumers, and transcended the Direct-Selling model.

By means of business model re-engineering, pure household consumption is developed to become household business consumption, achieving the dual-level wealth creation of consumption capital. Upon understanding the essence of direct selling, we can seize the opportunity of the rapid development of the internet, be aware of the dependence of household consumption on the network environment, develop the network-based the Direct-Selling supermarket to Direct-Selling e-commerce platform under the guidance of the household business consumption idea, which relies on but goes beyond direct selling, builds a global cross-border social e-commerce platform and achieves transcendence over direct selling.

CHAPTER 20

CONSUMPTION ECOLOGICAL CHAIN AND BUSINESS MODEL RE-ENGINEERING

An enterprise must take the changes of the target market into consideration for any form of transcendence. The formation of the consumption chain and the emergence of the consumption ecological chain create a major issue for Direct-Selling enterprises and also a major challenge to the Direct-Selling model.

SECTION 1
CONSUMPTION CHAIN AND CONSUMPTION ECOLOGICAL CHAIN

The re-engineering of the business model needs to be guided theoretically. The concepts of consumption chain, household consumption chain, consumption ecological chain and consumption ecosystem render theoretical support to the construction of the business model to a certain extent.

I. Consumption Chain

1. Concept of Consumption Chain

   To understand the consumption chain, we will start from the concept of the consumption unit. The consumption unit may be a person, a family or even a larger group. All products needed by the consumption unit constitute the consumption chain. The core for understanding the consumption chain lies in the consumption structure and its relevance, which reveals the different types of products in the consumption chain and the relations among different product types.

2. Two Perspectives to Study Consumption Chain

   There are two perspectives to study consumption: the micro economic perspective or the merchant's micro perspective. With the former perspective, we can see the allocation proportion of consumption funds in the national economic plan and the relation between consumption funds and investment funds. From the latter perspective, it is about the behaviours of consuming commodities provided by a specific merchant or manufacturer. At the macro level, the studies on consumption or household consumption are far behind the studies on production, circulation and distribution. At the micro level, the merchants change their perspectives to consumers or consumers' families to stimulate consumption, which creates a new concept of consumption chain from the view of the market.

3. Effective Analysis Tools
   The new trend of consumption development shows that consumers are paying increasing attention to holistic consumption. When commodities are in short supply, consumers will focus on the supply of some important consumers; but when commodities are sufficient, consumers will attach more importance to the rationality of holistic consumption. To express it in terms of economic concepts, consumers will acquire the same marginal utility from different commodities. As expected, the rationality of consumption will not contradict with the preferences of different consumers, since marginal utility is essentially a subjective judgment. The theory of consumption chain guides the enterprise's strategy for its product portfolio and sales. Compared to the previous market segmentation, the segmentation of consumption chain also brings more possibilities to the enterprise when it formulates a strategy for the product portfolio, locks the target market, and chooses the means of competition.

4. Recessive Characteristics of Consumption Chain
   Michael E. Porter's value chain theory describes an enterprise's activities throughout its product design, production, sales and delivery process, and connects these isolated links that deliver a product to the market with a complete value chain system, and then unveils the ultimate goal of an enterprise. If this system is considered a closed circulatory system, we will also think about how to withdraw a product from the market after its release. At the consumption level, the value chains of numerous enterprises correspond to the consumption chains of different consuming subjects. The collection of these consumption chains covered by the enterprise's products can describe the market faced by the enterprise more profoundly. The recessive characteristics of the consumption chain prove that consumer demands vary from time to time and will be understood by enterprises through market investigation. It is an art of operation for the enterprise to have its own unique understanding of the consumption chain, discover its structure and supply appropriate products and services.

II. Consumption Ecological Chain

1. The Consumption Ecological Chain Depends on the Consumption Chain and Consumption Pattern

The development of the consumption ecological chain is based on the dynamics of the consumption chain and consumption pattern. Simply put, it means to provide appropriate products to consumers, and produce and sell what consumers need. When formulating the product and service strategy, the enterprise must adhere to the ultimate goal of the demand of the target market. Only when the demand of the target market is satisfied can the enterprise earn profit and achieve further development. The consumption ecological chain is the sum of all enterprise measures to satisfy consumer demand.

The enterprise will also give consideration to the changes of the consumption pattern when drawing up the strategy of consumption ecological chain. The consumption pattern, big or small, may be a social concept, or the special properties of the target market. The consumption pattern itself constitutes an important part of the consumption chain. For example, to supply drinking water to employees, the enterprise can choose to either set up a boiler room to boil water for drinking or buy a water fountain and supplement bottled drinking water. In this case, the business opportunities may go to either the boiler manufacturer or the water fountain and bottled drinking water supplier. In the variation of the consumption pattern, the water fountain and bottled drinking water supplier beats the boiler manufacturer.

2. Consumption Ecological Chain Plays a Dynamic Role in Guiding Consumption

Instead of adapting to the adjustments of consumption and the consumption pattern passively, the consumption ecological chain can take the initiative to create consumer focus and change people's consumption habits. In other words, as a dynamic factor, the consumption ecological chain plays an important part in re-engineering consumption and adjusting the consumption pattern. In view of this, we can have a wilder imagination regarding the enterprise's consumption ecological chain strategy. We can argue whether it is the supermarket that changes people's shopping habits or whether people's shopping habits lead to the creation of the convenient one-stop supermarket. While the video recorder and compact discs squeezed on the cinema industry, upgraded cinemas have brought people back by improving acoustic effects, creating different seating modes, and adding popcorn and cold drinks. Due to this new concept, the consumption ecological chain, which describes the enterprise's ability to provide products and services, the re-engineering of consumption and the innovation of the consumption pattern become more creative, passionate and attractive. It is much more interesting than just referring to it as the content of the decision on the enterprise's ability to provide consumers with commodities and services.

3. New Concept of Household Consumption Ecological Chain
The e-commerce enterprise GOME put forward the concept of a 'household consumption ecological chain' in 2016. In view of the increasingly intensified competition in e-commerce, the enterprise that makes no innovation and discovers no new target market will necessarily decline. Centring on families, the household consumption ecological chain extends its upstream and downstream industrial chain to satisfy all-round household demands on commodities and services, which are general and personalized at the same time. The e-commerce enterprise provides the personalized service of one-stop shopping to household consumption. GOME has launched an online C2M (consumer-to-manufacturer) platform, replaced the previous commodity output platform with an information connection platform and has consumers directly contacting the manufacturers. Meanwhile, it has attracted designer teams into the platform to operate, match and recommend products, and provided functional services such as product search and order crowd funding. On one hand, it has collected market information on household consumption demand; and on the other hand, it has introduced first-class manufacturers, connected consumers with manufacturers through the platform, satisfied the personalized demand of families, and reduced the enterprise's inventory. It has rendered a rich practical experience in the household consumption ecological chain.

4. Consumption Ecological Chain of Direct-Selling Enterprises
Product interests make up the foundation of the consumption ecological chain of Direct-Selling enterprises, and economic interests constitute the centre of the consumption ecological chain of direct selling, which open up new space for wealth creation by household business consumption and increase consumers' profits layer by layer. The typical consumption ecological chain of the Direct-Selling enterprise provides two most representative types of products, health products and cosmetics, to satisfy the demand of the target market on healthcare and beauty. In line with the development trend of the consumption ecological chain, the Direct-Selling enterprise is constantly innovating the product series and launches products of the same or different category as a support to the key product series. Some Direct-Selling enterprises may run interdisciplinary businesses. With regard to product consumption, the product characteristics of health products, cosmetics and other products aiming to provide a high-quality life show little relevance to the channel selection based on consumption characteristics. The product

categories run by direct business enterprises are only accepted by the consumers who have confidence, so face-to-face information communication becomes an essential process for direct selling. During the development of distributors, advertising and education have been the vigorous tool that supports the development of the target market. The successful cases are the certification for product promotion; the accumulative interests realized by the points system become the important factors that drives the active participation of the target market; and product interests and economic interests constitute the basic framework for the consumption ecological chain of Direct-Selling enterprises.

SECTION 2
EXPANSION OF CONSUMPTION ECOLOGICAL CHAIN

Now, let's move on from the complicated concept talk and return to the analysis of the consumption ecological chain from the enterprise's perspective. In the age of networks, an enterprise must expand its products and services supplied to the target market, that is to say, adjust the enterprise's special consumption ecological chain or the product and service portfolio.

I. Specialized Expansion of Consumption Ecological Chain

Specialized expansion is the analysis of the consumption ecological chain from the perspective of the product portfolio. Specialized expansion shows a strong directive, which provides for services for a certain consumer group, or serves a certain type of demand of consumers. The enterprise can constantly deepen its production and operations associated with a certain category of products, such as increasing the categories of health products, or increasing the health products suitable for different groups. The factors of age, region and even gender can also be considered as strategic points for the expansion of the product portfolio. In other words, specialized expansion means to focus on the refinement of one production line while maintaining the relevance among products.

II. Diversified Expansion of Consumption Ecological Chain

The consumption ecological chain of diversified development shows a discrete structure of products and services or lower relevance among products. Several points are considered for diversified development. The first is about the choice of the diversified development interests, judging which is more important, spreading risks or seizing market opportunities. Second, the conditions that the enterprise embraces for diversified development, such as extensive resources, strong financial strength or talents' adaptability, will generate different diversified patterns. The third factor is the solution to or relief of management difficulties of diversified development, cross transmission and sharing of information, requirements of diversified businesses on resource allocation, and the integration and realization of diversified goals.

The diversified strategy and specialized strategy often constitute a major contradiction in an enterprise's decision. In most cases, diversified development manifests itself as a leap-forward development and creates more opportunities for the enterprise, like stepping from a familiar product area to a relatively unfamiliar one, or extending from consumers' food and beverages to consumers' clothing, from men's clothing to women's clothing, from small shops to department stores, from department stores to supermarkets, from eight hours a day to 24 hours a day, from physical stores to e-commerce platforms and from the children's market to the market for the elderly. Each step of diversification is a leap forward, which will develop from quantitative changes to qualitative changes. The alternating between diversification and specialization and the great integration of diversification and specialization will accumulate the great-leap development and finally realize the enterprise's self-transcendence. Transcendental development is not that mysterious.

SECTION 3
TRANSCENDING DIRECT-SELLING DEVELOPMENT CONCEPTS

I. Re-engineering of Consumption Ecosystem and Business Model

Consumption ecosystem is figuratively referred to as the business circle, which explains the consumption environment made up of different enterprises and enterprises of different forms, based on the competition and cooperation among their consumption ecological chains.

1. Relations between Consumption Ecological Chain and Consumption Ecosystem

The consumption ecological chains of different enterprises jointly constitute the consumption ecosystem. In the consumption ecosystem, some enterprises provide unique products and services, while some enterprises provide replaceable and competing products and services. The same products of different brands can easily be replaced, so every brand in the consumption ecosystem is attempting to convince consumers of their differences to other brands. They try to distinguish themselves by quality, price and convenience, and build up the threshold to their segment markets. They also compete with each other in terms of the business model. They may provide unique business models such as offering consumption loans for adopting zero-channel direct selling.

2. New Consumption Ecosystem
The age of network has modelled the new consumption ecosystem, which differs from the consumption ecosystem in a physical space. The collection of various business forms and business models in a physical space have been decomposed to numerous websites and e-commerce platforms on the internet, like a virtual consumption ecosystem formed in the neighbouring physical store. In a traditional consumption ecosystem, consumers personally visit the business district and walk from one shop to another; but in the new virtual consumption ecosystem, consumers browse websites and platforms one after another. In this way, the consumption ecosystem in a physical space is decomposed to e-commerce platforms on the internet.

The new consumption ecosystem has magnified the pros and cons of the tangible consumption ecosystem to the extreme. The e-commerce platform has a superior ability to gather products together that cannot be compared to by any physical store, as the product scale of an e-commerce platform far exceeds that of any supermarket. The e-commerce platform also features the great ability of integration and creates new logistics services and payment services. Meanwhile, the e-commerce platform breaks the spatial and temporal constraints that are imposed on physical stores. However, the original store design and layout is replaced by the webpage design and browsing rules; and the display of physical commodities is replaced by photos of different angles on the webpage, which makes the user experience more difficult. But this problem may be overcome by the application of 3D technologies. The personal exchange between sellers and customers is gone, so sellers have nowhere to use their knowledge and sales skills. Though the e-commerce platform has broken spatial and temporal constraints, the traffic ceiling has become a serious problem. The new consumption ecosystem is more sensitive to customer flow than physical stores are, and traffic seems to have become the only indicator of the success of an e-commerce platform. Hence, the traffic ceiling may become a fatal factor.

3. Re-engineering of Business Models
The interactive development of the consumption chain, consumption ecological chain and consumption ecosystem has become a catalyst for new business models. From the perspective of the consumption chain,

re-engineering of business models must adapt to ever-changing consumption habits and different shopping habits for different commodities of the target market, including commodity selection, commodity pickup, payment, after services and information delivery. The key to business model re-engineering is to follow up and lock the dynamic development of the consumption chain. From the perspective of the consumption ecological chain, the re-engineering of business models is embodied in the reshaping of the operations models, business forms, profit models and management models. From the operations perspective, the re-engineering of business models is the adjustment of an enterprise's internal business processes; from the angle of business forms, business model re-engineering adjusts the methods to save customers; from the angle of profit, it adjusts the rules for the distribution of economic interests; and from the angle of management, it is the adjustment of the ownership structure and the agent. From the perspective of the consumption ecosystem, business model re-engineering will adjust the relations among the three. It will adjust the categories of products and services and the supply methods based on the changes of the consumption chain and cultivate the new consumption ecological chain; and adjust the enterprise's competition positioning in the consumption ecosystem according to the changes of competitors, search for new partners and change the internal structure of the consumption ecosystem.

To sum up, from the consumption chain to the consumption ecological chain and to the consumption ecosystem, the interaction exerts influence on the enterprise's business models. We can summarize these specious concepts in a systematic, simple, logical and practical way as follows: First, the consumption chain that places emphasis on the consumption set and structure is the fundamental factor that determines the business models. Second, the consumption ecological chain focuses on the product portfolio supplied by the enterprise and the transportation method, which is the positioning of the enterprise in the consumption chain. Third, the consumption ecosystem attaches importance to the competition and cooperation inside the enterprise, revealing the position of the enterprise in the consumption ecosystem. Fourth, the business models pay attention to the integration of internal business processes, and any adjustment to the competition-cooperation relationship in the market finally depends on the development status of the consumption chain.

II. Development Stage of the Direct-Selling Model

The transcendental development of the Direct-Selling model has ushered in a new stage that transcends the development concepts of direct selling. This stage comes after the first two development stages mentioned below, before transcendental development is realized.

The first stage of the Direct-Selling model can be concluded as the stage of 'channel strategy.' Direct selling is essentially the direct meeting between the producer and the consumer. Zero-channel circulation is applicable for commodities that are less frequently consumed and need face-to-face communication, such as encyclopaedias and graveyards. This is about the decision of channels on selling products. In this stage, what people see as a typical representative of direct selling are not encyclopaedias or graveyards, but products in the cosmetics category. Avon is a typical representative of cosmetics direct selling.

The second is the stage of 'in-depth development of products + points system.' In this stage, the typical model of Direct-Selling enterprises is combining the development of the product portfolio and the utilization of the points system. In China, health products have been the new star of direct selling. The channel strategy is upgraded to be the product strategy and promotion strategy, transcending the Direct-Selling model focusing on channels. This is a transcendental development of the Direct-Selling model. As the typical representative of health products direct selling, Tiens has been constantly developing its internal business processes, as demonstrated by the consolidation of three networks, multi-network interaction and one body with multiple wings.

The current third stage of the Direct-Selling model transcends the Direct-Selling concept itself. In this stage, the biggest challenge that the Direct-Selling model encounters is the changes of the consumption chain and the follow-up of the e-commerce platform, which brings both business opportunities and survival challenges to Direct-Selling enterprises. This new transcendental development of direct selling must transcend the misunderstandings in the Direct-Selling concepts that are confined to their own characteristics; these enterprises develop themselves as Direct-Selling enterprises but fail to make use of the advantages of the Direct-Selling model to develop themselves.

CHAPTER 21

HOUSEHOLD CONSUMPTION: INTEGRATION OF FAMILY AND PRODUCT

Household consumption is a combined concept that can be viewed from the dimension of products and the dimension of family members and family quantity. The former can be considered as the connotation of household consumption, while the latter is the denotation.

SECTION 1
HOUSEHOLD CONSUMPTION: NEW CONCEPTS IN THE DIRECT-SELLING MARKET

In terms of the market, large-scale expansion of the consumption chain take place through two paths: first, emphasizing the relevance and driving force of products, and second, emphasizing the relevance and driving force of household consumption. These two paths present different characteristics. Household consumption means that the consuming subject develops from an individual to a family and then penetrates into another family. If developing from an individual to a family, it is the consumption expansion within a family, which is the denotation expansion inside a family. Meanwhile, consuming subjects may imitate other families, increasing the number of families involved. This process is the consumption expansion outside the family, the denotation expansion outside the family. The joining of either new family members or new families will facilitate the size expansion of the consumption chain in the target market. Direct-Selling practices stress on the expansion of consuming subjects of the same product or a few products. In other words, direct selling constantly increases the consuming subjects, from an individual to other family members, and from a family to another family. In this way, the market scale of the Direct-Selling enterprise expands.

The product-driven path mainly emphasizes the expansion of the product portfolio, aiming to encourage the consuming subjects who consume one product to consume another kind of product. For example, with ivory chopsticks, consumers will ask for fine food; and with a television, they will want varied TV programs. This effect may be seen among highly relevant products, or among some products showing little relevance. Essentially, this path targets the expansion driven by consumption behaviours and manifests it as the expansion of products, like the consumption of a villa resulting in the demand for a high-end resort. The villa and the resort seem to have no connection, but it will be perfectly logical and reasonable from the perspective of consumption behaviours. Direct-Selling products have limited motive force for the expansion of the consumption chain, as constrained by their special operations models.

I. Closed Nature of Household Consumption in the Direct-Selling Model

Household consumption in direct selling is closed and shows evident borders, which the business scale can never go beyond. Distributors in the Direct-Selling team always hold that their business expansion always targets household consumption, and the Direct-Selling market is the consumer subject they can explore. However, this idea has its limitations, as confined by the operations of distributors in the Direct-Selling model. Actually, there are two ways to integrate household consumption. The first is the connotation expansion of household consumption, which means to integrate all consumption demands with products and supply more products than just the Direct-Selling products. The second is the denotation expansion of household consumption, which suggests to break through the narrow scale of families, and start to cover more customers than just distributors' families in a practical way.

The closed nature of household consumption can be described from the two dimensions here. On this basis, we have drawn two square graphs of families and products for Direct-Selling enterprises.

1. Square Graph of Families and Products

Based on the standards in the two dimensions, the Direct-Selling families and nonDirect-Selling families, Direct-Selling products and nonDirect-Selling products are incorporated in the first square graph.

This square graph of families and products respectively divides families and products into Direct-Selling families and nonDirect-Selling families, Direct-Selling products and nonDirect-Selling products. It expressly draws the market border of Direct-Selling enterprises. A in the square graph represents the market of Direct-Selling enterprises, where enterprises run the business of Direct-Selling products and sell them to Direct-Selling families. Parts B, C and D are the markets that have not been covered by Direct-Selling enterprises. C denotes Direct-Selling families consuming nonDirect-Selling products and D represents nonDirect-Selling families consuming nonDirect-Selling products. B is a nonexistent market for Direct-Selling enterprises, since Direct-Selling products are only sold to Direct-Selling families as determined by the Direct-Selling model.

	Direct-Selling families	nonDirect-Selling families
Direct -Selling products	A	B
nonDirect -Selling products	C	D

Figure 21-1 Square Graph of Families and Products

2. Square Graph of Consumption-oriented and Business-oriented Families and Products
According to the two types of Direct-Selling families, the consumption-oriented Direct-Selling families and business-oriented Direct-Selling families, the second square graph of consumption-oriented and business-oriented families and products is drawn on the basis of the first square graph.

	Consumption-oriented Direct-Selling families	Business-oriented Direct-Selling families
Direct -Selling products	A	B
nonDirect -Selling products	C	D

Figure 21-2 Square Graph of Consumption-oriented and Business-oriented Families and Products

On the basis of the square graph of families and products, the square graph of consumption-oriented and business-oriented families further subdivides Direct-Selling families into the consumption-oriented and business-oriented Direct-Selling families, respectively denoted by A and B. The former only consumes Direct-Selling products, while the latter consumes Direct-Selling products and also encourages other families to purchase and consume Direct-Selling products. C and D suggest that both consumption-oriented and business-oriented Direct-Selling families consume nonDirect-Selling products.

The limitations of direct selling in product and market development are revealed by these two square graphs, as the Direct-Selling model only covers the market of A in Figure 21-1 and A and B in Figure 21-2. A and A+B in these two figures are essentially overlapped, and all other parts have not been covered by direct selling.

With the wide application of the internet in sales, the market becomes less regional and the products and target market show more extensive relations, so the Direct-Selling model with a strong directionality sees a reducing space for development. In this context, we have to emancipate our mind, break traditional ideas, give full play to the special advantages of direct selling while re-positioning the enterprise's products and market, for the sake of its transcendental development. Here two expansion strategies of Direct-Selling enterprises are discussed based on the two square graphs. The first is the expansion from market A to market B in Figure 21-1, and the second is the expansion from markets A and B to markets C and D in Figure 21-2. These two methods are essentially the breakthrough in family scope and the breakthrough in product scope.

II. The First Expansion Method of the Direct-Selling Model: Breakthrough in Family Scope

As mentioned above, distributors in the Direct-Selling model always target families to develop businesses. As a matter of fact, the families in their eyes are confined to market A in Figure 21-1. Though A will constantly expand with the development of the distributor team, the products are mainly sold to Direct-Selling families represented by A.

Nowadays, to break through the family scope, the key is to include the nonDirect-Selling families represented by B in Figure 21-1 as the sales objects of the enterprise through nonconventional approaches, thus to achieve a real breakthrough in and transcendence of families. The difference between the traditional approach and nontraditional approach lies in that the former turns the nonDirect-Selling families into Direct-Selling families before including them as the sales objects, but the latter directly incorporates nonDirect-Selling families as the sales objects and considers them as the market of the Direct-Selling enterprise. This is because the size of nonDirect-Selling families B is much bigger than that of Direct-Selling families A, making B the focus of market prosperity nowadays.

A new thinking pattern is needed to treat nonDirect-Selling families as the market of direct selling. An enterprise can easily get in touch with a vast market and the majority of customers depending on the internet.

By comparison, the number of families that distributors reach through great efforts in the Direct-Selling model is far smaller than the total number of families in the whole of society. Therefore, there is no way out if sticking to the traditional concepts of Direct-Selling families. We must re-examine the enterprise's market view to clarify who are the target customers the enterprise will approach and where they are. The traditional method depending on levels of distributors to explore the market starts to fall, since it develops slowly with a huge time cost, can no longer keep pace with the rapid development of the internet age and offends against the efficiency principle of market expansion. The Direct-Selling enterprise will put great efforts to change its idea of market exploration and directly include the so-called nonDirect-Selling families in the target scope of families. Based on the operations and management logic of the Direct-Selling enterprise, the traditional method is the foundation, and the nontraditional method is the transcendence.

III. The Second Expansion Method of the Direct-Selling Model: Breakthrough in Product Scope

To break through the product scope, we will firstly examine the nonDirect-Selling products consumed by nonDirect-Selling families represented by C in Figure 21-1. The Direct-Selling enterprise will draw up a plan and practically place the focus of product development on the so-called nonDirect-Selling products to achieve the transcendence of products. Product breakthrough is more practically significant than family scope breakthrough for the transcendental development of the Direct-Selling enterprise. As longitudinally shown in the first square graph, Figure 21-1, Direct-Selling families consume two types of products: Direct-Selling products and nonDirect-Selling products. According to the discussions on the consumption chain above, the length and structural relations of the consumption chain make it incomparably attractive than that of Direct-Selling products people can see now. By including nonDirect-Selling products as the target, approaching Direct-Selling families in a convenient way, and attaching importance to the consumption chain of Direct-Selling enterprises, it will create infinite development space and lower the cost for the Direct-Selling enterprise which is currently in difficulties. The enterprise strategy with household consumption as the target can only be truly realized when the enterprise delivers more nonDirect-Selling products to Direct-Selling families. Household consumption is nothing without product breakthrough. Direct-Selling with families as the target cannot be put on a par with the development with the household consumption chain as the object. The laws on the product categories for direct selling vary in different countries. As a Direct-Selling enterprise mainly running businesses in a multinational market, Tiens can take the lead to break through the product scope in the international market, which is a feasible way that can be immediately adopted for transcendental development.

In general, there are two ways to promote household consumption: the family breakthrough from A to B, and the product breakthrough from A to C in Figure 21-1. This is completely different with the refinement of A. In the traditional Direct-Selling model, A is slowly expanded mainly by the distributor's great efforts and the constant product development of the enterprise. When nonDirect-Selling enterprises are turned into Direct-Selling enterprises, and nonDirect-Selling families are turned into Direct-Selling families, they will naturally fall in the category of A and become a part of A. This result will manifest itself as an increment of A, which is still Direct-Selling families consuming Direct-Selling products. This is just the continuous replication of the results of the traditional Direct-Selling model, but not transcendence. To catch up with the development of the internet age, we must transcend Direct-Selling concepts and measures to apply them to nonDirect-Selling families and nonDirect-Selling products represented by B and C.

There is a need to avoid the classical path and mistake of family promotion in the Direct-Selling model. The classical path of family promotion in the Direct-Selling model is shown in the second square graph in Figure 21-2, which is to constantly turn consumption-oriented Direct-Selling families into business-oriented Direct-Selling families, and relies on the business-oriented Direct-Selling families to constantly turn common families into consumption-oriented Direct-Selling families. This circulation enables a stepwise promotion in the Direct-Selling model. While consumption-oriented Direct-Selling families only consume Direct-Selling products, the business-oriented Direct-Selling families not only consume Direct-Selling products but also actively develop new consumption-oriented Direct-Selling families, which will later be turned into business-oriented Direct-Selling families. Simply put, the classical path is to duplicate the high-end team of distributors. With this classical path of distributor development in the Direct-Selling model, the Direct-Selling enterprise develops its sales of Direct-Selling products, and distributors realize their dreams of getting rich. The motive force of this dream originates from the points system adopted by the Direct-Selling enterprise. Then, why do we also call it a mistake? Putting the two square graphs together, we find that A and B in the second square graph are the same as A in the first square graph. No matter how A is converted to become B in the second square, it is still A in the first square graph. In other words, it still falls in the category of Direct-Selling families in the eyes of distributors. Distributors fail to see the scale of nonDirect-Selling families, but only centre on the small circle of Direct-Selling families, being too short-sighted to think about transcendental development. They attach too much importance to the changes of the structure of Direct-Selling families, put great efforts to convert consumption-oriented Direct-Selling families to become business-oriented Direct-Selling families and, depending on the points system, turn more nonDirect-Selling families to Direct-Selling families. They only treat Direct-Selling families as customers, and they only think about the nonDirect-Selling families after they have been turned into Direct-Selling families. Therefore, household consumption is confined to Direct-Selling families, and the great consumption potential of nonDirect-Selling families has been neglected.

SECTION 2
NEW HOUSEHOLD CONSUMPTION CHANNELS

Regardless of family breakthroughs or product breakthroughs, the direct seller's understanding of household consumption must transcend the distributor's understanding of household consumption. Only in this way can the Direct-Selling enterprise truly understand the whole chain of household consumption and construct new concepts for the Direct-Selling market based on the household consumption chain and the consumption ecological chain of the enterprise.

II. New Household Consumption Channels

Family miniaturization, particularly the diversified consumption chain and decision points, will finally exert influence on the purchase methods of household consumption and play a decisive role in determining the enterprise's selling method. Compared to two decades ago, household consumption nowadays prefers the so-called one-stop shopping place, which was the physical supermarket 20 years ago but has become the e-commerce platform, the virtual online supermarket, in the last decade. The common characteristic of the two rests in the wide variety of products. Though the virtual supermarket is still called a supermarket, consumers' shopping habits here vary essentially from those in physical stores. While the physical supermarket satisfies consumers' demands of one-stop shopping, the virtual supermarket meets their needs in the selection of single products. Household consumption and consumers' shopping habits are exposed to new changes in the competition between the virtual supermarket and the physical supermarket.

1. Products and Leisure Services Bundled in Household Consumption

The supermarket attempts to cover all commodities of families' daily consumption by providing all ranges of products. One-stop shopping matches consumers' fast-paced lifestyles. From the merchant's perspective, bundled purchasing is a potential competitive means of the supermarket, and the price advantage acquired through bulk purchase also arouses the customer's buying desire. Therefore, the rise of supermarkets creates a win-win situation, from which both customers and merchants acquire benefits.

The shopping dependence on e-commerce has covered nearly every aspect of household consumption. Compared to the supermarket, the e-commerce platform multiplies its commodity varieties due to no restriction of physical space. In addition to daily consumption products, the e-commerce platform sells any type of commodity that is needed.

Considering the material base, the large shopping and leisure square replaces the large department store. Under the impact of e-commerce platforms, the changes of customers' shopping habits, the close combination of household consumption and leisure services, and the integration of shopping and consumption create favourable circumstances for the rise of large shopping and leisure squares. All these variations are changing household consumption methods.

2. Network Dependence of Household Consumption
Household consumption is increasingly depending on the development of the network. As the seller's market gradually turns into the buyer's market, the decision-making power of both parties in transactions is also silently changing. The view of product chain or value chain still rests on the enterprise-centred consumption cognition. The seller is trying to control the consumption activities by means of the integration of resources and products. However, as the idea of the consumption chain is put forward, buyers gain the initiative and customers start to determine their own consumption. The development of the network opens an important channel for the development of enterprises or Direct-Selling enterprises in the so-called YOU age. The network dependence of household consumption not only suggests that a large quantity of products are purchased through the network, but also means that the network is irreplaceable during consumption or purchasing behaviours. The information transmission through the network has replaced the traditional way of consumers seeking information during the purchase, which reduces the influence of information asymmetry on the purchase and the following consumption effect.

Convenience has always been an important consideration of consumers. In addition to the indicators of traditional commercial convenience, another important premise to convenience is the sufficiency of information, which is created by the network that transmits information quickly. The network provides full information on the whole process of purchasing, including the information on the product itself and the information on the product effect. The network brings word-of-mouth information into full play, significantly reducing the blind spots of purchase.

3. Signs of the Recovery of Physical Stores
   As demonstrated by Alibaba's strategic plan and initial practice of physical retail stores, consumers will not refuse to leave the keyboard and will personally visit physical stores to buy something that is rarely seen on the e-commerce platform. The development of the retailing industry always adheres to the principle of complying with consumers' lifestyles and consumption habits.

   Seen from the signs of the recovery of physical stores, the purchase itself constitutes an important part in consumption. Though 'shopping' is time-consuming, the behaviour of shopping itself is a part of consumption or can be directly viewed as a kind of consumption. In particular, in the large shopping and leisure square, shopping is a necessary part that bundles shopping with leisure services. Shopping, as a social activity, is essentially an innovative change of people's lifestyles. In the YOU age, they are no longer content with shopping by browsing the virtual world, but are inclined to enjoy this innovative shopping method.

   There are two potential reasons contributing to the recovery of the physical stores of e-commerce tycoons. First, they find that it will increase consumers' benefits by treating the purchase activity as a part of consumption. Second, they may have different opinions on the development of express services. The development of physical stores will certainly squeeze B2C express services and increase B2B logistics services. They can create favourable feelings among consumers by providing physical experiences for them.

   Lifestyle creates the consumption chain of a family; the household consumption chain guides the consumption ecological chain; and the consumption ecological chain shapes the consumption ecosystem. The Direct-Selling enterprise can find a path to expand the space of direct selling based on this logic. The above analysis shows that the Direct-Selling model is separated from these new channels of household consumption. What Direct-Selling model is the Direct-Selling model based on? The answer may be complicated. However, we confirm that the wide application of the network exerts great influence on household consumption, which is a great opportunity to integrate the Direct-Selling model and the e-commerce platform, for the sake of the current development of the Direct-Selling enterprise. Two paths can be adopted to develop the Direct-Selling model: family breakthrough or product breakthrough. In this way, the closed Direct-Selling model will become more open.

SECTION 3
RETURN AND INTEGRATION OF HOUSEHOLD CONSUMPTION CONCEPT

I. Return of Household Consumption Concept

The return of the household consumption concept means that to adapt to the age of e-commerce, the Direct-Selling enterprise has a full cognition of household consumption and introduces the concept of the consumption chain, from the Direct-Selling products consumption of distributors' families, to the total consumption of distributors' families, and finally to the total consumption of common families.

Product breakthrough constitutes the premise of the return of the household consumption concept. The breakthrough from A to C in Figure 21-1 is the expansion from the Direct-Selling products consumption of distributors' families to the total consumption of distributors' families. The Direct-Selling enterprise will focus on the full picture of the consumption chain of Direct-Selling families instead of focusing merely on Direct-Selling products in the Direct-Selling families' consumption chain.

The expansion from the total consumption of distributors' families to the total consumption of common families is to expand A to D directly in Figure 21-1. As expected, the enterprise can think over the path from A to C and finally to D to formulate a development strategy. It is safer to accumulate experiences in C to expand the target market and develop from Direct-Selling families to nonDirect-Selling families. This is because the Direct-Selling enterprise may not be familiar enough to run the business of nonDirect-Selling products, since the sales model of Direct-Selling products is completely different from that of nonDirect-Selling products. With the return of the household consumption concept, the Direct-Selling enterprise will not be confined to Direct-Selling products or a few links in the household consumption chain. Instead, the emphasis will be placed on all links of the household consumption chain. Therefore, the distributor's idea that their activities always target families is one-sided.

II. Integration of Household Consumption Concept

It is of profound significance for the Direct-Selling enterprise to break through the original family scope and integrate and choose family resources at the strategic level, which has transcended the Direct-Selling model. The key to the integration of the household consumption concept is to make choices. The enterprise will not take over all the demands in the consumption chain, but compare the enterprise's consumption ecological chain with the consumption chain and match the household consumption chain with the enterprise's resource advantages to make strategic choices. Simply put, the essence of integration is choice and priority. No enterprise can satisfy all of the requirements in the consumption chain merely relying on its own strength. Like the supermarket in the past could not display everything, the e-commerce tycoons nowadays cannot display all commodities on their platforms. We mentioned that lifestyle created a consumption chain. Choice and priority have already become the two major factors that influence the enterprise on how to create a consumption ecological chain. The choice is made upon the full understanding of the enterprise's strategic resources, while the priority plays a decisive role in the direction and border of product development.

If we treat the consumption chain as a whole, the integration of the enterprise's consumption ecological chain, the time, place, object and price of the product supply, and the categories of commodities are necessarily constrained by the enterprise's resources and challenged by competitors. The key to the integration of the household consumption concept is to determine the business direction of the enterprise.

III. Product Expansion in the Direct-Selling Model

With the health products run by Tiens as an example, in the household consumption chain, Direct-Selling products may show different consumption priorities due to different family structures. There are two basic factors that influence the consumption of health products: income and health. When income reaches a certain level, health issues become more important in life, the priority of which will be boosted; and when potential health issues become prominent, especially for the elderly, the likelihood of consuming health products will increase, increasing the priority of the products. In other words, high-income young families and elderly families are the target markets with the most potential for health products, and low-income and young families have a lower priority for these products. Some families may also top health products in the consumption list to provide against possible diseases due to the characteristics of the family structure. Hence, the priority of health products in the consumption list is never a scientific issue, but an issue about consumption desire.

The description and analysis of Figures 21-1 and 21-2 reveal the closed nature of the Direct-Selling model. On this basis, the Direct-Selling enterprise will explore the transcendence strategy of the Direct-Selling model in terms of families and products and seize development opportunities in the future by innovatively integrating the Direct-Selling model and the e-commerce platform.

Special Column 21-1: Online shopping malls never restrict consumers and commodities

As the three most representative comprehensive online shopping malls, JD, Tmall and Suning all supply hundreds of thousands of brands and dozens of millions of commodities from every corner of the world, including household electric appliances, mobile phones and digital products, computers, office supplies, furniture, home furnishings, kitchen utensils, clothing, shoes, hats, cases, bags, clocks, watches, outdoor sports equipment, maternal and infant products, toys, food, aquatic products, medicine, health products, artistic works, flowers, green plants, books, cultural and entertainment products, air tickets, hotels, financial insurance, installation maintenance, and cleaning services. Everything needed in a consumer's daily life is incorporated. By now, even some industrial products are sold in online shopping malls.

The sales models are also flexible here, such as flash sales, coupons, membership, flash purchases and auctions. In addition to the convenience, they also offer medical and tourism benefits to stimulate purchases and consumption.

They do not set a scope of commodities, as anything consumers need can be put in the online stores; or set a threshold to purchase, as anyone can browse, purchase, pay for and even rate commodities here to share their experiences and worries during the transaction.

These online shopping malls also provide consumers with their purchase records. For example, in pages such as 'My JD' and 'My Taobao,' consumers can see purchase management functions including the order centre, favourites centre, assets centre, special businesses and customer services to help consumers control the whole process of purchase and consumption.

How could it be possible for the open online shopping malls to set up thresholds and obstacles to exclude consumers or commodities? Any restrictions conflict fundamentally with the network-based distribution.

CHAPTER 22

HOUSEHOLD BUSINESS CONSUMPTION: CONSUMER SURPLUS FROM 'BUSINESS'

Household business consumption is an important concept of direct selling. The key to the development of household business consumption is the improvement of stickiness. The essence of Direct-Selling stickiness can be profoundly explained with the concept of consumer surplus and the analytical logic of management. Whether the points system of direct selling takes effect is determined by the consumer surplus from 'business' and the practice sublimation of consumption capital.

SECTION 1
HOUSEHOLD BUSINESS CONSUMPTION: DIRECT MARKETING DRIVES NEW SPACE

The key to household business consumption is the improvement of stickiness. The concept of consumer surplus can help us explain the practical logic of stickiness improvement.

I. Stickiness Improvement: Essence of Household Business Consumption

In the special context of household business consumption, to improve direct selling, the enterprise will put great effort, invest necessary human and financial resources, rationalize business processes, provide all-round education services, and turn the distributors' consumption-oriented families to business-oriented families. In other words, an increasingly number of families not only purchase and consume Direct-Selling products, but also promote Direct-Selling concepts to other families and participate in the Direct-Selling undertakings as a partner. Or we can say, it is essentially to achieve an in-depth integration of distributors' families and the Direct-Selling enterprise based on extensive interests.

II. Stickiness and Consumer Surplus

Consumer surplus is an economic concept. When this concept is applied to consumer behaviour research, it refers to the difference between the practical price and the expected price when the practical purchase price is lower than the expected price. The consumer surplus exerts direct or indirect influence over the consumers' purchases and determines the relevance between consumers and the products, which will further develop to the relevance between consumers and the enterprise.

The consumer surplus will play a role as a mechanism during consumers' purchasing behaviours, which will generate a sense of acquisition or making profits among consumers. These feelings will improve the consumer satisfaction about the purchase or consumption of certain commodities, and make them attracted or inclined to these commodities. When the consumer surplus is fixed in a certain form of concept, it becomes the stickiness. Stickiness here is essentially loyalty, the loyalty to the brand, to the enterprise and, in the Direct-Selling industry, to the Direct-Selling model. The consumer surplus can be acquired by purchasing products and, more importantly, by developing distributors, by purchasing from other distributors. When the consumer surplus is gradually expanded, stickiness is improved. With increasing loyalty to the Direct-Selling model, the consumption-oriented distributors will become business-oriented. Their loyalty to the Direct-Selling model is the start to guide household business consumption, as well as the key to and transcendence over the wealth creation by household business consumption

III. Consumer Surplus from 'Business'

Consumption-oriented Direct-Selling families obtain a fixed consumer surplus, and business-oriented Direct-Selling families obtain an incremental consumer surplus. The so-called fixed consumer surplus is the part the consumption-oriented Direct-Selling families acquire from the points given by the Direct-Selling enterprise. The consumer surplus in this case is determined by the consumption amount and the points system of the Direct-Selling enterprise, and is therefore relatively stable. The incremental consumer surplus is the benefits from the enterprise's points system earned by business-oriented families by developing new distributors (consumption-oriented Direct-Selling families).

The characteristics of the acquisition of consumer surplus. According to behavioural science, consumer surplus is derived from the seller's price adjustment that makes the price lower than the buyer's expected price, instead of from the buyer's request. The seller takes the initiative. This relationship is determined by the seller's behaviours. In other words, the seller takes the initiative to lower the price, 'presents' the buyer with the gap between the buyer's expected price and practical price and has the buyer gain a consumer surplus.

The consumer surplus from business has two meanings. First, the consumer surplus is the benefit derived from the seller's price policy. For example, in a batch pricing policy, the more consumers buy, the bigger price referential they can enjoy. They can acquire a constantly increasing consumer surplus if they purchase products ceaselessly. However, the quantity of a certain kind of product consumed by a consumer is limited, so the interest space under the policy is also limited for the consumer. However, in this case, the buyer obtains certain initiatives to decide the scale of the consumer surplus.

Second, in the Direct-Selling model, the seller's price policy renders the possibilities for the buyer to 'run business.' In short, the buyer can sharply expand the space of the consumer surplus by developing a new buyers' group. The buyers' group in the Direct-Selling model refers to the distributors' group that is created and developed through the buyers' efforts, like providing education services, products and services. Apparently, a consumer surplus can be reached through the buyer's subjective efforts.

These two meanings show essential differences. In the former case, the consumer surplus is determined by the buyer's purchase quantity. To acquire more consumer surplus, the purchase quantity must be increased. However, the consumption of a certain product is always limited for a consumer. Over-purchase not only makes consumer surplus a false benefit, but also causes consumer wastes and losses since the consumer cannot consume all the products purchased. The 'business' that can be done here is nothing more than increasing the purchase quantity within the limits to increase consumer surplus. In the final analysis, it is merely a purchase decision within the scope of rational consumption and rational purchase, instead of a business decision. The latter is completely different. In this case, the consumer surplus is expanded not by the consumer's overpurchase of certain commodities but by the development of the distributor team. With the special points system in the Direct-Selling model, unlimited consumer surplus can be achieved through the business operations of the distributor team and the price system offered by the Direct-Selling enterprise to the distributor team.

Evidently, stickiness is derived not only from the interests from product consumption, the consumer surplus constantly offered by the seller to the buyer through the purchase of products, but also from the development of the distributor team itself. It means to constantly turn nonDirect-Selling families into Direct-Selling families and turn consumption-oriented Direct-Selling families into business-oriented Direct-Selling families, thus to acquire consumer surplus from the business.

Stickiness has become a motive force for direct selling. Consumer surplus here explains the source of profit of distributors. The basic economic concept of consumer surplus is used to explain how distributors make profits, which is the benefit from household business consumption and the new perspective to observe consuming subjects' behaviours, instead of being merely a method or perspective to calculate economic interests. The Direct-Selling model fixes the profit from household business consumption through the points system. Once the interest from household business consumption is fixed by the points system, the active-passive relationship between the Direct-Selling enterprise such as Tiens and distributors, subjects of household business consumption, may be changed and even reversed. Originally, it seems that the enterprise organizes distributors together as the external resources of the enterprise; the distributors survive and grow depending on the enterprise; and the enterprise provides various services to distributors including education, logistics and financial services. When the relations are fixed by the points system, the enterprise will increasingly depend on the development of the distributor team for survival and development. Seeing the change and reversal of this relationship, the consumer surplus can be considered as the goal that distributors independently pursue after, which makes it possible to get rich through household business consumption.

IV. Dual-level Wealth Creation of Consumption Capital

As a wealth stock of the owner, consumer surplus from business will be realized with the advancement of the business. However, it features another property, the mechanism of wealth stock appreciation, which can be described with consumption capital.

1. Theoretical Value of the Consumption Capital Concept

Consumption capital is a concept describing how different subjects consider the potential uses for the subjects of the currency they hold during social production, which will help us understand different subjects' behaviours to use their currency. The theory of consumption capital considers consumption capital as a certain amount of currency possessed by consumers, which can be applied to reinvestment in production. It is an extension from the consumption area to the production or business area. The business results can be shared in forms of consumers' equity and options. When consumption capital is introduced to the enterprise, the enterprise will assign a certain proportion of the amount of products purchased by the consumer to the consumer's investment account at the enterprise. After a period of time, consumers can acquire consumer surplus from the balance of the investment account as well as the products. This method is similar to the supply and marketing cooperative in the early days, by which the quantity purchased or sold by cooperative members through the cooperative constitutes the basis for dividend distribution of the supply and marketing cooperative. The concept of consumption capital gives a description of the consumers' use of currency, which renders new thinking patterns for consumers to use currency on hand and for the enterprise to absorb currency capital.

2. The Dual-level Wealth Creation Role of Consumption Capital in Household Business Consumption

The points system of the Direct-Selling enterprise offers a brand-new choice for consumption capital. When either consumption-oriented or business-oriented Direct-Selling families leave their consumer surplus in the enterprise's records as the account balance, they are actually investing consumer surplus in the enterprise operations as a kind of consumption capital. From the perspective of the enterprise, this practice locks the target market; and from the perspective of consumers, they are realizing their dream of consumption creating wealth, business consumption creating more wealth, household consumption creating wealth and business household consumption creating more wealth, by investing their consumer surplus to the enterprise as consumption capital.

The consumer surplus left in the enterprise's records plays the role of consumption capital, motivating the two types of Direct-Selling enterprises to constantly be involved in the sales of the Direct-Selling products. However, the effect of the consumer surplus in the enterprise's accounts book, consumption capital in this case, varies between consumption-oriented and business-oriented Direct-Selling families. In other words, the consumption capital creates different amounts of wealth. The key lies in that the growth of the consumer surplus of consumption-oriented Direct-Selling families only depends on the enterprise's preferential batch pricing. However, when consumption-oriented families are turned into business-oriented families, they no longer consume products simply, but instead, they encourage more people to consume the enterprise's products, enable these newcomers to acquire the accumulated benefits from the consumer surplus resulting from the enterprise's batch pricing, obtain the consumer surplus from the business and then again leave the consumer surplus from business in the enterprise's records. In this case, their consumer surplus growth relies on not only the enterprise's batch pricing, but also the multiplier growth of the consumer surplus from their businesses. Considering the multiplier growth effect, the returns from consumption capital of business-oriented Direct-Selling families will be much higher than that of consumption-oriented Direct-Selling families. This dual-level wealth creation role of consumption capital in household business consumption makes up the essential driving force for the conversion from consumption-oriented Direct-Selling families to business-oriented Direct-Selling families.

SECTION 2
HOUSEHOLD BUSINESS CONSUMPTION: RETHINKING THE DIRECT-SELLING MODEL

I. Essential Connotation of the Direct-Selling Model

The growth of the Direct-Selling enterprise's interests is closely associated with the growth of distributors' interests.

1. Essential Connotation of Direct Selling as an Operations Model

The essential connotation of the Direct-Selling enterprise is to motivate distributors to pursue consumer surplus from business, thus to promote the enterprise's development. Since the concept of consumer surplus is applied here, it will be easier to understand the idea of 'consumption creating wealth' and 'business consumption creating more wealth.' On this basis, personal consumption and personal business consumption are respectively extended to be household consumption and household business consumption. Here a transcendental understanding of the Direct-Selling model emerges: direct selling is not only to purchase certain products directly from the manufacturer, but more importantly, means to introduce the products to others to engage them in the enterprise's business and earn profit from the business through great efforts. The so-called Direct-Selling operations model is trying to integrate customers in the enterprise's operations and enable them to make profit from the business.

On the face of it, direct selling is a kind of operations model, which is characterized by no intermediate circulation link during the sales of products and by the direct contact between the enterprise and consumers. It has the shortest distance for the enterprise to approach the market, by which the enterprise can rapidly acquire feedback information from the market, timely adjust the product and service portfolio, control the dynamics of the target market effectively and satisfy its demands. Meanwhile, through business in the target market, the enterprise can incorporate the circulation cost and profit of the intermediate links in the enterprise's scope of business and thus maximize its gross profit; and through the business run by the target market, the enterprise can share the circulation cost and profit of the intermediate links with the target market and achieve a win-win situation between the enterprise and the target market.

The Direct-Selling model has its own 'channels.' When getting deeper into the consumer group of the Direct-Selling enterprise, we can see that consumption-oriented customers are the real target market of the Direct-Selling enterprise, while the business-oriented customers are the middlemen, the channels, of the Direct-Selling enterprise. This is the basic characteristic and essential connotation of the Direct-Selling operations model. As a matter of fact, a key factor contributing to the success of the Direct-Selling enterprise is the choice of appropriate Direct-Selling products. As this factor has been widely discussed in many articles, we will not talk about it here.

2. Essential Connotation of Direct Selling as a Business Model
There are two key points to analyse the essential connotation of direct selling as a business model. First, it develops the distributor team, transforms the external resources to be internal resources and maintain distributors as the enterprise's assets. Second, the enterprise's profit is mainly derived from the circulation cost that is saved in direct selling; it is savedbecause there is no middleman in the Direct-Selling model. This circulation cost and the profit made by intermediate links are distributed to consumers and the enterprise. The specific rules for distribution are embodied in the design of the points system of the Direct-Selling enterprise.

The distribution of profits in the Direct-Selling enterprise is realized through the points system. This points system deals with the distribution from two levels: the distribution within the distributor system and the distribution between the enterprise and distributors. The former is about the operations model, while the latter is about the profit of the business model. People attach more importance to the former, which means that they pay more attention to the operations of direct selling. However, if direct selling is analysed as a business model, the latter distribution will be the focus.

As its most important characteristic, the Direct-Selling model has two levels of profit models as a business model. The first level is the profit model of Direct-Selling distributors. It cancels intermediate links and adopts the Direct-Selling method to sell products. The cost and profit of intermediate links constitute the distributors' profits. The other level is the profit model of the Direct-Selling enterprise, where the profit comprises the cost of intermediate links and another part of profit. These two parts are divided based on a certain percentage. The two parts show a positive correlation. The growth of one part will drive the growth of the other part. In other words, the growth of distributors' interests will boost the growth of the Direct-Selling enterprise's interests.

3. Transcending Direct Selling Based on Household Business Consumption
First, expand the product scope to transcend direct selling. The Direct-Selling products are an important means to motivate distributors to join the Direct-Selling activities. The Direct-Selling products correspond to part of the demands in the distributors' consumption chain, but there are many other demands in the distributors' consumption chain. That's why the Direct-Selling enterprise will provide more extensive product categories to cultivate its unique consumption ecological chain to satisfy distributors' demands.

Second, expand the family scope to transcend direct selling. The distributor team of the Direct-Selling enterprise is too small a part compared to the large number of consumers. The primary task of the Direct-Selling model is to promote Direct-Selling products to nonDirect-Selling families. However, nonDirect-Selling families also need more extensive products like Direct-Selling families do. Therefore, if the enterprise successfully transcends Direct-Selling products in terms of the product scope, it will naturally occupy the market of nonDirect-Selling families.

Third, broaden the enterprise's vision to transcend direct selling. Based on the operations model of direct selling, the enterprise will transfer the focus on the operations model to the business model to transcend direct selling and draw up the enterprise's strategies on the business model. Only with the transcendence of concepts and based on the characteristics of direct selling as a business model can the enterprise break through the family concept and product concept in the operations model, replace the concept of the operations model with the description of the target market in the business model. This vision will be much broader than that in the operations model. Similarly, the Direct-Selling model can only break through the original cognition of product concepts if treating the products of the Direct-Selling enterprise from the perspective of the business model.

II. Overcome the Weakness of the Direct-Selling Model in Speed

In the network age, the network speed has been drastically improved. An e-commerce platform may become the centre of people's consumption and change people's purchasing habits and channels overnight. By comparison, the Direct-Selling model shows an evident shortage in speed.

The speed of the development of the Direct-Selling model depends on the distributor team's expansion ability, which means to attract customers one by one and constantly provide education services on Direct-Selling products. The decisive factor here is the uniqueness of the Direct-Selling products, which are irreplaceable and have corresponding rigid demands. The development speed of this market exploration model falls far behind the e-commerce development speed in the network age, and the uniqueness and irreplaceability of Direct-Selling products are vanishing. Considering the speed of commodity development, consumers find it hard to believe that the functions of certain commodities are irreplaceable. Therefore, the education services that worked well previously can no longer reach the expected results.

Priority is given to speed in the network age. If an enterprise fails to speed up the development or break the product and family limitation, even a successful enterprise like Tiens, with its long history and rich experiences, has little room for the development of household business consumption based on the original product catalogue and the distributors' concept of household consumption. Faced with these difficulties, the Direct-Selling enterprise is impelled to make constant innovations. However, the fundamental innovation should be the re-recognition of the Direct-Selling model. If no rethinking takes place, then household business consumption is nothing here, not to mention the wealth creation by household business consumption.

SECTION 3
REPLICATION AND TRANSCENDENCE OF THE DIRECT-SELLING MODEL

I. Replicability of the Direct-Selling Model

Replicability of the Direct-Selling model means that this unique business model is replicated and applied to any business other than direct selling. Apparently, there is no need to discuss the replication of the Direct-Selling model itself, since any enterprise entering this field will design the effective points system, develop Direct-Selling products that attract distributors, compete in the market by means of lectures and education services, and construct its own distributor team, regardless of whether they can succeed. The key issue here is that the Direct-Selling enterprise will be cautious about applying the operations model of the Direct-Selling enterprise to any nonDirect-Selling business.

The focus of the business model of the Direct-Selling enterprise is to engage distributors, customers, in the interest distribution of the Direct-Selling enterprise. Then, can customers in the nonDirect-Selling business be engaged in the interest distribution of the Direct-Selling enterprise? The Direct-Selling enterprise does not acquire interests by adjusting the price, or we can say it does not obtain profit purely depending on consumer surplus. The interest distribution of the Direct-Selling model features two prominent characteristics: the interest distribution for direct participation and the interest distribution for accumulative sharing. The interest distribution for direct participation means that the distributors and the enterprise constantly acquire the profit from sales through the fixed points system. The interest distribution for accumulative sharing means that the business-oriented Direct-Selling families can acquire a certain proportion of the consumption of consumption-oriented Direct-Selling families and the lower-level business-oriented Direct-Selling families. The key to the replicability of the Direct-Selling model lies in the good institutional design for interest distribution.

There are two important points with the replicability of the Direct-Selling model. First, from the perspective of products, the restrictions on the application of the Direct-Selling model due to its interest distribution method and characteristics show no fixed relation with Direct-Selling products, so this model can be applied to nonDirect-Selling products. Since they are not locked with certain customers, this model can also be applied to nondistributors, general customers. Therefore, they are highly replicable. Second, from the perspective of the customer development model, the replicability of the Direct-Selling model in other channels is extremely low. In particular, the method to develop customers through one-to-one detailed education cannot be compared to e-commerce in terms of efficiency and speed.

II. New Room for the Development of Direct Selling's Advantages

'Direct selling + e-commerce' varies from 'e-commerce + direct selling.' These two concepts reveal the characteristics of the Direct-Selling enterprise, respectively, in the two stages after its combination with e-commerce. Direct selling + e-commerce applies the concept of direct selling to the e-commerce platform and is an extension of the Direct-Selling model in the nonDirect-Selling area. It centres on direct selling, retains the basic characteristics of the original form of direct selling, combines e-commerce as a means and seeks for the rapid development of the Direct-Selling operations model. E-commerce + direct selling focuses on e-commerce, where the Direct-Selling enterprise gradually turns into an e-commerce enterprise, adopts direct selling as a means and makes use of direct selling as an advantageous resource in the competition with other e-commerce platforms.

For the Direct-Selling enterprise, direct selling + e-commerce and e-commerce + direct selling are two stages of gradual development. Direct selling + e-commerce is the first step, which is a strategic choice made by the Direct-Selling enterprise as well as a leap-forward development. E-commerce + direct selling is the second step of the Direct-Selling enterprise, which may completely change the enterprise and lead to transcendental and even disruptive development. It may be the necessary result of the development of the internet age for the Direct-Selling enterprise to take the first step. However, the Direct-Selling enterprise will be more cautious about whether and when to take the second step, what conditions will be met, whether the original Direct-Selling distributors can accept this, what methods will be applied to realize wealth creation by household business consumption, and whether any consumer surplus can still be generated from the business as the driving force for performance development.

The combination of the Direct-Selling model and the internet has produced an e-commerce platform with Direct-Selling characteristics; JTMM, the so-called global cross-border social e-commerce platform, has become a pioneering undertaking for the transcendental development of Tiens. The key to the success of this undertaking lies in two aspects. The first point is whether it can break the limitations of direct selling and run businesses with a brand-new view of families and products. The second point is whether it can effectively apply the consumer surplus from business as consumption capital to the e-commerce platform, to help the customers of the platform create wealth through household business consumption.

CHAPTER 23

AGGREGATION AND TRANSCENDENCE OF THE DIRECT-SELLING MODEL

In the context of the internet and e-commerce, whether the Direct-Selling enterprise can succeed in strategically combining the network-based platform for development depends on the transcendence of this innovative business model over the Direct-Selling concept. The search for development opportunities in the Direct-Selling model leads to the strategic choice to integrate the advantageous resources commonly seen and recognized worldwide, the network platform, and the advantageous resources of the Direct-Selling enterprise, the distributor team. The awareness to make this strategic choice, the advantageous resources accumulated in the Direct-Selling model, the size of the distributor team, and the application of resources in Internet+ are key to the transcendental development of an enterprise.

SECTION 1
PRACTICE OF INTERNET+ IN THE DIRECT-SELLING FIELD

I. The Early Form of the E-commerce Platform in the Direct-Selling Model

Following Tianle Shopping Mall, Tiens created JTMM. This is a new e-commerce platform that leads the new development paths of breakthroughs in the product and family scope in the Direct-Selling model.

1. Direct-Selling E-commerce Platform: Basic Ideas and General Principles
As an exploration in the early stages, JTMM undertakes the important mission to explore the basic ideas and general principles of the Direct-Selling e-commerce platform and help the Direct-Selling enterprise to deeply understand the essence of consumption, where consumption is investment

and will acquire dividends. Since then, JTMM has started the disruptive exploration of the consumption concepts of the Direct-Selling e-commerce platform. Financially, consumption is always a subtraction of wealth. Adhering to the thinking pattern of the Direct-Selling model, JTMM puts forward the idea of personal consumption creating wealth, household consumption creating more wealth and more consumption creating more wealth. These ideas can be explained with the consumer surplus from business and consumption capital as discussed above. JTMM sticks to the basic principle of embodying the essence of the Direct-Selling model. It provides a platform that invites the majority of people, attracts nonDirect-Selling customers, targets the middle and high-end consumer groups, encourages customers' recommendations of new customers, promises customers lifetime benefits and prevents the simple simulation of the Direct-Selling system.

2. Market Segment Positioning: Starting Point of Household Business Consumption
   JTMM divides platform customers into five types based on their consumption amount. These different identities reflect the different relations between customers and the platform and determine the levels and activity for customers to engage in household business consumption. It will actively encourage customers to participate in consumption. Meanwhile, the market segment positioning also lays the foundation for the interests sharing system and is seen as the starting point for customers to join household business consumption.

3. Interests Sharing System: Institutional Design of Wealth Creation by Household Business Consumption
   JTMM's dividend mechanism reveals the core requirements of the above ideas and principles and reflects the economic logic for market segment positioning and a platform for customers' identities. JTMM's e-commerce platform offers various progressive incentive mechanisms such as red packets, dividends, tourism rewards and gross profit, which regulate the interests of and incentives for customers of different engagements. These incentives essentially encourage consumers to become distributors to share the e-commerce platform interests, consumer surplus and achieve the goal of wealth creation by household business consumption.

To sum up, as revealed by the basic ideas and principles of the Direct-Selling e-commerce platform, as well as its market segment positioning and interests sharing mechanism, JTMM e-commerce platform features the following advantages: 1) a large group of customers from the internet; 2) a large scale of sales from retailing; 3) the convenience and low cost for direct sellers to make recommendations; 4) and the convenience and low cost for direct sellers to acquire transformed resources. Among these four advantages, the most essential factors that we will focus on are the convenience and low cost for direct sellers to make recommendations and acquire transformed resources. These two points reflect an important principle of JTMM when it promotes the development of distributors depending on the e-commerce platform: 'swap of network resources.'

II. New E-commerce Platform of the Direct-Selling Model

After the exploration of Tianle Mall and the early form of e-commerce platform, JTMM by Tiens, JTMM has become a relatively stable and mature form.

1. Basic Characteristics of JTMM's New E-commerce Platform

JTMM's new e-commerce platform has integrated suppliers, online stores and customers, which is the same with general e-commerce platforms. The difference that distinguishes JTMM's new e-commerce platform from other e-commerce platforms lies in that it provides different subjects with different interaction interfaces. First, based on the supplier's interface about the products it supplies and the online store's interface about the products it is willing to distribute, an interaction platform that consists of product information, logistics information, price information and supply-demand information is established between the supplier and the online store. Through the virtual channel of the network platform, it develops transaction links between the supplier and the online store and offers a market choice at a new level, which guides the online store's understanding of market information. Second, based on the scale of product distribution between the online store and customer, it provides a platform to cultivate high-quality customers and a competition and cooperation platform to strive for preferential conditions. This competition and cooperation platform offers incentives to the online store and also provides preferential prices to the customer. Different from other e-commerce platforms, the incentives and preferential prices here assure a long-term transaction relationship between the two.

2. Diversified Engagement Structure of JTMM's New E-commerce Platform

Like all other transaction places, JTMM's new e-commerce platform consists of buyers and sellers. Sellers on the platform are the commodity suppliers. Online stores on the platform are buyers and sellers at the same time. Consumers of the platform have complex roles here, as they may change from buyers to sellers and can be buyers and sellers at the same time. In short, consumers may become online storekeepers, sellers, at any time. The participants of JTMM's new e-commerce platform, either buyers or sellers, can acquire corresponding performance points or the qualification to open a store on the platform based on the accumulated amount of commission or consumption within a certain period. In this way, the platform attracts all relevant parties to deeply engage in platform operations.

3. Diversified Interests Sharing Mechanism of JTMM's New E-commerce Platform
The diversified engagement structure undoubtedly corresponds to the diversified interests sharing mechanism. Based on the performance of JTMM's new e-commerce platform participants, this mechanism classifies sales grades and provides different prices and commissions according to the amount of products the supplier has distributed through the platform against both retailing and distribution. It also offers different platform service fees and consumption discounts to online stores and consumers based on their purchases and consumption amount.

The operations model of JTMM's new e-commerce platform seems simple, but it has seized a key driving force to enhance engagement. Incentive mechanisms have been set up at every transaction for suppliers, online storekeepers and consumers or their changed roles, which reflect the core operations concepts of Tiens that consumers create wealth. In addition to wealth creation by consumers themselves, online stores and suppliers are provided with favourable environments for the sake of consumers' wealth creation and thus make profit. The simpler process is always the more effective. The simple discount rate, seemingly an ordinary interest sharing mechanism, can stimulate all parties' enthusiasm to join the platform, and make JTMM a win-win e-commerce platform.

SECTION 2
AGGREGATION AND TRANSCENDENCE OF THE DIRECT-SELLING MODEL: CREATING NEW GLORY

JTMM's new e-commerce platform has been regarded as a part of the third start-up of Tiens and bears an important mission to achieve transcendental development. Whether it can accomplish this goal constitutes the key factor to judge its success by.

I. Aggregation: Realize Transcendental Development of the Direct-Selling Model

The strategic positioning of JTMM's new e-commerce platform is to promote and realize the aggregation and transcendence of the Direct-Selling model, and accomplish the third start-up of Tiens. Seeing the development trend of the Direct-Selling industry and the fierce competition among various distribution models, Tiens adheres to the following core goal and development path for the third start-up: breaking through the limits of direct selling, transcending direct selling, relying on direct selling and achieving the transcendental development of Tiens.

1. Break Through the Limits of Direct Selling
   If confined to the Direct-Selling model, it would be impossible for Tiens to progress to its third start-up. As seen by the development of global distribution models and the reform practices of circulation in China, e-commerce has dominated the selling model. The results of the pure Direct-Selling model are not as expected. Therefore, in the age of e-commerce, to seek new development opportunities, the Direct-Selling enterprise must be bold and far-sighted enough to break the limits of the Direct-Selling model in terms of the development ideas.

2. Transcend Direct Selling
   A practical path for Tiens to transcend direct selling is to establish a new e-commerce platform. The construction of JTMM's new e-commerce platform is essentially the transcendence of the Direct-Selling model, which aims to overcome the limits of the Direct-Selling model, open the product space, break the limits of household consumption and realize the idea of wealth creation by household business consumption in an all-round way. To transcend direct selling, the enterprise will need to have the courage and wisdom to practically implement the idea of wealth creation by household business consumption.

3. Rely on Direct Selling
   Breaking the limits of direct selling and transcending direct selling do not necessarily mean give up direct selling. It is unwise and irrational for a Direct-Selling enterprise such as Tiens, which has acquired advantages from the early development of the Direct-Selling model, to give up its advantages. Therefore, Tiens' third start-up must rely on direct selling as its advantageous resource.

   The combination of the Direct-Selling industry and the e-commerce industry offers a heaven-sent opportunity for Tiens to seek advantages in market resources, realize crossover competition and achieve innovative development. As a traditional Direct-Selling enterprise, Tiens embraces its strategic product portfolio, high-quality distributor team and high-efficiency education system. These advantageous resources of direct selling make up the foundation for the enterprise's development. No matter how the enterprise's development strategy is adjusted, the enterprise will depend on its understanding and utilization of these advantageous resources. The reliance on direct selling lays the foundation for the development of Tiens.

II. Transcendence: Realize Comprehensive Innovation of the Direct-Selling Model

As the innovation of the network Direct-Selling model, JTMM's new e-commerce platform is a new e-commerce model, which cultivates Tiens' new consumption ecological chain. It creates a kind of consumption ecological chain by which household business consumption can create wealth. This consumption ecological chain is created by breaking through the limits of direct selling, transcending direct selling and relying on direct selling as mentioned above. This e-commerce model with direct selling characteristics challenges direct selling from the perspective of the e-commerce platform, makes household business consumption possible; and challenges the e-commerce platform from the perspective of direct selling and makes wealth creation by household business consumption possible.

1. JTMM's New E-commerce Platform's Innovation of Customers' Identities
General e-commerce platforms can hardly imitate JTMM's new-ecommerce platform for how JTMM distinguishes and defines customers' (consumers') identities. General e-commerce platforms extend the same treatment to all customers. Despite the price or service preferential policies based on the purchase amount, customers are isolated from each other and show no connection. The purchase amount of one customer will not affect the price and service interest of another customer. Even when online storekeepers give certain benefits to old customers or friends who have recommended new customers, these benefits are one-time, without any institutional support. However, JTMM's new e-commerce platform takes different approaches. First, JTMM classifies and defines customers' identities, and then it adopts the identity of distributors in the Direct-Selling model and divides customers into consumption-oriented and business-oriented. Second, JTMM enables business-oriented customers to open stores online through the platform and thus effectively grade the interest system for different customer identities. Third, it adopts the open and transparent interests sharing system to promote the conversion from consumption-oriented customers to business-oriented customers, encourages customers to open stores online, indirectly replicates the development path of the distributor path in the Direct-Selling model, describes different ranks and levels for wealth creation by consumption by classifying customers, and builds the customer identity mechanism as an example.

2. JTMM's New E-commerce Platform's Innovation of Incentive Mechanisms
The incentive system is the lifeblood of the Direct-Selling model. The key to the success of JTMM's new e-commerce platform lies in how to rationally and effectively adapt the points system in the Direct-Selling model to the

new e-commerce platform and how to apply it to more products and more extensive customers. The core of the points system in the Direct-Selling model is to provide possibilities to expand the consumer surplus of business-oriented consumers. After the points system is converted to the incentive system of JTMM's new e-commerce platform, it must feature the following two characteristics. First, in addition to the common methods adopted by ordinary e-commerce platforms, such as the purchase stimulation, ratings mechanism and the pure incentives to storekeepers to create sales and profits, the interest sharing of JTMM's new e-commerce platform will inspire household consumption, encourage household business consumption and institutionally support the wealth creation by household business consumption with discount rates and rewards for an accumulated consumption scale. Second, the incentive system of JTMM's new e-commerce platform will provide diversified interests sharing mechanisms based on customers' different identities, realize the differences of the profitability of customers' business consumption, promote the conversion from consumption-oriented to business-oriented customers, encourage customers to open online stores and reveal different returns for different customer identities.

3. JTMM's New E-commerce Platform's Innovation of Competitive Advantages
The core of JTMM's new e-commerce platform's competitive advantage rests in its provision of a consumer surplus to customers. As mentioned above, the consumer surplus earned by customers in the Direct-Selling model can be actively applied to 'businesses' again, which complies with the basic property of JTMM as an e-commerce platform depending on direct selling. As guided by the interests sharing mechanism, customers of JTMM's new e-commerce platform can become business-oriented customers through self-consumption and directly or indirectly acquire constant interests.

Pointswin is an efficient instrument of competition created by JTMM's new e-commerce platform. According to Tiens, Pointswin is a points platform that attracts users, integrates resources and cultivates the resources of one body with multiple wings, and the connection between users and the resources of a comprehensive health ecosystem under one body with multiple wings. It boosts the realization of buying from and selling to the whole world and facilitates the development of partners' undertakings. Pointswin is a platform that constantly attracts newcomers to manage their points, which helps users acquire financial services, makes a payment method for them, and constitutes an integral part of the Star Program. From the customer's perspective, Pointswin helps them take the initiative to participate in the purchase and consumption activities of JTMM's new e-commerce platform and make profits, and reduces their cost to participate in those activities. Pointswin is a special form of consumer surplus.

4. JTMM's New E-commerce Platform's Innovation of Business Model
   Combining the Direct-Selling model and e-commerce, JTMM's new e-commerce platform for Tiens has broken the limits of both the Direct-Selling model and ordinary e-commerce platforms. The integration of the characteristics of direct selling and e-commerce has created the unique competitive advantage of JTMM's new e-commerce platform. On one hand, the traditional Direct-Selling enterprise cannot be compared to JTMM's new e-commerce platform, since JTMM makes it much more convenient to develop products and a distributor team. On the other hand, ordinary e-commerce platforms cannot be compared to JTMM, since JTMM has a stable and loyal distributor team that participates in the enterprise's operations and shares interests.

   As a special characteristic, JTMM's new e-commerce platform implants the e-commerce model in the Direct-Selling model, develops the e-commerce platform upon the Direct-Selling enterprise, and brings the concepts of household consumption, household business consumption and wealth creation by household business consumption to the e-commerce platform. Any distributor team without the Direct-Selling model or any e-commerce platform without the Direct-Selling interest mechanism can never grow to be a Direct-Selling e-commerce platform like JTMM. The breakthroughs made by JTMM's new e-commerce platform point out a new development path for traditional Direct-Selling enterprises. If the practice of JTMM achieves success within a short term, a considerable number of Direct-Selling enterprises may imitate this development model and place Direct-Selling advantages on the e-commerce platform. This practice of Tiens will become a useful experience for the Direct-Selling industry.

5. Rebirth of JTMM's New E-commerce Platform: Global Cross-border Social E-commerce Platform
   JTMM's new e-commerce platform for Tiens newly positions itself as the global cross-border social e-commerce platform. This is a leap made by Tiens through years of exploration in the network economy and e-commerce.

   The global cross-border social e-commerce platform focuses on maximizing the space to explore and swap resources. JTMM's new e-commerce platform for Tiens has realized crossover integration and the coordinated development of consolidation of three networks, multi-network interaction and one body with multiple wings, and has also made breakthroughs in the Direct-Selling model from two dimensions. Depending on network technologies and guided by the Direct-Selling model, it realizes the identity change of Linkers, has business expansion and customer expansion as the two driving forces for the development of the social e-commerce platform, attracts and cultivates Tiens makers by means of internet celebrities and fans, responds to the national strategy of mass entrepreneurship and innovation and the Belt and Road Initiative, and exercises multiple distribution models in Tiens' global cross-border social e-commerce platform. Meanwhile, it relies on block chain technology, promotes rapid development of the successful model through empowerment, assures reliable product quality, guarantees the safety of household consumption, and renders technological support to wealth creation by business household consumption.

SECTION 3
THEORETICAL REFLECTIONS ON THE INNOVATION OF THE DIRECT-SELLING MODEL

The combination of the Direct-Selling model and the e-commerce platform breaks people's traditional understanding of Direct-Selling products and families, and has the e-commerce platform take on a bright new look. Tiens' global cross-border social e-commerce platform, based on JTMM's new e-commerce platform, is faced with great challenges, but it is also the key to the success of Tiens' third start-up.

I. New Challenges to the E-commerce Platform

JTMM's new e-commerce platform, also Tiens' global cross-border social e-commerce platform, is the key measure for the third start-up and transcendental development of Tiens, which may have certain deficiencies and face huge challenges.

First, JTMM's new e-commerce platform will position itself as the frontier of Tiens' third start-up in terms of management concepts. The goal of establishing JTMM's new e-commerce platform is to open a new business sector, create a new business model and assist Tiens in achieving its third start-up and transcendental development.

Second, it needs to be established whether different requests from different customer groups can be satisfied in a coordinated manner. JTMM's new e-commerce platform mainly depends on two customer groups, the original distributor team, and the middle and high-end customer group. These two groups often show great differences in their interest demands. The original distributor team pays more attention to the benefits from the dividend distribution mechanism and wealth creation by business consumption. The middle and high-end customers stress more on consumption itself. Compared to the original Direct-Selling points system, the interests sharing mechanism of JTMM's new e-commerce platform lowers the incentive effect to the original distributors, so the problem is whether the platform can effectively retain them at JTMM. The third question is whether the specialized commodities and services supplied by JTMM's new e-commerce platform are attractive enough to the young middle and high-end customers, to bind them to the platform.

Third, whether the e-commerce platform can constitute favourable interaction with the internal resources of the enterprise, such as the business concepts of consolidation of three networks, multi-network interaction and one body with multiple wings. Since Tiens is a Direct-Selling enterprise, its value may considerably decline if the distributor system constructed in the Direct-Selling model is separated from the enterprise's three internal networks and some other networks.

II. New Thinking of the E-commerce Platform

In the e-commerce platform sector, a closed thinking pattern may pay excessive attention to the value chain inside the enterprise but ignore the utilization of and cooperation with external resources. The key to winning the market competition is to incorporate procurement, design, production, pricing, sales and logistics in the internal value chain. With an open thinking pattern, the enterprise will search for strategic partners based on the enterprise's internal value chain and even may outsource the work that was considered as the enterprise's internal affairs to partners. The partner today may even have been a competitor yesterday. With a closed thinking pattern, people only see the interest separation between the enterprise and partners; but with an open thinking pattern, the enterprise will be aware that the enterprise and other partners can create greater benefits jointly.

The Direct-Selling model is a result of a typical closed-thinking pattern. Its success has been deeply analysed by many people, but it now runs into historical barriers in the sharing economy and shared economy. To find a way out, the enterprise must break the original closed way of thinking in the Direct-Selling model and combine the Direct-Selling model with the sharing and shared economy through JTMM's new e-commerce platform. Literally, the sharing economy and the shared economy show certain differences. The sharing subjects in a sharing economy are equal; while the sharing subjects in a shared economy have different priorities. However, both economies set restrictions on the subject and expect for more subjects. The sharing economy sets no institutional threshold, but the subjects in the shared economy depend on institutional arrangements to decide their ranks. However, these institutional arrangements will never constitute any threshold for sharing. If Tiens hopes to launch the third start-up and achieve transcendental development through JTMM's new e-commerce platform, a business model with sharing and shared characteristics, it must keep an open mind.

III. New Models of the E-commerce Platform

The theoretical design of JTMM's new e-commerce platform will embody an open-thinking pattern to realize the transcendence of operations concepts. To realize a bright future for Tiens' new business model, JTMM's new e-commerce platform must accomplish transcendence in four aspects.

First, transcend the business scale. The key to the transcendence of the business scale lies in the expansion of market customers. As an open e-commerce platform, JTMM will not set up any institutional barriers for customers. While fully considering the role and interests of Tiens' original distributor team, JTMM will develop new business-oriented customers as the leading force of customer groups of JTMM. Household consumption will include the household consumption of both the distributor team and the new customers. New customers who strive for wealth creation by household business consumption make up the new force for JTMM's new e-commerce platform to promote the transcendental development of Tiens.

Second, transcend the scope of service. Transcendence over the scope of service is a breakthrough in the business concept. The commodity procurement, logistics system and payment system of JTMM's new e-commerce platform will transcend what Tiens provides and search for external service support. It can establish close strategic partnerships with other enterprises outside.

Third, transcend the scope of products. The transcendence of the scope of products, mainly means the transformation from a model of selling self-produced Tiens' products (including products labelled under Tiens' brand) to a product distribution model. JTMM will increase the products integrated into the household consumption chain. However, the transcendence of the scope of products does not mean blindly expanding the scope of products for distribution. A clear target market will be set up for the products. Therefore, choosing the products is essentially a kind of competitive policy.

Fourth, transcend customers' interests. This is difficult. On one hand, as JTMM's new e-commerce platform depends on direct selling for operation, JTMM will give consideration to the interests of Tiens' original distributor team; and on the other hand, the interest demands of new customers of JTMM's new e-commerce platform will be taken into consideration.

JTMM's new e-commerce platform, Tiens' global cross-border social e-commerce platform, is creating a new consumption ecological chain for Tiens. It is developing new customers. Based on original distributors and new customers, Tiens has extended household consumption to nonDirect-Selling families and nonbusiness-oriented Direct-Selling families. As an increasing number of products are introduced, the product chain consisting of Tiens' self-produced products and distribution products show more evident characteristics of household consumption.

JTMM is satisfying Tiens' new customers and their consumption chains with the new consumption ecological chain and expands the room for household consumption and household business consumption. Consumer surplus becomes less exclusive, as more customers acquire consumer surplus from not only the preferential prices but also the so-called business. In this way, the money in people's hands is activated as consumption capital, which finally helps more families realize the dream of wealth creation by household business consumption.

PART VII

GLOBAL EXPANSION CREATES THE FUTURE: SELF-TRANSCENDENCE PROMOTES SWAP PRACTICE

PENG LIHONG

In the international market, Direct-Selling enterprises have taken the initiative to choose the countries with a relatively favourable environment, experienced the enterprise-led, distributor-led and e-commerce platform-led development models in different stages of developments and realized the transcendence over traditional selling functions in multiple aspects by swapping markets and production capacities.

As challenged by the new round of industrial technology revolution and multinational operations and management, Direct-Selling enterprises are vulnerable to the shortage of international compound talents and the hidden risks caused by political and cultural differences in different countries. However, they also embrace the opportunities brought about by consumption upgrading, Renminbi internationalization and the Belt and Road Initiative.

Direct-Selling enterprises see broad prospects in middle and high-income countries, in the middle and high-income groups, and in the future. New global, systematic, innovative, entrepreneurial and human-oriented concepts have transcended traditional thinking patterns. Direct-Selling enterprises adopt trade-finance cooperations, direct selling + internet, localization and long-term talent incentives; they build cross-border social e-commerce platforms, gather new factors, show new vitality, construct high-quality ecosystems, and constantly improve their competitiveness in global exploration.

CHAPTER 24

GLOBAL EXPANSION OF DIRECT-SELLING ENTERPRISES

SECTION 1
GLOBAL EXPANSION PROCESS OF DIRECT-SELLING ENTERPRISES

I. Global Expansion Environment of Direct-Selling Enterprises

1. Global Development of Direct-Selling Enterprises

   Direct selling plays a positive role for enterprises, consumers and employment worldwide. Direct-Selling enterprises are popular in countries with a relaxed business environment for direct selling, where the Direct-Selling industry has grown steadily. With America as an example, Avon, founded in 1886, adopted direct selling in its early days and ranked in the World Top 500 Enterprises based on its rapid development. By 2017, approximately 18.6 million American people were engaged in direct selling, creating a retailing amount of over 34.9 billion US dollars[1]. To help Direct-Selling enterprises explore foreign markets, the World Federation of Direct Selling Associations (WFDSA) contacts government authorities, legislative departments and consumer organizations to open a channel for Direct-Selling enterprises. By 2017, the WFDSA included 65 Direct-Selling associations in member countries and regions and the European Direct Selling Federation, selling over a thousand types of products covering many different sectors. WFDSA announced the global Direct-Selling performance in 2017 to be $189.64 billion, where America contributed the most, compared to $34.29 billion from China, $33.68 billion from the EU and $15.33 billion from Japan. The number of direct sellers around the world reached approximately 117 million, where America ranked first again, compared to 6.96 million people from the EU, 5.35 million from China and 3.12 million from Japan[2].

1 https://www.dsa.org/statistics-insights/overview

2 https://wfdsa.org/wp-content/uploads/2018/06/Sales-Report-2017-June-12-2018.pdf

2. Domestic Environment for Direct-Selling enterprises

As to Chinese enterprises, direct selling is an imported product. In the late 1980s, a Japanese enterprise running the business of magnetic health mattresses entered Shenzhen and Guangzhou and adopted direct selling for sales. This new sales method was then copied by many domestic enterprises. On November 14 1990, Avon registered its first Direct-Selling enterprise in China, Sino-US Joint Venture Guangzhou Avon Co., Ltd., marking the official access of direct selling to the Chinese market. Since then, foreign Direct-Selling enterprises have rushed to take a place in China. Also, a great number of domestic enterprises began to copy this model. Direct-Selling enterprises sprung up in eastern coastal cities, which applied the multilevel Direct-Selling network to promote products.

With the rapid expansion of Direct-Selling enterprises in China, the whole Direct-Selling industry was chaotic. On one hand, these Direct-Selling enterprises did not have enough management experience, and the whole industry lacked self-discipline. On the other hand, the policies and regulations of the governments were relatively lagging behind, leading to the frequent occurrence of market chaos. Soon this situation extended to the inland market. To regulate the management of the Direct-Selling industry, the Chinese government had all enterprises engaged in pyramid selling registered for hierarchical management. Many domestically funded enterprises moved to countries with a relatively relaxed environment for direct selling for survival and development. *Regulations on Administration of Direct Sales* were officially released in 2005 to offer new management rules. However, its definition of direct sales showed some flaws and multi-level direct selling failed to get a legal status.

3. Direct-Selling Enterprises 'Go Global'

Compared to the strict control over the domestic Direct-Selling market, the institutional environment for Direct-Selling enterprises to go global was becoming relaxed. Before 1992, anyone planning to run businesses or make investments overseas had to complete complex approval formalities, and the investors could only utilize their self-owned foreign currency to make investments overseas and could not use any other foreign currency unless otherwise approved by the State Administration of Foreign Exchange. Detailed regulations were provided on the use of investors' foreign currencies for direct investments overseas and the management of foreign currencies they earned. These strict policies were relaxed after 1992. However, the approval procedures still made it very inconvenient for Direct-Selling enterprises to export products and make foreign investments. The process of the enterprises going global was slow.

After China's entry to the WTO, the government implemented policies that encouraged foreign investment and boosted the rapid growth of enterprises' foreign investment. The number of enterprises making foreign investments increased from 3,091 in 2001 to over 7,000 in 2007. In 2008, the Chinese government streamlined administration and delegated power to the lower levels, further relaxing the policies on enterprises' foreign investment. The complex approval process was replaced by a simple review and the approval formalities was reduced from 65 to 42. All formalities could be completed through the government affairs online service platform, which greatly shortened the approval process, increased transparency, and improved efficiency. After 2013, the Chinese government carried out the administrative system reform, to reduce the burdens of enterprises going global and rendered support in terms of policies, funds and services. Chinese enterprises were therefore greatly encouraged to go global.

II. Three Waves of Global Expansion of Direct-Selling enterprises

Through years of rapid development, Direct-Selling enterprises have accumulated certain strengths. However, the government has initiated classified governance over Direct-Selling enterprises since 1998 and has provided that "foreign-invested pyramid selling enterprises must run businesses through real stores." This regulation restricted the development of local Direct-Selling enterprises to a certain extent and put local Direct-Selling enterprises running businesses in the domestic market in a grey zone. These enterprises chose to transform, change the market or withdraw. The huge change of the policy environment for the domestic Direct-Selling industry restrained the expansion of the whole industry, caused the decline of the industry and impelled some local Direct-Selling enterprises to turn to overseas markets for survival. Therefore, the first wave of overseas expansion of Direct-Selling enterprises emerged.

After China's entry to the WTO, foreign-funded Direct-Selling enterprises rushed to the Chinese market. They expanded rapidly in diversified forms such as franchising, which supported the rapid recovery of the Direct-Selling market. In 2005, a high threshold was set for entry to the Direct-Selling industry. The government carried out more specific and standardized management over the Direct-Selling industry and started to license the enterprises approved to the industry, which led to the different development circumstances of Direct-Selling enterprises. The licensed and unlicensed enterprises showed completely different conditions. At this time, Amway's multi-level model of direct selling + store transformed to the single-level model. Some unlicensed enterprises had to turn to the international market again, which caused the second wave of overseas expansion.

After transformation, pilot projects and standardized governance in China, the enterprises that had acquired licenses in 2008 gradually got on the right track, vitalizing the market again. Despite the global financial crisis,

China had seen a vigorous economic growth and significantly improved the image of China by holding the Beijing Olympics. In this situation, Chinese enterprises found opportunities for global expansion, and many local Direct-Selling enterprises paid their attention to the overseas market again. Therefore, the third wave, also the largest wave of overseas expansion, appeared in 2009. China's opening had been exposed to evident changes after 2013, when the two-way opening balanced development became the focus. The Direct-Selling industry ushered in a rapid growth. The industrial size increased from 59.3 billion yuan in 2010 to 220.784 billion yuan in 2015, with a growth rate of 30.07%. The competition in the domestic Direct-Selling market was further intensified, and the overseas expansion of Direct-Selling enterprises significantly sped up.

III. Three Stages of Global Expansion of Direct-Selling Enterprises

1. Go Global Passively for Survival

   Expansion to overseas markets became a way for Chinese Direct-Selling enterprises to survive in the low period of China's Direct-Selling industry. The domestic Direct-Selling industry was exposed to ups and downs due to the difference between the enterprise's strategic selection and its market positioning at the micro level, as well as the backward policies and regulations in China that favoured foreign investment at the macro level. From 1998 to 2008, as strictly restrained by domestic policies and laws, Direct-Selling enterprises had to transform, went to the global market passively for survival and implemented the strategy of international development. Since these young enterprises had relatively weak strength and insufficient experience, and had no systematic plan or adequate preparation, many of them soon quit after they entered the foreign market as they could not adapt to local conditions. Direct-Selling enterprises had paid a high price for overseas expansion. However, in the meantime, they could study on and adapt to multinational operations in the foreign environment that was relatively relaxed for direct selling; absorb the international advanced concepts and incentive mechanisms of direct selling; be introduced to advanced management methods and production technologies; examine the product and service quality in the market competition in different countries; learn to understand the legal systems, international standards, international practices, religious beliefs and cultural etiquettes of different countries; act on international conventions; and cultivate a batch of talents who could adapt to global competition.

2. Go Global Actively for Development

   In the third wave of overseas expansion after 2008, many local Direct-Selling enterprises took the initiative to systematically plan for going global according to the overall environment. Enterprises with great strength made plans and consolidated domestic foundations before going out; young enterprises studied from others quickly and borrowed strength from others for exploration; and enterprises that had already participated in international markets further improved and deepened their exploration in them. Direct-Selling enterprises also formulated more detailed strategies of going global. They implemented different strategies in different countries and explored the more effective models for regional market selection and entry. For most Direct-Selling enterprises, their overseas exploration followed the route: from Hong Kong (of China) to Taiwan to Southeast Asia, and then to Eastern Europe and Africa. After a decade of practice, Chinese Direct-Selling enterprises established a stable overseas distributor network, became more familiar about the differences among different regional markets, fixed a supply system of Direct-Selling products and gradually optimized the bonus system. They paid more attention to product quality, were more cautious about global direct investments and launched entrusted processing and brand cooperation more frequently. At the same time, the overseas expansion of Chinese Direct-Selling enterprises was restricted by the increasing risks in global exploration and the evident lack of international talents.

3. Plan for All-round Layout to Seek Breakthroughs

The wide application of e-commerce technologies, the sharing economy, internet celebrity economy and new retailing exerts a great impact on the traditional Direct-Selling model and direct sellers are growing old or leaving. It is the only hope, as well as the realistic and ideal choice for Direct-Selling enterprises, to seek spanning development that transcends direct selling and helps them break out of their own shells. In recent years, domestic Direct-Selling enterprises have integrated their resources and have actively sought for transformation in succession. They are developing in an international, diversified and platform-based manner. Some enterprises have subverted themselves by planning for an all-round layout for both the international and domestic markets, combining Direct-Selling and nonDirect-Selling models and comprehensively upgrading the international competition strategy with innovative institutions, models, mechanisms, networks and platforms. Some leading Direct-Selling enterprises have spread their businesses from the comprehensive health industry to tourism, education and elderly support, and finally to financial services; built a platform deeply integrating all their business sectors; absorbed the advantages of direct selling; innovated the terminal model; collected and integrated resources as driven by greater interests; rebuilt their new competitive advantages in both the domestic and international markets; and facilitated business transformation and market exploration.

SECTION 2
GLOBAL EXPANSION MODELS OF DIRECT-SELLING ENTERPRISES

I. Company-led Model

Direct-Selling enterprises explore overseas markets for survival, development and expansion. However, they will adopt different models when exploring a new market due to the different driving forces behind them. Some are led by the enterprise, some are promoted by distributors and some are organized by the e-commerce platform. In the initial stage of overseas exploration, Direct-Selling enterprises mainly rely on their own layout. The enterprise will organize an investigation and design the overall plan, and decision-making, implementation and supervision in this process are completed by its relevant departments. They will open local branch offices of subsidiaries in the new overseas market, allocate corresponding human and material resources, and provide product and systems training, goods and sales settlement services to local distributors. The enterprise-led model is favourable for the overall strategic implementation, the cross-region and cross-market allocation of enterprise resources, and the cultivation and appointment of international talents.

In the early stage of overseas expansion, most domestic Direct-Selling enterprises adopt the enterprise-led model driven by an international strategy. They gradually establish the global branch office network which is managed by the overseas division or the regional subsidiary, and have achieved remarkable results. For example, Winalite has established subsidiaries in major countries and regions of the world since 2007 and has reached a sales amount of more than 200 million yuan merely in the Russian market. Only two years after its founding, CHANS opened subsidiaries in 12 countries including Kazakhstan, Uzbekistan, Ukraine and Russia. Tiens has marched strongly into the overseas market, established subsidiaries in 110 countries and regions, spread businesses to more than 190 countries, built extensive strategic partnerships with first-class enterprises from numerous countries, and earned 70% of its profit from the sales in overseas markets, making it an international enterprise mainly running businesses overseas.

II. Distributor-led Model

When going to the international market, some Chinese Direct-Selling enterprises adopt the lower-cost and flexible distributor-led expansion model. In this model, distributors take the lead to develop the market, penetrate the new market based on kinship and the Chinese circle, carry out Direct-Selling promotion activities in the early stage to attract new members and promote products, and start expansion by spreading influence from person to person. Seeing the rapid development of modern communication technology, distributors have also learned to use WeChat, WeChat Moments, Client and some other new tools to carry out international transmissions more effectively and conveniently. The headquarters or regional branch office nearby will support distributors' work or follow them to establish a branch office in the new market according to the enterprise strategy and business planning. Early entry is difficult, but stable development is harder. Direct-Selling products, systems and services must adapt to and satisfy the demands of different countries and regions of different nations, cultures, systems and laws. Only by doing this can the Direct-Selling enterprise truly survive in the newly developed overseas market.

In the distributor-led model, Direct-Selling enterprises make less investment in the early stage, while the experience in developing new markets and connections of individual distributors or the distributor team play a bigger role. However, considering the relatively low efficiency of communication and coordination between the Direct-Selling enterprise and distributors, as well as the low efficiency of services they provide to each other, service quality will be jeopardized if there is rapid expansion in the overseas market. Therefore, when the scale of the new overseas market reaches a certain level, the Direct-Selling enterprise will incorporate it in the subsidiary management network under the unified management of the enterprise. In 2007, as influenced by distributors' work, Merro International transferred its business focus to the overseas market. It recruited a large number of professional agents and distributors with overseas experience and took only two years to enter Russia, Vietnam, Eastern Europe and Southeast Asia.

III. E-commerce Platform-led Model

The e-commerce platform-led model depends on the Direct-Selling enterprise's cross-border e-commerce platform to explore the new market. Distinguished from the traditional distributor or enterprise-led expansion model or other general e-commerce development model, this model has introduced the consumption business idea and the Direct-Selling incentive system to the e-commerce platform, connects the international market through the internet platform, enables real-time online operations, breaks the spatial-temporal constraints, and builds a platform for more extensive communication and cooperation among direct sellers, thus achieving more convenient communication at a lower cost. In this way, the enterprise can be aware of the changes to market demands immediately, adjust marketing strategies accordingly and develop new products and even customized products. This is the new direct selling e-commerce platform.

The e-commerce platform-led model accumulates data resources during its operation. It can acquire precise information about consumers through data mining, rendering direct support for the Direct-Selling enterprise to explore the new market and for distributors to attract new members. This model will become the main method to explore global markets in the context of global platform connection and sharing in the future and is therefore of great commercial value and market prospects. The platform system will distribute interests to distributors based on their points levels determined by the consumers' individual and team consumption on the platform and communication contributions. Also, the platform will facilitate the rapid exploration of global markets through the conversion of online connections, offline experiences and study and interaction among distributors.

To adopt the e-commerce platform-led model, the Direct-Selling enterprise must embrace strong financial strength to develop and maintain the cross-border e-commerce platform, supply rich varieties of products and render the support of the complete ordering system, settlement system, electronic payment systems and the logistics and delivery system. If enterprises of weaker strength and immature conditions follow the trend blindly and excessively pursue personalized services regardless of their small customer base and limited management and risk control capability, the cost of platform operations will be so high that breakeven will hardly be realized. The online platform-led model may also result in conflicts between the e-commerce Direct-Selling network and the original direct-seller network in the distribution of product resources and interests. In this case, the enterprise will take control of the whole situation and make rational planning and systematic design.

SECTION 3
GLOBAL SWAP AND TRANSCENDENCE OF DIRECT-SELLING ENTERPRISES

I. Global Market Swap of Direct-Selling Enterprises

1. Market Swap Strategies

By overseas expansion, Direct-Selling enterprises are actually performing the cross-border swap of human, material and financial resources, as well as the institutional mechanisms by supplying good products, good prices, good brands and good services to foreign users, thus to win a broader market. When entering the international market passively in the early stage, Direct-Selling enterprises were seeking for a more stable and relaxed business environment. Tiens was one of the earliest Direct-Selling enterprises that explored overseas markets. During overseas operations, Tiens adhered to the concept of "promoting human health and serving the community," invested heavily to upgrade advanced equipment and select excellent products, and provide consumers with health, wealth and care. Moreover, Tiens also designed a competitive bonus system based on the practical demand of the international market; increased the proportion of sellers and improved the enterprise's vitality; organized distributors and managers to travel abroad and learn new knowledge; and recruited a large number of talents for the network for Direct-Selling operations and management in the international market including an international market education director, regional health supervisor, translators of multiple languages, education lecturers in foreign markets and many other types of international talents.

During the cross-border market swap, Direct-Selling enterprises mainly depend on globalization and localization to satisfy the local demands of the international market and pursue the enterprise's development goal with constant innovations adapting to market changes. Before the entry to Russia, Tiens conducted research on the Russian market for more than a year, analysed the economic situation and cultural influence there, established a large multinational subsidiary and invested 17 million yuan to hold a brand promotion presentation, to rapidly improve the local influence of Tiens. It implemented team training conscientiously and helped new distributors achieve success step by step. Responding to Russian people's preference for tangible benefits, Tiens transferred to use real rewards such as cars when designing the rewards system, which was welcomed by local distributors. They treated the rewards as the real benefits, as well as the respect. Through practical and meticulous work, the sales of Tiens in Russia soon reached 200 million yuan.

2. Transcendence of Market Swap

Direct-Selling enterprises are learning by doing during their overseas expansion. They accumulate experiences, innovate business models, constantly cultivate and improve their core competitiveness, and adapt to the changes of international market competition. By achieving transcendence of ideas, strategies, talents, institutions, culture and products throughout the enterprises' international development process, it will vigorously support their overseas expansion and significantly improve their cohesion and image overseas. Some small and medium-sized enterprises have rapidly grown to become multinational groups extending their presence to the whole world, playing a significant leading and exemplary role among domestic Direct-Selling enterprises running businesses in the local market.

Achieving transcendence through swap, Tiens ushered in its rapid development, demonstrated by the sharp rise of enterprise size and profits and a great international reputation. The income from Tiens' overseas businesses is far higher than that of the domestic market and at one time even occupied two thirds of its total income. At the end of 1999, Tiens had registered wholly owned subsidiaries in more than a dozen countries and regions, and expanded from Northern Europe, Eastern Europe and South Africa to the rest of Africa in just five years. At present, Tiens has constructed its own global Direct-Selling network, including the Eurasian region headquartered in Russia, Europe region headquartered in Germany, Africa region headquartered in Kenya, Latin America region headquartered in Argentina and Asia Pacific Region headquartered in Indonesia. Tiens has extended its businesses to over 190 countries and regions of the world, set up 20 subregion subsidiaries and key country subsidiaries, and has a stable consumer group of 40 million families.

II. Global Production Capacity Swap of Direct-Selling Enterprises

1. Domestic Production Capacity Swap

The overseas expansion of Direct-Selling enterprises essentially means that enterprises participate in the international market competition in a form of international trade. An enterprise's product output and profitability will be influenced by the political and economic relations among the countries, foreign trade surplus, logistics, costs and foreign exchange rate fluctuations to varying degrees. Those Direct-Selling enterprises that had marched to the international market early have already reached a certain market scale and economic strength through a decade of overseas exploration. To avoid international trade barriers, lower transportation costs and reduce the exchange loss incurred by the foreign exchange rate fluctuation, many Direct-Selling enterprises have started to seek opportunities for overseas production cooperation and direct investment, make plans for the global layout of production and swap domestic production capacity for overseas production capacity.

In the process of production capacity swap, Tiens regards the global financial crisis as important timing for the acceleration of internationalization. It has successively allied itself with enterprises producing health products, cosmetics and medicine from more than 20 countries including the US, France, Germany, Malaysia, Spain, Russia, Indonesia and India. More than 200 plants at home and abroad, including Pfizer, Formosa Plastics Group and Shiseido, supply OEM production services for Tiens. The products of commissioned processing make up 20% of the products for overseas sales. In addition, to speed up the circulation of the overseas supply chain, Tiens plans to build production bases in five major regions overseas with direct investment, to enhance its supply ability in foreign markets.

Direct-Selling enterprises swap domestic production capacity for foreign production capacity through greenfield investments. First, they choose the appropriate time for market entry. Direct-Selling enterprises have enjoyed years of experiences in international trade. China is strengthening open dynamics and encourageing private enterprises to go global. The host country should have a stable political and economic environment and offer preferential policies to attract foreign investments. Second, they choose a strategic region. Southeast Asia is a focus of foreign investments for the whole world, as well as a place where Chinese Direct-Selling enterprises can make investments conveniently. Choosing a region with a large population will exert great influence over the surrounding areas and satisfy the market demands of neighbouring countries. Third, they use the most advanced production equipment, production technology, management technology and international standards to assure safety, high efficiency and low cost. Fourth, they respect the special regulations of the host country; for example, the religious beliefs and cultural customs in Southeast Asia, where they adapt to local production and sales rules and pass the Halal certification. Fifth, they determine the investment amount according to the practical demands and purchasing power. They give consideration to the real and potential demands of central countries and practical demands and trade barriers of surrounding areas, to prevent excessively advanced layouts and trade restrictions. Private enterprises have their flexible mechanism for direct foreign investment but lack the awareness and capability to prevent risks.

2. Transcendence of Production Capacity Swap
   Direct-Selling enterprises are integrating themselves into the global industrial chain and joining the global production coordination system. They have realized the transcendence of domestic independent supply during the global allocation of production capacity. Among the products sold to more than 200 countries, some are produced in China, and some are produced by entrusted partners in North America, Europe and Asia and overseas production bases. By means of production capacity swap, Direct-Selling enterprises have transcended the original products supply from China only and realized the products supply from multiple countries; transcended product output and realized brand, technology and a standard system output; transcended standardized products and realized localized and diversified products; transcended export trade and realized capital exports; transcended on-site monitoring and domestic inspection and realized remote real-time online monitoring and third-party inspection for global production management; transcended the employment of domestic employees and realized the employment of local employees in foreign countries for international human capital accumulation; and transcended the worship of Chinese culture and realized the respect for multi-cultures for cross-cultural management that tolerates different cultures and religious beliefs.

III. Global Excellence Swap of Direct-Selling Enterprises

1. Featured High-quality Products

In either the domestic or foreign market competition, the product quality of an enterprise is the quality of the enterprise itself, as well as its 'name card' when it explores overseas markets. Some products have been long recognized by consumers, which suggests the enterprise has created values for consumers. The products of Direct-Selling enterprises embody their business principles and value pursuits. These efficient and safe products with a Chinese cultural essence and Chinese characteristics are only created based on the Direct-Selling enterprises' strict requirements on advanced production and inspection equipment, investment in R&D, international standards and optimum raw materials. Direct-Selling enterprises accomplish self-transcendence by constantly improving product quality, which is the most important foundation for overseas expansion. Tiens combines the traditional healthcare theory of "removing toxins from the body, regulating body functions, supplementing supplements and preventing diseases" with modern biomedical technology, selects high-quality raw materials exceeding national standards and independently develops series of products. Its first product, Tiens' high-calcium supplement, was launched in 1995; since then, Tiens has centred on the comprehensive health industry and has constantly increased its product categories. By 2016, Tiens had created over 1,000 products in five major categories. These products have been admitted to markets in dozens of countries worldwide and have passed the Halal Certification of China Islamic Association and Kosher Certification of the Kosher Supervision of America (KSA). Some products have also obtained the US FDA certification, EU certification and the certification of Japan Ministry of Health and Welfare. Tiens adheres to the business principle of 'independent intellectual property' and has cultivated a complete, scientific, practical and effective intellectual property rights management system. In October 2015, it was selected as the National Enterprise of Advantageous Intellectual Property Right.

2. Good International Image

The enterprise image is the outward performance of enterprise operations. The enterprise's brand, as a result of the enterprise's long-term behaviours, embodies its principles, values and responsibilities to consumers and society. Therefore, by deepening the brand connotation, improving the product and enterprise image, and enhancing the brand awareness and reputation, it is favourable for cultivating consumers' loyalty, bringing premium to product owners, and increasing product values. A good enterprise image is an extremely valuable intangible asset that will be elaborately created and maintained. Direct-Selling enterprises attach importance to credibility and social responsibilities, keep investing in charity, education and health, and spare no effort to create a good international image, which is more important than the pursuit of market scale and economic benefits. In 2003, Tiens invested 800 million HK dollars to establish Tiens Meijing International Love Foundation to launch long-term and systematic welfare programs. It contributed over 1.5 billion yuan in total to South Africa South Western Townships AIDS Orphans Aid program. In recent years, it has invested 10 billion yuan to build international Tianyuan University, which promotes international friendship, improves the social awareness and reputation of the enterprise, and creates a good image of Chinese enterprises.

3. Business Model Transcending Direct Selling
In the practice of diversified development, Direct-Selling enterprises have gradually transcended the limitations of the traditional Direct-Selling model. In the new business model, the coordination between Direct-Selling subjects and nonDirect-Selling businesses in terms of the management of organizations and institutions, operations, teams and the sales network has transcended that in the traditional Direct-Selling system. The traditional Direct-Selling businesses and nonDirect-Selling businesses are perfectly integrated to help enterprises participate in competition with this innovative model of lower cost, greater benefit and sustainable stability. Tiens has adopted the development strategies of consolidation of three networks, multi-network interaction and one body with multiple wings in the third start-up; has constructed the diversified experiential platform and global alliance that covers cross-border e-commerce, comprehensive health, hotels, education and training, and the barter network; has realized the resource swap and business interaction among multiple networks; has maintained the development of Direct-Selling subjects; has constructed the new social e-commerce platform; has created and shared values with other business networks; has formed a model of interactive development of multiple sectors; has established the internationally connected business mechanism; has seized new opportunities brought by the development of the digital economy; has explored new market space; and has created the new model of direct selling.

CHAPTER 25

GLOBAL EXPANSION OF DIRECT-SELLING ENTERPRISES: CHALLENGES AND OPPORTUNITIES

SECTION 1
DIFFICULTIES FACED BY GLOBAL MARKETING OF DIRECT-SELLING ENTERPRISES

I. Lack of International Talents in Direct-Selling Enterprises

Human capital is the driving force for innovative development, the source for value creation and the key to the competition among enterprises. The largest difficulty Direct-Selling enterprises encounter during overseas expansion is the lack of international talents. For the sake of global expansion, Direct-Selling enterprises will not only assign talents as demanded by global development, but will also have the competitive power to attract and cultivate global interdisciplinary talents. Therefore, Direct-Selling enterprises will cultivate talents internally and find talents from the international talent market rapidly. However, to permanently solve the talent shortage issue, the enterprise will institutionally reflect on the human capital contribution, create a corporate culture where talents are respected, and build a long-term codevelopment system of shareholders, customers and employees. It is a long-term systematic project to cultivate international talents, so Direct-Selling enterprises will integrate their talent resources, well manage their 'international talent bank' and incorporate the management of international talents in their global development strategies.

Global enterprises all face the management difficulty of how to perfectly integrate and effectively balance self-cultivation and market introduction and how to attract, retain and make the best of talents. A prominent issue here is the frequent loss of international talents introduced for important positions. In some Direct-Selling enterprises, the loss rate of international talents introduced from the market is as high as 80%. Hence, international talent management faces the difficulty to retain the enterprise's senior management, as well as the pressure caused by the possibility of the Direct-Selling team of rich international experiences hopping to competitors. The senior management of overseas branches are not localized enough, and may show inadequate tolerance, respect and trust to local talents with different cultural backgrounds. In particular, they have no long-term incentive mechanism designed for international talents.

During its global development, Tiens mainly relied on internal cultivation, with overseas recruitment as the supplement, and implements a localized talent development strategy. It employs excellent undergraduates from domestic universities every year, assigns them to overseas markets after two or three years of cultivation and puts the burden on them. In this way, they will gradually grow to be the backbone and support for the overseas expansion and talent development of Tiens. Tiens has 4,300 employees worldwide, including 2,400 employees at headquarters. In its subsidiaries located in 110 countries overseas, some local employees are employed, and many of them have served Tiens for over a decade. Tiens offers systematic training to local employees by inviting them to headquarters for study. Throughout the localization process, management teams of high quality, great affinity and multi-cultured have been cultivated. However, a great number of international management talents are still needed for Tiens to ascend to the Fortune 500 and explore the global market.

II. Risks of Foreign Exchange Market Fluctuation

There are multiple types of uncertainties Direct-Selling enterprises encounter during overseas operations due to different reasons. First, some uncertainties are partial, sudden or regular, such as natural disasters, regime changes and military conflicts. These would result in operations suspension or loss of investment. Second, some uncertainties are holistic, continuous and relevant, such as the fluctuation of product prices and the foreign exchange rate. When Direct-Selling enterprises remit their overseas income back to China, a great economic loss may be incurred due to the depreciation of foreign currency. The frequent fluctuation of the foreign exchange rate may lead to changes in commodity prices, further leading to foreign exchange economic risks. In this case, the overseas operating income and the value of assets will be jeopardized. In view of profound changes to world economic patterns, an increasingly complex great power competition and the influence of geopolitics and de-globalization, the fluctuation of foreign exchange rates of major international currencies has been intensified. Moreover, the marketization of the RMB exchange rate has accelerated, making two-way fluctuation a normal state. In 2016, the daily reference rate for RMB against USD dropped by 6.67% for the whole year, and the year 2017 saw the complete opposite, a growth by 6%. This rate dropped below 6.9 yuan/USD in October 2018. Being aware of the increasingly intensified fluctuation of the foreign exchange rate, Direct-Selling enterprises will combine their practical demands for development, formulate the hedging strategy systematically, including financing, settlement and exchange rate hedging, and adopt appropriate methods to effectively avoid the foreign exchange rate risks.

Though international financial service organizations are providing many types of foreign exchange financial products to enterprises, and hedging instruments including foreign exchange swaps, forward contracts, foreign exchange futures and options in the foreign exchange transaction market are available, Direct-Selling enterprises running businesses globally will search for a stable approach and long-term instrument to avoid foreign exchange rates on a larger scale and for a longer period. How to effectively maintain values and fundamentally avoid the loss incurred by foreign exchange rate fluctuations becomes a difficulty for Direct-Selling enterprises in their international operations, investment and financing, and tax planning. Direct-Selling enterprises can adopt the modern barter trade to avoid the exchange risk in currency settlement. Distinguished from the traditional barter trade method, modern barter trade is conducted on the barter trade platform based on the internet and therefore has no temporal or spatial restrictions. A barter quota is used instead of cash, which realizes the free B2B and even B2C exchange of commodities or services.

Among the Fortune 500 enterprises in 2010, 85% had established their barter divisions. Sixty per cent of the enterprises listed on Nasdaq were carrying out and developing barter trade. Barter trade has become a necessary means and method for great powers to avoid exchange rate risks in trade and resources. For example, Indonesia Department of Business Affairs traded coffee, palm oil and tea for 11 Sukhoi Su-35 fighter planes, and the value of planes supplied by Russia was expected to be USD$913 million. Tiens is also making use of the newly developed cross-border e-commerce platform to integrate the sales networks and high-quality products of 21 regions worldwide. By means of local sales and local procurement, the e-commerce platform buys from the world and sells to the world. The transactions here are settled with points and e-wallet, in a form of barter trade. By doing this, it can hedge the economic loss incurred by foreign exchange rate fluctuations, improve the use efficiency of foreign exchange funds and sell featured products worldwide for profit.

III. Higher Requirements of International Strategy

The enterprise's globalization strategy is a systematic response to the global political and economic changes, which require making a decision and action plan by forecasting the future. After entering the overseas market, the enterprise will be more competitive than it is in the domestic market.

Therefore, the enterprise's international strategy will be based on the enterprise's industry, development stage, goal, condition and capability, as well as the overall situation. Overseas exploration is not appropriate for all enterprises. In this stage, the entrepreneurs' courage, insight and strategic wisdom are extremely critical, as they will forecast the global development trend, organize a cross-cultural management team, and implement the global strategic layout and resource allocation. They search for a broader market and a more stable ecosystem, adopt more advanced technologies and management methods, and attract more innovative international talents.

The enterprise's globalization process will match its management capability. Some enterprises blindly enter the foreign market without an understanding of the host country's laws and market environment, in-depth investigation and adequate analysis, and therefore do not succeed. Faced with the global economic crisis in 2008, many state-owned enterprises rushed to the overseas market for layout. Wang Qishan, Vice Premier of the State Council at that time, questioned a central enterprise's overseas acquisition and said: "We dare to explore the world, but with a scientific spirit." The enterprises will act according to their ability after in-depth research is completed. Any excessively advanced strategic decision by the enterprise in direct foreign investment or acquisition may hurt the enterprise's vitality. For example, when Bridas, where CNOOC owned 50% of shares, acquired the shares of Argentina Pan American Energy from BP, the transaction was finally suspended due to legal reasons. During global development, enterprises will need to learn advanced production technology and mature management experiences from foreign enterprises in practice; study the rules and practices of international trade, investment and finance; effectively balance imports and exports; pay equal attention to introducing capital, technology and talents; and constantly improve the enterprise's international competitiveness.

Enterprises of global development will also encounter management difficulties of how to instruct, supervise and coordinate the networks and systems in different areas, countries and regions under the enterprise. With the changes of the enterprise's development environment, the efficiency of the principles and goals' guiding effect, the organization and systems' controlling effect and the compensation equity's incentive effect will also change. For the sake of overseas exploration, domestic enterprises will need to add international elements in their governance structure, organizational system, talent quality and cultural concepts, and construct an internal mechanism adapting to the international flow of production factors. As enterprises are expanding and deepening globalization, the quality, structure and efficiency of their international elements will assure their operations efficiency and strategic implementation. The efficiency of enterprises' subsystems and the synergistic effect among these subsystems make up the foundation for the high efficiency of the whole enterprise. Large global enterprises that are faced with diversified differences inside the enterprise system will carry out multi-layer and classified management centring on the overall goal and adopt appropriate incentive systems, which are considered as the important mechanism that promotes the efficient operation of the whole enterprise. As a premise of personalized and localized management, enterprises will adopt modern intelligent internet technologies to collect worldwide data in a transparent, real-time and efficient manner.

IV. Differences of Overseas Business Environments

When expanding globally, Direct-Selling enterprises see great differences in terms of politics, economy, culture and religion in different countries, a very complicated and diversified situation. The differences in the political systems and structures may give rise to macro risks. The differences in economic systems, development stages and development levels may produce market opportunities or cause market barriers. The differences in culture are associated with the countries' history and religion and will be embodied in laws, policies and people's habits. Different business environments of different countries inevitably exert great influence on the overseas expansion of Direct-Selling enterprises. In these different business environments, the main factors that restrict enterprises' development may also vary. According to a questionnaire on national competitiveness conducted by the World Economic Forum, the biggest issue encountered by entrepreneurs varies in different countries. For example, in America and Germany, entrepreneurs mainly consider the government's taxation system and tax rates, as well as government bureaucracy, as the biggest issue. Australian entrepreneurs mainly complain about the control over labour forces, high tax rates and government bureaucracy. British entrepreneurs think the taxation system is irrational, the infrastructure is insufficient and tax rates are high. Chinese entrepreneurs think the difficulty in financing, unstable policies and government bureaucracy are the most important issues. Japanese entrepreneurs worry about high tax rates, strict control over labour forces and inadequate innovation.

Special Column 25-1

In *Doing Business 2018: Reforming to Create Jobs*, published by the World Bank, 10 indicators were used to measure the difficulty of running businesses in a country: enterprise registration, construction license, access to electricity, property registration, credit acquisition, protection of small and medium investors, tax payment, cross-border trade, contract execution and bankruptcy handling. According to the research results, the top 10 countries with favourable business environments were New Zealand, Singapore, Denmark, South Korea, Hong Kong, America, Norway, Georgia and Sweden. China ranked 78th. India made the biggest progress in business environment improvements.

Direct-Selling enterprises will need to enhance their legal consciousness, pay attention to regulatory information and relevant laws and policies in different countries, and design better incentive systems and methods to give rewards to excellent distributors. Only by doing this can direct selling really integrate itself into the mainstream community. Negligence of due diligence, blind optimism, greedy excessive investment, or insufficient resource input may all cause damage and lead to missed opportunities, when the enterprises may even have to withdraw soon after their entry. To explore overseas markets, Direct-Selling enterprises will need to carefully study the special conditions of each country, respect and integrate into the country's culture, effectively communicate with locals, seek common grounds while reserving differences, avoid any conflict and reduce the risks. For example, Europeans uphold logic and rationality. Russians emphasize physical benefits, based on which the enterprise will adjust its training and reward system. The British are more conservative, and they refuse Direct-Selling businesses as they can depend on their good social security. The laws and regulations in some countries may directly affect the establishment of the Direct-Selling bonus system. The regulations on the contents of ingredients vary from one country to another. Some countries may show colour preferences. Some countries are greatly influenced by religion, so special local certifications must be acquired when producing and selling products.

Cross-border e-commerce is going global fast. Mobile terminal technologies, cross-border electronic payment systems, logistics and delivery, and after services overseas fall far behind that in the domestic market, and the product transportation, customs declaration, risk control and supervision are hard to handle. Therefore, cross-border e-commerce still faces many difficulties when going global. The pure replication of successful domestic models overseas can hardly succeed. The timing to enter the market is important, and the model will be localized according to specific conditions. For example, Tiens' e-commerce platform was successfully launched in Beijing in 2017. Tiens plans to replicate this platform in India, Russia and Kazakhstan, and will make adjustments according to the practical conditions in these countries.

SECTION 2 NEW CHALLENGES FACING DIRECT-SELLING ENTERPRISES

I. Profound Influence of Global New Technology Revolution

Along with the development and application of big data, artificial intelligence and block chain technology, de-centralization, disintermediary and de-boundary have become the mainstream, which profoundly alters human cognition, behaviours and ways of production and life. The intelligent development of cities, traffic, manufacturing, logistics, medical care, health and education, as well as the transformation and upgrading of industrial digitalization and digital industrialization exerts huge impact on traditional industries, models and business forms. The new round of industrial revolution will bring about new technologies, new knowledge and new mechanisms, which will be accompanied by new economies and new models emerging in an endless stream.

From the perspective of the micro economy, artificial intelligence will change the organizational structure. The original organizational structure of the whole enterprise is like a triangle, with leaders and experts at the top, business cadres and first-level managers at the middle, and grassroots employees at the bottom. However, this structure will become the shape of a diamond, and the repetitive work will be done by robots and artificial intelligence. Driverless cars, unmanned factories and unmanned retail stores will constantly emerge, and some professions may gradually disappear, such as drivers, security officers, translators, traders, bank tellers, cashiers and even doctors. Meanwhile, artificial intelligence may also produce some new positions like data analysts and modelling engineers.

As influenced by technological progress, various countries are pressed to transform and upgrade industries. The integrated development of different industries and the quality and cost of the whole supply chain system increasingly become a factor deciding the terminal competitiveness of the market. China proposed that it would become the leading artificial intelligence innovation centre of the world. China will rely on the advantage in data resources based on the internet applied to the huge market, combine big data as the new key production factor, centre on artificial intelligence, have everything connected, offer a constant driving force for the innovation of digital technologies and promote industrial integration. The new industrial organization will be typically characterized by the wide application of the network, platform and ecosystem. Online-offline integration will necessarily become the new direction of industrial development. In the future, the network data dividend based on the population dividend in China will be converted to advantages in hardware and software. In particular, China will establish advantages of independent innovation in core technologies including chips, software systems and big data analysis.

II. Radical Changes of Global Competition Environment

The global economic in-depth structure imbalance and interest conflicts pose a threat to the stable and healthy growth of international trade and world economy, and propose a new challenge to the swap and transcendence of Chinese enterprises. With the advent of the 21st century, the global competition environment has been exposed to radical changes. In particular, the financial crisis originating from Wall Street in America in 2008 spread to the whole world and heavily damaged the economies of all countries; major developed countries in Europe slipped into recession, further leading to the European debt crisis. To solve this crisis, China's 4-trillion investment, America's quantitative easing policy and stimulus plans in Eurozone countries significantly promoted the economic liquidity. The GDP growth rates of major countries in the world fluctuated dramatically. As the American economy gradually recovered, the Federal Reserve System gradually withdrew the easing policy and started increasing the interest rate and unwinding the balance sheet. As affected by the sudden increase and decrease of market liquidity, the prices in the global foreign exchange market and commodity markets saw ups and downs. Due to the relevant lower demands of the international market, some industries that had expanded rapidly in some countries were subject to severe over-capacity, which made it even more difficult to transform and upgrade the industry.

In the decade under the shadow of the global financial crisis, the economic status and strength of world major countries changed. From the perspective of the economic growth rate, China and India have maintained a rapid growth, while other major economies have been exposed to violent fluctuation and even negative growth. In 2008 the top 10 countries in terms of GDP were, respectively, America, Japan, China, Germany, France, Britain, Italy, Russia, Spain and Brazil. However, by 2017, Russia and Spain were excluded from this list and replaced by India and Canada. China ascended to second place after surpassing Japan; India moved five steps ahead; Canada improved by one place; and Russia and Spain dropped by four and five places. The imbalance of global economic growth and increasingly fierce competition among great powers lead to new variations of the world economic pattern. In the context of economic globalization and insufficient motive force for long-term growth, Brexit and the rise of far-right parties in Europe have aggravated the division of Europe.

'De-globalization' has become a new phenomenon in world economic development, and the multilateral trade system is challenged. According to a report from WTO, member countries of G20 had implemented 145 new measures on trade restriction between October 2015 and May 2016. America stirred up trade disputes with the severe imbalance of Sino-US trade as an excuse. The trade disputes between China and the US, the two largest economies of the world, not only hurt the enterprises and consumers in both countries, but also cause uncertainties in the world economy that has not stabilized yet. The external environment for Direct-Selling enterprises to participate in global development is becoming worse.

III. Increasing Risks of Global Expansion

In addition to the influential factors of technological progress and the international environment, Direct-Selling enterprises also face the challenges of peer competition and crossover competition during their global development. Also, consumption upgrading proposes higher requirements on the enterprises' self-owned resources. Direct-Selling enterprises must be flexible and adaptive. With more flexible mechanisms and being closer to the terminal, the enterprises will enjoy a greater advantage in resource integration. They need to judge the overall environment and timely adjust and upgrade their advantage combinations based on their judgments about the future business environment. The rigid core competence of enterprises has become a prominent issue that restrains on their adaptability. Adaptability is urgently demanded when enterprises implement risk management, respond to the uncertainties in the future, reposition the core competitiveness and perform strategic adjustments. The multinational enterprises that are going global are faced with more complicated international markets and more risks.

As predicted by the International Monetary Fund (IMF), the world economy will grow by 3.7% in 2018. Despite a generally favourable trend, partial national risks and political risks still exist. According to the global risk opinion survey in 2018 Global Risk Report published by the World Economic Forum, most experts predicted that future risks would further increase. In the risk opinion survey for 1,000 people, 59% believed that the risks would increase, compared to only 7% who considered the risks would drop. Ninety-three per cent held that political or economic confrontation between great powers would become more intensified, and approximately 80% believed in the rise of the possibility of war between great powers. The top 10 risks that are most likely to happen included: extreme weather events, natural disasters, network attacks, data fraud or theft, failure of relief and countermeasures against climate change, large-scale involuntary resettlement, environmental hazards induced by human beings, terrorist attacks, illegal trade and asset bubbles of major economies. Therefore, Direct-Selling enterprises also face the major challenge to prevent and avoid external risks.

The Belt and Road Initiative of China encourages private enterprises to go global and seek opportunities of cooperation and development in countries along the Belt. However, in view of immature markets, financing difficulties, lack of talent reserves, incapability of intermediary services, high entry thresholds for foreign investment and hidden barriers for investment, high regional investment risks and political risks in these countries, some Direct-Selling enterprises, which had marched to the market of the countries along the Belt and Road early, have seen the violent fluctuations of operating conditions. In particular, the countries along the Belt and Road generally suffer from a backward infrastructure, underdeveloped economy, unstable politics and complex religious conditions, making it difficult for Direct-Selling enterprises to explore the market. The investment returns and safety cannot be assured there.

IV. Numerous Challenges to Effective Multinational Management and Control

The development stage, income levels, people's quality, consumption preferences, cultural beliefs and infrastructure vary in a thousand ways among different countries. The global expansion of Direct-Selling enterprises mainly manifests itself as the expansion of the market scale, but behind it, the global operations capability of the enterprises is improved. They will allocate production factors globally and assure the effective operation of the supply chain system. Since the division of labour is highly developed in modern enterprises and the coordination among different departments becomes closer, Direct-Selling enterprises face the most direct challenge of how to effectively control branch offices and sales networks in different countries for multinational operations.

Where the modern market system is more perfect, the product, brand, technology, channel and equity markets are more advanced, and the entry and exit mechanisms are more flexible and diversified. For example, currently the wholesale and retailing industries have ushered in the omni-channel age based on mobile networks. Enterprises will adopt as many channels as possible to satisfy customers' comprehensive experience demands including shopping, entertainment and social demands. The channels include physical stores, invisible stores and information media (website, social media, Weibo, WeChat). The traditional sales model and the single sales model will be noncompetitive. However, in countries with backward information infrastructures, the control system adopted in developed countries can hardly be applied due to the lack of necessary software and hardware conditions.

Though having strengthened the incentives by adjusting the system, mechanism and equity structure, enterprises that are expanding globally still find it difficult to effectively manage themselves, since they have extended their presence to every corner of the world and have shown great differences inside. The key lies in whether the enterprises can act according to local conditions and their own abilities, construct a cross-cultural management team adapting to their abilities, and improve their cultural leadership and enable managers to perfectly combine local cultures with commercial factors despite the different cultural atmosphere. With a globalized thinking pattern and localized actions, capital can really suit itself to the overseas market. It is also a great challenge to maintain growth in the future. Take Tiens as an example. To satisfy practical demands in different regions, Tiens has developed an e-commerce model adapting to local infrastructures and customers' abilities after studying the conditions of the country. In the economically backward areas, where internet and mobile phone shopping are rarely seen, the e-commerce platform will promote the development model of group purchase; and in economically developed countries and regions, Tiens applies the internet-based wholesale and retailing model.

SECTION 3
NEW OPPORTUNITIES FOR GLOBAL EXPANSION OF DIRECT-SELLING ENTERPRISES

I. Income Increase Promotes Consumption Upgrading

The disposable income of a country mainly depends on the added value created by the country. The rise of per capita income level or per capita GDP will promote the increase of per capita consumption level. Consumption upgrading refers to the change of consumption demands from the material consumption of basic necessities of life to the spiritual life and life services at a higher level. Along with the increasing scale of consumption, the consumption structure will change and drive the adjustment of the supply structure and industrial transformation and upgrading. Major countries of the world are recovering from the impact of the global financial crisis, and China, America and Europe are seeing positive economic growth. From 2008 to 2017, the per capita GDP of China increased from USD$3,467 to USD$8,583 by 1.48 times, when America grew by 23%. Economic growth was also seen in Sweden, Ireland, Australia and Iceland. As expected, some countries have not returned to their per capita GDP before the crisis broke out, such as Norway, Denmark, France and Germany. In countries where the income increases, the demands on medical care, education and tourism are rising, bringing new opportunities to the global expansion of Direct-Selling enterprises.

As driven by consumption upgrading, enterprises will need to improve product quality, better their brand image, make constant innovations and provide more precise and personalized products and services to consumers. The enterprises are faced with both the great pressure from market competition and survival and the great opportunity for them to understand the market and customers, adapt to ever-changing market demands, improve market competitiveness, and reach development and prosperity. By satisfying the consumption demands formed after the rise of consumers' incomes, it will enable enterprises to earn more from producing high-quality products and supplying high-quality services.

Tiens has ushered in the great development opportunities in the new age when China's international economic strength and status are enhanced. This situation encourages Chinese enterprises to go global to win more market opportunities and creates a more favourable external environment for Tiens' domestic and foreign development. Tiens will seize the opportunity to go deeper into the international market, broaden the channels and find more options. The comprehensive health industry that Tiens has been devoted to is a sunrise industry vigorously supported by the government. As China's per capita GDP has exceeded USD$9,000, mainstream consumers' preferences have evidently changed and their consumption structure has been exposed to apparent upgrading; there will undoubtedly be huge market demands on the comprehensive health industry.

II. Acceleration of RMB Internationalization

Currency internationalization is a dynamic process by which the currency of a country develops from a domestic currency to an international currency, which is largely associated with the proportion of the currency in the international economy, trade and investment. It can be realized based on two conditions. First, the country has an economic strength powerful enough to satisfy the needs of foreign investment. Second, the country has an abundant trade surplus and foreign exchange reserve. The expanding trade scale produces demands on trade settlement, and the trade currency balance will promote international investment and the development of international financial products. The widely applied currency will be incorporated in the reserve currency by the central banks of different countries. The currency will be internationalized along with the constant improvement of international settlement, investment transaction and value storage. Despite small differences in the process, the USD, GBP and DEM were internationalized in the same way.

RMB internationalization is a national strategy. The US subprime crisis led to the fierce fluctuation of the global foreign exchange, so a new and more stable currency is needed. China has seized the opportunity and has actively promoted RMB internationalization. In July 2009, the People's Bank of China published the *Administrative Measures on Pilot RMB Settlement of Cross-border Trade*, allowing importers and exporters to use RMB as the settlement currency for cross-border trade. The measures have been officially implemented since June 2010. After 2010, the RMB offshore market in Hong Kong has seen an increase in variety and scale of RMB products, and the role of RMB in financial transactions and settlements has been constantly enhanced. RMB is now the fifth global currency for payment. In October 2014, the British government issued the first RMB sovereign bond. RMB is making its way to a reserve currency. By the end of 2017, over 250,000 enterprises and 245 banks were running cross-border RMB businesses, 195 countries and regions were using RMB for cross-border payment with China, and more than 60 central banks and currency authorities had incorporated RMB in foreign exchange reserves.

There is still a large room for the development of RMB internationalization. Trade partners are expanding their demands on RMB, making RMB the first choice for many countries and regions. After RMB is added to the global investment portfolio, the risks and benefits of the investment portfolio will be optimized. The construction of the Belt and Road puts forward great capital demands and also stimulates China's import of commodities and services, providing important strategic opportunities for RMB internationalization. In the future, with the improvement of RMB internationalization, the three functions of RMB in international pricing and settlement, investment transaction and value storage, will be further promoted. This situation is favourable for Direct-Selling enterprises to make settlement, investment and financial transactions with RMB during overseas expansion, and generally lower the foreign exchange risk caused by the fluctuation of the foreign exchange market.

III. Advance Economic and Trade Cooperation on the Belt and Road

China advocates the joint construction of the Belt and Road; founded Asian Infrastructure Investment Bank; actively advances the implementation of major interconnection and economic and trade cooperation programs in the countries along the Belt and Road; builds the cooperation platform, deepens the production capacity cooperation; attracts more investors; applies unified regulations on operations; and encourages the enterprises of great strength and reputation to explore international markets. China also accelerates RMB internationalization and promotes high-quality development by opening wider to the outside world. China strives to improve the two-way openness, bringing great development opportunities to Chinese enterprises and the countries along the Belt and Road. Infrastructure in some countries along the belt has been improved, significantly lowering the communication and logistics costs. China has set up a $40 billion US Silk Road Fund and has established international production capacity cooperation funds involving programs valuing hundreds of billions of RMB, including the China-Africa Fund for Production Capacity Cooperation, China-Kazakhstan Special Fund for Production Capacity Cooperation and China-Middle East Fund for Production Capacity Cooperation. In 2017, the trade amount between China and countries along the Belt reached 7.4 trillion RMB, having increased by 17.8% compared to the previous year, 3.6% higher than the growth rate of the whole country's foreign trade. In this number, exports were 4.3 trillion RMB, with a growth rate of 12.1%; and imports were 3.1 trillion, growing by 26.8%.

China actively advocates the construction of a community with a shared future for mankind, implements the diplomacy of great powers with Chinese characteristics and contributes Chinese wisdom to the reform of the global governance system. It advances the international cooperation of the Belt and Road, optimizes the structure of foreign investments, improves the openness of the west, inland and coastal areas, and explores the new space for economic cooperation. The construction of the China-Pakistan Economic Corridor, New Euro-Asia Continental Bridge Economic Corridor, China-Mongolia-Russia Economic Corridor, China-Central Asia-Western Asia Economic Corridor, China-Indochina Peninsula Economic Corridor and Bangladesh-China-India-Myanmar Economic Corridor has commenced. Gwadar Port has been initially completed and put into operation. The construction of highway, port, railway and hydropower station projects in the China-Pakistan Economic Corridor has been initiated. China promotes the liberalization and convenience of trade and investment, emphasizes the reform of clothes trade development mechanisms, encourages the application of internet technologies, and cultivates new business forms and models of trade. Meanwhile, it takes the initiative to expand imports, lowers the import tariff for cars and some daily necessities, improves the openness of the market, promotes industrial upgrading and the balanced development of trade, and provides more choices for consumers. China aims to enhance mutual understanding, trust and cooperation with people in countries along the Belt through communication and cooperation in education, culture and tourism.

Following the general trend of 'de-centralization' and 'disintermediary', the economic and trade cooperation in the Belt and Road will create a new platform for international cooperation; develop the 'Silk Road e-commerce'; encourage enterprises to supply services of e-commerce, big data, cloud computing and artificial intelligence in the countries along the Belt; and help these countries develop a digital economy. For Direct-Selling enterprises exploring overseas markets, the Belt and Road Initiative has not only pointed out the direction for going global, but has also constructed a platform with a favourable ecosystem for enterprises. It has become a new trend that Direct-Selling enterprises actively build and connect their online platforms, give full play to their offline advantages based on the Direct-Selling enterprise and encourage online and offline integration. The new innovative model of direct selling + internet rejuvenates traditional Direct-Selling enterprises. In June 2017, Tiens was selected as the Xinhua News Agency 'Excellent Enterprise of National Brand Communication Programs.' This award was presented to Tiens for spreading the new consumption e-commerce platform to countries along the Belt and Road including Kazakhstan, Russia and India.

CHAPTER 26

NEW BLUEPRINT FOR GLOBAL DEVELOPMENT OF DIRECT-SELLING ENTERPRISES

SECTION 1
NEW FOCUS OF GLOBAL SWAP AND TRANSCENDENCE STRATEGY FOR DIRECT-SELLING ENTERPRISES

I. Wealth Creation Effect in Middle and High-income Countries

Among more than 200 countries in the world, approximately over 60 have reached the standard for high-income countries. Europe has the largest number of high-income countries, accounting for 54.8% of all high-income countries, compared to 24.2% in Asia, 14.5% in America and 3.2%, respectively, in Oceania and Africa. Thirty-four out of the 45 independent European countries reached the high-income standard. All countries in Northern Europe, Central Europe and Western Europe had joined the club of high-income countries very early. Fifteen of the 50 Asian countries have reached the high-income standard. In Oceania, Australia and New Zealand are high-income countries. China is an upper-middle-income country with per capita GDP exceeding USD$8,000.

The world economic development shows an evident and increasingly intensified imbalance. According to statistics, rich people, accounting for only 1% of America's population, control 40% of America's wealth, and the richest rank taking up 10% of the population own 71% of wealth in America. The income gap is still increasing. Comparing the GDP of different countries to the world average level, we can see that the average per capita GDP of all countries in 2017 was USD$10,870.46, close to the per capita GDP of Turkey in 64th place; and the average number of world per capita GDP was twice of the median and only equal to 10% of the first place. Thailand's GDP in 2017 was USD$437.807 billion, ranking 26th in the world, which was close to the average number of all countries' GDP. The average number was only 2.2% of the first place and was 13 times that of the median number. This means that the GDP of most countries is far lower than the average level. The income of the poor (purchasing power parity) in 'moderately' wealthy countries will be five times that of the income of the rich in poor countries.

The actual purchasing power of a country's consumers is determined by the country's disposable income, which originates from the added values created by the economic subjects of the country. Therefore, the countries with higher per capita GDP embrace a greater ability to pay. For a long time, developed countries have been characterized by high income, high consumption and high welfare, making them the goal that many developing economies want to catch up with. High income, the foundation of high consumption, economically assures people's high living standards and happiness. From the global perspective, only the industry in the high end of the value chain can acquire great benefits from global participation. Developed countries have dominated the high end of the manufacturing value chain based on their technological advantages, and hence created high added values with small investments. The higher income level of the middle and high-income countries determines the greater market demand in these countries. Thus, enterprises can realize the economies of scale more easily in middle and high-income countries. The market positioning of Direct-Selling enterprises in overseas expansion decides the profitability of the enterprises. Therefore, if exploring the market of middle and high-income countries, Direct-Selling enterprises will create higher returns, bring more benefits to employees, and accumulate and create wealth more rapidly.

II. Wealth Creation Effect in Middle and High-income Groups and Families

The groups of different incomes play different roles in society and the economy. The middle-income group constitute the important driving force for consumption upgrading, industrial transformation, and social stability and development. The group generally have regular jobs and rigid demands and a desire for status improvement; they enjoy greater purchasing power and stronger consumption intentions compared to the low-income group. The main consumers in the future will have more knowledge and be more open-minded to new technologies and new models. According to research by American scholars on the consumption ideas and behaviours of the rich, the modern high-income group are more willing to spend money on invisible areas including education, medical care and food. In other words, the high-income group attach importance to invisible consumption.

Direct-Selling enterprises generally choose countries of a large population and high per capita income, and deeply penetrate the mainstream groups centring on education, tourism and health, which help them create more wealth. The wealth creation against the mainstream groups is mainly derived from the demands for high-quality products and services; stable purchasing power; basic conditions and abilities of innovation and entrepreneurship; and application of new selling skills and means to facilitate communication. Targeting the mainstream groups, Direct-Selling enterprises constantly acquire stable and high returns with high added values bases on their large-scale production, lower development costs, and diversified and high-quality products and services. Therefore, enterprises can enhance their international competitiveness while satisfying high-quality customers' demands. If developing products targeting middle and high-income families in all countries, Direct-Selling enterprises can expand their markets, increase diversity, share channels and save costs. The wealth creation effect lasts longer in families, since this effect is realized by an active household consumption of long-term stickiness. Stable blood ties can increase family members' confidence and make it easier to attract more family members as Direct-Selling members. With the family as a unit, the values of consumption rise; repetitive consumption increases; and demands will be extended to more types of products. Therefore, household consumption shows a more evident wealth creation effect.

Adhering to the concept of complete globalization, Tiens has targeted every country in the world during its overseas expansion. It will target middle and high-income families in all countries; adopt advanced models for global operations; supply internationally leading education systems and models including 80/90 CEO club, women's CEO club, second-generation winter-summer club, make a rich dad club and special forces club; offer featured high-quality products combining its comprehensive health network; and attract more middle and high-income families to join the Tiens talent network.

III. Wealth Creation Effect in the Future

If targeting mainstream consumers in the future, Direct-Selling enterprises will achieve a more potential and long-lasting wealth creation effect. If young people are positioned as the target, it will stimulate the enterprise to change and innovate adapting to the changing demands. These young people with greater consumption ability will bring enterprises longer and richer benefits in terms of market scale and added value. As revealed by a survey on 100,000 young people worldwide made by the US, the post-90s have higher requirements on life quality, a higher consumption amount and greater consumption ability compared to other age groups. According to *2017 Consumption Upgrading Big Data Report* jointly prepared by China UnionPay and JD Finance, the consumption amount of the post-90s has grown rapidly with an annual growth rate of 73%, much higher than that of the post-70s and post-80s. The increase of the post-90s' consumption amount is nearly double that of the post-70s' amount. The consumption contribution made by post-70s is declining, compared to the constant rise of the consumption contribution of post-80s and post-90s. Mobile internet consumption is popular among post-90s, which constitutes half of their total consumption. Post-70s propose greater demands on health equipment as they grow older. However, the demand of post-90s on health equipment is also high, since they like to present items such as blood pressure monitors and blood glucose monitors as gifts to the elderly.

With the rapid development of the internet and the popularity of network social interactions, customers can get into unmanned supermarkets through face recognition and make payments by sweeping the code. This proves that an interesting and fun consumption experience becomes an important factor that drives consumption. Young people like to gather together closely based on their circles of interest. With social networks, young people with the same interests will always find a circle to join in. When considering the increase of income level and consumption upgrading, young people can get in touch with different interests early and are economically able to participate in their circle of interest. It will be a future trend for people to have multiple interests, multiple circles and multiple identities. Young people are more willing to pay for their interests and will regard the interests as their development direction. Post-90s and post-95s have gradually become the mainstream consumers, so their consumption ideas are influencing and changing current business patterns. Tiens strategically fixes people around the age of 30 as the target customer, and produces products according to the rigid demands of the group, thus to seize the potential market of post-90s. In the future, the young and promising mainstream group will play an exemplary and leading role in the whole of society. Considering this, Tiens will acquire greater benefits from overseas expansion in the future.

After four decades of opening up to the outside world, China has become the second-largest economy, the largest goods trader, the largest investee of foreign capital, the second-largest investor of foreign capital and the largest outsourcer, making it the market with the greatest potential in the world. As China has been opening wider, the domestic market is increasingly internationalized, and people from every corner of the world visit China more frequently for study and business. Therefore, an important and efficient way of global expansion is to deeply explore the domestic market and achieve a linkage between domestic and foreign markets. As a strategic selection, enterprises pursuing international development will attach equal importance to introduction and output and perform two-way investments at home and abroad. China's Belt and Road Initiative brings a vitality to global economic development, paves the way to enterprises' global expansion, and lowers the entry risk and environmental cost for investment. Tiens also adheres to the development direction of buying from the world and selling to the world. As a representative of Chinese national brands, Tiens will actively explore the market in countries along the Belt and Road and will show the wealth creation effect of the Belt and Road with the gradual exploration of new markets.

SECTION 2 NEW THINKING OF GLOBAL SWAP AND TRANSCENDENCE FOR DIRECT-SELLING ENTERPRISES

I. New Concepts of Global Swap and Transcendence for Direct-Selling Enterprises

The business principles of an enterprise determine its development strategy. Every Direct-Selling enterprise is faced with a huge challenge: how to respond to this ever-changing world, the changeable market, the vast differences among different regions, and the complex domestic and foreign competition environment. Differing from small enterprises which just start businesses, global enterprises of multinational operations find it increasingly difficult to participate in global competition by simply imitating others and cannot merely rely on the advantage of large scale and low cost. Instead, they need to respond to ever-changing demands and solve management difficulties in enterprises' survival and development more effectively using new technologies, concepts and thinking patterns. Enterprises will need to explore or deepen both domestic and foreign markets and prepare themselves for the change before it comes.

The global swap of Direct-Selling enterprises is firstly embodied in the transcendence of business principles and the traditional thinking pattern. From the enterprise's perspective, it can make great achievements in overseas expansion mainly depending on the entrepreneur's spirit of innovation, the high-quality products recognized by the market and a good international image of the enterprise. Noel Tichy pointed out in *The Leadership Engine*: "A successful enterprise succeeds because of its excellent leaders, who guide the growth of other leaders at all levels in the organization." In any development stage, an enterprise demands the entrepreneur's strategic foresight and the willpower to sustain operations, which make what was strategically forecasted come true. This is the premise and subjective factor of the enterprise's constant growth. In the long-term, holistic and deep view, modern Direct-Selling enterprises must follow four principles: human orientation, user orientation, globalization and systematicness, and entrepreneurial and innovative thinking patterns (see Figure 26-1).

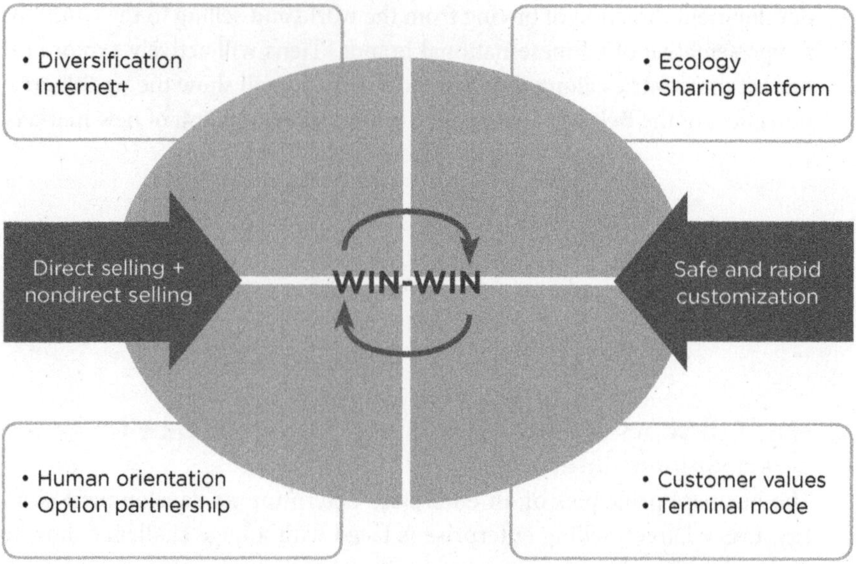

Figure 26-1 New Idea of Global Swap and Transcendence of Direct-Selling Enterprises

For global expansion of Direct-Selling enterprises, it is of great significance that they apply a global thinking pattern, embodied in how they respect and tolerate diversified differences of different countries and how they explore and satisfy customers' diversified demands in different countries. From the global perspective, enterprises need to stick to the principle of harmony in diversity, undertake their social responsibilities, make their judgments and selections, and attach more importance to long-term interests. With a global thinking pattern, the enterprises can plan for the global layout at the early development stage; emphasize diversity and localization; seek balance among different countries and regions; realize the overall interests of the enterprise in a broader global market; and actively build a global network based on internet technologies. President Li Jinyuan of Tiens, an enterprise with global thinking, put forward the slogan of "promoting human health, serving the community, developing undertakings and giving back to the country." Tiens focuses on the survival and development of mankind, evoking sympathy in different classes and different countries during its global expansion, and therefore wins respect and appraisal.

For global expansion of Direct-Selling enterprises, it is crucial that the enterprises have a systematic thinking pattern. A complete systematic thinking pattern is actually crucial for the enterprises' strategic layout and responses to all these major changes. Entrepreneurs' far-sighted ideas must be established on the systematic balance of the whole. The local optimum does not necessarily bring about the best results of the whole system. The rapid development of one single element may break the balance of the original system and cause extra coordination costs. The internal circulation and external supply chain constitute an interrelated ecosystem. Seeing the development of the industrial labour division, the competitive advantage of Direct-Selling enterprises lies in the high efficiency of the whole of the internal and external chain. The strength of the whole system depends on a systematic thinking pattern. For example, when Direct-Selling enterprises explore the overseas market, will they employ local internet enterprises to increase the traffic of the website? Will they employ professional providers? Will they cooperate with local warehouses, logistics and customer service enterprises? Or will they do all the things on their own? All these questions together make up a systematic logic for the rapid entry into a new market. Direct-Selling enterprises with systematic thinking generally stress on external cooperation and construct a highly effective ecosystem. Tiens' multi-network is actually the internal ecosystem of the group.

For global expansion of Direct-Selling enterprises, the innovative thinking pattern determines how long the enterprise can survive. The wide application of new technologies including big data, mobile internet, cloud computing and the Internet of Things has significantly changed people's lives and ways of thinking. In the age of reform, Direct-Selling enterprises will need to pay attention to the trends of the market, technology, business models and management, as well as the demand changes; inspire employees' creativity; implement the innovation results; provide high-quality, high-touch and personalized products and services; and create values for customers. Enterprises' innovation is implemented in a multi-level, multi-aspect and diversified manner, including the innovation of appearance, technology, process and procedures and the innovation of organization, management and business models. The investment in innovation will not create returns immediately, so enterprises will need to promote innovation resolutely and persistently for the sake of their survival and development. It is exactly because of differences in innovation ability that the average life of American and Japanese small and medium-sized enterprises is much longer than the average life of Chinese private enterprises. When making innovations in different levels and areas, most private enterprises focus on the function, appearance, cost, price, channel and supply chain of the product. This indicates that they stress on applied innovations that help them seize the market but pay less attention to fundamental and original innovations. Entrepreneurs' insight and innovation abilities are essentially the most important core competitiveness of an enterprise. Excellent enterprises are always brave enough to make disruptive innovations and show the willingness and capability to gather innovation resources, create innovation cultures and innovate the terminal models. While they create value for customers, they are actually receiving ceaseless returns from innovations.

For global expansion of Direct-Selling enterprises, enterprises will need to have an entrepreneurial thinking pattern. Only with entrepreneurial thinking can the enterprises be more passionate, more sensitive to crises and more innovative, and attach more importance to strategic and human capital management. Against the changing competition situation, the enterprises may need to enter or exit relevant industries at the proper time; integrate multiple industries; disruptively recreate the enterprises' strategies, organization, supply chain, value chain, products and services; create new business forms and models; deal with uncertainties and challenges with entrepreneurial thinking; and seek better opportunities in different industries and thus achieve long-term survival and development. Having been engaged in direct selling for over two decades and exposed to several business crises, under the guidance of the new swap theory, Tiens has adjusted its strategies fundamentally, experienced three start-ups and explored several sectors. The previous two start-ups were carried out for survival, development and business performance. However, in the third start-up, Tiens emphasizes the input-output ratio and profit rate and constantly innovates the management system, for the sake of the enterprise's rebirth.

II. New Strategies for Global Swap and Transcendence of Direct-Selling Enterprises

Localization is a competition strategy of low cost, low risk and high efficiency for Direct-Selling enterprises. The success of Direct-Selling enterprises' globalization depends on their localization. During global expansion, Direct-Selling enterprises basing their strategy on the concept of localization, offering jobs to local people and paying local taxes, can help enterprises build trust with consumers, win consumers' favour and enhance their international influence. The enterprises' globalization extends from trade to investment, marking a new stage for enterprises to overcome barriers among countries and pursue comprehensive advantages and high benefits in a deeper and longer manner. Enterprises can implement localization through greenfield investment, OEM/ODM under international cooperation, and cross-border mergers and acquisitions. Also, some enterprises choose to explore the overseas market as a group or invest in Chinese parks overseas. When entering the overseas market, Chinese Direct-Selling enterprises think highly of the communication and cooperation with local mainstream society, strive to draw support from local third-party organizations and adapt their management to local conditions. Tiens has tried greenfield investment but depends more on OEM/ODM cooperation for production localization. Tiens' localized production network that covers the whole world is now orderly implemented, to integrate small-sized service enterprises at home and abroad, form a pattern of e-commerce platform products + local services and enhance the integration and stickiness to local markets, to further promote direct selling and retailing businesses.

1. Linkage of Global Trade and Finance
   Direct-Selling enterprises link trade to finance to avoid foreign exchange risks. In terms of overseas incomes, Direct-Selling enterprises are mainly exposed to foreign exchange risks. Exporters mostly make payments in USD, so the fluctuation of the exchange rate of RMB to USD exerts a huge influence. Direct-Selling enterprises need to establish the correct risk awareness, control currency exposure, and manage foreign exchange risks. In case of violent fluctuations of the foreign exchange rate, enterprises will have to choose effective instruments to lock and reduce foreign exchange risks. Direct-Selling enterprises can combine the fluctuation of foreign exchange rate with PV/BV adjusting lever, give full play to the regulating role of the PV/BV to lower the influence of foreign exchange rate fluctuation, and avoid losses by requesting headquarters to adjust the time of remittance. In the future, with the deepening of globalization, Direct-Selling enterprises will manage the foreign exchange rate of currencies, interest rate and hedging instruments in the countries of overseas branches and production bases in a unified way; perform systematic appraisals in terms of brand promotions, R&D expenditure and investment and financing arrangements; select the optimum way to maintain or increase value considering the comprehensive income of the group; and fully discover the hedging value of the global sales, production and management network. Direct-Selling enterprises can also establish the global procurement network, purchase more profitable featured commodities and valuable resources with overseas incomes, and sell them to the regions or businesses of strong purchasing power, great demand and high market price to get a high return. They can also join the international economic circulation through the global sales network and conduct swaps of global commodities. The value of overseas-featured commodities in value preservation and appreciation can effectively relieve the risks brought by the violent fluctuation of foreign exchange rates of all currencies. Based on the 170 subsidiaries in 21 overseas regions, high-quality products, sales network, brand resources and trade platform, Tiens has transcended the original model of selling Tiens' products to the world and has started to select featured products and import products from the world under a unified planning strategy.

2. Direct Selling + Internet
   The fourth industrial revolution based on new technologies including cloud computing, big data, mobile internet, and the Internet of Things is mainly

characterized by the integration of multiple technologies, when a new industry and business innovation model is created. This new model will effectively lower the innovation threshold and enable a fairer, opener and more transparent market environment. Data become important means of production, and the applied data promote 'integration innovation.' In the 'new retailing' age, the emergence of new social e-commerce models, such as microbusinesses and e-commerce platforms, as well as remote online training, live broadcasting platforms, 100,000+ WeChat official accounts, are challenging the Direct-Selling industry to a certain extent. The Direct-Selling industry, mainly engaged in health products, has started its transformation to the model of direct selling + internet, facilitating the integration innovation of direct selling + internet. There are two ways to integrate Direct-Selling enterprises and the internet. First, teach distributors to run internet businesses. For example, the orders accomplished online through Amway Cloud Shopping take up more than 40% of Amway orders, suggesting that Amway distributors have combined the Internet+ element and have improved the operations efficiency. Second, lead the internet teams to Direct-Selling businesses. Dplus, which newly joined direct selling, had no direct sellers at the beginning. However, it turned its internet talents into a Direct-Selling team.

3. Human-oriented Long-term Incentives

The innovative development of Direct-Selling enterprises is realized essentially based on the accumulation of human capital. Talents are the foundation for the development of an enterprise, as well as the key to the competition among enterprises. Direct-Selling enterprises will need to establish a human-oriented corporate culture; introduce local talents overseas; make use of their advantages in language, profession and social recognition to promote cross-region and cross-border business development; and satisfy the needs of the enterprises' global development. Enterprises will have to adopt a differentiated human resources policy and reward employees who have created value with options. In the age of internet, enterprises will need to constantly motivate value creators through the multi-level partnership responsibility system and mobilize entrepreneurs' enthusiasm, and create value for society, employees and shareholders, in accordance with the innate character of the enterprise. Profit constitutes the guarantee and source for enterprises to sustain human orientation and enterprise development. Enterprises will provide incentives to those who create value, establish the awareness of cost and profit, improve the productivity of the labour force, and distribute interests while expanding the size. Overseas enterprises will be turned into profit centres, which will systematically improve the profit rate, expand to areas of high added value, and resist external market risks. The employment policies, scheduling systems, working hours, pay structures and incentive policies show different characteristics in different business sectors and departments.

Tiens mainly develops overseas talents through internal cultivation, supplemented by overseas recruitment. It employs excellent undergraduates from domestic universities every year, assigns them to overseas markets after two or three years of cultivation, puts the burden on them and sets up the distribution and promotion system. In this way, they will gradually grow to be the backbone and support the overseas expansion and talent development of Tiens. Tiens will strengthen its recruitment of overseas talents, adopt high standards, globally hunt international talents with work experience in the Fortune 500 or multinational groups, and attract and retain excellent talents with the strength and promising future of Tiens. Tiens will recruit local international professional talents from India, Pakistan, Singapore, Malaysia and Thailand to supplement talents for the Asia-Pacific and African markets and improve the structure of managers of different regions and branches. Thirty per cent equity will be transferred to options and given to high-potential employees who have made outstanding contributions as reward. As to the internal control of the Group, Tiens emphasizes the leadership responsibility system, organization coordination, project team and profit examination. Based on the new concept, the profit rate goal of the Direct-Selling division is set as 20%. Tiens will optimize the Direct-Selling threshold and system to assure "precise pricing, precise delivery, precise management and precise service."

III. New Measures for Global Swap and Transcendence for Direct-Selling Enterprises

Despite the slower growth of income in the domestic Direct-Selling industry, the number of Direct-Selling enterprises is constantly rising. According to the Direct-Selling industry management pages of the Ministry of Commerce's website, 89 Direct-Selling enterprises have acquired licenses in China, yet 46 'quasi-Direct-Selling' enterprises are in progress of public announcement, and over 260 enterprises have submitted application reports to relevant departments. All these indicate the increasingly fierce competition in the Direct-Selling industry, so products and services become the competition point of Direct-Selling enterprises.

Direct-Selling enterprises focus on customers' feelings, stress the extension of product value, innovate experiential consumption marketing and upgrade offline experience services. With the model development from previous nonstore operations to stores + employed direct sellers and to direct selling + experience stores, experience halls and experience stores are constantly emerging. Direct-Selling enterprises will innovate the marketing method, incorporate demonstrations in product experience, and combine education, training, lectures, and experiences to encourage consumers and direct sellers. Experience halls play an indispensable role for product display and service provision and become a standard part of Direct-Selling enterprises' marketing method. Seeing the rise of Direct-Selling enterprises, Amway (China) has come out from the crowd with its 'experience strategy' and has opened its fifth flagship experience hall in Guangzhou following Shanghai, Shenzhen, Chengdu and Beijing. Infinitus has also upgraded and transformed its experience centre. Tiens has changed the whole VI system of the enterprise and created a brand-new experience proposal.

Direct-Selling enterprises will continue to improve their brand image and stress the word-of-mouth effect of their products. Based on the demands of global markets and direct sellers, the enterprises choose/develop hi-tech products of high added value, quick results, good demonstration effects and a good story; and products that can be easily approved, choose/develop high-quality products of fashion, excellent quality, high price and gross profit, high grade and high value; introduce products of repetitive sales and attach importance to both business-oriented and consumption-oriented direct sellers. Direct-Selling enterprises will also increase emotional engagement, improve the quality of after service and enhance consumers' loyalty and satisfaction. Tiens provides precise service experiences to direct sellers, where they can enjoy the medical care services of a specialist department, the care services of a sanatorium, the concierge services of a five-star hotel and health preservation services of private clubs. This helps strengthen the communication of the Chinese traditional health preservation culture and Tiens' culture, and promotes the communication and interaction between Tiens' culture and the local culture. When promoting products to customers, Tiens not only sells products, but also helps people develop their causes. Tiens' products have won consumers' trust and favour with the products meeting market demands and having advanced marketing means. Tiens bears the mission of "putting love first, promoting human health and serving the community." It is dedicated to promoting multi-business development, planning for global layout, and achieving the long-term goal of ascending to the Fortune 500; Tiens aims to cultivate an international comprehensive health group under a national brand.

Direct-Selling enterprises innovate the terminal model and provide systematic solutions. In the new age, guided by a new concept, Tiens innovates multi-network interaction and one body with multiple wings, and constructs an internal ecosystem for sharing. The key to multi-network interaction lies in creating a business model with terminal competitiveness, to realize interconnection, mutual swap, mutual linking and benefit overlapping. In this way, a new model of lower cost, lower risk, higher benefits and greater stability that increases benefits of multiple parties is created. The new model replaces the traditional 'low risk and low return' with 'low risk and high return.' Through the swap of profit points of multiple business sectors, it assures direct sellers' benefits, lowers the operating risk, and has direct sellers get profit from multiple business sectors. Tiens also innovates the consumption method. Consumers benefit from the repetitive sales incentive mechanism, as well as from the points and invited consumption system. It also innovates the organizational structure, connects the business, finance and personnel information among multiple networks, and guarantees the smooth flow of products, customers, information and cash.

For the third start-up, Tiens has formulated a three-year strategic plan, to guide all departments to implement the global layout and global swap strategy. Tiens is expanding globally based on the interaction of the seven terminal networks and the one body with multiple wings strategy. It adheres to the new concept, adopts the new model, ushers in the new age of globalization, expands the market, improves diversity and local services, and generates increasing marginal revenues for mainstream groups. It also integrates product experience, marketing and education support together, converts the profit points among different business sectors based on a certain calculation method, measures customers' consumption contributions to each sector, and constructs the new mechanism of invited consumption. In 2019, Tiens upgraded and launched JTMM, the platform integrating direct selling and social e-commerce, to build the user-centred Linker net and seek new crossover breakthroughs that transcend the traditional Direct-Selling model.

SECTION 3
NEW VISION OF GLOBAL SWAP AND TRANSCENDENCE FOR DIRECT-SELLING ENTERPRISES

I. New Platform for Global Swap and Transcendence for Direct-Selling Enterprises

The two centenary goals are the focus in the new stage. People's sense of acquisition, happiness and safety are indispensable from health. By vigorously developing the health industry, direct selling will welcome in spring. In addition to expanding globally and opening wider, Chinese Direct-Selling enterprises will still need to constantly explore and build a broader and higher development platform and search for newer and better opportunities for development. Under the impact of new concepts, new ideas and new strategies, Direct-Selling enterprises will rise to new challenges. In this process, they will be brave enough to subvert themselves, thus seizing new development opportunities through transcendence.

The constant and healthy development of the Direct-Selling industry is of great significance for improving people's lives and promoting social progress, since it can increase employment, create product value, and promote technological progress and human health. As Direct-Selling enterprises are becoming modern, the e-commerce platform with Direct-Selling DNA plays a decisive role here. Seeing the global expansion of Direct-Selling enterprises, the e-commerce platform carries the new function of global swap and transcendence. Products are released online for sale, terminal experiences are presented all over the world, production factors are allocated globally, production capacity is arranged at the international level, and local services are provided at very corner of the world. In other words, the global network-based super platform featured with Direct-Selling DNA that serves small and medium-sized enterprises and consumers, has realized the network-wide interconnection of commodities all over the world.

This new platform is the transaction centre of featured commodities worldwide, the stage for the entrepreneurship of global distributors and the shopping paradise for all consumers of the world. More importantly, this new platform is the important support for Direct-Selling enterprises to transform and upgrade themselves in the new age. Modern Direct-Selling enterprises will continue to attach more importance to customer value, build the new platform for global swap and transcendence oriented on customers, and vigorously create new models, collect new elements, provide new products, explore new markets, cultivate new abilities, create new values and realize new strategies.

II. New Patterns of Global Swap and Transcendence for Direct-Selling Enterprises

With highly flexible marketing and operations models, direct selling provides personalized services, enables sellers to take the initiative to make sales and makes services more convenient. Moreover, the operations strategy is concealed in these models. Direct-Selling enterprises will follow the trend of global economic transformation and upgrading and the new wave of the digital economy; support the Belt and Road Initiative; take the initiative to participate in economic globalization; forecast the future of the Direct-Selling industry; apply new business models, management systems, incentive mechanisms and world leading digital communication technology; develop customized products and logistics services based on the big data on customers; perfectly integrate the mobile internet, fan economy, community network, featured products and intelligent services; think highly of users' experiences; contact users face to face; provide customized services; maximize customer value; combine direct selling and nonDirect-Selling and create the new closed value chain.

The new patterns of Direct-Selling enterprises can be created when the enterprise enhances the motive force for development. Direct-Selling enterprises will overcome cross-border and cross-region barriers to deliver better products and undertakings to all countries of the world. They will initiate expansion in economically developed countries and then gradually cover developing countries. They will transcend the limits of products to only six types, try to cover all areas associated with comprehensive health and household consumption demand, deepen the traditional Direct-Selling businesses, and meanwhile explore the new space for development. With the new patterns, Direct-Selling enterprises will take the initiative to create a human resources network of integrated interests and realize the smooth flow of commodities, services, talents and currency on the super swap platform. The enterprises will focus on high-quality markets, elements and customers, re-shape the structure, create new Linkers, explore its commercial values and explore the profit space.

As required by the new patterns, Direct-Selling enterprises will go steady and go far. Seeing the rapid development of China, Direct-Selling enterprises will observe the laws and regulations, fulfil their social responsibilities, and make themselves the important force to promote consumption upgrading and boost economic prosperity. They will take the initiative to communicate Chinese culture and positive energy and lead this loving undertaking on the road of sustainable development. Direct-Selling enterprises will keep the pace with the country; rely on national development strategies; adapt to the trend of technological progress; make constant innovations to maintain market vitality; create high-quality products and services based on craftsman spirit; become the excellent representatives of private enterprises through diversified and integrated development; play the role of backbone to support national rejuvenation; and build themselves into world-class enterprises of international competitiveness.

III. New Vision of Transcendence-driven Swap for Direct-Selling Enterprises

The transcendence and swap of Direct-Selling enterprises show the trend of a spiral rise and constitute quantitative change-qualitative change relations. Transcendence is the goal of swap, while swap is the tool and approach to realize transcendence. When transcendence is realized, the level of swap is upgraded, and the new swap becomes the new starting point of a new transcendence. In these years, department stores have been closed; fresh e-commerce markets have emerged; convenient and fast goods delivery assures delivery quality at the same time; the 'sharing economy' always shows a win-win result; third-party payment methods such as Alipay and WeChat Payment are highly appraised by Chinese common people and envied by foreigners for their high efficiency. We can predict that Direct-Selling enterprises will improve swap throughout self-transcendence, and new transcendence will be achieved through a higher level of swap. The blueprints we drew are becoming real, and the prospects are definitely inspiring.

As China's market mechanism will play the decisive role and the government's governance system and capability will be improved and modernized, the more open, standardized, transparent and efficient market economy will bring Direct-Selling enterprises a favourable business environment and realize fair and orderly competition. Direct-Selling enterprises will feel freer when 'bringing in' and 'going out.' Through the two-way flow, Direct-Selling enterprises will see the improvement of globalization, informatization, marketization and publicity. Faced with the rapidly changing international competition, Direct-Selling enterprises will seize new opportunities; rise to new challenges; accumulate new elements based on new concepts, strategies and platforms; show new vigour; construct high-quality ecosystems; and constantly improve the ability to create value. By deeply integrating themselves in the international division of labour, they will attempt to ascend to the high end of the value chain and realize the great dream of making contributions to the country by setting up great enterprises.

EPILOGUE

Tiens Group continues to develop, to adapt and, most importantly, to innovate using the notions of swap and transcendence. Under the new situation, the strategy of 'taking the shop into the internet and taking the internet into the shop' is the next innovation of swap and transcendence, and also the important support point of the one body and multiple wings global strategy in new marketing.

This approach will guarantee entrepreneurship, employment, security and health, as well as drive the involvement of stakeholders, and promote economic development and social progress! Tiens' first venture through the 'network within a store, store within a network' strategy quickly realized a big development in the world,

More than 20 years ago, in the new marketing approach of Tiens, global logistics and payment were underdeveloped, and relied on authorized stores to build a good framework for network development, rapid cross-regional, cross-border network team operations and development. Today, authorized stores are an important supporting point for global network development but are being reformed and upgraded. Today global development, logistics and payment are no longer a problem, and the mobile internet has made online shopping mainstream. The 'experience' stores of Tiens have adapted to keep ahead of this way of modern life.

The pace of people's lives is accelerating, but the core elements of experience, presentation and service cannot be replaced completely online. How to provide better experience and service is particularly important. Under this new situation, we are upgrading our authorized stores to experience stores; to experience strong service products to assist customers and to enhance their commitment and loyalty. At the same time, this will enhance the profitability of the experience store itself, the formation of the intermediate experience store, senior experience store and super senior experience shop, layer by layer, to better support the development of the network both in person and online in the new marketing approach of Tiens.

Tiens has introduced slimming and shaping experience service projects, becoming the first service content in the store. This involves a series of marketing and service strategies; as long as the experience store attracts a certain number of experience users, that will help the store achieve a quick return and fast profit. As long as the important support of the experience store through the experience service means fast profit and fast turnover, it will be able to drive the rapid sales of products, thus driving rapid development.

For Tiens, this slimming and shaping approach is only the beginning of our future development around the world. The follow-up will increase a series of service products such as health inspection, health monitoring, health maintenance, beauty enhancement and beauty presentation. At the same time, through the combined internet and the experience store model, Tiens will achieve cross-regional, cross-border development, and the formation of the third venture 'shop within network, network within shop' strategy.

Tiens Group has always had its base in quality products, committed people, targeted marketing, excellent customer service, great education and focused training, as well as a strong standing in the world. This has allowed Tiens to achieve success. That success is continuing through huge digital system engineering and the creative use of the internet. Tiens will continue to succeed through new breakthroughs, new leaps, new developments and new marketing.

Li Jinyuan
Tiens Group

BIBLIOGRAPHY

Bai, Mu. (2008). "The Advent of the Third Wave of Direct Selling in China – Deduction of the Law and Trend of *Direct Selling Development* in Current China." *Direct Selling in China*, Issue 121.

Bao, Tongzhen. (2018). "Investigation and Countermeasures of Existing Problems in Direct Selling Industry – with Direct Selling Company Was an Instance." *Hebei Enterprises*, Issue 2.

Bei, Jin, & Jianjian, Gong. (2014). "Economic Trends and Policy Regulation and Their Influence on Enterprise Competitiveness – Empirical Analysis Based on Panel Data of Chinese Industries." *China Industrial Economics*, Issue 3.

Berle, Adolf A. & Means, Gardiner C. (2005). *The Modern Corporation and Private Property* (Chinese version). Beijing: The Commercial Press.

Bi, Hongyi, & Shi, Ying. (2013). "Growth Conditions and Growth Paths of Chinese Multinational Enterprises." *Theory Journal*, Issue 12.

Blackford, Mansel G. (2001). *The Rise of Modern Business* (Chinese version). Beijing: Economy & Management Publishing House.

Blair, Margaret M. (1999). *Ownership and Control: Rethinking Corporate Governance for the Twenty-first Century* (Chinese version). Beijing: China Social Sciences Press.

Cao, Qianman. (2017). "Consumption Orientation, Wealth Gathering and Conditions for High-income States." *Reform*, Issue 1.

Centre for China and Globalization (CCG). (2017). *Report on Globalization of Chinese Enterprises.* Beijing: Social Sciences Academic Press.

Chaffey, Dave, et al. (2004). *Digital Marketing: Strategy, Implementation and Practice* (2nd edition) (Chinese version). Beijing: China Machine Press.

Chen, Rui. (2017). "Seven Major Trends of Direct Selling in China." *Knowledge Economy*, Issue 3.

Chen, Wei. (2003). *Study on Competition Strategy-based Enterprise Value Chain Management Model*, Harbin Engineering University dissertation.

Chen, Wei. (2009). "Network Direct Selling Research Review." *North Study*, Issue 8.

Chen, Yayun. (2006). *Primary Exploration of Enterprises' Core Competitiveness*. Xiamen University dissertation.

Chen, Yonghua. (2006). "Tiens Expansion to Health Equipment." *Medical and Health Equipment*.

Chen, Yu. (2008). *The Theory of Consumption Capital*. Beijing: China Statistics Press.

Chen, Yuchai. (2004). *The Amway Empire of Legend*. Beijing: Qunyan Press.

Cheng, Xirong, Li, Pengbo, & Liang, Han. (2016). "Sharing Economy and Emerging Human Resource Management Model – with Airbnb as an Instance." *Human Resources Development of China*, Issue 6.

China Consumer Journal. (2017). "Tiens: Creating Brand with Top Quality, Winning the Future with One Body with Multiple Wings." [DB/OL], [2017-04-19], http://dy.163.com/v2/article/detail/CID9FE0U0512AKQV.html.

China Investment Consulting. "2016-2020 China's Logistics Industry Investment Analysis and Forecasting Report." https://wenku.baidu.com/view/f30d3934ce2f0066f53322fe.html.

"Congratulations! You Made the Right Choice Again: Infinitus Topped Direct Selling Performance Again in 2016." [DB/OL], VCCOO Net, [2017-2-16], http://www.vccoo.com/v/x106k0.

Dine, Janet. (2008). *The Governance of Corporate Groups* (Chinese version). Beijing: Peking University Press.

Easterbrook, Frank H. & Fischel, Daniel R. (2005). *Economic Structure of Company Law* (Chinese version). Beijing: Peking University Press.

Editorial Office, 2018: "Grand Opening of the 13th China Direct Selling Chart." *Knowledge Economy (Direct Selling in China)*, Issue 1.

Fan, Libo. (2011). "3L Path for the Growth of Chinese Multinational Enterprises." *Contemporary International Relations*, Issue 8.

Felson, Marcus, & Spaeth, Joe L. (1978). "Community Structure and Collaborative Consumption: A Routine Activity Approach." *American Behavioral Scientist*, 21(4), pp. 614–624.

Gao, Hongye. (2001). *Western Economics*. Beijing: China Renmin University Press.

Gao, Li. (2011). *Research on the Generation Mechanism and Management of the Enterprise's Ecosystem*. Hefei University of Technology dissertation.

Guo, Yifu. (2009). *Innovation of Business Model and Enterprise's Competitive Advantages: Internal Mechanism and Empirical Study*. Donghua University dissertation.

Hamilton, Robert W. (2008). *The Law of Corporations in a Nutshell* (Chinese version). Beijing: Law Press China.

Han, Xiushen, Chen, Ming, & Guo, Jing. (2015). "Comparative Study on Chinese and American Direct Selling Industry – with Amway as an Instance." *Foreign Investment in China*, Issue 21.

Huang, Maokai. (2009). "Similarities and Differences of Core Competitiveness and Dynamic Competitiveness." *Journal of Industrial Technological Economics*, Issue 11.

Jin, Bei. (2001). "On the Nature of Enterprise Competitiveness." *China Industrial Economics*, Issue 10.

Jin, Yongsheng. (1997). "On the Theory and Historical Trajectory of Organizational Evolution of Western Retail Industry." *Journal of Hebei University of Economics and Trade*, Issue 6.

Jin, Yuan. (2003). *Li Jinyuan and Tiens*. Beijing: Chinese Literature and History Press.

Keller, Kevin Lane. (2006). *Marketing Management* (12th edition) (Chinese version). Beijing: Shanghai People's Publishing House.

Kang, Zhijun. (2016). *Business Partner: Way of Enterprise Management in the Age of Knowledge* [M]. Beijing: China Machine Press.

Khalifa, M., Limayem, M. & Liu, V. (2002). "Online Customer Stickiness: A Longitudinal Study." *Journal of Global Information Management* (JGIM), 10(3), pp.1-14.

Li, Donghao. (2008). "Reform of Company Governance Structure of Japanese Enterprises – Analysis Based on Diversified Reforms in Recent Years." *Review of Industrial Economics*, Issue 4.

Li, Junhua. (2015). "Path and Optimization Direction of Industrial Development Model Transformation in China in the New Normal." *Modern Economic Research*, Issue 2.

Li, Yang. (2015). "On Internet+ Strategic Transformation of Direct Selling." *Price: Theory and Practice*, Issue 9.

Li, Zhiying. (2005). "Comparison of Multi-level Direct Selling Model." *Commercial Times*, Issue 23.

Lin, Qian. (2014). "On the Incentive System of Direct-Selling Enterprises – with the Direct Seller Incentive System of Amway as an Instance." *Modern Economic Information*, Issue 11.

Lin, Xiaochun. (2013). *Study on E-commerce Models of Direct-Selling Enterprises*. Xi'an University of Science and Technology dissertation.

Liu, Bin, Wei, Qian, & Lv, Yue. (2016). "Service-oriented Manufacturing and Value Chain Upgrading." *Economic Research Journal*, Issue 3.

Liu, Jixing. (2002). "On Core Competitiveness of Enterprises." *Guide to Business*, Issue 2.

Liu, Sheng. (2006). "Amway vs Avon: Variations of Direct Selling in China." *China Business Review*, Issue 2.

Liu, Yingqiu, & Li, Jinyuan. (2003). *New Swap Theory*.

Liu, Yufeng. (2012). *Research and Innovation of Amway (China) Direct Selling Business Model*. Southwestern University of Finance and Economics dissertation.

Lu, Shan. (2008). "Supply Chain Synergism: Analysis Based on Core Competence Theory." *Enterprise Economy*, Issue 11.

Miao, Weisheng. (2017). *Outlook Report on Foreign Investment of Chinese Enterprises*. Beijing: China Economic Publishing House.

Mo, Zhenzhen, & Li, Shiyang. (2017). "Platform Economy: New Economic Growth Model." *High-Technology and Industrialization*, Issue 8.

National Bureau of Statistics – Data Interpretation of "*Fundamental Role of Consumption Constantly Improved and New Forces for Development Rapidly Enhanced*," http://www.stats.gov.cn/tjsj/sjjd/201707/t20170706_1510401.html.

National Bureau of Statistics of the People's Republic of China. (2016). "Statistical Communique of the People's Republic of China on the 2016 National Economic and Social Development."

OCN. "Investment Analysis and Prospect Forecast Report on China Logistics Industry 2016-2020," https://wenku.baidu.com/view/f30d3934ce2f0066f53322fe.html.

Otsuka, Hisao. (2002). *History of Joint Stock Company* (Chinese version). Beijing: China Renmin University Press.

Ouyang, Haonan. (2005). "Reflection on the Development of Direct Selling in China." *China Market*, Issue 5.

Penrose, Edith, translated by Zhao, Xiao. (2007). *The Theory of the Growth of the Firm*. Beijing: Shanghai People's Publishing House.

Pine, B. Joseph & Gilmore, James H. (2016). *The Experience Economy*. Beijing: China Machine Press.

Porter, Michael E. (2014). *Competitive Advantage*. Beijing: CITIC Press Group.

Qian, Yanwen, & Sun, Linyan. (2003). "Research on Classification of Operation Models." *Science of Science and Management of S.&T.*, Issue 9.

Qu, Yanxia. (2015). "Strategic Analysis of the Transformation from Traditional Logistics to Modern Supply Chain Management." *Arts and Sciences Navigation Journal*, Issue 12.

Ran, Zhiyuan. (2016). "Tiens Builds One Body with Two Wings." *Knowledge Economy (Direct Selling in China)*, Issue 3.

Rifkin, Jeremy. (2014). *The Zero Marginal Cost Society*. Beijing: China CITIC Press.

Romer, Paul M. (1986). "Increasing Returns and Long-run Growth." *Journal of Political Economy*, 94(5), pp. 1002-1037.

Ruan, Shaojun, & Chen, Jia. (2005). "Direct Selling – New Forces of Sales in China." *Market Modernization*, Issue 25.

Schultz, Theodore, translated by Jiang, Bing and Zhang, Heng. (1990). *Investment in Human Capital* (1st Edition). Beijing: Beijing Economic College Press.

Schumpeter, Joseph. (1991). *The Theory of Economic Development*. Beijing: The Commercial Press.

Shen, Jie. (2017). "Top 10 Hot News of Direct Selling Industry 2016." *China Association for Quality Promotion*, Issue 1.

Shi, Jiewei. (2011). *Empirical Research on Amway's Direct Selling Model Based on Supply Chain Management*. Zhejiang University of Technology dissertation.

Shihua, Ma, & Yong, Lin. (2015). *Supply Chain Management*. Beijing: Higher Education Press.

Shuyan, Ma, & Chenghua, Deng. (2014). "Sources of Enterprise Competitiveness." *China Quality Supervision*, Issue 12.

Su, Liping, & Zhou, Mengyao. (2017). "Literature Review of Enterprise's Competitiveness and Its Appraisal." *Science & Technology Economy Market*, Issue 9.

Sun, Yuguo. (2006). *Legal Regulations on Direct Selling*. Shandong University dissertation.

Sun, Zilai. (2018). "Manufacturer's Selection of Sales Model Considering Direct Selling Cost and Platform Transaction Cost." *Chinese Journal of Management*, Issue 1.

"Taking Advantage of the Belt and Road, Direct-Selling Enterprises Will Meet New Development Opportunities and Challenges." http://www.zx58.cn/news/10326832

"Tiens: One Body with Two Wings Promotes Transformation [DB/OL]." *Economic Daily*, October 31, 2016.

Tiens. "Tiens Launches E-commerce Platform JTMM for the Layout of Mobile Internet" [DB/OL], *Direct Selling City Net*, [2017-10-09], http://www.zx58.cn/news/10358735.

Wang, Baoshu. (2004). *Development of Modernization of Japanese Company Law*. Beijing: Social Sciences Academic Press.

Wang, Li, Yang, Jian, & Chen, Caixiang. (2011). "Logistics Management Innovation Based on Supply Chain System." *Fujian BBS (Social Sciences and Education edition)*, Issue 4.

Wang, Pingping. "National Residents' Income Steadily Grew and Residents' Consumption Further Increased in 2016" [R/OL], [2016-1-20], http://www.stats.gov.cn/tjsj/sjjd/201701/t20170120_1456174.html.

Wang, Xin. (2015). "Analysis of the Application of Fractal Theory in Enterprise Management." *Technology Innovation and Application*, Issue 15.

Wang, Zhiqiang, He, Yi, & Lian, Lu. (2008). "Application of Flat Management in Modern Enterprises." *Network Health*, Issue 11.

Wu, Hong. (2011). "Brand Strategy and Enterprise Competitiveness." *Business Culture Monthly*, Issue 9.

Wu, Jian'an. (2011). *Marketing*. Beijing: Higher Education Press.

Wu, Yin. (2006). "Secrets of Tiens New Favorite: Cosmetics." *Knowledge Economy*, Issue 2.

Xiao, Xiangyu. (2003). *Research on the Evaluation of Enterprise Competitiveness*, Jiangxi University of Finance and Economics dissertation.

Xie, Hongwu, & Ma, Chi. (2017). "New Collision and New Development of Traditional Direct Selling and E-commerce in the Context of New Media." *Market Modernization*, Issue 18.

Xu, Guolan. (2007). "Research on Network Direct Selling Models." *Journal of Zhejiang University (Humanities and Social Sciences)*, Issue 5.

Xu, Zhongrong. (2007). "Research on the Direct Selling Models Based on Network Platform." *Market Modernization*, Issue 31.

Xue, Cuiping. (2015). "On the Application of Fractal Theory in Modern Enterprise Management." *China Market*, Issue 10.

Yingqiu, Liu, & Jinyuan, Li. (2003). *New Swap Theory*, Beijing: China Social Sciences Press.

Yoshimura, Norihisa. (2008). "Dynamics of Japanese Company Governance Reform." *Review of Industrial Economics*, Issue 4.

Yu, Jinshan. "Development of 'Internet' Direct Selling Combining E-commerce [DB/OL]." *Direct Selling City Net*, [2015-05-14], http://www.zx58.cn/news/9872434.

Yu, Zude, & Chen, Junfang. (2009). "Theoretical Overview and Commentary on the Source of Enterprise Competitiveness." *Science and Technology Management Research*, Issue 6.

Yuan, Jin. *Li Jinyuan and Tiens*. Beijing: Chinese Literature and History Press.

Yuan, Pan. (2015). "Table of Chinese Direct-Selling Enterprises' Performance 2004-2014 [DB/OL]." *Direct Selling Encyclopedia Net*, [2015-04-03], http://www.askci.com/news/data/2015/04/03/144941g5b0.shtml.

Yuan, Xiao. (2012). *Study of Amway (China) Direct Selling Strategies*. Jilin University dissertation.

Zhang, Hongyan. (2007). "Manifestations of Hierarchy of Needs in Consumer Demand." *Science and Management*, Issue 6.

Zhang, Qidi. (2012). *Research on Operator Enterprise Application Platform Based on Platform Economy Theory*. Beijing University of Posts and Telecommunications dissertation.

Zhang, Yingxin. (2016). "Microanalysis of Repeat Sales Rate on E-commerce Platform." *China Glasses Science-Technology Magazine*, Issue 21.

Zhang, Yunxia, Li, Xin, & Chen, Yiwen. (2015). "Research Review on Online Customer Stickiness." *Chinese Journal of Ergonomics*, Issue 4.

Zhuang, Wenjing, & Xie, Dandan. (2013). "Amway: All Younger." *Sino-Foreign Management*, Issue 3.

ABOUT LI JINYUAN

A highly successful entrepreneur, **Li Jinyuan** is founder and Chairman of Tiens Group Co Ltd, a private company headquartered in Tianjin, People's Republic of China. One of the world's largest health-focused organizations, Tiens Group operates online, in person and in stores and has millions of customers in most countries of the world. Mr Li is also a philanthropist who has given many millions for humanitarian, education and health causes globally. A graduate of Nankai University, Mr Li has received many awards and honours for his business activities and for his contributions to society in China and around the world.

Li Jinyuan
Courtesy of Tiens Group